# LA Rising

# KOREAN COMMUNITIES ACROSS THE WORLD

## Series Editor

Joong-Hwan Oh, Hunter College, CUNY

*Korean Communities across the World* publishes works that address aspects of (a) the Korean American community, (b) Korean society, (c) the Korean communities in other foreign lands, or (d) transnational Korean communities. In the field of (a) the Korean American community, this series welcomes contributions involving concepts such as Americanization, pluralism, social mobility, migration/immigration, social networks, social institutions, social capital, racism/discrimination, settlement, identity, or politics, as well as a specific topic related to family/marriage, gender roles, generations, work, education, culture, citizenship, health, ethnic community, housing, ethnic identity, racial relations, social justice, social policy, and political views, among others. In the field of (b) Korean society, this series embraces scholarship on current issues such as gender roles, age/aging, low fertility, immigration, urbanization, gentrification, economic inequality, high youth unemployment, sexuality, democracy, political power, social injustice, the nation's educational problems, social welfare, capitalism, consumerism, labor, health, housing, crime, environmental degradation, and the social life in the digital age and its impacts, among others. Contributors in the field of (c) Korean communities in other foreign lands are encouraged to submit works that expand our understanding about the formation, vicissitudes, and major issues of an ethnic Korean community outside of South Korea and the United States, such as cultural or linguistic retention, ethnic identity, assimilation, settlement patterns, citizenship, economic activities, family relations, social mobility, and racism/discrimination. Lastly, contributions relating to (d) transnational Korean communities may touch upon transnational connectivity in family, economy/finance, politics, culture, technology, social institutions, and people.

*Transnational Communities in the Smartphone Age: The Korean Community in the Nation's Capital*, by Dae Young Kim
*Medical Transnationalism: Korean Immigrants' Medical Tourism to South Korea*, by Sou Hyun Jang
*Transnational Return Migration of 1.5 Generation Korean New Zealanders: A Quest for Home*, by Jane Yeonjae Lee
*LA Rising: Korean Relations with Blacks and Latinos after Civil Unrest,* by Kyeyoung Park

# LA Rising

## Korean Relations with Blacks and Latinos after Civil Unrest

Kyeyoung Park

LEXINGTON BOOKS
*Lanham • Boulder • New York • London*

Published by Lexington Books
An imprint of The Rowman & Littlefield Publishing Group, Inc.
4501 Forbes Boulevard, Suite 200, Lanham, Maryland 20706
www.rowman.com

6 Tinworth Street, London SE11 5AL, United Kingdom

British Library Cataloguing in Publication Information Available

**Library of Congress Cataloging-in-Publication Data Available**

ISBN 978-1-4985-7705-2 (cloth : alk. paper)
ISBN 978-1-4985-7707-6 (pbk : alk. paper)
ISBN 978-1-4985-7706-9 (electronic)

♾™ The paper used in this publication meets the minimum requirements of American National Standard for Information Sciences—Permanence of Paper for Printed Library Materials, ANSI/NISO Z39.48-1992.

To my husband, Roberto, and
to the memory of my brother, Ickwhan

# Contents

# List of Figures

# List of Tables

# Acknowledgments

I would like to acknowledge the people in South Los Angeles: Korean immigrant merchants and their African American and Latino customers and residents, who despite much stereotyping and objectification from the media and popular culture, shared their personal stories providing insight into their everyday lives, whose struggle is also my own in some senses. I learnt a lot from their interpretations and analysis, and I hope this book does some justice to their experiences. I also would like to thank Jeff Saito, Jocelyn Henry, Helen Na, Caroline Kim, Sharon P. Kim, Kathryne Cho, and Dave Kim for their outstanding research assistance.

Although I take responsibility for the final product, I would like to pay special thanks, warmth, and appreciation to a number of friends and colleagues who encouraged me to start this work, persevere, and finally publish. In New York, Thomas Burgess always listened to my analysis and provided critical feedback. Prof. Roger Sanjek encouraged me to work on Black-Korean tension as my postdoctoral research project. In Los Angeles, I am sincerely grateful to Profs. Laurie Hart, Jessica Cattelino, Sherry Ortner, Akhil Gupta, Carol Browner, Karen Brodkin, Lane Hirabayashi, Thu-Huong Nguyen-Vo, David Yoo, Min Zhou, many other colleagues and my students, past and present, at University of California, Los Angeles; also Scott Kurashige, John Lie, Min Hyung Song, and Jenny Banh, who read different chapters over the years. It is wholeheartedly expressed that your advice was a milestone in accomplishing the end product. Thank you to Jinqi Ling, Keith Camacho, Mariko Tamanoi, Aomar Boum, Franklin Ng, Shirley Hune, and Cheong Huh, whose reminders and constant motivation encouraged me to meet important deadlines. I am thankful to the chairs of the Department of Anthropology, Jason Throop, the Department of Asian American Studies, Victor Bascara, and Karen Umemoto, Director of the Asian American Studies Center, and their amazing staff, for their vital support and assistance. In addition, Tyler Lawrence provided necessary technical support and help with preparing the manuscript. John Yong Cheun did the map, and Arc Indexing, Inc. helped me with the index. I just wish to recognize the valuable help provided by everyone during my research. In Seoul, I am grateful to my friends and colleagues, Jeong Duk Yi, Kyung Koo Han, Eun-Ju Chung, and members of the joint research project, entitled "Diversity, Agency, and Transnationality among Korean Americans," Myung Suk Oh, Eunyoung Kim, and Hye Sook Park, all of whom never stopped challenging me and helped me develop my ideas.

I thank the University of California, Los Angeles, for the special leave that made it possible for me to spend a year at the Russell Sage Foundation as well as take sabbatical leaves. I offer special thanks to the Russell Sage Foundation for their financial support that made the year at the foundation possible and to its staff for their support. I also received research grants from the Institute of American Cultures, UCLA; Academic Senate Grant, UCLA (multiple times); Division of Graduate School, UCLA; and The Academy of Korean Studies. This work was also supported by the Program for Studies of Koreans Abroad through the Ministry of Education of the Republic of Korea and the Korean Studies Promotion Service of the Academy of Korean Studies (AKS-2016-SRK-123-0005).

During the final stages of preparation, I thank Rebecca Bodenheimer for her superb editorial skills and insightful feedback. I thank also Lynn Itagaki, Peter Wissoker, Kerry Truong, and Sahra Su for proofreading and providing editorial suggestions. I wish to present my special thanks to the series editor Dr. Joong-Hwan Oh, the press editor Courtney Lachapelle Morales, and other colleagues at Lexington Books, an imprint of Rowman & Littlefield, for sharing their confidence in my work in addition to their patience and help. Dr. Oh proved to be an excellent series editor, whose help and sympathetic attitude at every point during my research helped me throughout. Morales was equally an excellent press editor for her support and patience, even when I had difficulty with preparing my manuscript when my office flooded multiple times due to unexpected heavy storms in January and February. Readers for the press offered very helpful comments, too.

Finally, I would like to acknowledge with gratitude the support and love of my family—my parents and my late parents-in-law, my sister Min Sook and her family, my sister Kyewhan, and my husband Roberto. They all kept me going, and this book would not have been possible without them.

*Part I*

# KOREAN, AFRICAN, AND LATIN AMERICANS IN SOUTH LOS ANGELES

# Introduction

## *Theoretical Interpretations of Ethnic Tension*

A year before the verdict in the Rodney King beating trial (1992) was an-nounced, I set out to study the social and cultural construction of tensions that had developed between Korean merchants[1] and Black residents of South Los Angeles (hereafter South LA), an area south of downtown Los Angeles that is referred to as the "first large suburban ghetto" (Scott and Soja 1996, 10). When I started my research, there were heated debates about the fatal conflict between a Korean grocer, Soon Ja Du, and a Black 15-year-old girl, Latasha Harlins. In South LA on March 18, 1991, Harlins was shot dead by Du in a dispute over a $1.79 bottle of orange juice. Eventually, Superior Court Judge Joyce Karlin fined Du $500, sentenced her to probation, and ordered her to perform 400 hours of community service (*Los Angeles Times*, January 16, 1992). The decision by Judge Karlin provoked widespread furor within the African American community, who perceived the sentence as too lenient.

In the aftermath of this case, a not-guilty verdict against the four police of-ficers accused of beating Black motorist Rodney King triggered what would become the 1992 Los Angeles unrest, which became the worst incident of civil unrest in US history.[2] In addition to causing 54 deaths, 2,383 injuries, and the damage and/or destruction of 4,500 businesses, the unrest signaled a new chapter of ethnic conflict in the city. During past riots, it was "whites who typically attacked and killed black newcomers who threatened white la-bor unions" (Mumford 2003, 2804). In the 1960s, it was African Americans who fought back against neighborhood businesses, government representa-tives, and law enforcement agencies they perceived as unfairly targeting them.[3] The 1992 unrest, however, pitted people of color against one another, with Korean merchants suffering over half of the total property damage, which was committed largely by Blacks and Latinos.

The Los Angeles unrest in 1992 proved devastating for the Korean community and the city, attracting national and international attention. Even today, parts of the city have not fully recovered. In the wake of the incident, Korean immigrants were perceived differently in America. They had previously been viewed as the model minority, but during the unrest they were seen as the oppressor, which resulted in a decline in Korean immigration to the United States. More significantly, the beating of Rodney King and the subsequent acquittal of the officers became a touchstone for discussing race relations and the criminal justice system in this country.

Only a few days before the King verdict, I had conducted an ethnographic interview with the Korean manager of Tim's Liquor Store on the corner of Florence and Normandie, an intersection that would become a focal point for the violence. A few days after the unrest, I returned to my field site and stood speechless at the magnitude of the destruction and the disappearance of my interviewees' businesses. I witnessed people scavenging for burnt metal with bloody hands and felt guilty that, as a researcher, I could not prevent this devastation in some way. To make matters worse, I struggled with an increasing level of criticism from the devastated Korean community, who insisted that academics were exploiting the violence by giving high-profile interviews and serving as experts on national news outlets. Despite these critiques, I continued my research for over a decade after the unrest.

In this book, I seek to revisit the Los Angeles unrest of 1992, focusing on the related interethnic and racial tensions. While there has been ample media coverage and a number of scholarly books and articles on the subject, this study is unique in several ways. First, I focus on how structural inequality impacted relations among Koreans, African Americans, and Latinos.[4] Second, race, citizenship, class, and culture were axes of inequality in a multi-tiered "racial cartography" that affected how Los Angeles residents thought about and interacted with each other. Third, although race and class are often considered the foundations of social inequality, I argue that one is not necessarily more influential than the other, nor can they be considered separately from each other. Fourth, race, class, citizenship, and culture are interwoven in hierarchical power relations among groups, as evidenced in processes of social inequality and conflict.

I propose a conceptual framework of "racial cartography"[5] that offers insight into intergroup tensions and relations within the context of the changing demographic contours of the US. This conception moves beyond political scientist Claire Kim's notion of "racial triangulation" (1999) to extend to the interactions of race, class, citizenship, and culture. My book will demonstrate the value of a unitary approach, which will encourage further discussion and research. Furthermore, this is a comparative work that delves into the complexities of multiracial and multiethnic relations in American cities remade by immigration during the past five decades. I make a case for treating race and ethnicity as categories that cannot be reduced to single variables for the purposes of expedient, but ultimately misleading, quantitative analysis. My book aims to add the ethnographic nuance that quantitative analysis can't offer, to really examine the interconnections. I suggest that the meanings of race and ethnicity emerge only through a complex web of cross-referential signs.

This book will draw on neo-Marxist scholarship through its emphasis on racialized capitalism and its deployment of cultural studies methods and theories in examining multiracial/ethnic tensions in South LA. Its theoretical stance owes much to critical race theory and critical ethnic studies. It is a processual analysis, because the tension that exploded during the LA unrest had long been simmering due to structural inequality. I began my empirical research on structural inequality in the US vis-à-vis Korean-Black-Latino relations before the unrest and continued for over a decade until 2002. Thus, the main research question of this book does not revolve around the LA unrest itself, but rather focuses on the interethnic relations in South LA that provided the groundwork for it. The book uses the LA unrest and its aftermath to understand the racial, ethnic, and class relations of the 1990s and 2000s. It also explores how different Angelenos think about race, class, and culture at the end of the second millennium. My main objective is to explore how different axes of inequality—race, citizenship, class, and culture—have made an indelible impact on racial minorities and their relationship with one another.

I argue that different positions in relation to US racial hegemony, capitalism, and national identity tend to create sociopolitical barriers and obstruct potentially meaningful social relationships among African Americans, Latinos, and Koreans. Race, class, citizenship, and cultural difference disadvantage these groups relative to the mainstream White population, although in different ways. Discourses on differential access to power, resources, and legitimacy have played a central role in establishing distinct categories of belonging, worthiness, and respectability.

The LA unrest involves two primary ethnic antagonisms—Black-Korean and Latino-Korean relations—which are conceptualized here as racialized class (and cultural) conflicts. As Korean immigrant merchants appeared to play the paradoxical role of both oppressed and oppressor within the ghetto/barrio, they were often treated with hostility, largely because of the exploitative relationship between Korean merchants and Black and Latino customers and employees. Therefore, I analyze Korean American, African American, and Latino constructions of race and culture before and after the riots, and I explore how these constructions relate to class relationships across ethnicity.

This book is less concerned with whether racial minorities' attitudes toward other minority groups have improved or become more tolerant; rather, it critically examines historical and structural processes that inform shifting racial articulation. In utilizing these analytical categories, I aim to understand race, class, etc. as interconnected systems of oppression in the US.

While it is important to consider the interrelations between race, class, and culture, it is also necessary to specify the dynamics of these interrelationships. As Allen and Chung state,

> Each hierarchical system [race, class, citizenship, or culture] is conceived as both autonomous and overlapping with other systems, yet the degree to which each system may influence the material lives of social actors is not linear, homogeneous, nor universal. . . . Depending on the context and the way in which they are organized and applied, different stratification systems are themselves hierarchical and diverse in effect. (2000, 799)

In other words, not all intersections are homologous. Furthermore, as Claire Kim (2015) suggests, we should think not just about the way in which systems of difference are "interlocking," but rather how they operate "synergistically," deriving power from one another. Following this model, my study aligns with more recent work on social inequality and explores the compounded nature of the interaction between race and class in the US.

I have found in my research that race, class, citizenship, and culture are entwined and produce oppression differently than when they operate separately. To better understand these relationships, I examine the tension among Korean immigrant merchants and Black and Latino customers and residents in South LA. I also analyze the varying constructions of these four dimensions of inequality before and after the unrest.

Finally, I look at how race is mutually determined by both ideational and material factors that later shape class and cultural relations. This will involve assessing the way minorities describe racial, ethnic, and cultural differences and determining whether their descriptions reflect different moments in the sociohistorical juncture of race. This project also investigates how race and ethnicity both impact and are impacted by changing class relations. Specifically, this refers to the material entitlement Korean small business owners represent in relation to poor and dispossessed Black and Latino ghetto/barrio customers.

My analysis will highlight the continuing significance of race, but it will not reify the concept. I disentangle the strategic role of race and relate it to class and culture. Race (and ethnicity) is not a form of false consciousness or a "phantasmal" mystification of class. Rather, when "ascribed" cultural differences rationalize structures of inequality, race and ethnicity take on a cogent reality. By identifying the classist nature of racial and ethnic tensions between immigrant merchants and other working-class minorities, I hope to give readers a better understanding of the causes and consequences of those three horrific days in 1992.

## A UNITARY CONCEPTUAL FRAMEWORK OF INEQUALITY: RACE, CLASS, AND CULTURE

Two main explanations have been advanced regarding intergroup hostility between Blacks and Koreans. The first is a cultural-psychological explanation. Focusing on the ideational level, this perspective looks for the root of racial antipathy in areas such as cultures,[6] preferences, or psychology of the groups involved.[7] In their analyses of Black-Korean tensions, Ella Stewart (1989) and Benjamin Bailey (1996) focus on cultural differences and language barriers between Korean merchants and their Black customers (see chapters 4 and 5). Cultural and psychological factors alone are limited in explaining how over-the-counter disputes between Black customers and Korean store owners sometimes developed into boycotting. It becomes crucial then to pay attention to both micro- and macro-level processes (see chapters 2 and 5).

The second explanation advanced by other scholars attempts to examine Black-Korean tensions from a material and structural (political, economic, and ideological) foundation. Nancy Abelmann and John Lie (1995) provide a critique of what they call "American ideological assumptions" about Black-Korean conflict as framed by the Los Angeles riots. They indict the media of constructing and reifying the Black-Korean tension. Jennifer Lee (2002) explores how civility, not conflict, characterizes most interracial commercial interactions between Jewish, Korean, and Black merchants and their customers. Patrick Joyce (2003) argues intergroup violence is less likely to occur in cities with strong political institutions because group tensions and grievances are channeled and given voice through existing organizations.

The most widely used and canonized structural explanation of the Black-Korean conflict and the 1992 Los Angeles unrest is Pyong Gap Min's (1996; 2008) application of Edna Bonacich's middleman minority model (1973) to Black-Korean tension.[8] Min explores how the Korean immigrant merchant's economic "middleman" role is often caught between the conflict of low income minority customers and large corporate suppliers.[9] However, in recent decades, this middleman minority hypothesis has been criticized. Claire Kim (2000) registered the strongest criticism of the middleman minority hypothesis, calling it a "racial scapegoating argument" that obfuscates racial power: "the middleman economic formation as given . . . asks only how Blacks and

Koreans act within this formation, rather than asking, say, how the middleman economic formation might itself have come about as a result of racial power" (C. Kim 2000, 4).

Importantly, Claire Kim (2000) contends that boycotts are best understood not as a campaign to scapegoat Koreans or as an irrational misdirection of group anger against an innocent yet racially vulnerable target, but instead as a social movement involving the intentional exercise of collective agency in the pursuit of specific political goals.

Several books have been published on the Los Angeles civil unrest. Robert Gooding-Williams (1993) and Mark Baldassare (1994) provide useful analyses of what happened in late April and early May of 1992: the former emphasizes political-economic and cultural aspects, and the latter discusses demographic and sociopsychological perspectives. Darnell Hunt (1997) examines the way different races—Latinos, Blacks, and Whites—interpreted the media coverage of the 1992 riots. Although not about the unrest, João H. Costa Vargas (2006) focuses on ethnographic fieldwork of African Americans' struggle for empowerment in South LA, focusing on gang violence, drug abuse, unemployment, and inadequate schools. Finally, Brenda Stevenson (2013) focuses on the neglected Du-Harlins shooting.

Although my work is clearly in conversation with this literature, I studied the area affected before the riots occurred, which offers a longitudinal perspective. Moreover, instead of looking for one causal factor, my approach considers the political, economic, social, and cultural dimensions of ethnic antagonism, as well as the multilayered development of conflict between these groups. In using this process-oriented analysis, I identify the multiple variables involved in the emergence of this conflict.

In existing literature on Black-Korean tensions and the Los Angeles civil unrest, the concepts of race and class have not been well-discussed—except C. Kim's 2000 work—with little attention paid to the question of inequality. This study engages with race, class, and national belonging as an intersectional nexus (Crenshaw 1989, 1991). Intersectionality as an analytical approach emerged initially as a mechanism for revealing how power works in uneven and differentiated ways. Legal scholar Kimberlé Crenshaw uses it to demonstrate the limitations of the single-axis frameworks that dominated antidiscrimination regimes and antiracist and feminist discourses (Carbado, Crenshaw, Mays, and Tomlinson 2013, 311).[10] Similarly, sociologist Evelyn Nakano Glenn argues against treating race and gender as separate fields of analysis, stating, "in the United States race and gender have been simultaneously organizing principles and products of citizenship and labor" (2002, 236). Thus, intersectionality has moved from its foundation in Black feminism to a notion adopted by critical race and feminist studies more broadly.

What makes an analysis intersectional is "its adoption of an intersectional way of thinking about the problem of sameness and difference and its relation to power," while "conceiving of categories not as distinct but as always in the process of creating and being created by dynamics of power" (Cho et al. 2013, 795).

In the United States, where race intersects with class, citizenship, and other axes of power to shape people's access to resources and social networks, class often operates as an invisible social structure, and most people experience their class position through race. Intersectionality can allow us to identify how different groups are racialized in related yet distinct ways, while simultaneously helping us to analyze the importance of social class, citizenship, and culture in structuring interactions. Following Crenshaw's notion of intersectionality, I explore the complex and cumulative interactions between multiple factors—race, class, citizenship, and culture—in the making of social inequalities and how these converge in people's everyday lives to constrain and enable human agency. One of my main goals is to develop a unified theory regarding the intersections of ethnicity, race, and class with a materialist approach to these phenomena.

What the racial triangulation model tends to overlook is that race never operates alone; rather, it articulates itself through gender, sexuality, class, nation, ethnicity, culture, and other differences that form heterogeneous identities and crosscutting social hierarchies. I am advocating an approach that emphasizes "the dynamic, independent, yet intersecting quality of race in relation to other systems of oppression" (Allen and Chung 2000, 799). As Charles Tilly (1998) writes, differential access to advantages are not due to "individual differences" in ability, but rather to oppression that exists across binary groups, such as "black/white, male/female, citizen/foreigner" (7). More importantly, these inequalities are the result of processes such as "exploitation, opportunity hoarding, emulation and adaptation" (Tilly 1998, 13). Durable inequalities such as racism arise via systems of social closure and exclusion as well as exploitation. While exploitation is mostly practiced by elite groups, opportunity hoarding is often practiced by non-elites and does not require the cooperation of those who are exploited. Instead, it consists of the monopolization of valuable resources by one group and the exclusion of other groups. Thus, many minority ethnic groups set up networks of information to benefit their own members at the expense of outsiders. This book attempts to subsume race, class, citizenship, and culture under a unitary conceptual framework that recognizes the intersections of different forms of inequality.

The configuration of race is not relevant only to other forms of collective identity; it also informs an understanding of history/memory, place, forms of production, and systems of political belief. This problem of intersectionality has been partly addressed by Aihwa Ong (1996), who examines the impact of transnational capitalism on citizen-making; she goes beyond Michael Omi and Howard Winant's popular theorizing of racial politics in terms of American citizenship and the nation-state. As Ong (1996, 739) argues, we need to study the shifting constructions of racial politics with attention to normative performance or schemes of cultural assessment. In a later work (2003), Ong examines the racial formation of Cambodian refugees in terms of cultural citizenship via medical, judiciary, religious, and economic institutions in the US. Similarly, I focus on the dimensions of race, class, and culture entangled in the everyday experience, in the racial and class formations in public and political spheres, and in market sectors that feed into Black-Korean-Latino tensions.

Ong also notes that hierarchical schemes of racial and cultural difference intersect in a complex, contingent way to locate minorities of color—in Ong's case, Asian immigrants—from different class backgrounds. Comparing the experiences of rich and poor Asian immigrants in the United States, she discusses the way immigrants of color are subjected to one of two "processes of normalization: an ideological whitening or blackening" (1996, 737). Whether an immigrant group undergoes ideological whitening or blackening is determined by the "human capital and consumer power" that they bring with them to the US (1996, 737). Ong's insight can be applied to my South LA case study. One relevant question my book asks is, are new immigrants from Asia and Latin America with diverse class backgrounds subjected to different kinds of racialization such as ideological whitening and blackening?

## RACIAL CARTOGRAPHY

Claire Kim defines racial power as the process by which the white status quo reinforces its dominance over people of color through a variety of "political, social, and cultural processes" (2000, 2). This racial power creates a social order within which Koreans are a "triangulated" group: they possess a favored cultural position as a model minority and enjoy relative economic success, but they are still permanently foreign and "unassimilable" (2000, 450). C. Kim's study is a crucial intervention, especially because most studies on conflict between Black residents and Korean merchants focus on the "dyadic relations" between the two groups without considering the broader context of race relations in the United States or the role of a hierarchical racial order.[11] C. Kim (1999) also problematizes the concept of racial hierarchy, which, as a vertical ranking, does not consider the ways non-white groups are racialized differently (C. Kim 2004, 998).

While C. Kim's study relates to race, the analysis needs to be expanded, as Korean immigrants' commercial activities in Black neighborhoods have as much to do with their transnational class resources as well as with the racial ordering process (see chapter 1).[12] There are various forms of inequality underlying Black-Korean tensions in addition to racial power/order, such as class, citizenship, and culture, and it is important to include them in analyzing important social phenomena (see chapters 3, 4, 5, 8 and 9). I find C. Kim's notion of a "field of racial positions" to be useful for locating racialized groups on a plane defined by at least two axes of inequality in order to better grasp the mutual constitution of group racialization processes and their rankings. According to C. Kim, public discourse about racial groups and their relative status generates a field of racial positions within a given time and place. She argues that Asian Americans have been "racially triangulated" vis-à-vis Whites and African Americans in this field of racial positions:

> Racial triangulation occurs by means of two types of simultaneous, linked processes: (1) processes of "relative valorization," whereby dominant group A (Whites) valorizes subordinate group B (Asian Americans) relative to subordinate group C (Blacks) on cultural and/or racial grounds in order to dominate both groups, but especially the latter, and (2) processes of "civic ostracism," whereby dominant group A (Whites) constructs subordinate group B (Asian Americans) as immutably foreign and unassimilable with Whites on cultural and/or racial grounds in order to ostracize them from the body politic and civic membership. (C. Kim 1999, 107)

Drawing on this insight, I have developed the concept of a racial cartography based on a contemporary study of South LA. My criteria for the racialization of various minority groups differ from C. Kim's superiority/inferiority and insider/outsider categories, since I do not believe these dimensions are mutually exclusive. In addition, because they are based on a triangular formation with an unknown point and two known (Black and White) points as the vertices (see figure 0.1 below), racial dynamics cannot go beyond the two fixed points, as seen with the conventional White/Black bipolar framework.[13]

My own research focuses on how structural inequality—specifically, race, citizenship, class, and culture—impacted relations among Koreans, African Americans, and Latinos before and after the unrest. These four axes of inequality make up a multitiered "racial cartography" that affected how the Los Angeles residents thought about and interacted with each other. With its emphasis on cognitive mapping, this model represents the most effective way to analyze my interviewees' discourse on the dynamics of interracial relationships.

The notion of "cognitive mapping" is adopted from Fredric Jameson, but the idea was developed in the 1940s and 1950s—culminating in the work of Kevin Lynch (1960)—and was very popular with geographers in the 1960s and 1970s.[14] While Jameson refers to cognitive maps as "our individual social relationships to local, national, and international class realities" (1991, 52), I extend the relationships to include race and citizenship. Similarly, sociologist Wendy Roth argues that people use cognitive schemas to help them organize cultural understandings of race (2012). How do regional (specifically South LA) racial hierarchies and relationships shape the contours or cognitive maps? How do individuals whose bodies are differentially racialized, gendered, and classed experience cognitive maps? Racial cartography is a mental roadmap where people chart out their historical relationship to each other, and this framework foregrounds the dialectical relationship between Whiteness, Blackness, Latino-ness, and Asian American-ness. Racial cartography is full of unequal and differential power relations, not just between Whites and African Americans, but also between other racial categories, pertaining to race, class, and citizenship in different institutional contexts.

My goal was to visualize a discussion on interracial relationships among my interviewees in South LA that involved the issues of racial status, rights and entitlements, racial distance, and racial tension. With Whites at the top and African Americans and Native Americans securely positioned at the right and bottom (see figure 0.1), Asian Americans and Latinos have not yet been fully granted national belonging and symbolic integration into the US nation-state, even though they have over a century of presence, contribution, and struggle in the US.

Racial cartography constitutes a set of orienting social maps that people carry in their heads to negotiate reality, but these maps are both social and spatial (given that segregation plays such an important role in race relations).[15] They are built via social experience (including common stereotypes, media input, etc.), class position, and gender, as well as personal interaction in the real world of urban space. Moreover, they are not dualistic in structure (Black-White, Latino-Black), but they exist within a landscape of racial hierarchies that are dynamic, often noncongruent, and contested (i.e., the hierarchy is not universally agreed upon or stable). I focus on selected variables in the creation of these cognitive maps, including the question of priority of occupancy (territoriality). My model is more of a hologram or a layering, which comes into play situationally; in that sense, it is truer to real lived experience. It is landscape that people both live in and have a role in creating.

There are several assumptions that undergird my model of racial cartography. First, racial positions are mapped out along the axis of local schemes: specifically, economic indicators (Y-axis) and rights of prior occupancy

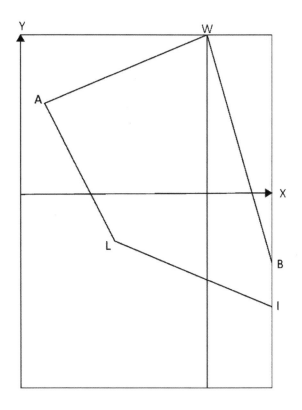

X: Centuries present within U.S. since 1776

Y: Household income above taxable minimum

     W: White

     A: Asian American (1840-50s)

     L: Latino

     B: Black

     I: American Indian (pre-1700s)

Figure 0.1.   Racial Cartography

(X-axis).[16] Significant gaps in socioeconomic status between these groups (Y) imply that the US is becoming multipolar.

Race has long been the modality in which class is lived, as well as the determining factor for participation in the "national" economy, including which sectors and jobs people have access to and with/against whom they identify and struggle (Hall 1980, as cited in Jung 2009, 391). The politics of national belonging intertwine with race, class, and other categories in the making and remaking of the nation. For precision, let us say that Y = household income above taxable minimum and X = centuries present within the US since 1776. The Y dimension requires a different strategy from conventional thinking about socioeconomic indicators. Instead of employing median household income, in this model, real income after taxes is used in order to emphasize the fact that all minorities except for Asians earn below the cost of their own social reproduction (i.e., they do not earn enough to support themselves).

According to a study by the Urban Institute-Brookings Institution Tax Policy Center, 46 percent of US households did not pay federal income taxes in 2011, although most paid other federal taxes, including Medicare and Social Security. About half of people who don't pay income taxes are simply poor, and the tax code explicitly exempts them.

Furthermore, Black wealth is only one-twelfth of White wealth, and Black financial assets are, at the median, zero (Oliver and Shapiro 1995). The 1990 Census median family income for Asian Pacific Americans (APA) was $36,000, higher than that of Whites ($31,000), Latinos ($24,000), and African Americans ($19,000). However, 14 percent of the APA population lived below the poverty line, which is one and a half times higher than the poverty rate for Whites. This lowers Asian Americans' position on the Y dimension.

Second, a consideration of Asian Americans and Latinos adds complexities that redefine traditional relationships between race and power. Race and power are intrinsically related, as race assumes meaning only when it becomes a criterion of stratification. As Robin Kelley notes, race has always been about supremacy and one group oppressing another (2012, 87). Therefore, this racial cartography is full of unequal power relations, not just between Whites and African Americans, but also between other racial groups, which implicates class and citizenship in different institutional contexts.

Third, the model is flexible: it can be modified depending on the time, place, and changing nature of relations. For instance, economic improvement or cumulated records of residency in the US will facilitate a better position for a group.

Fourth, unlike African Americans, Latinos and Asian Americans do not have a legacy of slavery in the US, and therefore, they do not experience the same kinds of systemic discrimination (Lee and Bean 2004, 233). "Black" is an unambiguous racial label in the US. The "African American" census label is often "an expression of solidarity, of shared heritage, of the shared discrimination and oppression they experience at the bottom of the US racial order" (Jaynes and Williams 1989, as quoted in Hunt 1997, 77). The term "Latino" is popular in LA, with its large population of Mexican and Central American immigrants. Although few interviewees referred to themselves as "Latinos," preferring instead terms related to their national origins, American society writ large tends to lump Latin American immigrants and their children into a large, pan-ethnic group and distribute rewards and punishments accordingly: "As representation, this panethnic label becomes a racial one, attributing bodily and other characteristics to members of the group, explaining/justifying the group's relative position in the racial order" (Hunt 1997, 54). As is evident, people do not always identify themselves with a racial category; rather, it is often assigned. Despite intra-racial variation, people seem to know what the norm or general attitude toward a certain racial group seems to be.

My ethnographic interviews with African Americans suggest that economic indicators (Y), a proxy for class, alone cannot explain the presence of the racial status quo. As shown in figure 0.1, African Americans promote a "right of prior occupancy" (X), a proxy for citizenship, and "the politics of national belonging" as the alternate tool of analysis. In other words, they believe they are owed more because of their rights of prior occupancy. African Americans' insistence on rights of residency in the US partly explains why they are not always sympathetic toward immigrants, who they often view as doing better than Blacks economically despite their shorter presence in the US. In other words, economic indicators and rights of prior occupancy might be conceived as being encompassing and hierarchical, rather than oppositional. US society has allocated racial status, rights, and entitlements based on socioeconomic indicators, culture, political power, and symbolic integration, including citizenship.

Explaining the model requires a brief comparison of immigration/citizenship status. African Americans were not citizens until 1868, and African American men could not vote until 1870, except in the American South (Stevenson 2013, 87). In the case of Latinos, around half of the current population arrived before 1965—with some Mexican citizens being granted US citizenship as early as 1848 in the aftermath of the Mexican-American War—and half arrived after. Asian immigrants are the most recent group to enter the US. From its first deliberations about citizenship in 1790 up until 1952, Congress restricted naturalization to White immigrants (in addition to extending citizenship to Blacks in 1868), and it did not truly dismantle racial restrictions on immigration until 1965 (Goodman et al. 2012, 70). Latinos and Asian

Americans have undergone differential racialization. Latinos generally confront more overt racial discrimination than Asian Americans (Jimenez 2008).

Given the struggles African Americans overcame to gain both physical
freedom and citizenship, they at times relegate Latinos and Koreans to the
categories of "immigrant," "foreigner," or "undocumented worker," which
are categories that highlight their un-Americanness. The question commonly
raised by Black interviewees was whether other groups had suffered as much
as African Americans, whose ancestors contributed to the creation of this
country and fought to attain civil rights, and which groups still have not
gained full equality. At the same time, both Latino and Korean immigrants
viewed African Americans as advantaged by their US citizenship and English
fluency. Korean riot victims and their allies painfully recognized that their
political, social, and cultural power was no match for that of Blacks. From
Blacks' point of view, they were true Americans, while Koreans represented
unwanted, politically impotent immigrants who subsisted in the shadows (N.
Kim, 2008). Both Korean and Latino respondents reported their belief that
Blacks held "forever foreigner"-type prejudices against them (I elaborate on
this in chapter 2) and that their negative attitudes toward African Americans
were shaped by these tensions.

## RESEARCH STRATEGY

This study is based on in-depth ethnographic interviews and informal conversations with Korean immigrant merchants and their Black and Latino customers, as well as participant observation conducted from 1992 to 1997 and
again in 2002. In addition, I relied on a comprehensive archive of documents:
newspaper reports, TV clips, government reports, magazine articles, and various published histories. My fieldwork was prolonged because of difficulties
related to finding Korean immigrant interviewees after the riots. I also had to
pause my interviews with Latino participants due to a brief relocation to the
East Coast (1996–1998). From January 1992 to 1997, my research assistants
and I conducted both interviews and nonparticipant observation. In 2002,
as a follow-up, my research assistant conducted participant observation of a
Korean-owned liquor store for eight months.

According to the city planning department, South LA is bounded by Pico
Boulevard to the north, 120th Street to the south, Figueroa Street to the east,
and Arlington and Van Ness Avenues to the west; this constituted my research area.[17] For my ethnographic research, I surveyed the geographic area
of Figueroa Street to the east, Western Avenue to the west, the University of

# Major Areas Affected During
# The 1992 Los Angeles Civil Unrest

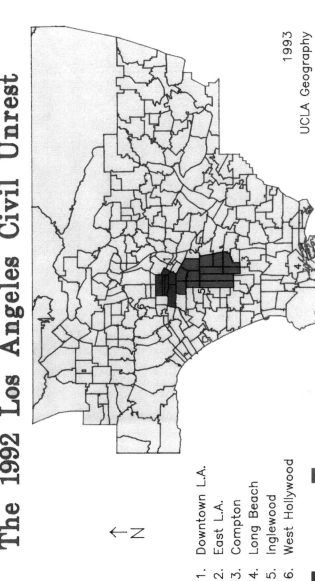

N ←

1. Downtown L.A.
2. East L.A.
3. Compton
4. Long Beach
5. Inglewood
6. West Hollywood

■ Koreatown    ■ South Central L.A.

Boundary File:   L.A. Zipcodes.

1993
UCLA Geography
John Yong Cheun

**Figure 0.2.   Major Areas Affected during the 1992 Los Angeles Civil Unrest**

# Sample Distribution Of Korean Businesses Damaged During The 1992 Civil Unrest

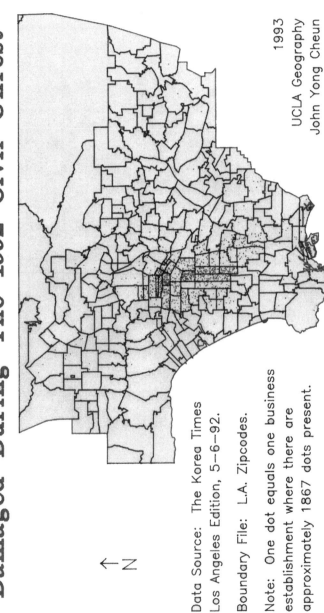

1993
UCLA Geography
John Yong Cheun

← N

Data Source: The Korea Times
Los Angeles Edition, 5–6–92.

Boundary File: L.A. Zipcodes.

Note: One dot equals one business
establishment where there are
approximately 1867 dots present.

**Figure 0.3.   Sample distribution of Korean Businesses Damaged during the Civil Unrest**

Southern California to the north, and 90th Street to the south (see figures 0.2 and 0.3), taking into consideration the distribution pattern of Korean-owned businesses. Before the 1992 unrest, most of the interviews focused on the 1991 Soon Ja Du/Latasha Harlins incident. Du's Empire Liquor Market was located at 9172 South Figueroa Street in the city of Compton, in the suburb adjacent to the research area. The remaining interviews were conducted later, with a focus on the events of 1992, and were expanded to include Latinos.

I was interested in analyzing South LA residents' moral arguments and political debates about Black-Korean-Latino relations surrounding the 1992 unrest, as well as the merchant-customer interactions at various Korean business establishments. Interviews and informal conversations were the most appropriate methods for collecting data, especially because residents and merchants lived and worked in various places. This study includes 142 life histories and ethnographic interviews, with the following participant breakdown: fifty-one African Americans, sixty-six Korean immigrants, eighteen Latinos, and two Chinese people. Five Korean immigrant merchants interviewed before the unrest were re-interviewed after the unrest. Of the forty-nine interviews before the unrest, there are thirty interviews with African Americans and nineteen with Korean immigrants. Of the ninety-three interviews after the unrest, there are twenty-one interviews with African Americans, fifty-five with Koreans, eighteen with Latinos, and two with Chinese people.

I held interviews with Korean immigrants and conducted nonparticipant observation at their liquor stores and grocery markets from January to April 1992, and from July 1992 to March 1994. I sought interviews with any willing Korean immigrant merchants in my research area. I also interviewed Black and Latino customers living or working in South LA (or Pico Union) and also customers of Korean-owned stores. Black customer interviews were held from January to April 1992 and from July 1993 to January 1996. While before the unrest my research assistants regularly visited a Black-owned beauty salon for non-participant observation and interviews, in the aftermath we resumed these interviews in their homes and community organizations. This beauty salon was burnt down during the unrest and later relocated to Koreatown. Latinos, both US-born and immigrants, were interviewed at Latino-run businesses, community organizations, churches, and parks. We also attended a number of dinner parties, picnics, weddings, and graduation ceremonies between May 1995 and May 1997.

Among Korean immigrant interviewees, thirty were male and thirty-six were female. There was a wide range in age with a slight predominance of people in their fifties. Forty-four graduated from or attended college, seventeen graduated from high school, and five had postgraduate education. Fifteen were either 1.5- or second-generation immigrants, while the remainder were first-generation immigrants. The length of time since immigration varied from two to twenty-three years. Two-thirds of the Korean immigrant interviewees owned liquor stores, grocery markets, or supermarkets, and seven were community organizers.

Among Black interviewees, twenty-five were male and twenty-six were female. Nearly half of them were in their twenties and thirties; the rest ranged in age from their forties to their sixties. Merchant-customer disputes often involved younger customers; thus, I included a larger sample of young people among my Black interviewees. Most of these interviewees identified themselves as either Black, African American, or both, with the exception of two Belizean immigrants and one Afro-Mexican American. Two-thirds graduated from or attended college. The occupation of my respondents varied, with ten college students and graduate students, seven secretaries, five unemployed people, four beauticians, and three community organizers; the rest were employed in various professions, including teaching, nursing, the postal service, janitorial, delivery services, or car repair.

Among Latino interviewees,[18] nearly two-thirds were male and the rest were female, with most of my respondents falling between the ages of twenty-three to forty-eight years old. Except for a few second-generation Mexican Americans, they were all first-generation immigrants. The length of time since immigration varied from six to twenty-three years. The majority of interviewees were high school graduates, with a few having either a college or just an elementary education. In terms of occupation at the time of interview, there were five community organizers, three unemployed, two pastors, and two market workers; the rest were employed in car repair, construction, security, sales, or clerical work.

This study makes no claim of generalizability based on a random or representative sample of Korean merchants and their Black and Latino patrons. I tried to include a crosssection of people from South LA to examine the state of race relations in the aftermath of the riots. Given the media's propensity to stereotype the Black community as unemployed or gang-affiliated, I sought to obtain a substantial sample of working- or middle-class African Americans.[19] In terms of educational attainment, Latino immigrants' educational level was considerably lower than that of the other two groups. Although Korean immigrants' educational level was higher than African Americans, 25 percent of Korean immigrants and 33 percent of African Americans were only high school graduates. Most of my Korean interviewees had lived in the US for more than ten years, although they had often run businesses in South LA for less than five years.

I was able to employ the conventional method of participant observation to a limited degree. First, high crime and personal safety issues made it difficult for me to reside in South LA. Second, Korean-immigrant-owned stores were already heavily scrutinized by the media and the public after the unrest. In fact, many stores were equipped with multiple security cameras (see chapter 5). The ethnographer can become "an additional 'eye' of the panopticon" (Gounis 1996, 114). At the same time, my research strategy may well have impacted the reception of the African American and Latino research subjects. My initial fear of South LA may have shaped how I conducted my study, and my ability to relate to poor Black and Latino residents might have been affected by this fear. However, once I began spending time in South LA, I quickly found it to have a strong sense of community—much more so than my own West LA neighborhood that is dominated by a university population. I regularly commuted to South LA to make observations during weekends and summers.

I conducted all the interviews with Korean merchants in Korean and conducted some of the African American and Latino customer/resident interviews; the rest were conducted by research assistants (see below). Chapters 2 through 4 and chapter 6 draw on nonparticipant observation at African American-run businesses, such as hair salons, and at Korean immigrant business establishments and community organizations. Chapter 5 particularly features ethnographic detail stemming from participant observation of Korean merchants with their customers. Chapter 7 draws up community participation observation at meetings, rallies, public hearings, and other social gatherings.

Field researchers of various racial and ethnic backgrounds were used to assess the interracial dynamics between researcher and subject, as well as their reception by the community. African American research subjects often indicated their discomfort with Asian American interviewers. In response, I matched the race/ethnicity of our research subjects with those of the researchers to a certain extent in that most interviews with African Americans and Latinos were conducted by African American and Latino research assistants, respectively. A racially mixed researcher, Jeff Saito—his father is Japanese American and his mother is Mexican American—was received positively by Black interviewees, perhaps because Jeff's family lived in Watts. Jocelyn Henry, a Black researcher, came from a middle-class background and was initially apprehensive about entering South LA. Nonetheless, she managed to conduct interviews successfully, as she was introduced to research subjects by friends.[20] Caroline Kim and Helen Na, Asian American assistants, accompanied me to most of the interviews with Korean immigrant merchants. Two other Asian American assistants, Sharon Park Kim and Kathryne Cho Yoon, also conducted interviews.[21] Finally, Dave Kim, who had worked at his family's liquor store in South LA for 7.5 years, provided participant observation notes (see chapter 5).

While Korean merchants were receptive to me and the Korean American research assistants, Black and Latino residents showed more varied responses. In one instance, we were able to conduct informal group interviews when community members listened in on the interview of a Black woman at a hair salon. The researchers began to pose questions, and it was only a matter of time before the others joined the conversation. One man was interviewed while he styled a patron's hair. The place was filled with excitement and laughter. Everyone had something to say, and the interviews multiplied. Interaction among participants became an important source for significant insights concerning our investigation, which might not have been possible with private, individual interviews. Public spaces like the hair salon allowed individual interviews to become informal focus groups rich in anecdotal data.

While my main research questions concerned African American and Latino interviewees' interactions with Korean Americans, particularly Korean merchants, I also inquired about their race relations with Whites and people of other races/ethnicities, as well as their own communities. Topics included how they were affected by change occurring in South LA, their perspectives on problems in South LA, feelings about national belonging, and work and immigration history. However, it must be stressed that no narratives from Black or Latino interviewees granted me the intimate level of knowledge I have of Korean shop owners.

## INTERCESSORY ETHNOGRAPHY

The events of 1991 and 1992 solidified my belief that feminist, postcolonial, and minority ethnographers should engage with what I call "intercessory ethnography." There are at least four steps in this process: 1) Ethnographers should radically unlearn those privileges that make them witting or unwitting accomplices to subject positions of "Western" theory (Scott 1989, 84); 2) Instead of collecting answers to the given question, ethnographers should commit themselves to communicating with interviewees and allow for critical exchanges (but only after becoming familiar with the field situation); 3) Ethnographers should try to intervene selectively and cautiously in evoking responses from interviewees; and 4) Ethnographers should thoroughly reflect on and integrate the challenges and even opposition voiced by research subjects during the entire process of conducting and writing ethnography. Ethnographers must become agent provocateurs, if necessary, and take calculated risks. Otherwise, they are only patronizing the people they study and reinforcing negative views of ethnographers as self-promoting or opportunistic.

My conception of intercessory ethnography comes from the idea of the social sciences as a social intervention. As an educator in the Korean and Asian American community in Los Angeles, I do not conduct and write ethnography solely as an objective observer. Rather, I try to take a more active, dialectical, and intercessory role and develop a critical consciousness about the people I study. I look to Paulo Freire, who employed a dialectical method in organizing and liberating the oppressed people of various Third World countries (Brazil, Chile, Guinea-Bissau, and Mozambique). Furthermore, Hegelian dialectics envision the interplay between ethnography and theory-making. "Dialogue" in this sense is no longer a conversation between two people, but rather the display of cross-arguments that become a social basis for efficacy, authority, or utility. Nevertheless, the question remains as to what role an active/critical/intercessory ethnographer can assume.

An intercessory ethnographer should be sensitive to what might be potentially offensive to research subjects. An ethnographer who comes from an underrepresented background is often concerned with fighting against existing stereotypes about their community. A critical understanding of oneself can help the process of community empowerment. However, such critical representations potentially cause ethnographers to embody historical stereotypes that have been used to justify marginalization. The position of the feminist/postcolonial/minority anthropologist is necessarily an ambivalent one, as James Clifford and George Marcus (1986) put it, since ethnographic truths are inherently partial and incomplete.[22]

Ultimately, intercessory ethnography can function as a productive and meaningful way for a minority researcher to engage in critical dialogue with the construction of historical narratives and the politics of collective remembering. For instance, the initial interpreters of the 1992 LA unrest—the media and journalists—were the first to foreground Black rage. The higher incidences of Latino arrests and the gravitation of violence to Latino neighborhoods later challenged this representation, showing that this issue did not exclusively affect African Americans. Similarly, another popular explanation of the cause of the unrest, Black-Korean tension, was refuted by many of my interviewees. At the same time, young Korean Americans who neither experienced nor remember the unrest possess an overly simplistic understanding of the events of April and May 1992: they tend to blame it entirely on Korean immigrants and their racism. This new generation has a radically different perspective than that of the Koreans who experienced it personally, and I found my position as an intercessory ethnographer crucial to acting as a bridge between these two groups.

## The African American Response

In conducting my research, I received three different kinds of reception from Black informants. As most of my ethnography was conducted in local venues, such as African American-run barbershops and hair salons, Black interviewees seemed comfortable with sharing their opinions. The first category of response was somewhat positive, with some African Americans surprisingly initiating conversation with me. Many Black men had been stationed in Korea during the Korean War and probably had sustained interactions with Koreans. As war veterans, they held complex views that had been shaped by their understanding of racism and its impact on other people of color worldwide. Some veterans complained about Korean merchants' lack of respect for African Americans in their own neighborhoods, even though Black veterans had fought on their behalf during the Korean War. Other veterans, however, felt comfortable around Koreans and offered their assistance. Some refused to support the Black boycott of Korean stores, which was then occurring under the leadership of Danny Bakewell.

In contrast to Black war veterans, other community members responded negatively, treating me as if I were guilty of a crime similar to that committed by Soon Ja Du. "Yeah, that was the sentence for the death of a colored woman," one respondent told me, referring to Du's sentence of time already served, community service, and only $500 restitution to Harlins' family. "I wrote a letter in support of recalling that white bitch Judge Karlin." The woman who said this tried to spit on me.[23] These responses, while uncomfortable, are understandable, especially given the Black Lives Matter movement that highlights the ways Black lives have always been devalued. Nonetheless, this reaction made me anxious about my safety in South LA in the weeks following the unrest.[24] The atmosphere was very tense, and as a Korean American woman, I stood out. In addition, some Black interviewees were skeptical about the positive impact a study exploring the aftermath of the unrest might have on their community. Aaron, a Black hairstylist, said that researchers had conducted interviews with him in the past, but they had never made any difference. He argued that researchers are part of the status quo and had forgotten about the communities we originally wanted to help. Aaron commented that people like us buy into the "false psyche that the white man instills in us."

The third response was the most common, neutral or nuanced. African Americans eloquently commented on the changes that had occurred in their community, including the influx of Korean merchants. At some point, it became difficult for me as a Korean American ethnographer to listen to anti-immigrant and anti-Korean sentiments. I learned that some of my informants preferred interacting with my research assistants who were Mexican American or African American.

## The Korean American Response

Many Korean immigrant interviewees saw me initially as a young, female student. Some said I reminded them of their educated, unmarried daughter with whom they had a difficult relationship. In addition, they had trouble believing I was a professor because of the small number of female professors in Korea.[25] Notwithstanding these assumptions, I benefited from their overall respect for educators and education.

While conducting ethnographic interviews at Korean-run stores, I tried to explain Black sentiments to Korean merchants and passed on business strategies of other Korean merchants in South LA. During our encounters, I became concerned with the prejudiced remarks of some Korean immigrants. Faced with a difficult situation, I recalled the standard guidelines for conducting interviews or oral histories: an emphasis on "objectivity" discourages ethnographers from engaging in dialogue with their interviewees. Although I originally aimed to foreground people's voices, especially those that were underrepresented, I also felt a strong responsibility as an educator and community leader/activist to engage them in dialogue. As Dell Hymes delineates, the ethnographer plays both a critical and scholarly role within the academic world: that of working for communities, movements, and operational institutions, and that of direct action as a member of a community or movement (1969, 56). I conducted my interviews by relying on the Korean oral performance tradition *Sinse T'aryong*,[26] which requires listeners to comment on the subjects' often bitter storytelling. Therefore, the context of my interviews with Korean immigrants actually required my active participation in their storytelling. When my interviewees were young Korean Americans, either 1.5[27] or second generation, I could not pretend to be silent.[28] One 22-year-old, college-educated Korean American who worked at his parents' liquor store told me:

> I really do not understand why African Americans keep boycotting the Korean-run stores and the Korean community, particularly Danny Bakewell.[29] Why do they say Koreans are wrong? The only wrongdoing by Koreans is that they work too hard. I do not understand and hate them. Sometimes, you know, I feel like killing them.

I was taken aback by his violent statement. I mentioned that not all African Americans supported the boycott, led by Bakewell, of Korean-run stores,[30] and I immediately asked him, "If Koreans came to America as slaves some centuries ago, do you think we could make it in America now?" He replied quietly: "No, I don't think so." After this incident, I felt compelled to carry out a critical exchange with the interviewees, from which I developed the idea of intercessory ethnography.

My anthropological dilemma took a turn for the worse when I started to write the ethnography. Especially after the three-day burning and looting in April 1992, the Korean American community responded passionately to my work. At a forum about the Los Angeles riots, I explained various interethnic encounters on a broader community level, as well as possible solutions to race relations in the larger American society and between Korean and Black communities. As a member of the Korean American community, I felt comfortable discussing what Korean Americans could do. However, the Korean American community leader on the panel challenged me. "I am sick and tired of hearing what Koreans did not do right. That's enough. Koreatown was reduced down to ashes and the whole Korean American community has been uprooted. All the time Koreans have been beaten up and discriminated enough by the American society," she stated. She argued that Korean merchants and Black customers lacked mutual respect and that they needed to start respecting each other.

Although I agreed with her assessment, she believed I was betraying the interests of the Korean American community. After this fierce backlash, I became very upset. On the one hand, among my academic peers I was suspected of breaking "objectivity" as a native anthropologist and of violating norms of "native" talk; on the other hand, I was having difficulty getting support from my own community for my research. However, being a native anthropologist does not necessarily entail having to praise or celebrate everything about a given culture. One should keep in mind that "there will never be a single community view or monolithic 'insider' reaction to an ethnographic text" (Brettell 1993, 21). I do not think my role is to glorify the past or blindly agree with the communities I study. If I did, my work would just be another form of Orientalism, colonialism, or nativism.

For me, the most important goal was to locate the tensions in Black-Latino-Korean American relations and to explore them within the broader context of the US political economy and its capitalist system. In exploring these tensions, I am examining the different attitudes from all three parties. As a researcher studying Korean immigrant merchants in South LA, I can critique Korean American ideology and its emphasis on upward mobility, while as an immigrant researcher, I can provide insights into the American capitalist system. Both critiques converge in the context of Black and Latino views on Korean American ideology. From this unique perspective, I attempt to understand the position of African Americans and Latinos through locating and dislocating myself from the position of Korean American merchants in the US political economy.

## ORGANIZATION OF THE BOOK

This book is organized into four parts. Part I (Introduction and chapter 1) explains my fieldwork in South LA and provides theoretical and historical background regarding ethnic tension among Blacks, Latinos, and Koreans. Part II (chapters 2–4) examines Black-Korean tensions as they relate to race, class, and culture. Parts III and IV, using intersectional analysis of ethnic tension, investigate the nature of the interrelationships between these variables (race, class, culture, and citizenship). Part III (chapters 5–7) explores the aftermath of the unrest through a discussion of Latino-Korean and Black-Korean relations, and it illustrates how race and ethnicity often stand in for class relations. These chapters examine various sociocultural arenas: merchant-customer interactions, business practices and ideology, and post-unrest ethnic tension. Chapters 8–9 address racial, ethnic, and class relations within Los Angeles in the new millennium. I argue that unlike Black-Korean tensions, Korean-Latino conflicts relate more to ethnic distancing than to "othering" and "racializing." While comparing Black and Latino perspectives on the unrest, I attempt to draw a new racial and class cartography in Los Angeles at this current juncture.

The manuscript explores African American-Latino relations and Latino-Korean relations, going beyond the usual Black-Korean emphasis in discussions of the LA unrest, and highlights how race and citizenship as well as class and culture affect these relationships.[31] Through my analyses, this book attempts to understand how Korean immigrants' encounters with other minority groups are constitutive of and contribute to the making of new, broader racial and ethnic relations.

## NOTES

1. Throughout this book, I use "Korean immigrants" interchangeably with "Korean Americans" and "Koreans." I use the term "Korean Americans" to refer to the large population group of Korean descent, but I specify when I am speaking about immigrants.

2. I am using the term "unrest" because it entails a structural process.

3. The Watts riot in 1965 signaled this change; since then, it has often been Black communities rebelling against law enforcement and espousing Black nationalism.

4. For heuristic purposes, I use the term "Latino" to indicate more recent immigrants from El Salvador, Guatemala, other parts of Central America, and Mexico. I also use Latino to refer to US-born Latinos, but I specify when I am speaking about immigrants.

5. This concept has been previously used by a few scholars; however, it has often referred to the conventional meaning of cartographic representations of human beginnings or human races.

6. Here, "culture" is used in the narrowly defined sense of the word, not in the anthropologically inclusive sense of the word. Typically, anthropologists' use of "culture" goes beyond mental phenomena.

7. Jo (1992) applies a prejudice hypothesis in explaining Black-Korean conflicts in Philadelphia. Yoon (1997, 219–45) also comments on the prejudices held by Korean Americans. Drawing on empirical research, Weitzer (1997) reports anti-Black prejudice among Korean immigrant merchants.

8. Broadly, this hypothesis focuses on the commercial role of the outsider, the middlemen merchants, as a causal factor of intergroup hostility. Immigrant merchants typically distribute goods produced by the host society to minority customers because of rigid stratification systems that create a status gap between the elite and the masses, thus necessitating a third group to perform intermediate, degrading, and often despised roles in trade and in services such as tax collecting and moneylending (Blalock 1967). As a result, triadic relationships are observed between a middleman group's ethnic solidarity, the middleman's economic/commercial role, and host hostility (Bonacich 1973; Min 1996).

9. This middle position makes it easy for them to get involved in the conflict via boycotts by Black customers, discriminatory treatment by White wholesalers, commercial rent hikes by White landlords, and disadvantageous regulations imposed by government agencies.

10. In 1976, several Black women sued General Motors for discrimination. Crenshaw uses this case to develop her theory. Although the court dismissed their claims because they couldn't prove them, the women's argument was that what happened to them was not just like what happened to White women or Black men; in other words, the specific discrimination they faced could not be explained by existing frameworks (Crenshaw 2015).

11. C. Kim's study was drawn from observations of Black-Korean tensions in New York. The case of Los Angeles, where Black boycotters have been limited to "Black [capitalist] nationalist" advocate Danny Bakewell and his group the Brotherhood Crusade, is different. In addition, the interracial dynamics, politics, and the role of the media in Los Angeles and New York differ significantly.

12. Although some social scientists integrate class into their analysis of ethno-racial relations, no one has done so with regards to Black-Korean relations.

13. Despite the qualitative distinction C. Kim draws between the two (Black and Asian American) racializing logics, there is a connection between them, as the racialization of Asian Americans is derived from a "white supremacist ideology" that was created in tandem with an economy based on slavery (Lye 2008, 1733). Although C. Kim's racial triangulation perspective most clearly illuminates the interests and actions of Whites in constructing the relative positions that subordinated groups occupy and the common discursive frames that represent them, as sociologist Vanesa Ribas also notes, "it does not properly describe the dynamics by which subordinated groups themselves construe interests and exercise agency vis-à-vis one another, do so not as isolated minority groups but rather from within the field of racial positions" (Ribas 2016, 199).

14. Personal communication with Peter Wissoker, February 22, 2011.

15. Kevin Lynch's idea (1960) was fundamentally geospatial: the idea that people's mental maps were based on the experience of moving through space, their interests in particular places, and their dependence on landmarks, which did not conform to formal maps.

16. There are other dimensions that affect a group's social status, rights/entitlements, and treatment by others. These may include geopolitics between the US and country of origin, media images, religious differences, and/or role in US economy.

17. South LA at its most geographically expansive is considered the area south of the 10 Freeway, north of the 91 Freeway, east of Crenshaw Boulevard, and west of Long Beach Boulevard (Sides 2012).

18. My research assistants Eddie Gomez, Lourdes Castro, and Billy Shin conducted most of the interviews with Latinos.

19. I did not want to generalize about who was involved in the riots. However, I wanted to present perspectives of African Americans whose views had not been included in media accounts.

20. Molly Des Baillets conducted additional interviews with African Americans, in particular young ones.

21. Thomas Hong and Soyun Cho conducted additional interviews with Korean immigrant merchants.

22. This is, of course, true even for white, male ethnographers.

23. I felt hopeless after this response. These interviewees responded similarly to my Korean American assistants.

24. None of my Korean interviewees resided in South LA. Thus, Korean merchants were criticized for lack of commitment to the South LA community. However, it is important to emphasize that many African American merchants do not live in South LA either.

25. This situation is changing slowly.

26. *T'aryong* is a kind of storytelling performed to the rhythmic beat of a drum. It is an account of one's fate or circumstances, and the term connotes self-pity or a sense of sadness. Thus, *Sinse T'aryong* is the telling of one's experience to obtain sympathy from listeners (K. Park 1997, xiii).

27. See K. Park (1999a).

28. As a member of the Korean immigrant community, where respect for the elderly is very important, it was hard for me to question similar statements made by people older than me.

29. See Tong (1992) for info on Bakewell.

30. Nevertheless, no Black community leader disagreed with Bakewell in public.

31. There were no large-scale Latino-Korean tensions before the 1992 civil unrest. During the unrest, Korean-owned stores were looted by Latinos and Blacks, but these tensions did not continue after the unrest.

*Chapter One*

# The Political Economy of Ethno-Racial Identities in South Los Angeles

Los Angeles has long symbolized the last frontier of the American Dream. John Laslett (1996, 39) notes that by the 1970s, Los Angeles was fast becoming America's second largest and most prosperous metropolitan area and aspired to be a global city with visions of multicultural diversity. However, in subsequent decades, after a series of human and natural disasters, Los Angeles seemed to represent the opposite: an American nightmare. Mike Davis's *City of Quartz, Excavating the Future in Los Angeles* (1990) and David Rieff's *Los Angeles: Capital of the Third World* (1991) vividly portray this troubling picture of the city, positing that Los Angeles has come to constitute a paradoxical symbol of utopia and dystopia in the context of advanced capitalism.

South LA, formerly "South Central,"[1] has a long history of marginalization in which residents suffer from limited access to basic resources (education, work, health care) that perpetuates poverty and violence in the community (Gonzalez 2014, iv). Decades of racially restrictive housing covenants; the lack of greenery, public space, and public transit; and the freeways' destruction of previously stable middle- and working-class neighborhoods all led to the "ghettoization" of South LA (Kurashige 2008). In the post-war period, South LA was one of few places in the city where Black Americans could buy homes and operate businesses. Black people migrating to Los Angeles—where during WWII the defense industry created a high demand for laborers in ship, plane, and steel production—from the Southern states were confined to areas like South LA by racially restrictive covenants, discriminatory practices, and redlining policies.[2] The name "South Central" was applied to the Black community, which flourished along South Central Avenue from the 1920s to 1950s.

Although the 1992 civil unrest affected many areas, it was South Central, the epicenter, that was inscribed into the national consciousness, bolstering impressions of a community embroiled in chaos, just as Watts was in 1965 (*LAT* January 3, 1993). Since the 1992 unrest, South Central's boundaries have expanded to include any neighborhood where African Americans and Latinos live south of the 10 Santa Monica Freeway, east of Crenshaw Boulevard, north of the 91 Freeway, and west of Long Beach Boulevard. On the west side, residents are predominantly Black and middle class; further east, most inhabitants are Latino immigrants. Many media images, as Dionne Bennett (2010) notes, perpetuate prevailing discourses about South LA: that it is steeped in danger, yet also "authentic" because of its violence and musical talent. The stereotyping of South LA as a center of urban gangs and drug culture, or an area mired in poverty, unemployment, and violent crime, has heightened feelings of despair among residents, although younger generations tend to defiantly embrace this stereotype, particularly in hip-hop songs. The large influx of Latinos into South LA has altered this reputation somewhat; however, some Latino residents I interviewed for this book experienced similar prejudices and feelings of despondence as those of African Americans.

With this drastic transformation in mind, it is important to understand the structural changes that occurred due to the city's growth and to examine what has occurred in South LA demographically, socioeconomically, and politically in recent decades. Drawing on a Marxist critique of political economy to examine "the distribution and accumulation of economic surplus, and the attendant problems of determination of prices, wages, employment, and the efficacy or otherwise of political arrangements to promote accumulation" (Bottomore 1983, 375), I pay special attention to the political-economic analysis of Los Angeles' racial and ethnic complexity. However, to understand the racial minorities that live in Los Angeles, we need to explore the varied trajectories of ethno-racial identities as well.

## ETHNO-RACIAL COMPLEXITY IN LOS ANGELES HISTORY

Today, Los Angeles is known as one of the most racially segregated cities in the US, characterized not only by the separation of Whites and people of color, but also of various racial minorities from each other (Kun and Pulido 2014, 12). LA has an extensive history of both racial conflict and interracial coalitions that predate the demographic transitions of the last quarter century. Prior to 1965, racial conflict was characterized by White aggression against racial minorities. For example, race riots took place in 1877 when a band of marauding Whites massacred 19 Chinese people, and much later in 1943, when White servicemen attacked Latinos, African Americans, and Filipinos in the Zoot Suit Riots (McWilliams 1973).

However, the Watts Revolt of 1965, "the largest urban uprisings to hit the United States in modern history" (Alonso 2010, 143), differed from the earlier violence: this time, an oppressed group initiated the major actions. Sides (2003) states, "African Americans—mostly young men—rampaged through the streets of Watts and South Central, looting and burning retail stores, beating passing motorists, and attacking the firefighters and police officers" (169). Provoked by what might otherwise have been a routine traffic stop of a Black motorist by the California Highway Patrol, the people who fomented the rebellion were protesting merchant exploitation, substandard housing, unemployment, inadequate social services, racial discrimination, and the neglect of White policymakers in addressing quality of life issues in the Black community (Sears 1973). Both the 1965 McCone Commission, which investigated the Watts Revolt, and the 1968 Kerner Commission, which investigated the 1967 civil disobedience in other American cities, identified poverty, unemployment, poor housing, inadequate schools, inaccessible health care, widespread perception of police abuse, and the deficiency of consumer services as the principal grievances that led to the riots of the 1960s. Citing these two reports, the Assembly Special Committee on the Los Angeles Crisis (California Legislature, Assembly Special Committee 1992, 10) noted that even in 1992, "[l]ittle has changed" since 1965.

It is important to note that despite these eruptions of racial violence, interracial coalitional politics have also been in place in LA for decades. Conservative WASPs (White Anglo-Saxon Protestants) dominated city government throughout the first half of the twentieth century, excluding the growing Jewish, African American, Latino, and Asian American communities from municipal power. Political scientist Raphael Sonenshein's study (1993) documented the rise and fall of the biracial liberal coalition between Jewish and Black Democrats from 1963 to 1993 that gave Black mayor Tom Bradley an unprecedented five consecutive terms in office and elected three Black city council members. Jews and African Americans shared not only a common political ideology, but they also developed, through interaction and communication, trust and effective leadership.[3]

## IMMIGRATION AND URBAN RESTRUCTURING: NEW FORMS OF SOCIAL INEQUALITY IN SOUTH LOS ANGELES

Any discussion of contemporary politics in Los Angeles must begin with the tremendous demographic changes the city has undergone over the last several decades. The most important cause of the demographic shift was the Immigration Act of 1965 and its 1978 amendment, which ended racially based quotas in US immigration policy and emphasized global economic and humanitarian concerns, especially family reunification.[4] As the full force of this reform took hold in the 1970s and 80s, international immigration from Mexico, Central America, and Asia transformed Los Angeles, which quickly became the destination of choice for the greatest number of post-1965 immigrants. In addition, the 1986 Immigration Reform and Control Act provided amnesty for recently arrived undocumented immigrants, and Mexico's economic crisis and peso devaluation pushed new immigrants north (Kun and Pulido 2014, 7).

Demographers predict that by the middle of the twenty-first century, the nation as a whole will reflect the racial demographics of Los Angeles. In the 1970s, 70 percent of LA residents were White, 15 percent Latino, 11 percent African American, and 3 percent Asian. Two decades later, 41 percent were White, 36 percent Latino, 12 percent Asian, and 11 percent African American. By 2000, Latinos had surpassed Whites as the largest racial group in the city and county. As of 2010, Los Angeles County was 48 percent Latino, 28 percent White, 14 percent Asian American, and 9 percent African American. It is important to note that as the number of minorities increases, Whites in Southern California have increasingly moved to the outskirts of the city, abandoning many post-war suburbs like South LA that they founded, and isolating themselves in affluent enclaves. As a consequence, most Whites did not experience the unrest in the same way as minorities did.

It is also noteworthy that many historically Black areas, such as South LA, were becoming predominantly Latino prior to the unrest. South LA was 14 percent Latino in 1980, 45 percent in 1990, and 54 percent in 2000. Mexican Americans constitute the majority of Latinos, accounting for nearly 72 percent in all parts of the county, including South LA. Central Americans (primarily Salvadorans, Guatemalans, Nicaraguans, and Hondurans) make up 13 percent of the Latino population in Los Angeles County and 26 percent of the Latino population in South LA.[5] For perspective, the population in South LA is made up of less than 0.1 percent of Koreans (341 in 2000, up from 330 in the 1990 Census).

## Anti-Immigrant Sentiment and Demographic Shifts

Although conflict and discord does not overwhelmingly characterize inter-ethnic relations, the increasing proximity of different communities of color to each other has had significant consequences. Latinos have often been the ignored minority in South LA, as low rates of citizenship and political participation have allowed African American political leaders to advance an essentially Black agenda in districts where the population is as much as two-thirds Latino. It was only during the unrest that the Latino community began to be noticed.

The controversy surrounding the Martin Luther King, Jr. Medical Center, built from the ashes of the 1965 Watts Revolt, is a relevant case. By 1990, most of the patients and visitors to the hospital were Latinos, not African Americans. Latinos pressured the hospital to hire doctors and administrators with linguistic and cultural sensitivity to Latinos, but their demands were ignored.[6] Similarly, in 1994, Latino parents in Compton charged that although they made up more than half of the city's 91,600 residents, the Black-run school system discriminated against Latinos. Latino students complained of being ridiculed and even beaten by Black teachers and security guards (*Newsweek* November 21, 1994). In 2010, there were still no Latinos on the Compton Unified School District's board, even though they made up at least 75 percent of the district's student body (*LAT* December 20, 2010).

Many would attribute this local discord to the increasing heterogeneity of urban communities, especially as backlash to immigration emerged as the contemporary form of racism or racial *nativism* before and after the unrest. For example, James Johnson and Melvin Oliver (1989) lay the blame on Latino and Asian immigrants for diminishing Black political, economic, and demographic capital. In contrast to this rhetoric, various studies, both pro- and anti-immigrant, have concluded that "immigrants have little or no real economic impact, especially on African Americans and other native-minorities" (Garcia 2000, 4); rather, their impact is greater on other, less recent immigrants. However real or imaginary the effects, immigrants have been scapegoated by both the traditional majority (Whites) and native minorities (Blacks). Modern restrictionists deny that race is the reason for their dismay with immigration and employ other, non-race-based arguments—that too many people are immigrating to the US, that immigrants (particularly "illegal aliens") take jobs from US citizens, that immigrants contribute to overpopulation that damages the environment, that they overconsume public benefits and adversely affect already-strapped state and local governments, that they engage in criminal activity, and that they cause interethnic conflict and refuse to assimilate. (K. Johnson 1997, 174)

Notwithstanding this rhetoric, new immigration and the proximity of distinct ethnic groups to each other are only partial explanations for the escalation of interethnic tension in Los Angeles (I elaborate on this in chapters 8 and 9). Before discussing the nature of interracial relations, it is necessary to understand the historical context in which racial minorities both were assigned ethno-racial identities and developed their own.

Along with rapid demographic change, there was also an increase in economic inequality in the 1980s and 1990s. The percentage of people with an income of $50,000 or more increased from 9 to 26 percent; at the same time, the percentage of people making less than $15,000 increased from 30 to 40 percent. However, the percentage in the intermediate income category was reduced from 61 percent to 32 percent, indicating the shrinking strata of middle-class Angelenos. This economic inequality was correlated with racial and ethnic inequality, as well as inner-city urban poverty. According to one study conducted between 1979 and 1989, two-fifths of the jobs created in Los Angeles County paid less than $15,000 annually (Meyerson 1991, 26). Accordingly, before the unrest, Black male earnings amounted to 69 percent of the median income of White males. Even more alarming is the fact that Latino males earned only 46 percent of what Whites did.

Concentrated poverty matters because it leads to increased crime rates and poor health outcomes. Violent crime rates tend to be higher in economically distressed neighborhoods. Gang-related homicides increased through the 1980s and peaked between 1991 and 1993, when more than 3,200 people were murdered, mostly young Black men (Sides 2012, 4). In 1993, young black men died of homicide in Los Angeles County at a rate that was twenty-five times the national average (Leovy 2012, 200). Although crime has decreased significantly for more than a decade, reflecting the national trend, violent crime in LA is still nearly twice the rate of the country as a whole (Sides 2012, 47, 7).[7]

Although this region has changed demographically, nearly 60 percent of African Americans in the city of Los Angeles still lived in South LA in 1990 and were directly affected by events both during and after the 1992 unrest. During my first visit to South LA in 1991 after having lived in New York City, it was hard for me to view South LA as a ghetto in the sense of New York's Harlem. This was partly because much of the Leimert Park section of South LA is comprised of single-family homes owned by the Black middle- and working-class people.[8] Even less well-off neighborhoods in South LA still retain their original suburban street layouts: manicured lawns, well-kept single-family stucco homes, and low-density populations. However, inside the local stores and houses, living conditions were visibly impoverished. The few strip malls I saw on Western Ave were barred up and closed in 1992. Some homes, despite having charming architecture, were run down, with ugly bars covering the windows and trash in the yards.

South LA has been the heart and soul of the largest Black community in the western United States. Just before the 1992 unrest, South LA was the place where African Americans and Latinos lived as neighbors and fellow job seekers, while Korean Americans operated small businesses that served both

Black and Latino customers. After the unrest, as both Black and Latino residents observed, there was an influx of Latino residents and merchants, what historian Josh Sides called "Latin Americanization." Between 1990 and 2000, Black people went from being the majority population of South LA (55 percent) to 39.8 percent, and Latinos went from 45.5 percent to 58 percent (Sides 2012, 44). Almost one-quarter of the Black population of South LA left, while the Black populations of Orange, Ventura, Riverside, San Bernardino, and Imperial counties continued to grow (Sides 2003, 201). Storefront Latino Evangelical churches had been established next to Black Baptist churches and soccer had begun to rival basketball as the sport of choice at neighborhood playing fields. Finally, four South LA high schools that had overwhelming Black student populations in 1980—Fremont, Jefferson, Jordan, and Manual Arts—now had Latino majorities (*LAT* May 3, 1990).

There's not a huge difference between the assessments of Black and Latino informants—yet some Latinos were seriously concerned about the future of South LA. A Black research assistant, Jocelyn, felt that many Black interviewees did not want to express negative feelings; it was as if they were embarrassed to tell her the truth. Perhaps this was because Jocelyn let her interviewees know about her middle-class background and they were afraid it might be hard for her to understand what was going on in their neighborhoods. Perhaps interviewees felt an obligation to positively represent the place they call home. For example, a 20-year-old Black male who had lived all his life in South LA was slightly defensive when he was asked what he thought of his community in 1993:

> This is my neighborhood. There's nothing wrong with it. There's nothing wrong with it. The same stuff happens in all neighborhoods. It just happens a lot more here. It's more obvious. People get killed. It's because of the type of people that stay in my neighborhood.
>
> (Like who?)
>
> Gangsters I guess. They hang out more.

A 19-year-old Black female, a college student and hairstylist, was interviewed in 1993. Her house had a bullet hole in the front living room window. She shared: "This particular area [54th and Crenshaw], I would prefer not to live here. But I feel safe. If I had an option to move, I would take it. I am content. I get along with the neighbors." Regarding the business people in her community, she stated: "Everybody was pretty rude before but now they [Koreans] are trying to be real nice." Similarly, an 18-year-old Black male, a UCLA student who was interviewed in 1993, said: "It's getting better. It used to have a lot of gang members and drug dealers. It was kinda bad at one time, real bad. But the police are cleaning it up. I think gangbanging is going out."

A 64-year-old Black woman, a community organizer who was interviewed in 1996, pointed out that the ethnicity of merchants became much more diversified in the aftermath of the 1992 LA unrest: "In my area [52nd and Vermont], liquor stores are Korean, there are some East Indians, let's see . . . the carpet store is Black, gardener's Mexican, uniform place Black, it's pretty well mixed." However, she was indignant about the lack of safety on the streets: "Well, it needs some help with gangs; my neighbor couldn't go to the liquor store two blocks away because it was out of his territory. Two blocks! That really bothers me."

A 41-year-old Mexican male who had emigrated from Guadalajara in 1982 was interviewed in 1994. He expressed relief that things had changed, stating that when he first moved to South LA, Black people acted as if it was their community and Latinos were infringing upon it. Despite reduced racial tension, he complained, "Black people tend to blame Latinos and Latinos blame Black people." In the same vein, a 23-year-old second-generation Mexican American female clerical assistant who was interviewed in 1995 was worried about Black/Latino gang fighting:

> I like my community because I was born here and I grew up here. Of course there are problems like gangs, homelessness, and one needs to worry when you're out in the street, but it's different from block to block. My street [23rd and Central] is calm, but the next one isn't. In the future there might be problems because we see more gang members on our street. Sometimes there's gun shots between rival gangs like "Loco Park" and "Low Bottom Crips" fighting over who is to control the park.

## POLITICAL ECONOMIC TRANSFORMATION

In the post-war period, the manufacturing sector provided the economic foundation for a Black middle class in South LA: 24 percent of African American men and 18 percent of Black women worked as manufacturing operatives in the region's booming automobile, steel, and rubber tire industries (Sides 2003, 180). However, starting in the 1970s, American corporations witnessed decreasing profit margins when confronted with foreign competition and responded by cutting costs: outsourcing labor, developing labor-saving technologies, and ultimately closing plants. The loss of industrial jobs decimated working-class communities nationwide. For South LA, the consequences of the loss of well-paying manufacturing jobs was catastrophic.

Deindustrialization, along with the transnationalization of capital and labor and the relocation of businesses out of the area, devastated the economy of South LA, the traditional industrial core of the city, and shattered the dreams of postwar prosperity for many Black workers, fueling bitterness and disillusionment (Sides 2003, 185). Specifically, the recession and the end of the Cold War in the late 1980s precipitated structural shifts in LA's economy that had previously been marked by fairly steady growth in employment. These shifts included the decline of unionized, high-wage, heavy manufacturing and service sector jobs. By the end of the 1970s, LA had lost more than half of the manufacturing jobs in the county (Alonso 2010, 154). Around 300 South LA plants closed, which put many African Americans, and to a lesser degree Latinos, out of work (Johnson and Oliver 1989). The Tucker committee reported that the LA area lost more than 300,000 jobs between June 1990 and February 1992, accounting for 60 percent of statewide job losses during the period. For instance, in August 1992, the shutdown of the Van Nuys General Motors plant displaced 3,000 workers, two-thirds of whom were Black and Latino (Omatsu 1995, 87).

In addition, manufacturing industries began to leave South LA for other suburban areas in pursuit of lower taxes, larger plants, and more profitable markets as early as 1963, representing the first phase of the deindustrialization of Southern California (Sides 2003, 180). In the 1970s and 1980s, heavy manufacturing companies such as General Motors, Goodyear, Firestone, Bethlehem Steel, and American Can also left for the suburban area. These industries had provided more than 25,000 unionized jobs and had supported job growth in related industries. Their abandonment of South LA "literally pulled the plug on the entire economy of the area" (Labor/Community Strategy Center 1993, 8).

Meanwhile, unlike Rust Belt cities, Los Angeles was simultaneously experiencing industrialization in two sectors. First, the military-centered Keynesian economy facilitated by the Cold War entailed a massive growth in the aerospace and electronics industries. However, many African Americans did not benefit from this development because of mismatches between their skills and the occupations available in these industries. A second area of industrialization entailed the development of very low-skill manufacturing industries as well as low-wage jobs in light industry and service occupations, which remained in Los Angeles proper. African American workers were likewise excluded from this trend because employers preferred Latino immigrant workers (I elaborate on this in chapter 8). Thus, while heavy-industry jobs disappeared, low-wage and non-durable manufacturing jobs increased by approximately 25 percent between 1972 and 1990. Consistent with national trends (Bluestone and Harrison 1982), low-wage service and retail-sector employment also doubled between 1972 and 1990 in Los Angeles (Soja et al. 1983). This trend had a detrimental impact on minority workers, as it left them with few options outside of below-poverty-level employment or underemployment.

In addition, many of the high-paying corporate jobs in the growing sectors of high technology, information services, real estate, and corporate finance moved to the suburbs, predominantly populated by White employees. Although the large number of well-paid technology jobs for highly skilled individuals led to a heavy concentration of White engineers, executives, managers, and supervisors in communities such as Santa Monica, Latino immigrants occupied low-skilled, low-wage jobs in the technology sector, living in neighborhoods including Pico Union, South LA, and East LA.

The political corollary to this economic restructuring[9] was the post-"War on Poverty" racial politics of the Reagan and Bush administrations. For instance, "the decline of more than one-third in the value of Aid to Families with Dependent Children (AFDC) payments adversely affected all poor people," (Lipsitz 1998, 16), in particular non-Whites. The de-investment in public spending devastated African Americans in South LA by severely downsizing the Great Society-inspired social programs that had been vital to the survival of poor inhabitants since the 1960s. When Reagan took office in 1980, community-based organizations received an estimated 48 percent of their funding from the federal government (Oliver et al. 1993, 126). During that decade, however, California politicians chose to build prisons rather than fund education, health care, housing, or human services. While the city government had been able to provide some benefits to poor residents through the use of federal grants, it was now forced to reduce funds allocated to social welfare and community development programs. As the city government increasingly depended on private sector capital rather than federal funding, the development of poor neighborhoods like South LA was overlooked in favor of a corporate-oriented, downtown redevelopment project.

Black political leadership in Los Angeles County had helped bring about significant economic advances by creating a dynamic, Black public-sector job base. During the last decade of the twentieth century, African Americans made up about 10 percent of the population of Los Angeles County, but they still held about a quarter of the jobs in city government and a third in county government. African Americans have held three seats on the fifteen-member City Council since the 1960s, and three of the region's representatives in Congress in Washington have been Black. However, the acme of Black power has since faded.

In his obituary, former LA mayor Tom Bradley (serving from 1973 to 1993) was described as a non-confrontational man who worked to build coalitions, revive the storefronts and small businesses that had been wiped out during the Watts Revolt, and position the city as the unofficial capital of the Pacific Rim during an era of growing international trade. However, he was also remembered for the negative consequences of this exponential growth, such as pollution and traffic jams (*New York Times* Sept. 30, 1998, B7). As a moderate integrationist, Bradley generated visible economic advances for African Americans, appointed numerous African Americans to his administration, implemented successful affirmative action programs in city hiring, and succeeded in moderately reforming the LAPD (Sides 2003, 194). Nonetheless, he did little to address the city's loss of well-paying jobs and its widening economic disparities. He became increasingly reliant on developers and investors, including the elite sectors of Los Angeles Black society, and began to neglect his base of working-class Black voters. While $2 billion of city resources financed the corporate renaissance of downtown LA during Bradley's time as mayor, South LA's social programs were gutted, which was a fact demonstrated by the drastically reduced funding for the city's Redevelopment Agency and other community-based organizations prior to the unrest (Freer 1994). Funding for anti-poverty assistance, vital human services, and job training in South LA lagged far behind that of West Los Angeles and the Valley (Davis 1990, 304).

Partly due to the relocation of businesses out of the area, there was a marked increase in unemployment and crime, and an emerging gang population in South LA's Black community.[10] While there were 45 Black gangs in 1978, by 1982—when "crack" cocaine hit the streets of Los Angeles—the number had grown to 151 (Alonso 2010, 154). Years later, the Black community was justifiably outraged over allegations that the US government was involved in selling crack in LA to finance the CIA-backed, Nicaraguan right-wing guerilla campaign to overthrow the left-wing Sandinista government (Alonso 2010, 156). In 1990, more than one in every three South LA residents lived below the poverty threshold, with a median income of $20,820; over a quarter of all households received public assistance. Only 59 percent of South LA adults worked, 42 percent were not in the labor force, and 9 percent were unemployed. In addition, almost 70 percent of Black men between the ages of 25 and 35 with less than a high school education were unemployed in South LA (Vargas 2006, 35). Nearly 15 years later, in Los Angeles County, one in three young Black men was under the supervision of the criminal justice system (Vargas 2006, 14). By 2000, 43 percent of LA's Black, working-age population was unemployed, while 29 percent were employed in low-wage jobs (Bonacich et al. 2010, 364).

Equally important was the growth of the Latino "working poor" in Los Angeles in the late 1980s and 1990s. Latino workers, who accounted for more than one-fourth of California's labor force, lagged behind all other groups in wages and educational attainment, even among third-generation Latinos (Telles and Ortiz 2008). In 1989, the per capita income for Latinos living in LA was $7,111, which was less than half the city's average. For recent immigrants from Mexico, El Salvador, and Guatemala, the average income was even lower in South LA: $4,461(Pastor 1993, 48). Although Latinos had high rates of labor force participation in addition to "low labor force deser- tion, strong functional families, and other positive indicators," they experi- enced difficulties in areas of "language, immigration status, documentation, restricted access to public services, and lack of access to capital" (Latino Coalition 1993, 113). In South LA, only 18 percent of Latinos graduated from high school, compared to 61 percent of the Black population (Pastor 1993, 50). About 29 percent of Latino residents twenty-five or older had less than a ninth-grade education, compared to 18 precent citywide, according to the 1990 Census.

Confronted with the rapid growth of drug trafficking and accompanying gang turf wars, the political and economic elite of Los Angeles turned to a militarization of physical space and everyday life. In *City of Quartz*, Davis (1990) evokes an image of LA as a fortress, brutally divided between "'forti- fied cells' of affluent society and 'places of terror' where the police battle the criminalized poor" (224).[11] By 1990, the combined forces of the Los Angeles Police Department (LAPD) and the Los Angeles County Sheriff's Department had picked up as many as 50,000 suspects (Davis 1990, 277), indicating an increase in number of arrests. In South LA, the Vermont and Slauson Complex (a mall) became notorious for its unprecedented security measures, which included "a seventy foot iron fence around the perimeter, only two driveways, dozens of security guards, infrared motion detectors, and a security tower and nighttime security illumination three to five times the standard" (Sides 2012, 39).

The militarization of the LAPD was accompanied by increasing incidents of police abuse. In July 1991, after the Rodney King beating was aired across the nation, the Christopher Commission released a scathing probe of the LAPD that exposed patterns of excessive force, lax internal discipline, and a core group of 44 "rogue officers," who were the subject of frequent complaints or lawsuits (Webster, William H. [Special Advisor] Report 1992). The report recommended that Police Chief Daryl Gates step down and that term limits for the office of police chief be instituted. Latinos joined African Americans in calling for federal monitors to oversee the department because of allegations that police routinely violated the rights of Latino and Black youth.

## Korean Immigrant Merchants in South LA

First-generation Korean immigrant merchants have been in South LA since the 1970s. Utilizing various types of sociocultural capital as well as class resources—the Korean American bank, Korean rotating credit association (*kye*), human capital, and family/kin (as well as Latino) labor—Korean immigrants showed the highest rate of small business ownership in the 1990 and 2000 censuses and became increasingly portrayed in the national media as "the model minority" or "successful immigrant entrepreneurs."[12] In Los Angeles, the median family income in 1989 for Blacks, Latinos, and Korean Americans was $14,930, $15,531 and $20,147, respectively (US Bureau of the Census, Washington, DC 1990). However, in the 2000 Census, Korean American household incomes ($37,957) were only slightly higher than those of African Americans ($33,526) and Latinos ($36,154) in Southern California (N. Kim 2008, 141).

There was a major transfer of small business ownership to Korean American merchants in South LA in the mid- to late 1980s. The number of Korean-owned grocery and liquor stores in LA County increased by 750 percent between 1977 and 1991, and by then Korean small business owners owned 39 percent of grocery and liquor stores in the county. This rate of increase was five to six times higher than that of the Korean American population nationally during a similar span of time (*KTLA* June 13, 1991). Existing store owners, including many African Americans, preferred selling their stores to Korean immigrants because Korean buyers often offered higher purchase prices or required less credit than other prospective buyers (*LAT* May 5, 1992). The picture becomes clearer if other retail businesses are considered. In 1992, there were at least 20 swap meets in South LA. In leased stalls at these swap meets, almost 1,000 Korean American merchants were selling either products imported from Korea or other Asian countries, or clothing supplied largely by the Korean garment industry in Los Angeles (*KTLA* January 1, 1992). In addition to the swap meets, about 200 gas stations and 100 dry cleaners, hamburger stands, wig shops, and beauty shops were owned by Korean immigrants. In total, almost 80 percent of all retail stores in South LA were thought to be Korean-owned. The flight of large, chain supermarkets from the inner city to the suburbs, which began in the late 1950s and 1960s, exacerbated this trend.[13]

To make matters worse, South LA also suffered a loss of small retail stores. Most small corner stores were Jewish-owned before 1965. In the 1950s, tensions abounded between Black residents and Jewish merchants, who were often accused of price gouging and loan-sharking. The Watts riots of 1965 caused significant damage to these businesses and stimulated a massive Jewish flight from South LA, leaving a void that would be filled by Black merchants (Horne 1997; Fogelson 1967). This change in ownership was also assisted by the US Small Business Administration (SBA). After a series of urban riots in the late 1960s, alcoholic beverage outlets came to be seen as one of the few successful types of minority-owned businesses.[14] The US government provided significant monetary assistance to stimulate the overconcentration of liquor stores in South Central LA, and the withdrawal of large supermarkets from the area left these outlets a captive customer base. Black-owned grocery and liquor stores thrived during the 1970s. Many owners made a profit by selling their stores after the deregulation of liquor prices in 1978.

Like supermarkets and small corner stores, many banks also chose to abandon the area. In the late 1980s, nearly 1,200 bank branches closed and only 61 opened in LA County. South LA was in an even more precarious situation: only 20 bank branches served about 260,000 residents, while 21 branches served about 50,000 in Gardena, a more affluent nearby city (California Legislature 1992, 12). The relocation of bank branches contributed to the development of Korean small businesses, as these merchants expanded their offerings to include basic banking and check-cashing services. Thus, the abandonment of the inner city by retail stores, large grocery stores, and banks provided opportunities for Korean immigrants; their entrance into this market was thoroughly shaped by the dynamics of urban restructuring.

Korean merchants also developed indoor swap meets. Traditional swap meets (or flea markets) are outdoor mobile markets usually held on weekends where customers can buy cheap or second-hand goods. Korean immigrants moved these gatherings indoors, simulating open-air markets in South Korea (Abelmann and Lie 1995, 140). The first swap meet in the area was the Compton Fashion Center, with 350 booths. Now a Walmart, the Compton Fashion Center opened in the space of what had been a Sears in 1983. Korean developers purchased buildings abandoned by chain department stores such as Sears and J. C. Penney in South LA and converted them into indoor swap meets.

Despite their apparent economic success, it should be noted that Korean immigrants suffered from a lack of political power and generational wealth, and they often faced downward mobility compared to their white-collar work in South Korea. Although they lived outside of South LA, Korean inner-city entrepreneurs had stores in areas with high poverty and crime levels, and thus were subject to redlining and higher rates by insurance companies and banks. In 1991, nine Koreans were murdered by non-Koreans in Los Angeles (Chang and Yu 1994, xvi), and in 1993, 19 Korean store owners were murdered by non-Koreans in Los Angeles (see chapter 7 regarding the escalating tensions post-unrest).

## ETHNO-RACIAL IDENTITIES AMONG AFRICAN AMERICANS BEFORE AND AFTER THE CIVIL RIGHTS MOVEMENT

William J. Wilson (1979) argues that the "life chances" of Black youths were generally determined by their class position, not by the color of their skin.

However, as Robert Blauner (1989) notes, the Black underclass is not simply a product of shifts in the economy and changes in the type and location of available jobs: "That Blacks without marketable skills live in inner-city ghettos is also the result of centuries of overt discrimination and today's more subtle institutional racism" (170). In addition, Mary Pattillo-McCoy (1999), writing about Black middle-class youths, makes the case that racial segregation persists even among the middle class.[15] Therefore, the status of African Americans in American society has been determined by both racial stratification and class.

Manning Marable writes that "the politics of racial identity have been expressed by two great traditions of racial ideology and social protest—integrationism and Black Nationalism" (1995, 187). As an alternative to this bifurcated view, Marable (1995) divides Black identity politics into three ideological camps. The first, "inclusionists," not only incorporate the traditional integrationist perspective of the earlier twentieth century, but also the neoliberal and pragmatic elements of the post–Civil Rights period, as seen in the 1970s and 1980s in writings by Thomas Sowell and William Julius Wilson. On the other hand, the "nationalists"[16] included Afrocentrists such as Molefi Asante, Leonard Jeffries, and Niara Sudarkasa, and more broadly, the rap and hip-hop generation, the Black working class, and the entrepreneurial elite. The third group, the "transformationists," advocated a "radical multicultural democracy" that Marable supports. Transformationism is an eclectic mixture of social theories that includes militancy, socialism, trade unionism, feminism, and internationalism.

Black community leaders and activists have historically employed a variety of strategies—nationalism, integration, coalitions with left-wing and labor groups, and/or interracialism—in combating employment and housing discrimination or school segregation. In the post-1965 era, Black residents expressed an increasing sense of self-worth, pride, and positive identification with blackness, culminating in the Black Power movement, which was an alternative means of combating the racism that persisted despite the gains of the Civil Rights Movement (Alonso 2010). Alprentice "Bunchy" Carter, a founding member of the Southern California chapter of the Black Panther Party, formerly a leader of the Slauson street gang, South Central, aimed to transform young Blacks into revolutionary soldiers against police brutality and agents for social change by organizing Black high school student unions and forming the Black Congress in South LA. Many street gang members also joined an LA-based cultural nationalist group, the US Organization, led by Maulana Karenga (Alonso 2010, 146). After various Black Panther leaders were murdered at UCLA in 1969, many Black nationalist groups were rendered ineffective, partly because they were targeted and infiltrated by the

FBI's Counter Intelligence Program for their opposition to the Vietnam War, their support of assassinated leader Malcolm X, and their radical rhetoric (Alonso 2010, 148, 147). As Black youth witnessed the deaths of their key leaders, the loss of jobs, increase in poverty, and the overall deterioration of their quality of life, many turned to gang activity for protection (Gonzalez 2014, 190).

Many African American community leaders in LA worked in the Civil Rights Movement to integrate Blacks into mainstream American life, fighting to achieve social, political, and economic equality with Whites, while producing a new racial image. When the Supreme Court banned the legal enforcement of racially restrictive covenants in 1948's *Shelley v. Kraemer*, Black people began to move into areas outside the already overcrowded Slauson-Alameda-Washington-Main settlement area of South Central. This, however, did not prevent Whites from utilizing informal methods of exclusion. In 1968, the federal government enacted its own fair-housing legislation, and today minorities have the right to file complaints against acts of housing discrimination. The LA Branch of the NAACP, established in 1913, desegregated the LA Fire Department as well as the county's nursing school. Through consumer boycotts and picketing, they forced countless banks, stores, and even some larger industrial firms to hire African Americans. In local and state politics, Black people began to yield significant influence, culminating in the Fair Employment Practice Commission (1958) and the Rumford Fair Housing Act (1963) (Sides 2003, 167).[17] During the 1960s, United Civil Rights Committee marches, Congress of Racial Equality sit-ins, and Black representatives in local politics all contributed to African American freedom struggles in Los Angeles.

African Americans—who suspected that integration was essentially a top-down project that supported rather than countered the status quo—confronted White racism in the form of discrimination in employment and city services, overcrowding in housing, and police brutality. Early ethnographies of Black communities speak of the regular occurrence of race riots, which were often precipitated by the tensions of postwar adjustment and competition for jobs among ethnic Whites and Blacks. The "Red Summer" of 1919, in which Whites attacked African Americans who they accused of Bolshevik sentiment, occurred in more than three dozen cities—notably in Chicago.[18] The Harlem Riot of 1935, the first modern race riot, was sparked by rumors of the beating of a teenage shoplifter. The violence was directed almost entirely against property, but it included struggles between the police and the Black population. In the 1930s, Harlem activists organized boycotts against White-owned retailers who refused to hire Black employees, and they later protested against discrimination in retail services. African Americans in Los Angeles joined Blacks in other northern and western cities in "Don't Spend Where You Can't Work" campaigns (Sides 2012, 36).

In contrast to histories about Black-White relationships, few studies examine Black attitudes toward Asians and Asian Americans, and even fewer specifically examine attitudes toward Korean Americans. Like other cities, as Sides (2003) notes, before WWII, Los Angeles was clearly divided by a color line: on one side was a White population, while on the other was a large patchwork of races and ethnicities. Black workers lived alongside Mexicans and Asians. Whites and Mexicans worked in manufacturing industries, but Blacks usually worked with other Blacks. Blacks interacted with other races, not just as neighbors, but as classmates, fellow parishioners, club members, consumers, friends, and even spouses (Sides 2003, 33, 18, 19).

African American attitudes toward Asian Americans have been mixed: "In the nineteenth and twentieth century, a few African American leaders opposed Asian immigration, while others such as the nineteenth century abolitionist Frederick Douglas, were more receptive" (McFerson 2006, 19). Other studies have pointed out a shared past oppression (Okihiro 1994): African American support for Japan during World War II (Lipsitz 1998): Asian American intellectual influences on Black political and material culture, such as Ho Chi Minh (Thornton 2011, 1292); and the impact of the Black Power movement on the Asian American ("yellow power") movement in the 1960s (Wei 1993). Thornton and Taylor (1988) draw upon data from the National Survey of Black Americans to identify subgroups of African Americans who feel a kinship with Asian Americans; about one-fifth of respondents felt this connection (486), particularly among men, rural residents, older respondents, and those in the secondary employment sector. In a recent study, Thornton (2011) examined how the preeminent Black newspaper in LA, the *Los Angeles Sentinel*, changed its coverage of Black-Asian American relations from 1993 to 2000. The *Sentinel* criticized local Black leaders for being silent on how members of the community attacked Asian Americans during the Los Angeles uprising (2011, 1276). Additionally, the focus and breadth of coverage changed from highlighting antagonism between Korean merchants and African Americans to emphasizing inter-minority collaboration and inclusion.

The existing literature on Black-Asian American relations often reproduces a binary logic of Afro-Asian alliance or conflict. Helen Jun (2011) offers an alternative by creatively exploring the Afro-Asian nexus in newspapers, novels, and films. According to Jun, the rallying of White laborers against Chinese immigrants defined the contours within which African Americans could articulate claims to citizenship in the nineteenth century. Her analysis shows how Orientalism included a sub-discourse called Black Orientalism, in which essentialist representations of China, Chinatown, and alien, backward Chinese people became the backdrop for the formation of a Black national identity during Reconstruction. Conversely, Asian Americans positioned themselves as possessing good citizenship values and skills, in contrast with Blacks. This instance of cross-racial discrimination displays the "discursive constraints" of a racialized and hetero-patriarchal institution of American citizenship (Jun 2011, 48). Jun's analysis enables us to look at the contradictions arising from racialized subject formation as a fundamental condition of US citizenship. In this book, I will be extending her analytical angle beyond the question of citizenship to that of class and culture.

Historian Scott Kurashige (2008) broke new ground in studies of Black-Asian relations. He examined how Japanese Americans and African Americans in the mid-twentieth century in the Crenshaw district of South LA both competed and cooperated with each other as they struggled to improve their lives in a city that celebrated whiteness. Mayor Bradley hailed from the Crenshaw district, which had integrated only after World War II. Crenshaw was also an incubator of the Asian American movement, which launched the pan-ethnic notion of a unified Asian American identity. Despite occasional fighting over turf, Kurashige suggests convivial interactions among Blacks, Asians, and Whites in everyday neighborhood social interactions. Residents formed leftist coalitions to fight for housing, employment, and political power. He attributes some of the antagonism between the groups to the dominant White power structure (e.g., American nationalism and Japanese incarceration during WWII), which exercised a modus operandi of divide and conquer. Although Japanese Americans and African Americans engaged in common, if largely separate, efforts to gain access to housing and jobs in the 1920s and 1930s, their glaringly dissimilar struggles during WWII placed them on divergent paths. Japanese Americans gradually became a "model minority," thanks to Japan's new role as a Cold War ally, in contrast to Black people, who remained a stigmatized and ghettoized minority.

## ETHNO-RACIAL IDENTITIES AMONG KOREAN IMMIGRANTS

Dating back to the pre-modern world, Korean and Japanese people shared a Sino-centric conception of peoplehood. From at least the Han dynasty (206 BC–220 AD), the Chinese felt their culture would prove so attractive to "barbarians" (*yi* or *fan*) and other "outsiders" that they would willingly pay tribute and adopt Chinese ways. The operative assumption was one of Chinese cultural superiority, not necessarily racial superiority.[19] Moreover, the Confucian tradition of self-cultivation and the civil service exam system were understood as allowing for "class" mobility in ways that were ethnically "neutral." The Chinese might have had discriminatory views of other Asians (e.g., Japanese and Koreans) but they would not consider them to be of another race, but rather a different ethnic group. Confucian societies have historically been concerned with cultural superiority, not Eurocentric notions of racial superiority (which include evolution, phenotype, skull measurements, permanent inferiority by virtue of race, etc.). Rather, there is a focus on cultural prejudice and notions of merit. Fundamentally, the distinction the Chinese have made between themselves and foreigners has always been cultural.

Influenced by Chinese notions, Koreans have long believed themselves to be more civilized than any other nation except China. Historically, they have not used the Western notion of race, although there are other hierarchies that were later adapted to include race. Thus, Koreans dismissed Whites as *yangi* (Western barbarians) until the late nineteenth century, when Korea was confronted by the military power of the supposedly inferior *yangi* and *waenom* (a derogatory term for the Japanese). Korea is often considered to be a country composed of one ethnic group, and some have discussed the "ethno-nationalist" belief in the superiority of Korean blood relative to other nations, each seen as having its own pure bloodline (Robinson 1988). Such ethno-nationalist discourses might be linked to Confucianism, which naturalizes and mandates inequality between social classes, age cohorts, and genders (albeit not races) as the means to social harmony.

However, anthropologist Kyung-Koo Han has found that "traditional Korea did not consider itself to be an ethnically homogeneous state, and did not discriminate against foreigners simply on the basis of their ethnic origins" (2007, 12). Instead, Korean nationalism, although superficially focused on ethnic homogeneity, was actually based on "a profound sense of cultural distinctiveness and superiority," in order to emphasize that the history of Korean political and cultural life is as old as that of China (Han 2007, 12). Nevertheless, as sociologist Gi-Wook Shin (2006) points out, premodern forms of community on the Korean peninsula from at least the tenth century onward seem to have laid a strong foundation for the construction of modern nationalism: well-defined territory, a centralized state, and relatively little linguistic variation. In the twentieth century, Korean society became fervently nationalistic, in part as a response to Japanese colonialism (1910–1945), and later, US neocolonial control.

With the introduction of Western notions of science, Korean society was exposed to Herbert Spencer's evolutionary theories of human difference. Spencer's notion of "the survival of the fittest"—progress as a necessity or destiny—advocated the study of evolution as an overarching principle from physics to ethics. Each society was identified at different stages, from savagery to civilization, while increasing its adaptability to changing conditions. In this world view, Europeans were considered the most civilized and innately superior to those they conquered. Spencerian Social Darwinism was introduced to Korean intellectuals in the last years of the Chosun dynasty,[20] chiefly through Liang Chi-chao (1873-1929) and other Chinese intellectuals, and by Yu Kil-chun (1856-1914), the first Korean student to study in Japan and the United States. Historian Kwang-rin Lee argues that "as Korea was about to fall, her intellectuals could readily accept Darwinism, which taught the rule that the weaker fall prey to the stronger and only the fittest could survive. . . . Darwinism helped them establish a nationalist view of history which grasped the national history with nation and competition (struggle) as main theme" (1978b, 48). Korea became a colony of Japan from 1910-1945 and Korean nationalism developed in reaction and resistance to the racist oppression of Japanese expansionist nationalism.

Despite this resistance, Korea was heavily influenced by Japanese notions of itself as a homogeneous mono-ethnic nation, specifically as the superior "Yamato race"—one that was superior to the rest of Asia and the West—in the period leading up to and during World War II (N. Kim 2008, 24). Paradoxically, Japanese immigrants and their descendants in the US were, at the time, excluded from that national community and subject to what historian Takashi Fujitani called "vulgar racism" or an explicitly race-based discrimination throughout the pre-Pacific war years.[21] The Japanese ethnoracial framework can also be traced back to Western intellectual influences, especially "Fichte and advocates of German nationalism, who emphasized common blood as well as a common language and culture" (Han 2007, 23). When both the West and Japan challenged Koreans with their "superior" technology, scientific knowledge, and industrial power, "Korea had to resort to the idea of a 'Kultur'-style German nationalism and solidarity in the forms of a symbology based on myths of a common language and blood" (ibid., 27).

In addition to Spencerian scientific racism, as well as a Sino-centric Confucian hierarchy, Euro-American racial ideology contributed to emerging Korean conceptions of identity. Since the Korean War (1950–1953),[22] the US has been a hegemonic force in South Korea. Sociologist Nadia Kim charts how South Koreans are racialized through "imperialist formations" such as the central importance of the US military and US cultural domination. For instance, in 1970s South Korea, White soldiers admitted that they heard Koreans repeat their anti-Black epithets without full comprehension of their meanings or the level of animus (Moon 1997, as cited in N. Kim 2008, 93). South Korean society has often viewed Black soldiers more negatively than White soldiers, as they observe a racial hierarchy within the military and the assignment of Black soldiers to the most dangerous missions. Equally important, Black soldiers have at times fanned the flames of animosity by adopting stereotypes and abusing their power over citizens, for instance, by assaulting local citizens in public places (Roth and Kim 2013, 349, 350). More generally, US soldiers have been accused of violent assaults against Korean sex workers and accidental killings of teenage girls.

Like other Asian immigrants, Korean immigrants have historically been racialized both as "forever foreign" and "model minorities." Korean immigrants have been racialized as dependent, feminine, and fundamentally foreign since the early 1900s (Espiritu 1997). More recent manifestations of anti-Asian sentiment include the 1980s Japan-bashing related to the success of the Japanese auto industry that led to the murder of Chinese American engineer Vincent Chin (1982) by two White autoworkers; they were given only three years of probation with no jail time. In addition, there were a host of post-9/11 crimes committed against South Asian Americans mistaken for Muslims.[23] The racialization of Asian Americans includes the "model minority" ideology, which has been buttressed by post-1965 immigration laws favoring educated Asians (Park and Park 2005). The "forever foreigner" and "model minority" ideologies mutually constitute one another, for often, once the model minority becomes too successful, exclusion and racial vilification can result (Cho 1993). Moreover, although Korean Americans, like Asian Americans more generally, are thought of as middle class in the US, many working-class Koreans, just like Latinos, suffer from language barriers and find it hard to negotiate with authorities and access crucial instrumental resources (Kwon 2015, 637).

Through the process of racial acculturation, immigrants become socialized into US-based racial meanings and race relations, largely through social networks, the mass media, and official institutions (Roth 2012); this also means their conceptualizations of self-identity might shift in their encounters with other ethnicities. Post-1965 Korean immigrants have benefited from the Civil Rights and racial minority movements,[24] and thus are subjected to a subtler form of racism than earlier East Asian immigrants. N. Kim's (2008) argument that Korean Americans' racial ideologies are influenced by US military and cultural domination in Korea is partially true. The US media's simplistic and negative depiction of African Americans as lazy, immoral, violent, or buffoonish tends to make Korean and other immigrants wary of Blacks. However, even without US military presence, other Asian immigrants have a similar understanding of US racial hierarchy, which indicates the salience of the global Euro-American hegemony in the nineteenth and twentieth centuries. When Koreans immigrated to the US, they were further exposed to the negative perceptions of African Americans, on top of the already familiar stereotypes. As Toni Morrison argues, in the US national identity has been constructed through racist strategies, and becoming American often means buying into "the rhetorical experience of Blacks as noncitizens, already discredited outlaws" (1994, 98–99).

The experience of running small businesses appears to also structure emergent ideologies of race and ethnicity among Koreans (K. Park 1997).[25] Pyong Gap Min asserts, "Korean merchants' prejudice against blacks . . . developed mainly through their contact in Korean-owned stores" (2008, 85). Notwithstanding the fact that the Black-White binary is still hegemonic in many parts of the US, I believe the Korean immigrant view of race is more gradational and not as polarized. They acknowledge being influenced by Euro-American racial ideology, which assigns Korean Americans to the racial category of "Asian American," or "*tongyangkye*" (people from the Asian continent). They also notice the complexity and diversity within racial categories such as Black and White. Overall, the numerous nationalities and languages and heterogeneous physical appearances of Americans have led many Korean immigrants to shift from a narrow racial analysis of US society to a more complex one. Nonetheless, their understanding of racial structure in the US is often uneven and class-specific in ways that reflect their interactions with other racial minorities and the urban poor (K. Park 1997). Lacking knowledge of the Civil Rights Movement and the taboo of being openly racist, they are more likely than others groups (particularly Whites) to admit to prejudices (Roth and Kim 2013, 346).[26] At the same time, Korean immigrants increasingly empathize with subjugated groups such as Blacks and admire their political and cultural power (ibid., 345).

In brief, Korean immigrants have been exposed to Euro-American racial ideology and are therefore produced as racial subjects, even while their understanding of this ideology remains incomplete. In this process, the old Sino-centric Confucian hierarchy seems to recede, however uncomfortably. In some senses, postcolonial Korea, with its Confucian, hierarchical sociopolitical systems intact, has embraced new notions of racism in the form of an American White privilege model without much contestation. Nonetheless, it is not until they immigrate to the US that this ideology becomes pertinent to their everyday lives.

## ETHNO-RACIAL IDENTITIES AMONG LATINOS

For heuristic purposes, I use the term "Latino" to indicate more recent immigrants from El Salvador, Guatemala, other parts of Central America, and Mexico.[27] Latino is a term of self-reference generated by people from Latin

America. It does not necessarily imply feelings of pan-ethnic identity among these recent immigrants, although (similar to the emergence of the term "Asian American") a Latino pride movement emerged in the 1960s and 70s that emphasized unity among people of Latin American descent. [28] As I will discuss in later chapters, in the aftermath of the unrest, there was also coalition building that took place between the established Mexican American community and Central American immigrant communities. Notwithstanding the differences between the various countries in Latin America, Latinos' common linguistic heritage; history of subjugation via Spanish colonization and US imperial expansion; and their own stories of resistance, survival, solidarity, and love are often identified as a source of unity and common identity (Oquendo 1995).

Latinos are descended from 500 years of *mestizaje*, or racial mixing between Indians, Europeans, Africans, and (to a lesser extent) Asians. Census counts in Latin American countries, like in the US, categorize people by race, with the main difference being that mixed race has been an official category since the large-scale independence movements of the nineteenth century. Thus, it should be emphasized that the terms "Latino" or "Hispanic" are not racial categories; they refer to Latin American origin. In other words, Latinos can be white, Black, mixed race, or indigenous.

In the 1850 US census, the newly conquered Mexican population in the American Southwest was classified as "White"; nearly 110,000 Mexicans who remained in the territory that was ceded by Mexico one year after the ratification of the Treaty of Guadalupe Hidalgo (1848) became US citizens. However, at the time Whites often referred to Mexicans as a "mongrel Spanish-Indian and Negro race" (Cobas, Duany, and Joe Feagin 2009, 4). In 1930, Mexicans were removed from the White category and placed in a separate racial designation as "Mexican," which coincided with the mass deportation of Mexicans from Southern California. By 1940, however, Mexicans were once again redefined as part of the "White" population, due to outcry from both Mexico and "persons of Mexican birth or ancestry who were not defined as Indian or some other nonwhite race" (Almaguer 2012, 146). In 1970, the census introduced the category "Hispanic" to capture the diversity of the various Latino nationalities in the US.

During the Chicano movement in the late 1960s, Mexican Americans began to redefine themselves as a "brown" population, claiming and celebrating their Indian ancestry (Almaguer 2012, 153). Nonetheless, in the 2000 Census, more than half of the Latino population racially defined themselves as "White." Reflecting the fact that most ethnic Mexicans are considered to have a mixed-race ancestry (typically Spanish and Indian), 41.2 percent of Latinos opted for "some other race," indicating such intermediate racial categories as *mestizo, mulato, trigueño,* or *moreno* in the space provided (Almaguer 2012, 149). Despite the high presence of both indigenous and African populations in countries formerly colonized by Spain, few Latinos identified as either Indian or Black (Almaguer 2012, 148). Notwithstanding these census statistics, racial categories such as *negro* (Black), *chino* (Chinese, or Asian more generally), and *indio* (Indian) are widely used by ethnic Mexicans to designate individuals with African, Asian, or Indian phenotypical features: "They were generally ranked below mestizo (because they were less White) and placed near the bottom of the racial hierarchy . . . the most derisive term and devalued racial category invoked was the term Indio" (Almaguer 2012, 153).

Rodriguez (1992) notes, in relation to racial categories, that "Latinos have emphasized, in addition to biological inheritance, dimensions that are freely varying, such as physical appearance, social class, and cultural modes of behavior" (Rodriguez 1992, 931). For example, although some Latinos are mistaken for African Americans because of their dark skin color, others are as fair-skinned as non-Hispanic Whites and often "pass" if they do not exhibit other markers of ethnic distinction (Telles and Ortiz 2008, 233). However, it should be noted that, at least with respect to Mexican Americans, although the law did not permit their racial segregation, many schools segregated Mexican children under the auspices of culture or language and subsequently emphasized vocational and Americanization curricula (Garcia and Yosso 2013, 68). In both Texas and California especially, district lines isolated Mexican American students until the mid-twentieth century.[29]

As with Asian Americans, there have been debates about the merits of pan-ethnic versus national identity among Latinos. The single most important advantage of pan-ethnic identifications is the strength-in-numbers factor it provides and the possibility of leveraging large population numbers for political strength. However, the disadvantages include the fact that the label "Latino" obscures the enormous diversity among people who come from two dozen countries. In Los Angeles, where Latinos have represented more than half the population since 2000, there are major differences in terms of class, citizenship, culture, and other factors: Latinos can be either immigrants or American-born, working or middle class, and of Mexican, Central American,[30] or other Latin American descent.

It is also important to understand how pan-ethnic identity labels are used by civic society and mainstream political institutions. Latinos are identified as a distinct racial/ethnic minority group by the US government in Civil Rights legislation and the Voting Rights Act, as well as in affirmative action programs (Lee and Bean 2004, 224). Mainstream institutions, marketing agencies, and the growing Latino media have reinforced this trend by addressing the Latino population as a homogeneous entity with a distinct culture identity. These media trends in turn impact the formation of identity among recent waves of immigrants. Notwithstanding the use of these terms by large institutions, however, recent studies find that only 19 percent of Mexican Americans chose a pan-ethnic term to represent themselves, and a full 69 percent preferred Mexican or Mexican American (Telles and Ortiz 2008, 219). In addition, national/ethnic identification for Mexican Americans remains strong across generations (ibid., 236). Telles and Ortiz (2008) state, "Even in the fourth generation most Mexican Americans continue to have Mexican-origin spouses, live in mostly Mexican neighborhoods, and have mostly Mexican-origin friends, though they report considerable social contact with others, especially Anglos" (183). Mexican Americans also feel the least social distance between themselves and other Mexican Americans, followed by low to moderate resistance to Mexican immigrants, other Hispanics, and non-Hispanics. While the social distance from Anglos declines notably with successive generations—for instance, no objection to marriage or school integration—they are more hesitant to marry or form social relationships with Asians and African Americans (ibid., 183).

As opposed to the long history of Mexican immigration to the US, the majority of Salvadorans and Guatemalans began arriving in the 1980s as part of a massive migration of Central Americans. Migration was a result of various political upheavals in Central America, including a socialist revolution and counter revolution in Nicaragua; the political violence, human rights violations, and economic devastation of the 1980–1992 civil war in El Salvador; and a decades-long civil war in Guatemala (Hamilton & Chinchilla 2001; Coutin 2007). This influx of immigrants can be traced back to Cold War interventionist policies of the US (i.e., the support of authoritarian dictators and the overthrowing of a popularly elected president in Guatemala in 1954), together with US economic policies, which led to the erosion of subsistence agriculture and resulted in peasants being pushed off their land (Ochoa and Ochoa 2005, 9).[31]

In spite of these different histories, Mexicans and Central Americans share similar experiences (Chavez 1992). Both groups face challenges related to the constraints of their immigration status and limited economic opportunities. They also share a common language, albeit with regional variations.[32] In addition, there is a history of extensive social interaction between Central Americans and Mexicans, including intermarriage, and because in the 1990s many Central Americans lacked the long history of migration and well-established communities, they often turned to Mexicans for social and cultural resources (Chavez 1992, 137). Mexicans and Central Americans often work together on issues of common interest, for instance, combating anti-immigration legislation in the aftermath of the civil unrest (see chapter 9). Institutions such as the Coalition for Humane Immigrant Rights of Los Angeles and One Stop Immigration assist both groups in efforts to legalize their status. However, there are also tensions. Hamilton and Chinchilla (2001) report that Mexicans' long-established history in the region leads some to resent the "new" Latino groups. In turn, Central Americans tend to be resentful of the sense of superiority exhibited by some Mexicans.

As the Latino population has grown to nearly 50 percent of some major metropolitan areas such as Los Angeles, media outlets have sprung up and urban culture has adapted. With five major television networks broadcasting in Spanish, 13 radio stations, 37 newspapers, and dozens of magazines, the Latino public of Los Angeles has many options for media consumption. The emergence of cultural phenomena such as lowriders, *banda* music, and dances (from *Punta* and *soka* to *quebradita*) demonstrate the increasing significance of Latino culture (Hayes-Bautista et al. 1993, 447). Despite the fact that the term is somewhat problematic in glossing over ethnic differences, Latino identity and culture is flourishing in LA and beyond.

This chapter has demonstrated that Los Angeles' ethno-racial history contains both antagonisms and alliances among racial minorities.[33] The four primary ethno-racial groups and their livelihoods have been structured in a way to avoid direct confrontation over residential, educational, and occupational segregation and segmentation along with anti-miscegenation laws.[34] Nevertheless, there have been racialized conflicts, such as the race riots of 1965 and 1992, but fewer conflicts directly related to class, notwithstanding the already discussed anti-Chinese sentiment White workers displayed in the nineteenth century. That said, relationships between Whites, Blacks, Latinos, and Korean immigrant groups in South LA should be understood within the context of political economy, where immigration and urban restructuring has allowed the ruling elite to manipulate perceived differences between ethno-racial groups to maintain an "us" versus "them" mentality; this antagonism has given the capitalist elite a new means of production and surplus extraction. African Americans have suffered greatly from the decline of the Southern California industrial economy and have been almost wholly left out of booming suburbanization. The exodus of industrial employment has been accompanied by a marked increase in unemployment, crime, and gangs. Global neoliberal capitalism has led to the relocation or drying up of industrial jobs and has crippled industrial unions.

In the next three chapters, I'll discuss three major analytical dimensions of social identity in relation to Black-Korean tensions and the 1992 LA unrest—race and racism, class and class conflict, and culture and culture clashes—which I argue are the building blocks of inequality in a multitiered "racial cartography."

# NOTES

1. "South Central" is made up of 25 neighborhoods (and three unincorporated ones). As of April 10, 2003, South Central was renamed South Los Angeles in order to downplay collective memories of violence and blight; however, most residents still use the old name.

2. Racially restrictive covenants were used nationwide to prevent people of color from buying, leasing, or occupying property in White communities, as property owners agreed not to sell to certain people, particularly African Americans (Pastor 2014, 38).

3. Black-Jewish relations haven't always been harmonious, particularly when it comes to certain topics like Israel.

4. The 1965 Act made it difficult for Latin Americans to immigrate to the United States, while immigrants from the Eastern Hemisphere benefited from this law. A visa limit of 170,000 was set for the Eastern Hemisphere. Three years later, an amendment established a visa limit of 120,000 for the Western Hemisphere, but only in 1978 did another amendment establish a fixed, per-nation quota. The 1978 amendment reduced the number of authorized immigrants that could come from Latin America, especially Mexico (Telles and Ortiz 2008, 94).

5. Compared to Mexicans, more Central Americans live in the city than in the suburbs.

6. In addition, an Indian doctor at King Medical Center filed a lawsuit, alleging that he was continually passed over for promotions because he was not Black (Washington Post 1998, A01).

7. From April 2012 through September 2012, the six-month crime rate for South LA was 20 crimes per 1,000 residents, higher than the average citywide crime rate, 13.5. However, the violent crime rate for South LA was 5.4—more than double the average citywide crime rate (2.5 per 1,000) (Los Angeles Department of City Planning 2013, 145, 146). Average annual homicide rates in some higher income neighborhoods on the west side of the city were nearly zero, compared to more than 20 homicides per 100,000 residents in South LA (Los Angeles Department of City Planning 2013, xiii).

8. The Crenshaw/Leimert Park Village emerged as the new center of Black Los Angeles following the 1992 civil unrest (Chapple 2010, 74).

9. See Davis (1990), Omi and Winant (1993), Winant (1994, 73), and Freer (1994, 187) regarding the reactionary racial politics during the Reagan-Bush years and Bradley administration.

10. When it was founded, CRIPS, the most renowned gang in South LA, was meant to be a community survival group that protected African Americans from violence by White neighbors (Gonzalez 2014, 190).

11. Davis is critical of contemporary social theory's silence—in discussing the role of electronic technologies precipitating "postmodern space" or the dispersal of urban functions across poly-centered metropolitan "galaxies"—on the militarization of city life (1990, 223).

12. Nationally, self-employment among Korean immigrants increased significantly from 18 percent in 1980 to 27 percent in 1990, but it slightly dropped to 24 percent in 2000 (Min 2008, 30).

13. In 1963, there were 17 Vons (Southern California's largest supermarket chain) and Safeway stores in South Central LA. Between 1963 and 1991, the two chains relocated 82 percent of their branches to the suburbs (Ashman et al. 1993, 111).

14. Until the late 1960s, according to Mosher and Mottl (1981, 450), the SBA did not grant any loans to "suspect" businesses like liquor outlets, for which the sale of alcoholic beverages comprised more than half their gross income.

15. I thank Maureen Mahon for this reference.

16. In the early twentieth century, Black Nationalism was represented by the Universal Negro Improvement Association of Marcus Garvey and subsequently by the Nation of Islam, led by Elijah Muhammad. The separatist movements of the 1960s included several variations: the revolutionary nationalism of the League of Revolutionary Black Workers in Detroit and the Black Panther Party in Oakland; the Booker T. Washington-influenced Black capitalist nationalism of Roy Innis and Floyd McKissick of the Congress of Racial Equality; the cultural nationalism of Maulana Karenga and Amiri Baraka, who argued for the establishment of rituals such as Kwanzaa; and the political nationalism manifested in the Gary Black Convention of 1972 and the National Black Political Assembly (Marable 1995, 211).

17. However, in 1972, the Wakefield Amendment proposed to outlaw these systematic desegregation efforts, arguing against forced integration. In 1979, the Robbins amendment (Prop 1) declared that school boards were not obligated to the Equal Protection Clause of the Fourteenth Amendment regarding school transportation, which ended busing and student reassignments (Gonzalez 2014, 107–8).

18. The riots were extensively documented in the press, which, along with the federal government, conflated black movements with Bolshevism.

19. Since the Tang dynasty (618–907), the imperial family has had significant non-Han ethnic origins.

20. During the decade of the 1890s and 10 years after Yu Kil-chun introduced Darwinism to Korea, Korea was challenged both internally and externally. Internally, Korea's government crumbled and the country was plunged into chaos in the wake of the Tonghak Revolution and the Kabo Reform in 1894. Externally, China was defeated by Japan in the First Sino-Japanese War; Korea thus became an arena for competition among imperial powers and faced the possibility of territorial partition by the encroaching powers (Lee Kwang-rin 1978a, 38). I thank Walter T. Lew for this reference.

21. The Immigration Act of 1924 ended almost all Japanese immigration until passage of the McCarran-Walter Act in 1952; naturalization laws allowed only "free white persons and those of African descent to become naturalized citizens; state-level alien land laws prohibited those ineligible to become naturalized citizens from owning land; the numerous state anti-miscegenation laws; and the like" (Fujitani 2007, 28).

22. More accurately, as the 1945 truce granted the US administrative control of the southern part of Korea, the US armed forces, which landed to drive out the Japanese, introduced racial ideologies and iconology.

23. Although it emerged for the purposes of anti-racist organizing, it should be noted that the term "Asian American" is particularly problematic, perhaps even more so than "Latino," in the way it lumps together a large geographic area with very different languages and histories.

24. Most Korean immigrants were not aware of the history and legacy of the African American struggle against racism.

25. In most Korean American communities, more than one-third of immigrants engage in small business activities.

26. Korean immigrants also have little knowledge of social desirability norms, such as how they are expected to talk about racial differences in the US.

27. According to the US Census Bureau, a person is of Hispanic origin if he or she identifies his or her ancestry as Mexican, Puerto Rican, Cuban, or other Spanish origin or culture, regardless of race. Those who identify with the term Hispanic tend to seek assimilation into the dominant Anglo-American culture, whereas those who use the term "Latino" generally seek to modify a system that they see as wanting to change them (Murguia 1991). However, the use of one term or the other is not always such a politicized choice. Regional variation exists in the use of the terms: "Latino" is used more frequently in California and on the East Coast, while "Hispanic" is more prevalent in Texas and Arizona.

28. I view both pan-ethnic identity terms—Latino and Asian American—as strategic (i.e., for the purposes of building a movement for civil rights across ethnic differences) and as recognizing some cultural similarities, while at the same time being aware of major distinctions. If anything, pan-Latino identity is more cohesive than Asian American identity because of the shared language and history of colonization by the Spanish.

29. According to David Garcia (2013), the schools were "integrated," but all of the classrooms, hallways and bathrooms were segregated.

30. The Central American immigrants in Los Angeles are scattered throughout the city. Less than 10 percent of Salvadoran and Guatemalans in Los Angeles County live in the Pico-Union area, which contains the largest number of Salvadorans and Guatemalans (Chang and Diaz-Veizades 1999, 21).

31. Another recent issue, which I cannot discuss at length, is the Deferred Action for Childhood Arrivals (DACA) program and the crisis of unaccompanied minors from Central America. California has the largest proportion of DACA recipients in the country, and this issue has undoubtedly impacted LA's Latino population.

32. This is not always the case, particularly for Guatemalan immigrants, some of whom are indigenous and do not speak Spanish very well.

33. I discussed Black-Asian relations but didn't touch on Latino-Asian relations or Black-Latino relations at all. In chapter 8 and 9, I'll address these relations.

34. The government has been involved in redlining, etc.

*Part II*

# BLACK-KOREAN
# TENSION BEFORE THE UNREST

# Chapter Two

# Disentangling Race and Racism

They don't respect us, don't redistribute money into the community, and don't even bother to live near us! During the civil unrest, our anger for the system, and the police department it created, manifested itself in the form of breaking down what we saw as unfair, the embracing of this new nigga at the expense of the little dignity and pride we had left. (Nia, 1992)

In no way was the death of Latasha Harlins trivial or forgotten . . . however, this was not so cut and dry a racial case of the aggressor on an innocent victim. Both sides contributed to this tragedy. . . . The black eyes and split lip on face of Soon Ja Du wasn't just a little catfight. It contributed to the reasoning for the judgment at the time. (Thomas 2013)[1]

Although different racial and cultural discourses constitute the principal framework for understanding the conflict between Korean merchants and South LA African American and Latino residents, the state and the accumulation of capital are the principal forces in everyday power relations between groups. When the state becomes directly involved in race issues, it redefines racial conflict through the dual functions of instigating social change and maintaining social control. Social control is enforced through policies involving civil rights, immigration policy, welfare reform, and political restructuring. The state and social movements are thus linked in a single framework of racial formation (Omi and Winant 1994, 78). In my Gramscian analysis, as mediated by the work of Stuart Hall (1986), institutions and processes within civil society—such as cultural organizations, family, churches, and religion—"play an absolutely vital role in giving, sustaining and reproducing different societies in a racially structured form" (26) via consent.

The media depicted conflicts such as the Harlins-Du incident and the 1992 LA unrest as racial confrontations between African Americans and Koreans, arising from cultural differences, contentious daily experiences, and racial bigotry among both groups. Headlines in the *Los Angeles Times* stated: "Boycott: Business Has Plummeted in a Store Where Korean American Owner Killed a Black Woman" (*LAT* July 2, 1991) and "Korean Stores Firebombed; 2 of 3 Hit Have Seen Black Boycott" (*LAT* August 19, 1991). An editorial argued that while protesters had a right to be upset, "in the long run, boycotts rarely address the real, core problem and only add to community tension" (*LAT* October 25, 1991). However, while boycotts may not lead directly to solutions, they certainly address the economic basis for such tension.

In the Du-Harlins incident, media attention was high[2] because the shooting happened after a series of incidents involving Korean grocers in Black neighborhoods around the country, one of which included a yearlong boycott in New York City. In order to better understand race relations in Los Angeles, we need to look for the missing link in this issue, which is not represented by the media or either side: where do White people fit into the Black-Korean conflict? Are Koreans simply considered a dominant White-adjacent group? What kind of racial discourse did the media create, and what role did race play in this conflict?

In contrast to the media interpretations of the conflict as a racial one, Korean and, to a lesser extent, Black community leaders explained the tensions in terms of culture. They claimed that cultural differences accounted for the majority of the disputes involving merchants and customers. Responding to the boycott in New York, a Korean staff member of the New York City Human Relations Commission testified:

> Korean merchants' seeming attitudes toward their customers are the source of many tensions. . . . It is in their frustration that . . . they appear arrogant and rude. . . . Western culture is very open. It is kind, always smiling, that is the tradition. But we are very different. If a Korean woman smiles at an unknown man, we would think she is a prostitute. Even if they do not smile, it is not their intention to be rude or arrogant. . . . They are not trained to smile.[3]

Black media critic Earl Ofari Hutchinson, while acknowledging the racist practices of some Korean merchants, agrees with this assessment, arguing that "the dispute and friction between Blacks and Koreans is caused more by differences in customs, culture, and language than racism" (1991, 554–55). Still, while there are cultural differences between Korean merchants and Black residents, it is unclear whether these differences are the root of the problem.

Scholars have stressed the importance of structural forces within race relations. In their view, Black-Korean tensions include a range of phenomena, including altercations over daily transactions between merchants and customers, boycotts of Korean-run stores, and the potential for arson by customers. C. Kim (2000) and Lee (2002) offer a more complex analysis. Lee suggests that everyday interactions between merchants and customers are civil, but that "race can inflect merchant-customer relations in diverse ways, sometimes polarizing the simplest interactions and, in extreme cases, becoming the source of protest motivations that lead to intergroup conflict" (2002, 143). Merchants and customers are also members of racial groups that have long-held beliefs about one another. Specifically, Lee argues, "It is precisely when groups question their position in the ethnic hierarchy that social order breaks down" (2002, 163). Macro-racial narratives infuse every commercial interaction, not just when disputes arise. What is important here is that political protest is not separate from, but rather intertwined with, everyday relations.

C. Kim challenges the conventional argument that Black boycott leaders misdirected their rage at defenseless Korean merchants. She interprets the Flatbush Black boycott of Korean stores (1990) as an expression of Black political resistance to racial oppression by the White power structure in New York City (2000, 3). White elites use Korean and other Asian Americans as buffers between Blacks and themselves by celebrating Asian Americans' cultural superiority to Blacks. At the same time, they emphasize Asian Americans' "foreign" and "inassimilable" characteristics. Unsurprisingly, the mainstream media, White political and economic leaders, and judicial institutions sided with the Korean community in squashing Black boycott organizers' resistance, using integrationist, colorblind rhetoric that "transformed what had begun as a neighborhood scuffle into a major political crisis" (C. Kim 2000, 3).

However, the mainstream media and White leaders have not always criticized boycott leaders and supported Korean merchants. Korean community leaders felt that during the unrest the media gave mostly favorable coverage to the concerns of Black protesters over their own. As C. Kim notes, the *Los Angeles Times* depicted Korean immigrant merchants as rude, disrespectful, greedy, and exploitative of the Black community. The media also praised Danny Bakewell, a leader of the Black Nationalist movement in Los Angeles, as a significant voice for the Black community. In extending this discussion, I suggest that we consider this issue in relation to the limitations of political participation by Koreans and African Americans in the White-dominated spheres of media, criminal justice, policy-making, and leadership. While fully acknowledging that racial ordering shapes the dynamics of Black-Korean tensions in the US, I also consider racial attitudes and racial distancing as salient dimensions of my model of racial cartography (see chapter 9).

In this book, I frame Black and Korean comparative experiences in terms of the defining axes of inequality in the US: race, citizenship, class, and culture. This chapter explores how White racism is reconstructed in institutions associated with the public and political spheres (the media, police, courts, government, educational settings). I consider what role race plays in Black-Korean tension and the nature of racism between minorities. Most of the interviews used in this chapter were reactions to the 1991 Du-Harlins incident and the 1992 unrest, the most deadly and costly race riot in US history, which began only eight days after the appeals court affirmed Judge Karlin's sentence of Du. I present the Du-Harlins incident as a case study of Black-Korean tension and then shift to Black and Korean racial discourses. In describing the boycotts, I pay special attention to how they came to be organized; how both the Black and Korean immigrant communities were mobilized; and how Blacks and Koreans have differential access to public and political spheres aligned with the state and civil society that "are implicated in setting these conflicts into motion" (Gold 2010, 2).

The prevailing political, economic, and cultural conditions in South LA at the time put Black residents in conflict with Korean American merchants. The economic success of the Korean community distanced them from the economically strained residents of the South LA area. However, economic disparity alone cannot explain "distancing" or "othering"; cultural and racial differences also played a significant role. This "otherness," according to Freer (1994, 182), was a critical variable in explaining how two relatively resource-poor, stigmatized groups could come to view their differences as more important than their similarities.

## THE MODEL MINORITY MEETS THE UNDERCLASS

The popular stereotype of Koreans as a model minority not only touts their success, but it also highlights the failures of other groups, especially poor African Americans.[4]

An article in *Newsweek* (May 18, 1992) about the aftermath of the 1992 LA riots used Koreans as an example to reject the view that poverty and joblessness lead to the failure of minority groups. The article explains that because Koreans have "made it," violence, crime, and poverty in inner cities are not inevitable. The discourses about African Americans and Korean Americans reflected in such media portrayals cultivate misconceptions, which contribute to interracial antagonism.

During the height of the unrest, Black residents accused Koreans of overcharging, being rude, taking over Black businesses, taking dollars away from the Black community, and giving little in return. African Americans further complained that Koreans seldom hired them or contributed to community services. Many African Americans believed that the US government was providing money and other resources to these "newcomers" while ignoring their own needs (Jo 1992, 398). In addition, African Americans often felt that Koreans too readily accused them of shoplifting and other criminal behavior (Stewart 1994). In response, members of the Korean immigrant community expressed outrage and contempt toward boycott organizers for these seemingly unfair attacks, as was evidenced in the quote at the beginning of this chapter.

Many Koreans also expressed frustration over the lack of attention given to the killing of fellow immigrant merchants, and they resented being scapegoated in the media (Freer 1994, 190). Federal mediator and former Chair of the LA County Commission on Human Relations (LACCHR) Jan Sunoo, a third-generation Korean American, expressed his thoughts about the Black community in our interview (1991): "Korean Americans are not the cause of the dismal economic plight of African Americans. Nor are they the cure. It is wrong to scapegoat Korean Americans for what hundreds of years of historical discrimination have left in its wake."

Notwithstanding the tense relations, both communities had been making strides to reduce hostilities long before the unrest. In 1983, members of the LACCHR founded the Black/Korean Alliance (BKA), which became more active following the deaths of four Korean merchants in South LA in 1986. The BKA served as a multifunctional community organization that provided (1) community education and cultural exchange programs; (2) crime prevention seminars; (3) joint ventures and economic development; (4) mediation; and (5) religious activities. However, it was set up primarily as a reaction to racial tension and was "ill-equipped to strike preemptively to prevent conflicts, because its members had few resources, little political support—and most importantly—few grassroots community ties" (Joyce 2003, 130).

Along with the BKA, the Asian Pacific American Dispute Resolution Center (APADRC) and the Martin Luther King Dispute Resolution Center (MLKDRC) emerged as key players in the effort to address Black-Korean tensions. These two organizations grew out of a national movement to divert disputes from the civil courts to less costly alternatives.[5] With limited funding (an annual budget of less than $100,000 each), both programs relied on volunteers to handle the 40 to 75 cases per month involving disputes between landlords and tenants, employers and workers, neighbors, family members, and merchants and consumers. Both groups mediated interracial disputes, including those between Koreans and African Americans (Ong et al. 1994b, 284). Despite these achievements, their efforts were not successful in substantially reducing the level of hostility.

Korean merchants also tried to respond independently to community needs in several ways by: (1) extending credit, accepting coupons, cashing checks, and selling money orders; (2) employing African Americans; (3) participating in customers' social events (e.g., funerals,[6] weddings, birthdays, and other occasions[7]); (4) throwing block parties, sharing Korean *pulgogi* or *kalbi* barbecues, and exchanging food or gifts with customers on holidays; and (5) donating money or refreshments to various Black community organizations, youth and elderly sports teams, churches, local schools, and the police.

When I first began my research prior to the 1992 unrest, there was much heated discussion by both Koreans and African Americans about the Du-Harlins case. Some interviewees suggested that a few Black militant protesters were rabble-rousers attempting to lead people into conflict. "But the average person in South Central has better things to do with their time," commented one interviewee. Most interviewees believed that the media, by focusing on the Du-Harlins case, exacerbated the Black-Korean conflict. However, Black informants still believed Du should have received jail time. In addition, when most Black interviewees were asked about their interactions with Korean Americans, they commented that encounters were generally pleasant but that merchants were often rude.

## Black Boycotts of Korean Stores in Los Angeles

Beginning in the early 1980s, Black boycotts of Korean shopkeepers in New York and Los Angeles began to draw national attention. Less widely publicized boycotts were held in cities such as Chicago,[8] Washington, DC, Philadelphia, Atlanta, and Columbus. Most boycotts occurred in low-income minority neighborhoods and targeted businesses selling food products.

The Du-Harlins incident was hardly the first Korean-Black conflict in Los Angeles. Long before then, Korean and Black high school students clashed in 1974 (Chang and Yu 1994). Increasingly, African Americans began to feel that they were treated badly by a wave of Korean merchants who had come into South LA to open liquor stores, markets, clothing boutiques, and swap meets. In 1983, a major Black newspaper, *The Los Angeles Sentinel* (*LAS*), ran a five-week series urging the boycott of Korean-owned stores:

> [B]lacks are angry because here are a bunch of foreigners, a bunch of folks who don't speak English, who can't vote, who come here with money, and that is how it is perceived. . . . The Black community has literally been taken over by Asians in the past five years. . . . We urge fellow Blacks to boycott Korean owned stores. (*LAS* 1983)

The *LAS* also condemned Korean merchants for mistreating Black customers, further intensifying the interethnic tension.

Following the shooting of Latasha Harlins, the Brotherhood Crusade (BC), a Black Nationalist organization led by Danny Bakewell, and Mothers in Action (MIA) began a boycott against Du's store, reminiscent of the "don't shop where you can't work" protest campaigns led by prominent Black leaders several decades earlier in LA and major northern US cities. Other boycotts were initiated in New York, such as the eight-month boycott of Red Apple Market in the Flatbush neighborhood of Brooklyn in 1990, which was the result of a physical altercation between a Haitian customer and a Korean proprietor who had accused the former of stealing.

As for Korean merchants, they were resentful toward African Americans who had robbed or shoplifted at their stores. Many Korean immigrant inter-viewees reported having been held up a dozen times by African Americans while conducting business in South LA. Moreover, as noted earlier, 19 Ko-rean merchants in Los Angeles were killed in their stores between 1988 and 1991. What was too often an issue of class was read by many Korean infor-mants as an issue of race, and violent behavior was perceived as characteristic of all African Americans. However, the violent incidents are only one aspect of the relationship between Korean merchants and Black customers: the mu-tual distrust developed from their everyday interactions.

By the late 1980s, a number of reported incidents reflected hostility to-ward Korean merchants in Los Angeles. In 1989, the Organization of Mutual Neighborhood Interests (OMNI) staged a two-day boycott against the Slauson and Inglewood Indoor Swap Meets in South LA to protest the mistreatment of African Americans. They urged Koreans to hire more Black employees and to contribute to local community efforts. There were more specific demands, such as a 72-hour exchange policy for merchandise; dressing rooms; price tags on merchandise; a return policy for damaged goods; and a procedure for registering complaints.[9] Other instances were violent and sometimes fatal. Even before the Harlins shooting, the LACCHR had reported a 150 percent increase in anti-Asian hate incidents in 1990, identifying Asian Americans as the second most victimized ethnic group in LA after African Americans. On July 17, 1990, two Black youth beat and shot a Korean man in South LA. The police classified the incident as an anti-Korean hate crime because the attackers did not rob the victim, but taunted him as a "Yellow Monkey" (*Se-gye Times* [ST] June 19, 1990). In the same year, several Korean swap meet owners in the area were attacked by Black gang members in their stores (*ST* August 16, 1990). Finally, in February 1992, a Thai woman was pulled from her car and beaten because she was thought to be Korean.

## The Du-Harlins Incident

A year later, events at two separate Korean stores in South LA escalated racial tensions between Korean and Black communities.[10] The subsequent Black boycotts and individual acts of anti-Korean violence paved the way for the massive destruction of Korean businesses during the unrest in 1992.

However, thirteen months before the unrest (and thirteen days after the police beating of Rodney King), on March 16, 1991, Soon Ja Du, the 51-year-old Korean owner of the Empire Liquor Market on South Figueroa Street, shot Latasha Harlins, a 15-year-old Black girl, after an over-the-counter scuffle involving a bottle of juice (*LAT* October 21, 1991). The descriptions of the event remain controversial. Black and Korean interviewees differed on the details of the event and how and why it occurred. For instance, Korean immigrant merchants challenged the media's version of the events and accused it of airing a particular segment of the security video.

The security videotape became key evidence in the investigation: it showed Du and Harlins scuffling over the bottle of orange juice. Du had been watching Harlins in the security mirror and erroneously concluded that Harlins was attempting to steal, evidently not seeing the money Harlins held in her hand (*LAT* March 20, 1991). She accused Harlins of trying to shoplift the juice, which Harlins had stuck in her backpack before approaching the counter. Harlins then turned around to show Du the juice in her backpack and told her she wanted to pay for it (*LAT* March 22, 1991, B1). After Du grabbed her backpack and demanded payment for the juice, Harlins punched Du four times in the face, and Du fell down twice. When she stood up the first time, Du threw the stool that was behind the counter at Harlins, but she missed. When Du stood up the second time, she grabbed the gun her husband kept behind the counter and pointed it at the girl. Harlins picked up the orange juice, which had fallen to the floor during the scuffle, and threw it on the counter. As she turned to walk out of the store, Du shot her in the back of the head. When the police arrived, they found Harlins dead, clutching two dollar bills in her left hand. Six months later, in November 1991, Du was convicted of manslaughter, but a judge sentenced her to probation; no time would be served.

During the trial, Du's lawyers argued that she was defending herself after Harlins struck her and that the gun had fired accidentally. Du and her family testified regarding the hostility they had experienced since purchasing the store in 1989: robberies, burglaries, threats of arson and murder, and extortion, as well as constant shoplifting. Du's family contended that the weapon had been stolen and recovered but had also been modified, unknown to them, to have a hair trigger, which was a fact that police seemed to corroborate. Du testified that she thought she "was going to die" after Harlins hit her. Du's son Joseph testified that the store, which the family had owned for two years, had been robbed on three occasions and burglarized 30 times per week.[11]

The morning following the incident, representatives from the BKA, the LA chapter of the NAACP, the Southern Christian Leadership Conference (SCLC), the LA Mayor's Office, the LACCHR, the Southern California chapter of the Korean American Grocers Association (KAGRO), and other civil rights organizations met and issued a statement stressing that the shooting was not racially motivated and asking people to remain calm (*KTLA* March 20, 1991). On March 22, Mayor Tom Bradley brought twenty leaders into a closed-door meeting at an SCLC office to discuss solutions to minimize racial tensions (*KTLA* March 24, 1991). Despite these meetings, antagonism increased. Although the Empire Liquor Market was closed immediately after Harlins' death, approximately 150 African Americans picketed in front of the store two days later. The demonstration was organized by Danny Bakewell and the Reverend Edgar Boyd, pastor of the Bethel African Methodist Episcopal (AME) Church, which was located in the same neighborhood. During the press conference, the participants shouted slogans such as "Send Koreans home," "Get rid of Koreans," "Stop murdering our young children," and "We want justice" (*KTLA* March 23, 1991).

Danny Bakewell, a millionaire businessman, activist and philanthropist who acquired the *Los Angeles Sentinel* in 2004,[12] cofounded an LA-based community development organization called The Brotherhood Crusade, one of the largest nonprofit organizations in Southern California. He had been "a member of the Nation of Islam during the 1970s and continued to embrace the Nation's self-help philosophy and acceptance of capitalism" (Joyce 2003, 127). While condemning the judge presiding over the Du-Harlins case, Judge Karlin, as a racist, Bakewell took "a Black nationalist, self-determination stance that included holding community business owners to a respectful protocol with their black customers on threat of losing their businesses" (Stevenson 2013, xxi).[13] As discussed in the previous chapter, Black nationalists have often drawn on a "community control" framework to condemn Korean-owned shops they see as stymieing the development of Black entrepreneurship and to envision a geographical base for greater Black economic power, which is a legacy of the Garveyites of the 1920s.[14] While Bakewell stressed the power of Black entrepreneurism and the need to recycle Black dollars back into the community, his concern did not move beyond a somewhat narrow and simplistic emphasis on Black capitalism. Neither did he directly challenge White supremacy as an oppressive system or analyze its economic or psychological impact.

The Harlins Family and their supporters formed their own activist organization called the Latasha Harlins Justice Committee (LHJC) before the trial took place. The LHJC helped persuade District Attorney Ira Reiner to appeal Karlin's sentencing of Du, held candlelight vigils, mounted protest rallies outside of Karlin's courtroom, petitioned the Justice Department to file a civil rights violation case against Du, and organized two petition campaigns to remove Karlin from the bench (Stevenson 2013, xxi).

As with the Rodney King beating, the criminal court's decision angered the Black community more than the incident itself, "resurrecting the long, black memory of whippings, lynching, dismemberment, rapes, and burnings" (Stevenson 2013, 287). Most Black interviewees noted that they experienced increasing tensions only after the controversial sentencing. Citing Du's lack of a criminal record, Judge Karlin handed her a suspended 10-year sentence in the state penitentiary—six years for the murder and four for the use of a firearm. Du was also ordered to perform 400 hours of community service, pay a $500 fine, pay for Harlins' funeral and medical expenses, and she was placed on probation for five years (*LAT* November, 16, 1991).

Karlin's decision gave African Americans the impression that Koreans were being protected by the White-dominated criminal justice system; activists strongly protested this perceived special consideration. Legal scholar Neil Gotanda notes: "The cultural attributes of defendant Du are favorable, and portray a sympathetic, Korean 'model minority.' Placed in opposition is the more familiar cruel stereotype of African Americans as criminals and gang members" (2000, 381). Calling Harlins a martyr, Ray, a family friend, said, "I'm not mad at any Korean person—I want that clear. . . . I'm angry at the justice system . . . African Americans don't get justice in the United States today" (*LAT* November, 26, 1991). Legal experts not involved in this case were divided over whether the sentence was unusually lenient. However, *Los Angeles Times* journalists noted that according to the results of a survey of 1,831 Los Angeles Superior Court criminal sentences in the summer of 1990, probation without prison time for a violent crime was rare (*LAT* November 26, 1991). In addition, this sentence was one of the most lenient imposed on a felon convicted of voluntary manslaughter with the use of a gun in California that year. LA City Councilman (and current county supervisor) Mark Ridley-Thomas called Karlin's sentence "another assault on the quality of life and the dignity of African Americans. . . . It will be read as the court having turned its back on what is obviously a senseless killing of a teenager by an adult—by a merchant directed at a consumer" (*LAT* October 12, 1991). Following the decision, thirty civil rights, religious, political, and grassroots leaders, led by Danny Bakewell, picketed in front of the Compton Municipal Criminal Court asking for Judge Karlin's resignation. Five hundred Black participants, including the mayor of Compton, attended the protest, criticizing the verdict and alleging anti-Black racism (*KTLA* November 23, 1991).

Bakewell's protest was also supported by Black churches. Sponsored by the Black Women's Forum and led by Representative Maxine Waters (D-Los Angeles), more than 300 Black activists gathered at Bethel AME Church in South LA to channel their anger into a campaign to increase Black political and economic strength in the community (*LAT* November 17, 1991). There, the Reverend Cecil L. "Chip" Murray, pastor of the First AME Church in South LA, encouraged residents to express their frustration not only in protest but also in coalition building. In a town meeting at the Bethel AME Church, the anger was readily apparent. One man was wearing a T-shirt that said, "Fuck the judge. Justice B damned!!!" Wilbur Thomas, wearing a Malcolm X cap, stood in the street waving a sign that read, "Enough is enough" (*LAT* November 17, 1991).

While church leaders tried to direct their congregations' anger toward political organizing, some Black residents held more violent protests. On November 26, 1991, Molotov cocktails were thrown into the Korean-owned Ace Liquor Store (*KTLA* November 27, 1991). On December 15, young African Americans smashed the windows of nine cars parked at a Korean Catholic Church in San Diego while the car owners were attending a service inside (*KTLA* December 18, 1991). In addition, Joyce (2003) reported the following cases of violence between African Americans and Koreans in Los Angeles, 1986–1995: the shooting of two Korean merchants and one Black customer, the Dennis Lee Young Song shooting, the 7 Days Food Store altercation, the Juri Kang shooting, the Century Liquor Store shooting, the Paul Park shooting, and the Yong Tae Park shooting (147). Some of the violence on the part of African Americans could be attributed to the revelation that in response to the sensationalized media coverage of the Du-Harlins case, many Koreans throughout the US and the Korean government had submitted letters petitioning Judge Karlin to give Du a lenient sentence (*KTLA* October 26, 1991). They complained that as shopkeepers they felt threatened by their customers, and their anxiety was based on a history of violence: in September 1986, four Korean merchants were murdered by Black people during robberies in South LA, and 15 were killed in the 18 months before Harlins' death.

Many Koreans characterized Du as a victim of inner-city crime, arguing that her actions, based on fear, were justified as a means of self-defense. When the news of Du's five-year probation sentence was released, many Koreans considered it a victory for their community. However, not all in the community offered unconditional support for Du. Attorney T.S. Chung, a former candidate for the California State Assembly, voiced a widely shared concern that by painting Du as a symbol of Korean immigrant identity, it was no longer one woman on trial, but the entire Korean American community: "It's just one case . . . a sad case . . . but it should not have any greater significance attached to it . . . we haven't had a demonstration every time a Korean shop owner gets killed" (*LAT* October 12, 1991).

Koreans also questioned whether Du had been arrested and charged with first-degree murder as a kind of "peace offering" to African Americans after the LAPD beating of Rodney King. The Du family gave the shop's security video to the LAPD, hoping it would vindicate Du, but the Department instead released it to the media. John Lee, who covered the Harlins case for the *Los Angeles Times*, stated about this decision:

> The police were feeding the media through the very calculated press conference [Monday after the weekend shooting], while calling for "Murder One"—a premediated homicide charge . . . The calculation was to take away from the Rodney King incident and to displace their racist beating—to displace some of that shock of the racism—and put it on a Korean merchant. (*LA Weekly* July 10, 2013)

As politicians, community leaders, government officials, the criminal justice system, and the media became involved in the dispute over Judge Karlin's verdict, the Du-Harlins incident became more overtly politicized. Ira Reiner, the district attorney at the time, fought desperately against Karlin's sentence. He tried to have it overturned and threatened her career as a judge, calling the sentence "a stunning miscarriage of justice." He said he would order his deputies to exercise an option allowed by state law to automatically remove Karlin whenever she was assigned to a criminal case (*LAT* November 24, 1991). Even some members of the Black community questioned Reiner's populist rhetoric, as they did not want the DA to use this case to accrue more power vis-à-vis the general discretion judges exercised (Stevenson 2013, 247). Months later, in a 26-page opinion paper, the second District Court of Appeals rejected claims by Reiner that the sentence was illegal and that Karlin had abused her discretion in issuing it (*LAT* April 22, 1992). To the disappointment of Reiner and the Black community, the state appeals court held 3-0 in April 1992 that Karlin had not exceeded her authority, noting that judges have broad discretion in sentencing (*LAT* July 13, 1992). Black activists were dealt another blow when Karlin defeated three challengers and won reelection by a narrow margin in June 1992.[15] Furthermore, the LA County Bar Association's Criminal Justice Section awarded Joyce Karlin the "Trial Judge of the Year" title and Charles Lloyd, Du's defense lawyer, the "Trial Attorney of the Year" title for their roles in the Du trial (Stevenson 2013, 259).

Seven months after Du's trial and eight days after the decision by a higher court to uphold the sentence, five White officers were acquitted of beating Rodney King. LA erupted into violence on April 29, 1992, with fifty-four people ultimately killed and $1 billion in damages to businesses. Approximately half of the businesses destroyed in the riots were Korean-owned, with those located in South LA suffering even higher rates of damage. Some people burned Korean stores invoking Latasha Harlins' name, as the case was still fresh in the minds of many in South LA, and retribution was taken primarily on Korean merchants. The Empire Liquor Market was one of the first to be firebombed, although it had closed long before; a sign had been hung on its door: "Closed for Murder and the General Disrespect of Black People."

## THE INSTIGATING ROLE OF WHITENESS

### The Criminal Justice System

Black interviewees firmly believed that there are a range of forces (e.g., discrimination from the financial institutions and the government) that limit Black business opportunities and encourage the influx of Korean shopkeepers into Black communities. From the perspective of those who boycotted Korean-owned stores, anger against Korean merchants was linked to their frustration with American society and government as a whole. The presence of Korean merchants was seen as proof of preferential treatment toward Koreans as contrasted with continuing, pervasive racism against African Americans. As one of the leaders of the 1990 Church Avenue boycott in New York remarked: "Now they [Koreans] are acting as agents of the White racist establishment to control the African American community" (*Village Voice* May 29, 1990). In this context, Korean merchants came to symbolize many social injustices African Americans have historically suffered in the US.

Seen in this light, the Black-Korean interracial discourse was actually a tripartite relationship, with White-dominated institutions mediating this relationship and playing a key role in shaping tensions. Asians—Koreans in particular—hold neither a White nor Black position in US race relations; this is the case not only for small business ownership, but also in the criminal justice system, as exemplified by the court's sentencing of Soon Ja Du. Numerous interviewees identified the enduring anti-Black racial implications of Du's sentencing:

"The judge was unfair. A Black postal carrier received six months in jail for beating a dog but this woman receives probation for killing a human."

"If it was a White child, she would've done time. People go to jail for parking tickets. People go to jail for less."

"If the situation had involved a Black store owner and an Asian girl, the Black woman would have been put in jail . . . "

"The judge's sentence sends out a message that Black life is worth less than a White life. The sentence should be overturned. The woman should serve time. You mean to tell me that Mike Tyson is going to do 3–7 years time for supposedly raping, date-raping a woman when they were the only two there, and this woman killed a Black child, and she is not going to serve a day in time? That's insane. That's the beast working."

For her part, Judge Karlin argued that the rules against probation should not apply in the Du-Harlins case:

> There are three reasons that I find this is an unusual case. First, the basis for the presumption against probation is technically present. But it doesn't really apply. The statute is aimed at criminals who arm themselves when they go out and commit other crimes. *It is not aimed at shopkeepers who lawfully possess firearms for their own protection.* Second, the defendant has no recent record, in fact, no record at any time of committing similar crimes or crimes of violence. Third, the defendant participated in the crime under circumstances of great provocation, coercion and duress. Therefore, this is, in my opinion, an unusual case that overcomes the statutory presumption against probation . . . Mrs. Du is a 51-year-old woman with no criminal history and no history of violence. But for the unusual circumstances in this case, including the Du family's history of being victimized and terrorized by gang members, Mrs. Du would not be here today. Nor do I believe Mrs. Du would be here today if the gun she grabbed for protection had not been altered. This was a gun that had been stolen from the Du family and returned to them shortly before the shooting, and I cannot ignore the reason Mrs. Du was working at the store at that day. She went to work that Saturday to save her son from having to work. Mrs. Du's son had begged his parents to close the store. This was because he had been the victim of repeated robberies and terrorism in that same store. (*LAT* November 22, 1991, my emphasis)

Karlin's legal papers repeatedly called the events an attack and labeled it brutal, violent, and vicious (*LAT* February 25, 1992). She also described Harlins as Du's assailant, and briefly noted that the teenager, with her athletic build, was much stronger than the 51-year-old grocer.

As is evident from the Du-Harlins case, racial inequality is routinely played out in judicial sentencing, usually in favor of Whites against Blacks. African Americans know well that Whites who kill African Americans get lesser sentences than Blacks who kill other Blacks, and that Blacks who kill Whites get the most stringent sentences. Given this racialized bias, Black community members perceived that Du received judicial sympathy as an "honorary White" because she killed a Black person. Conversely, it is unlikely that Du would have received the same lenient sentence if she had been a Black person who dared to kill a White customer. However, we should not overlook Karlin's reasoning in arriving at a final sentence. She invoked aspects of capitalist social relations in the US, including the right to engage in free trade and to defend oneself, one's property, and one's livelihood. In addition, gender played an important role in this sentencing (Stevenson 2013). While characterizing Du in feminine terms, stressing her vulnerability and her role as wife and mother, Karlin viewed Harlins not as an innocent girl, but as a threatening figure. In this way, a White-Asian-Black hierarchy was made visible through racialized, gendered, and classed sentencing.

## Media, Police, Politicians, and Government Officials

The criminal justice system is not the only institution with a racialized agenda. LeGrand Clegg II, City Attorney of the City of Compton and Chair of the Coalition against Black Exploitation in Compton, wrote incisively:

> Racism is not inherent. The national and international attitude of non-Blacks toward African Americans is largely shaped by misconceptions gleaned from the mass media. No matter how law-abiding, churchgoing, and patriotic the masses of Black people are, if others view us in great measure through "Soul Man," "In Living Color," crime reports on the 6 o'clock news, and other media stereotypes, these non-Black people—who generally have only minimal contact with African Americans—will subconsciously disrespect us as individuals and as a collective. Hence, a market owner *assumes* that a Black girl is shoplifting, police *assume* that every Black male driver is violent, Japanese leaders *assume* that African Americans are the bane of this society, and White Americans *assume* that most of us are drug addicts, criminals and welfare recipients. (*LAT* March 29, 1991)

Wayne, a 35-year-old retired mail carrier, gave his opinion about the way media influences Korean perceptions of African Americans:

> They are normal people. They only know about us from what they see on TV when in Korea, and they then perceive us as such [in a negative way] when they come here. They are struggling to survive just like anyone else—humble, but they don't understand Black ethnic ways. They come from a poverty-stricken country and value a penny.

Earl Ofari Hutchison writes in a similar vein:

> African Americans and Koreans should demand that the media stop inflaming the tensions. Much of the press played the story of the Black-Korean conflict nationally as if it is a case of the "poor, besieged Koreans" being put upon by African Americans. There is no effort to discuss the issues that plague both groups: high unemployment, poor educational and social services, and inability to get business loans and credit. . . . There is little mention of the meetings, coalitions, and task forces that many Korean business persons and Black community organizations have organized to resolve their problems. (1991, 3)

In the aftermath of the Du-Harlins incident, interviewees' perceptions of the media deteriorated. In July 1993, a 20-year-old Black man said:

> The media causes ignorant people to take their rage out on innocent people . . . From this incident, other people will respond by stealing from other merchants. Remember the incident when a Japanese woman was mistaken for a Korean woman and assaulted at a stoplight. This is called "getting back." This is ignorance.

These comments can be contrasted with those of Korean merchants regarding the influence of race. Several indicated that race was not a real factor, that it was an incident between a shopkeeper and a customer, and that the media had injected race into a situation where it was not relevant. A 52-year-old grocery market owner privileged cultural differences over racial differences in the Du-Harlins controversy:

> This Du Soon Ja incident has nothing to do with race. This is not so much a racial confrontation but rather a problem between merchants and customers. I see cultural differences producing similar conflicts. I find fault with the American media. They kept spreading a message along racial lines and exaggerated the incident in order to satisfy themselves, which is often their job. It is like doctors who keep warning you that you are ill [when you are not ill].

Similarly, many Korean merchants believed that for many years the mainstream media had inflamed the Black community against Koreans through superficial, insensitive, and unbalanced coverage of incidents involving customers and shopkeepers. Kapson Lee, editor of the *Korea Times Los Angeles, English Edition*, wrote:

> First, the media unduly emphasized the Korean ancestry of Du, thus indirectly, and perhaps inadvertently, contributing toward a negative image of Korean Americans in the eyes of Black people. Second, the media played into the hands of those whose vested interest it was, and is, to exploit such fallacious images. (1994, 255)

Within hours of the King verdict, most media coverage was projecting crude depictions of the Black-Korean conflict, attributing the extended period of violence and destruction in 1992 wholly to this factor (Kurashige 2008, 42); it was as if King had been beaten by Korean merchants. Indeed, the tape that showed Du shooting Harlins was the second most played video during the week of the most intense riots. Blacks were criticized for blaming others for their poverty, while Korean store owners were reprimanded for neither investing in the Black community nor paying respect to Black people. Thus, as one Korean American wondered, "Was there any conspiracy among the white-dominated media to pit one ethnic group against another and sit back and watch them destroy one another?" Furthermore, police and media outlets conspired to conflate the LAPD's racist beating with the Korean merchant's shooting of Harlins. After police released the videotape, many news outlets edited it to show only the shooting of an unarmed Black girl, and not what happened before the gun went off. Journalist John Lee indicted the media:

> Mainstream media such as the *Los Angeles Times* had a part in it. This case was put on this Korean family who barely spoke English and were not in a good position to defend themselves. . . . I do feel like the portrayal of how Latasha Harlins was killed and how the trial went down contributed to people's righteous indignation and fueled a lot of violence directed at Korean merchants. The way media simplifies things, it was pointing an arrow at Korean merchants. Whatever grievance you have with the justice system, this is your enemy. Here's your target. (*LA Weekly* April 26, 2012)

Korean Americans were also critical of LA Mayor Tom Bradley. Bong Hwan Kim, former executive director of Koreatown Youth and Community Center and a member of the BKA, believed that Mayor Bradley had not done enough to alleviate Black-Korean tension:

> I was in a meeting with Mayor Bradley when the boycotts [of John's Market] occurred. We were asking him to come out and take a public stand, something visible. He would never do it. He said it was a justified homicide after the boycott was over. The mayor didn't attempt to stop [the] boycott until after there were some firebombings of Korean stores. . . . By then, it was too late. . . . The Korean as the bad guy was already formed in the minds of too many people. By the time he came out, it wasn't credible anymore.

Jay Lee Wong, another BKA member and former member of LACCHR, also critiqued Mayor Bradley:

> He has done very little for the Korean community. He refused to take a position about the boycott. As mayor of LA, he has to make a public statement saying that Koreans have a place. It's not a Black city. It was a pure incident of suspected robbery. It was justified homicide. To abuse that kind of a situation given the racial tension that exists is opportunistic . . . he should have taken a stand saying it was wrong to boycott the store.

Despite these feelings of lack of support, quite a few African Americans felt that Mayor Bradley supported the Korean American community over them because Koreans had "a lot [more] money than the black community to give" (Stevenson 2013, 241). Other Koreans interpreted themselves as victims in the struggle between Whites and African Americans. As one interviewee put it, they were small shrimp caught in the fighting between large whales. David Kim and Jeff Yang wrote, "Daryl Gates wanted the Blacks to let out their outburst toward the Koreans, because he knew that the Blacks didn't feel good toward the Koreans. I do believe there must have been some conscious politics, because [the police] just weren't there" (*Village Voice* May 12, 1992).

While both sides were keenly aware of the role of the White power structure in influencing the conflict, Koreans and Blacks also noted prejudices between each other. The boycott leaders in New York City believed that Korean merchants were not merely pawns of the "White power structure," but rather "active participants" within it. Thus, they saw Korean merchants as legitimate targets of boycotts (C. Kim 2000, 110).

## SUBALTERN RACISM

### Anti-Black Prejudice among Koreans

Black communications scholar Ella Stewart reported that African Americans felt subjected to the same kind of racism in Korean-owned business as they experienced in those owned by Whites. Black customers felt they were being watched by Korean shopkeepers: "They are reminded of how they have been treated all of their lives and view the Korean merchants/employees as just another racist element in society and a part of a racist system contributing to the perpetuation of discrimination against Blacks in general and low-income Blacks in particular" (Stewart 1989, 93). Anti-Black sentiments held by Korean merchants often color their negative experiences with Black customers (Lee 2002, 185). (I present anti-Black comments from Korean interviewees directly in the next chapter and in chapter 6). A 28-year-old Black female vital statistics clerk (1992) stated[16]:

> They [Korean store owners] have to look within themselves for basic respect. They have to try not to look at them as just Black but as human beings. . . . They need to look at them and treat them as they would treat White people that would walk in their stores every day.

Some African Americans believed these prejudices were a product of the larger society, which, according to a 40-year-old law firm manager, portrayed African Americans "as belonging to gangs, uneducated, and as people who steal." For another Black resident, this perceived prejudice explained the actions of Korean merchants: "Korean Americans always watch you. They are very suspicious. They think Blacks are thieves." Korean Americans, according to a 45-year-old African American female hairstylist, "have a negative attitude towards African Americans because of the way television portrays us." A 20-year-old Black male (1993) made similar comments: "Koreans and Whites are scared of Blacks. They expect any Black person to rob them. If they're going to open a store in a Black community, they shouldn't act like that."

Whether these perceptions of anti-Blackness are accurate or not, when combined with the history of economic exploitation and racial injustice between merchants and customers, they play a powerful role in the magnification of individual conflict (Ong et al. 1994). Although Korean merchants in early 1990s LA may have only been actors in a play scripted by larger forces, they nonetheless made the decision to open businesses in Black neighborhoods. High prices, poor-quality merchandise, and no-return policies were seen as small but persistent examples of discrimination and exploitation. Given the relative lack of power of Korean store owners, many of these practices were understandable. Owners were often forced to cut services and operating costs to stay in business, but customers found it difficult to disregard these practices when repeatedly confronted with them.

The perceptions held by Korean merchants were also shaped by daily exposure to potential crime. Frequent shoplifting was regarded not simply as a petty crime, but also as a sign of disrespect toward Koreans and a drain on meager profits. The racial interpretation was reinforced by continuing coverage in the Korean newspapers, which often played up race (Chang 1990, 199–200). Race-based perceptions, along with anxiety over the lack of personal safety, made some Korean merchants react defensively to their Black customers, thus adding tensions to daily transactions.

In short, Black interviewees identified various types of anti-Black prejudice among Korean merchants. However, a few factors that play a central role in shaping Korean immigrant merchants' understanding of America's color line should be brought to the forefront. First, quite a few Korean immigrant merchants uncritically internalized anti-Black racism as a feature of American culture. Second, they racialized class-specific urban issues such as poverty, crime, violence, and substance abuse. Fearing for their physical safety and property, Koreans treated their inner-city customers as products of these urban problems.

## Anti-Korean Prejudice among African Americans

Some Korean merchants viewed themselves as victims of racism by African Americans. African Americans' anti-Korean sentiments include two related components: Orientalism and nativism. Helen Jun demonstrated via a wide range of cultural texts how the logic of citizenship has compelled racialized subjects such as African Americans to reproduce xenophobic narratives of inclusion in the effort to achieve political, economic, and social incorporation since the mid-nineteenth century. She states, "the formulaic narration of Black military service, Christian morality, and nationalist identification to represent Black people as unambiguously *American* subjects became a repetitive and frequent refrain with respect to discourses of Chinese exclusion" (2011, 28, emphasis original). She extends her analytics to Black-Korean tension a century later:

> What seemed to be a driving force in the mobilization of Black inner-city communities against merchant exploitation was the perceived audacity of new Asian immigrants who were practicing American racism and were getting away with devaluing Black life, just as White Americans had done for centuries. The opposition of Black residents to Korean merchant racism expressed an Orientalized indignation that was informed by racialized conceptions that these alien outsiders barely belonged here at all, much less had the right to start thinking and acting like American racists. (2011, 3)[17]

Another key element was nativist racism. The presence of anti-Asian and anti-immigrant sentiments in the larger society provided ready-made frameworks into which African Americans could place their negative personal experiences with Korean merchants (Lee 2002, 185). Black interviewees clearly labeled Korean immigrants as "foreign" or "oriental" for many other reasons besides language and cultural barriers, and they did not see them as belonging in the US. For instance, they observed that many Koreans use chopsticks and eat rice, take off their shoes upon entering a room, and enjoy different music. "They are Oriental. Little, short people. Poverty-stricken peasants," one informant said. Among the older generation of African Americans, images of Koreans or other Asians constructed through the lens of the Korean or Vietnam War were still vivid, because some of them were veterans.

Some Black interviewees commented extensively on Korean merchants' language barriers, dismissing merchants as foreign and un-American. "Different accent," "Can't understand a word they say," and "Hard to understand" were how some of them described casual exchanges with Koreans. A 22-year-old Black male who worked as a security guard was asked how Koreans are different: "They're just not like us. They just seem hella foreign, like they can't even speak English." Similarly, a 19-year-old Black female college student answered, "I used to get offended because they talked so loud, and I didn't understand why. But my mother explained to me that that is just the way they are." In this case, the language barrier corresponded to a cultural barrier, and furthermore, a racial barrier.

Taeku Lee, a political scientist, examined public attitudes on race relations and Asian Pacific Americans (APA) using media polls and academic surveys. His results showed that all respondent groups held stereotypes of APAs as inscrutable perpetual foreigners and harbored feelings of hostility toward them. African Americans exhibited the greatest tendency to stereotype APAs, followed by Latinos and Whites (2000, 128). However, Lee made it clear that anti-Asian stereotypes and anti-Black stereotypes were not equally damaging: being viewed as inscrutable or exotic is not the same as being seen as mentally inferior, morally dissolute, or criminally disposed (ibid., 132).

Although some African Americans viewed Korean merchants as surrogate Whites, others believed they had their own racial status. Long-time resident and community activist Nia (1992) criticized how they were inserted into and perhaps took advantage of a racist exploitative system. "Hell yeah, Blacks were pissed off! We saw this new nigga come into our community, do well, and then displace us. They didn't ask or even care, for that matter, how we felt." Whereas anti-Black prejudice among Koreans contained elements of biological racism, anti-Korean (and more broadly, anti-Asian) prejudice among African Americans reflected elements of Orientalism and nativism, which have a long history. Booker T. Washington thought poorly of Chinese people because they "lacked moral standards and could never be assimilated to occidental civilization" (Fuchs 1990, 296, as cited in Yoon 1997, 203). Washington's sentiments were indistinguishable from White prejudice toward Chinese and Japanese people, who faced various immigration bans before World War II. As will be discussed in detail in later chapters, older Black populations in particular often expressed this type of nativism toward immigrants, which formed another important dimension of this racial conflict (Cheng and Espiritu 1989; Yoon 1997, 203–4). Finally, due to the post-1965 influx of Korean immigrants, some African Americans believed Koreans were unfairly profiting off the achievements of the Civil Rights Movement (Jo 1992). It was these sentiments that Danny Bakewell played on, along with a Black Nationalist form of nativism, to mobilize boycotts of Korean immigrant-owned stores.

## THE PRODUCTION OF RACE AND RACISM

In *Racial Formation in the United States: From the 1960s to the 1990s*, sociologists Michael Omi and Howard Winant place racialization and racial awareness at the heart of social relations, both at the macro-structural level and in everyday life. They define race as an "unstable and de-centered complex of social meanings constantly being transformed by political struggle"

(1994, 57). In other words, race and politics are connected, and racial categories are created and transformed for the purposes of organizing and ruling society (1994, 57). These political categorizations of race are useful in relation to my analysis of interethnic tensions, particularly the reification of racism in the media, criminal justice system, and educational system. While the notions of racial formation and racial projects are valuable to this study, my analysis contributes something new by focusing on the role of non-state racial formations, particularly those enacted through culture and economics.

Mediated by shifting constructions of race and culture, African Americans and Koreans, as well as White institutions, interpreted the Black-Korean conflict in different ways. African Americans generally attributed problems to racist exploitation and discrimination, while Koreans focused on business practices and communication. The White establishment reflected a White-Asian-Black racial hierarchy and the biases of capitalism (property owners over customers). Meanwhile, media discourse largely portrayed the Black-Korean conflict as a racial confrontation, describing it in terms of cultural differences, but seldom mentioning the systematic failures to address urban problems such as racism, poverty, unemployment, and underperforming schools. Whether the media blamed the problem on race or culture, their coverage was generally ahistorical, focusing on the symptoms and not the causes. There was no consideration by the media of the legacy of discrimination in Los Angeles that lay behind the interracial conflict. Media discourse further racialized the tensions by focusing on Black hostilities toward Koreans, fueling the brewing discontent of Korean merchants, and contributed to Korean prejudice against African Americans through the reproduction of stereotypes about Black people.

Local media also showed a bias—more sensitivity and empathy—toward African Americans, perhaps reflecting the binary racial alliances in Los Angeles. In addition, by repeatedly showing the edited videotape of Du shooting Harlins in the aftermath of the King beating, the media displaced the rage that should have been directed at the LAPD's brutality onto Korean merchants. Drawing on an experimental study conducted about college students, sociologist Darnell Hunt (1997) critically examines how local television news coverage about the unrest was received and interpreted among Whites, African Americans, and Latinos in LA. He argues that television disseminates hegemonic assumptions that support dominant social groups, although his research findings include the combination of White/Latino espousal of hegemonic positions and Black ambivalence toward those same positions.

The media's collusion with state apparatuses, especially the criminal justice system, contributed to the escalation of the tension. In the Du-Harlins case, the judiciary system applied a racialized formula. As a consequence,

Black-Korean tension was intensified more drastically by state intervention than by the actions of African Americans or Koreans. Drawing on insights from Jürgen Habermas (1989), who critically examined the development of the bourgeois public sphere from its origins in the eighteenth century through its transformation and influence by capital-driven mass media, we can see how the political and public spheres played an integral role in the Black-Korean conflict. However, the bourgeois public sphere, like political spheres, operates on exclusionary grounds: there may be barriers for ethnic minorities and subordinate classes to gain entry into the bourgeois public sphere. Both African Americans and Koreans have differential access to public and political spheres than Whites do, which has resulted in significant losses for Korean immigrant merchants from the unrest and boycotts and continued institutional racism for African Americans. State agents, such as Judge Karlin, were important players in the development of racial tension and reinforced the American capitalist racial order. However, it is inadequate to pinpoint only the racialized nature of such spheres. I suggest instead that we understand how they are also classed (and gendered) entities, which is a subject I discuss in more depth in chapters 4 and 5.

As discussed in this chapter, the structural location of Korean immigrants in early 1990s LA was embedded in the contemporary racial landscape as neither White nor Black; rather, Asian Americans acted as a buffer between the two. To "focus on the Black-White racial paradigm is to misunderstand the complicated racial situation in the U.S. . . . It ignores the complexity of a racial hierarchy that has more than just a top and a bottom" (Chang 1994, 27). In this vein, I present a multipolar racial paradigm in the concluding chapter of this book.

The White-Black racial paradigm also ignores intergroup racism. In the unfolding of the Black-Korean conflict, subaltern forms of racism between Koreans and African Americans were evidenced.[18] Subaltern racism must be differentiated from institutional racism, as racial minorities generally lack the power to enforce their prejudiced notions. Nonetheless, both Blacks and Koreans acted on racist notions, albeit from relatively disempowered positions, engaging in looting, burning down stores, shoplifting, and shooting either shop owners or shoplifters. Korean merchants expressed notions of biological racism and reinforced stereotypes about violence-prone, urban Blacks. African Americans, on the other hand, expressed Orientalist and nativist sentiments that contested the citizenship and presence of Korean immigrants in the US.

The Black-Korean conflicts contributed to the creation of a new racial discourse: race as culture and culture as race. Moreover, this interracial conflict also evoked larger issues involving the reproduction of capitalist relations in

America and the redefinition of race and culture in a multiethnic society. In subsequent chapters, I will address other dynamics centering on culture and class.

## NOTES

1. Take Two "The contested murder of Latasha Harlins" 89.3 KPCC, August 26, 2013. http://www.scpr.org/programs/take-two/2013/08/26/33413/the-contested-murder-of-latasha-harlins/

2. Nancy Abelmann and John Lie (1995) indict the media for constructing and reifying Black-Korean tensions. However, as Nopper points out, there is actual conflict between Blacks and Koreans and a material basis for this antagonism (2006, 105).

3. Meeting minutes, November 1989, Community Conciliation Center, New York City.

4. The underclass thesis, as formulated by William Wilson (1987), tends to portray life in the inner city as an a priori characterization of otherness. The underclass thesis ignores adaptive nature and other noncultural causes of poverty. The alleged underclass behaviors that do exist are symptoms of the inequities of the changing political economy more than of a depraved culture of poverty.

5. California's Dispute Resolution Act of 1986 enabled counties to set aside civil court filing fees to establish and maintain community-based dispute resolution centers (Ong et al. 1994, 284).

6. For Korean immigrants, funerals are particularly important. Deaths in South LA are often caused by drive-by shootings, and Korean merchants expressed their condolences through monetary offerings.

7. They often celebrated together when customers were released from prison.

8. The Chicago boycotts were relatively small-scale and short-lived. See In-Jin Yoon's *On My Own: Korean Businesses and Race Relations in America* (1997, 176–79).

9. Interview with Jan Sunoo, March 21, 1991.

10. Three months after Harlins' death, there was another violent incident. On June 4, 1991, Tae Sam Park, the Korean owner of John's Liquor Store on Western Avenue and Seventy-Ninth Street, killed Lee Arthur Mitchell, a Black man, during a suspected robbery. A boycott was initiated within a week by Rev. Edgar Boyd of Bethel A.M.E. church. He was joined by Danny Bakewell. What prompted the protest was the belief that the killing was unwarranted because Mitchell was unarmed. Feelings intensified after the judicial system found the owner innocent of murder. The boycott lasted for three and a half months.

11. Police records report only three robberies and three break-ins.

12. Danny Bakewell, Sr., was the founder and chairman of the Bakewell company, one of the largest African American commercial and real estate development groups in the western United States. He was also chairman of Bakewell Media, which owns the oldest west coast African American newspapers, the *Los Angeles Sentinel*, the

*LA Watts Times*, as well as WBOK radio station in New Orleans. Bakewell was a three-time NAACP Image Award winner and a Southern Christian Leadership Martin Luther King, Jr. Award recipient. He has been inducted into the International Civil Rights Walk of Fame and has received numerous other awards, including JFK Profiles in Courage Award from the Democratic Party, the US Congressional Black Caucus Adam Clayton Powell Award, and the Roy Wilkins Award (*Los Angeles Sentinel*, May 18, 2017, A1, A8.

13. Similarly, in 2016, Bakewell sent an open letter to Toyota criticizing the auto giant for placing ads in white-owned media outlets thanking customers for standing by it during a safety recall, but bypassing Black-owned newspapers and advertising agencies. Toyota got the message and began advertising with Black media outlets (*New York Beacon* June 2012, 4).

14. By the 1990s, "gangsta" rappers from South Central LA echoed these themes of self-determination and black nationalism, thus linking the past and the present and joining Black Power advocates like Bakewell. As ethnomusicologist Rebecca Bodenheimer notes, NY-based hip-hop artists like Public Enemy and KRS-One had previously espoused Black nationalist views in the later 1980s (personal communication, December 19, 2017).

15. Charles Lloyd, the Black defense attorney who successfully defended Du, received many threats from African Americans. After the Los Angeles riot, Du paid $300,000 to the parents of the victim as an out-of-court settlement in a civil suit filed against her. The Allstate Insurance Company, which insured her grocery store, reportedly covered the entire amount.

16. Hereafter, I indicate the year of the interview.

17. Black Orientalism, as Jun notes, "is a heterogeneous and historically variable discourse in which the contradictions of Black citizenship engage with the logic of American Orientalism" (2011, 18). She also reports the persistence of nineteenth-century Black press representations of China, Chinese immigrants, and Chinatown ghettos as embodiments of premodern alien difference (ibid., 6).

18. The term "subaltern" is derived from the work of Antonio Gramsci, referring to social groups who are subjected to the hegemony of the ruling classes. Here I am referring to prejudices and racism among oppressed racial minorities.

## Chapter Three

# Culture, Race, and Clash

During the Black-Korean conflicts of the 1990s, the media often discussed the hostilities in cultural terms, invoking differences between African Americans and Korean Americans in terms of language, behavior, customs, ideologies, and values (*LAT* March 24, 1991). Conflicting groups often have very distinct "conceptions of the world" (Gramsci 1971, 335). In the context of this particular conflict, culture was not subordinate to or a mere reflection of race or class, but rather greatly contributed to politicizing Black–Korean tensions. Using the Gramscian concept of "hegemony,"[1] I will illustrate the ways that stereotypes about the cultures of Koreans and African Americans were incorporated into hegemonic understandings of them.

Few scholars have addressed the question of culture with respect to Black-Korean conflicts, mostly because of the repercussions of advancing under-developed culturalist arguments. Attributing conflicts to cultural differences can be used as a convenient way to avoid charges of racism and redirect attention away from more "important" issues (K. Park 1994). However, in my analysis, "culturalism" refers to the "process of stipulating acceptable cultural differences among ethnic groups, establishing equivalence across groups, and taking moral readings from them" (Chock 1995, 308). In other words, we still need to understand the role and meaning of culture in the conflict. Korean merchants attributed the incidents to social and cultural differences, such as difficulties in communication with customers, poverty in the Black community, situational and psychological factors, or media portrayals. For instance, when many African Americans complained that Korean merchants were rude, Sung Soo Kim, a New York Korean immigrant community leader, responded[2]:

Confucian teachings dictate that a woman may not touch a man's hand—that it is deemed unseemly. Many cashiers often plunk down change on the counter,

89

avoiding the customer's proffered hand. Some customers interpret this as a personal insult when none was intended. In addition, the meager grasp of English by many Koreans often comes across as "rudeness" and "arrogance." (*Daily News* July 2, 1988)

In sum, he attributed conflicts to Korean cultural differences.

In contrast, some Black residents, despite their awareness of cultural differences, did not agree with this explanation for Black-Korean tensions. Father Lucas, who led a 1988 boycott against a Korean merchant in Harlem, argued: "None of the boycotts started over 'cultural differences' or 'language barriers.' Vicious assaults, especially against African women and babies, were the last straw after long patterns of disrespect and verbal abuse of African people" (*Amsterdam News* October 6, 1990). He was convinced that disrespectful treatment of Black customers, not cultural or linguistic barriers, was the true catalyst for Black boycotts of Korean stores.

In this chapter, after briefly examining how Korean merchants' language and cultural barriers and business practices contributed to miscommunication and disputes between them and their customers, I will analyze Black and Korean cultural representations of each other via racial and cultural discourses. Doing so will provide analysis that moves beyond the hegemonic understandings of the causes of the events in early 1990s LA.


## RACIAL AND CULTURAL DISCOURSES

Much of discourse about culture may entail aspects of racial discourse. Race theorist David Goldberg writes, "race is coded as culture, what has been called 'the new racism,' making no reference to claims of biology or superiority" (1993, 73). If we understand culture as "the interpretive, performative process by which humans make sense of the world largely in relation to group identities" (Hartigan 2010, 208), culture shapes social interactions. The term "culture" denotes discrete customs, religious practices, aesthetic preferences, artistic and folkloric traditions, and languages other than US English (Chock 1995, 312).[3] Anthropologists generally believe that all human conduct is culturally mediated and all cultures are equally valuable (Rosaldo 1988).[4] However, many interviewees seemed to speak about and understand culture in quantifiable terms, from a lot to a little, from thick to thin, and from elaborate to simple (1988, 78). Their views of culture were also defined in terms of an opposition to (White) American culture. In other words, many interviewees defined "culture" as traits or practices considered non-American or inferior to American culture.

Surprisingly, there have been few investigations of the folk notion of culture in American public discourses. As Rosaldo states, from a pseudo-evolutionary framework, people begin without culture and grow increasingly cultured until they reach the post-cultural point where they become transparent to "us" (1988, 80). In the dominant US racial discourse of the early 1990s, Koreans were seen as cultured (meaning traditional) and having the potential for class mobility, while poor or working-class African Americans appeared to "lack culture" (Rosaldo 1988, 82).[5] Koreans also argued that if they had been born in America, they would not have possessed culture. Some were worried that their children would be conscripted into the White/Black (American) paradigm and become susceptible to laziness, selfishness, arrogance, Eurocentrism, and loss of culture. Korean interviewees explained their economic successes in terms of having "more culture" (family unity, ethnic solidarity, education) than African Americans. Thus, Korean perceptions reflected their notions of a cultural hierarchy where they "had" culture and African Americans did not. Interestingly, African American informants also presented Koreans as having more culture than they did (exotic, strange, or un-American). Korean immigrants and African Americans thus both deployed a politics of cultural difference.

The Black-Korean conflict of the early 1990s contributed to the creation of a new racial discourse, where race talk was produced as culture talk. In other words, since neither group wanted to be criticized for racism, some attributed their conflicts to cultural differences. As a result, unfulfilled social obligations were explained simply as features of culture, while racism was glossed over. This conflict involved relations between African Americans and Korean immigrant merchants, but implicated larger issues, namely the reproduction of capitalist relations in late twentieth century America and the redefinition of race and culture in an increasingly multiethnic society. In fact, interviewees' cultural conceptions echoed Gramsci's proposition that "cultural processes unfold within a sharply divided society, a hierarchy of class domination backed by political power. Culture becomes part of the process of domination" (Alexander and Seidman 1990, 6). The Black-Korean conflict created a new racial discourse that benefited White-dominated power structures, and it was one that highlighted hostilities between racialized groups instead of the history of Black-White relations, the political-economic relations between the US and Korea, and the power of the US nation-state and capitalism.

This chapter will critically examine the "cultural" characteristics and practices that marked the Korean American and Black communities in 1992. Given the essentialist nature of the discussion of these isolated cultural traits, it is important to understand the underlying implications of such a discourse.

The cultural traits discussed refer to the different ways Koreans used their bodies and beliefs during the conflict. John Szwed observes that to most people, motor habits—the way one moves, blinks, stands, etc.—are seen to be rooted in some mysterious racial or at least "instinctive" fact (1975, 23). Observation of different bodily gestures in everyday interactions is an important mode of analysis, although I must note that I find it troubling to focus on whether Koreans smiled and placed change directly in the hands of their customers. These gestures tend to essentialize Koreans and their culture. In addition, it is important to consider the historical specificity of culture. Culture undergoes transformation, and "too often today we implicitly think of culture as what is completed, as works, not the working" (Hymes 1969; 33). Therefore, in my analysis, "Korean American culture" specifically refers to cultural traits expressed in the Korean American community, not the contemporary culture of Korea or the Korean culture of a century past.

## BUSINESS PRACTICES

It is difficult to assess the overall relationships between Korean merchants and African American customers in south LA during the 1990s. Nonetheless, based on me and my assistants' observations, most Korean merchants attempted to address problematic aspects of their relationships with customers. I observed mostly positive interactions, with negative or problematic interactions in the minority.[6] Furthermore, although Korean immigrant merchants' business practices may be labeled "parochial" and considered by some to have been a source of the Black-Korean tensions, some female Korean merchants adopted African American women's dress, hairstyle, and makeup. Thus, it is difficult to present a generalized portrait of this relationship.

On January 25, 1992, my research assistant Jeff Saito left a beauty salon on Crenshaw Blvd and walked next door to what appeared to be a Korean-owned donut shop. As he approached the counter, he noticed an Asian woman and man behind the counter and wrote in his field notes:

> The woman asked if she could help me. She smiled and asked if I was a student. . . . (I was carrying my school backpack.) I noticed that they also sold hot food. I ordered lunch and a donut. The woman was friendly and thanked me for my business. The man stood expressionless behind the counter. . . . An African American man dressed in street clothes entered and ordered some hot food. The store owner spoke in a plain, monotone voice and his face was expressionless. The woman smiled as she helped him, and her husband behind the counter still stood expressionless. After he received his food, he departed the donut shop. A few minutes later, an older African American man entered the store. He

had gray hair and was dressed raggedly. He spoke loudly as he ordered some donuts. A debate occurred. In a loud voice, the male customer accused the woman of overcharging him. The woman explained that she had not. Upon her husband's insistence, the woman gave the customer the change that he believed he should have received. During the entire episode, the woman's facial expression remained constant, and the man behind the counter continued to stand undisturbed. The African American man looked irritated and left abruptly. . . .

(Although the woman received me with more warmth than when she had received the other customers, overall, she was professional. I speculate that my status as a student impacted her in some manner. . . . The Asian woman was more receiving of the first African American man. Since the first African American man appeared better clothed than the older African American man, this characteristic may have accounted for the difference in the woman's approach to the two individuals. In addition, the older African American man spoke in a much louder voice; this might have also affected the woman's behavior. But despite the older African American man's complaint, the woman maintained her composure and professional appearance.)

In the shopping center, I noticed a dry cleaning store. Judging from the writing, I assumed that it was Korean-owned. . . . Behind the counter, there were two Asians, male and female. Their faces resembled expressions by individuals who smelled something rotten and were angry. The woman was helping an African American woman at the counter. The Asian man approached me and handed me a paper pad. He motioned for me to write. I asked the man if he could clean a leather jacket. With his facial expression the same, he responded: "No." I thanked him, returned the pad, and left. (Jeff Saito, fieldnote January 25, 1992)

As Jeff notes, the interactions at the first donut shop did not seem to be uncommon. Dress is perceived as an indicator of socioeconomic status and was regularly used to differentiate customers.

On February 29, 1992, Jeff entered a swap meet in South LA:

As I entered the swap meet, I approached a stand selling compact discs, tapes, and other music items. . . . An Asian woman and man, casually dressed, were behind the counter. The woman was assisting a heavy-set African American woman . . . [who] danced to the beat of the music that came from the stereo system of the stand. The African American woman seemed lively and friendly and smiled frequently. As the Asian woman assisted the African American woman, her face was expressionless. The Asian woman didn't smile or frown, but continued to help the African American woman . . . .

As I continued along the center aisle, I came to a clothiers stand, attended by an Asian woman. The woman was casually dressed and appeared to be middle-aged. As she assisted two young African American women, she smiled and laughed. She also seemed to be eager to help her customers. Two African American women seemed to appreciate the Asian woman's efforts. The two young women smiled and laughed with the Asian woman.

At this point, I turned east and headed towards the eastern aisle and continued south. I came across an Asian man selling hardware items and a young Asian woman, who was also working at the stand. She wore a T-shirt and shorts and seemed to be of high school age. I determined that she could be the man's daughter. While I looked over the merchandise, they both smiled. I returned the greeting. A few moments later, an African American man approached the stand. He was dressed in jeans and a Black T-shirt. The African American man approached the Asian man and explained that he purchased the wrong sized bolt from the hardware stand. The Asian man took the bolt, smiled, and then exchanged it. The young woman also smiled. The African American man smiled, thanked the Asian merchants, and then left . . . Later I confirmed that most of the Asian merchants in the swap meet were Korean. Throughout the entire time I was in the swap meet, two African American security guards patrolled the swap meet.[7] They were both male, and both were armed. Most of the patrols in the swap meet were African Americans.

From Jeff's description of Korean-run business establishments in South Central, we noted a few things: (1) interactions between merchants and customers can vary from positive to negative; (2) inexperienced or newer merchants seemed to have more problems with their customers; (3) class markers seem to influence the way Korean merchants treat their customers; (4) the race of customers seems to play some role in affecting the merchants' attitude.

Given these descriptions, how did African Americans explain their shopping experience at Korean-owned business establishments? A 42-year-old African American female janitor who had a Korean landlady argued that Korean merchants should give their customers receipts. She believed that Korean merchants did not give receipts to avoid taxes and told us that it is difficult to exchange items without receipts. She also complained that the different Korean merchants use the same black bags to pack purchased items, which made it difficult for customers to identify the right store when exchanging items.

Similarly, Penelope, a Black hairstylist, had bad relations with Korean merchants. She had been to a Korean-owned (perhaps Vietnamese-owned) nail salon located in West LA on Pico and Overland. On one of her visits, the female manicurist that usually helped her was busy, so she referred Penelope to a male manicurist who worked in the salon.[8] When Penelope asked him if he could paint her nails according to her specifications, the man shouted at Penelope. According to Penelope, he said: "You don't like the way I paint? I paint the way I paint." Penelope called him a "thing-a-ma-jig" and proceeded to exit the nail salon. Her regular manicurist chased after her, apologized for the man's behavior, and asked Penelope to return, which she agreed to do later. Despite this experience, Penelope indicated that she had developed good relations with the Korean cleaners located close to her salon: they did not normally accept checks, but since she was a regular customer, they accepted checks from her. She also patronized the Korean-owned video store next door to her salon.

There are certain cultural traditions that inform Korean Americans' approach to business. Their reliance on family labor means that individuals work long hours, which can lead to fatigue and irrational responses. One of the Korean merchants who had known the Du family before the Harlins shooting discussed this issue:

> That shooting occurred as they were overworked and under lots of stress. They might be too tired to control themselves, even over very trivial things. Like other Korean immigrant families, Mr. Du relied upon family labor, especially his wife, Du Soon Ja. I find it problematic to rely on family labor heavily. You might save some money on wages, but you do not realize that family members force themselves to work beyond their capability. I know this from my own experience of running a drugstore in Korea. That's why I do not allow my wife to work here. Mr. Du used to be dressed in a beautiful suit and always went to the bank and took part in other activities in the Korean community. Therefore, it was always Mrs. Du who ran the store. They own another store. In this context, I really want fellow Koreans to reflect on the way they operate their stores. Even a small store should hire at least part-time local help, if possible African Americans, instead of just exploiting family labor.

Since most of the Korean-run small businesses were labor-intensive, profit depended on whether they mobilized labor intensively and efficiently. Thus, Korean immigrants pushed family members, workers, and themselves to the limit, as other immigrant employers do.

The award-winning writer Chang-rae Lee articulated how Korean merchants might be victimized by their own strategy:

> [Y]ou worked from sunrise to the dead of night. You were never unkind in your dealings, but neither were you generous. Your family was your life, though you rarely saw them. You kept handsome sums of cash close by in small denominations. You were steadily cornering the market in self-pride. You drove a Chevy and then a Caddy and then a Benz. You never missed a mortgage payment or a day of church. You prayed furiously until you wept. You considered the only unseen forces to be those of capitalism and the love of Jesus Christ. My father knew nothing of the mystical and the neurotic; they were not part of his make-up. (1994, 123)

The long and intensive work results in many health complications and most Korean small business owners do not take regular vacations. Common complaints from interviewees were leg, back, shoulder, or stomach pain (Yi 1993,

120). Lacking health insurance and the spare time, these small business own-ers found themselves sick once it was too late to be cured. Church ministers mentioned attending many funerals of men in their 40s.

## CULTURAL HABITS OF KOREAN MERCHANTS

### Eye Contact

Korean merchants were largely criticized by Black interviewees for their lack of eye contact with customers, which gave them the impression of being dis-honest or unfriendly. Stevenson states, "African Americans would view this kind of treatment as cold at best, disrespectful and offensive at worst" (2013, 70); they might also perceive it as racist, as they are used to being shunned at store counters by White clerks. However, for many Korean immigrants this was a standard cultural custom, especially when interacting with elders and strangers. Koreans are generally socialized to cast down one's eyes or risk be-ing seen as challenging the authority of others. However, eye contact in itself should not be considered an independent cultural element, but instead should be considered in conjunction with different concepts of friendship and other social relationships. The ways Koreans form friendships are distinct from those of the US, and it is not culturally appropriate to smile at strangers unless they are sure the relationship will become a lifelong friendship.

### Smiling

Smiling should also be considered in relation to the gender and class back-ground of Koreans. For instance, if a woman is from the countryside, she will not smile in her encounters with strangers, lest she be perceived as promis-cuous or improper in a traditionally gender-segregated society. In contrast, as Stevenson notes, "In African American culture, speaking—saying hello, how are you? Or even a slight nod of the head and eye contact are important indicators of respect" (2013, 230). Given the fact that in 1992, most Korean immigrants came from cities and had middle-class backgrounds in Korea, this cultural argument might be somewhat less relevant. In addition, I have observed that Koreans with businesses in middle- or upper-income neighbor-hoods in the US tend to smile more. I can only assume that their behavior is different in low-income areas such as South LA because of the higher crime rate and riskier business environment. Clearly if they're smiling in more wealthy neighborhoods, it's not only a matter of cultural difference, but also their own perceptions about South LA, race, and crime.

In Korean culture, the act of smiling or not can have diverse meanings depending on the context. For example, like other individuals, Koreans might smile when they are embarrassed or feeling abashed. Ideally, merchants want to project professionalism in business transactions and maintain a serious appearance. They are not educated to smile during business transactions; otherwise, customers may think they are being cheated. In addition, merchants work long hours. Most of the Korean merchants I interviewed worked far more than full-time, often seven days a week, 16 hours a day. A Korean merchant's smile, like eye contact, should be contextualized in relation to their understanding of social relationships. Nevertheless, I found that women who played a significant role in running stores in South LA were generally better at interacting with customers: they smiled more and were friendlier to customers than Korean men.[9] Both Korean women and Black male customers agreed on this point.

## Handling Change

At Korean business establishments, change is often given to customers on a small plastic tray. I asked Korean interviewees how they hand change to their customers. Some told me they put the change on the counter. They explained to me: "Otherwise, our customers might drop the change on the floor or cannot receive their change properly if they are absent-minded." That is, Korean merchants assumed that this method was most convenient for both parties and intended no disrespect to their customers.

Both Koreans and African Americans also wondered whether the other party hesitated to touch them during a business transaction. When I asked Black residents how they perceived this way of handling change, they wondered: "Why the lack of contact?" They believed that Korean merchants were reluctant to hand them change in order to avoid physical contact with their Black hands. One female Korean merchant gave me a completely different interpretation, stating that customers did not want her to hand change to them, demanding instead that she put it on the counter. In this case, she wondered whether this was due to customers' aversion to her "yellow hands." Thus, the financial transactions between Korean merchants and their customers also involved a materialization of racial difference.

In brief, customers with their own behaviors and perceptions often interpreted Korean merchants' behavior as continuing a long tradition of racial discrimination and class prejudice. Nonetheless, several years later, when I returned to observe South LA businesses, I noticed that most Korean merchants were attempting to put change directly into the hands of their customers.

## BLACK-KOREAN REPRESENTATION

Lacanian psychoanalysis helps explain how the desire for domination, dependence, fear, and rivalry is at the root of the constitution of "self." How people construct their (political) identity or interpret themselves is partly unconscious, and the rationalizations this involves are key to the analysis of conflict. One way to understand Black and Korean perceptions of each other is through Jacques Lacan's concept of the "mirror stage" and his explanation of the development of the ego. This stage occurs in babies between the ages of 6 and 18 months, during which time the child is first able to imagine him or herself as a coherent and self-governing entity. It also involves constructing a particular image and identity of the Other, which is supposed to reveal displaced or condensed elements of the Self. The subject is made and remade in this encounter with the Other. It is from the Other that the subject receives the message that they emit. However, this image is mirrored and reversed, and therefore inaccurate.

Although Lacan's Other may stand for the unconscious, by analogy, it can be applied to other or foreign cultures. Thus, in understanding the racial dynamics in South LA, Korean Americans and African Americans represent the Self and the Other, and vice versa. In other words, this image may not be their own—it is the play of light on mirror, the gaze of a completely separate subject that may seem to represent the self, but it is equally the property of others. This concept of mirroring provides insights into each community.

By and large, the respective discourses of Koreans and African Americans operate in a larger framework of power, hegemony, and unequal power relationships. Here, power, in Foucauldian terms, refers to the subject's ability to control both the ordering of knowledge and the signification (production of meaning) of relations of production. Thus, Korean merchants' power to manipulate relations of production, such as commercial property in South LA, defines signification in this discourse. Moreover, as in Lacan's "mirror stage" theory, Koreans and African Americans are influenced by concepts of each other which have been constructed by White supremacy in order to pit them against each other (Sexton 2010, 96). This is what Brackette Williams calls "the ghost of Anglo-European hegemony" (1991, 127). Postcolonial studies have reminded us how the impact of Anglo-European hegemony has been felt and persisted in interethnic relations long after the end of formal colonialism. For instance, the Anglo-European elite in Guyana used race and ethnicity as a potent way to define the enslaved Africans and, later, Indian and Portuguese immigrants to defend the status quo. With the withdrawal of the elite from Guyana in 1966, the two primary non-White groups, African and Indian descendants, have often struggled bitterly over power relations in the nation-building process (Williams 1991).

What, then, were the racial images and identities held by African Americans and Koreans, the mirror images they reflected back to each other in South LA in the early 1990s? Stereotypes often focus on the very domains of human behavior and values that are basic to a society's maintenance and order. Thus, they relate to "work practices, health and eating habits, means and style of communication, sexual and kinship conceptions, notions of etiquette and law, notions of the supernatural and the eternal" (Szwed 1975, 22). The stereotypes reveal attitudes about racial ordering and cultural values in US society and provide a new dimension for understanding interethnic conflicts.

Interviewees were asked a variety of questions, including: their perspectives on the changes occurring in their neighborhoods; the history of contact and interaction with other racial groups; their thoughts on their own culture; and their thoughts on other cultures. In this way, I attempted to avoid the clichéd representations of the Black-Korean conflict put forth by the media and other dominant discourses, and also to place other groups in the broader context of community change.

## African Americans and Koreans as the Friendly "Other"

A good number of Korean merchants and Black customers had either positive or neutral impressions of the other group. African Americans commented on Koreans' communication style, food, music, dress, demeanor, lifestyle, cohesiveness, work ethic, study habits, and other "model minority" characteristics. It is important to note that both Black youth and community organizers have distinct perceptions than the rest of the Black community in South LA; these two groups tended to have Korean American school friends or community organizer colleagues, which positively affected their perception of Korean immigrant merchants. Black business owners also tended to be more understanding of Korean immigrant merchants.

Trina (1993), a middle-aged Black female department store manager, was sympathetic to the situation of Korean immigrant merchants in her neighborhood: "They usually treated me with respect. I've seen a few interactions with others—young Black guys, boys—that were not very friendly. However, personally I don't blame them. They were hoodlums anyway, and they were stealing."

A 28-year-old Black statistics clerk (1992) commented on the benefits of a racially diverse community. Exposure to different cuisines and cultural practices made her interested in Korean culture, and food served as a tangible cultural connection. Regarding differences in communication style, she continued:

> What I've noticed about the Asian community on a whole, or wide scale, is that they interject a lot. They speak harshly. They speak curt, and they use many hand gestures. This is especially true of those that have recently arrived in the US. This is part of their culture, and if one is not familiar with their culture, this behavior comes off as rude.

Language barriers between Korean merchants and their customers often hindered the merchants' abilities to communicate or resolve misinterpretations. Therefore, many store owners were highly dependent on non-verbal communication such as hand gestures, repetition, interjection, or writing. To make matters worse, their reliance on Korean speech manners sometimes escalated a minor problem into a major dispute with their customers. Nonetheless, a middle-aged Black female teacher (1992) living in Compton said that because her stepfather was Chinese, she was not irritated with Koreans' accented English:

> There are differences in communication style, definitely their language. I'm accustomed to heavy Asian accents because my stepfather is from "Red China" almost 30 years ago and has a heavy accent. I don't have a communication problem with Korean merchants. I know many Filipinos and Japanese with accents.

A 30-year-old Black male machinist (1992) and self-identified "born-again Christian" said that his own experiences with Korean merchants were usually pleasant. However, he later gave an example of how Koreans stereotyped African Americans: once he went into a Korean-owned store to buy sunglasses, and the merchant immediately gave him a pair that the interviewee considered "gangster" glasses. Despite this stereotyping, he calmly stated:

> The Koreans are the same as the Blacks, Hispanics, etc. . . . they are all people. I don't look at them by race and [don't] pass judgment on them . . . however, they have a learned culture of being brought up intelligently. They learn to take advantage of the opportunities in America and use them to the fullest. This I admire in them . . . the Koreans look different—skin color and hair, as does any other race. The Koreans are harder on themselves than most, though. For example, they study hard when others slack off.

Overall, my interviewees' images of Korean immigrants reinforced the "model minority" myth: Koreans were intelligent, hardworking, and took full advantage of the system while maintaining a strong faith in it.

Young African Americans often had fond memories of their Korean American school friends, considering them full American citizens. Iyanna, a young junior college student (1993), said, "[My Korean American friends] were pretty cool. I went to school with them but I didn't take the time to get close to them. I knew some that were into dating Black guys. I get along with them. If they respect me, I respect them back." Another Black university student (1993) stated that he had a "pretty good relationship with [the Koreans]." He characterized the business people in his community in a friendly way and attributed some Korean merchants' suspicion of Black customers to gangbanging:

> On the whole, the Koreans are pretty cool. A few blocks down from my house, there's a swap meet with a lot of Koreans. They are good business people. They have a good heart. Some have stereotyped Black people and they watch you and hawk [follow you around and crowd] you and treat you bad. However, I can see why sometimes. The gang members go in and they don't have respect, so the Koreans have a reason to act that way sometimes. Therefore, there are a few bad apples in the bunch, but that's people in general. . . . They are getting better at distinguishing between you and gang members.

Young African Americans also tended to have more social interactions with Koreans. A Black male college student (1993) had Korean friends in high school and also spoke about a friendly Korean supervisor at work: "She was real cool, real professional. She was friends with my mom in high school, and that's how I got the job." Similarly, a Black male community organizer in his mid-twenties (1996) brought up generational differences and noted clear differences between Korean immigrants and their Korean American children (some of whom he was friends with):

> The music is different, both have different instruments, the food is different. They are really into their studies, pressured by their parents. Therefore, they are doing well academically. . . . There is a difference with Koreans and Korean Americans. I don't have anything against Korean Americans. Korean Americans are more normal, regular.

His distinction between Korean Americans and Koreans stemmed from his social contact with the former; he felt he had more in common with them because they were born here. He also felt the need to separate Korean immigrants from his "more normal regular" Korean American friends, which was understandable as the latter were much more assimilated to American culture.

Some Korean immigrant merchants appreciated African Americans for their warmth and concern, and acknowledged that they had reaped benefits from the Black-led Civil Rights Movement. A middle-aged married Korean American woman (1992), the owner of Gee Gee Liquor Store, discussed a Black employee, using the Korean cultural emphasis on education as a frame of reference:

> As long as [African Americans] are educated, they are the same people. For instance, my Black manager calls us "ma" or "pa" and asks whether or not I am tired. When he got married, we bought him a nice watch and my son attended his wedding ceremony.[10] We also gave him a paid week leave for his wedding. Later when we retire, we would like to leave our store with the Black manager.

She differed from other interviewees in that she had some in-depth understanding of Black history, although she still relied on ethnocentric views related to education:

> I try to understand them better. Thanks to their Civil Rights Movement, we Koreans, as *yakso minjok* [a lesser nation], are able to live now in America. Because Blacks have been oppressed for a long time, they have accumulated their hostility toward others, including us. Both Koreans and Blacks are the same. However, our social background and way of thought are drastically different from theirs. For example, as far as children's education is concerned, it is common for Korean parents to sacrifice themselves to educate their children, which you cannot find among either Whites or Blacks.[11] White parents do their duty to a certain extent, but not fully like Korean parents, and Black parents seem to ignore their children's education. For example, I raised my children to go to graduate school. Strong family ties and respect for their parents are virtues, which one cannot find in America due to its welfare system.

## BLACKS AND KOREANS AS STEREOTYPED OTHER: "UPROOTED PEASANTS" VERSUS THE "UNDERCLASS"

Notwithstanding the relatively positive perceptions some Blacks and Koreans had of each other, many interviewees fell back on common stereotypes. Szwed stated that the average person is not so much bothered by physical differences, but rather with their seeming co-occurrence with behavioral differences (1975, 20). According to Szwed, there are two distinct forms of stereotyping:

> The first is the reading of a person or a group of persons as being known by a set of physical characteristics or behaviors, which are quite concrete and subject to some kind of verification. Thus, a person may be said to have red skin, or blue eyes, or to be musically inclined, or to avoid facing each other when they talk. . . . But there is also a second level of stereotyping, one which offers observations

about a people's laziness, ugliness, childishness, stupidity, dishonesty, lack of self-control and the like. In these latter forms, we see virtual moral ascription or accounts of deviancy, assessments of how far another people's behavior is seen to vary from the observers', and even a sense of how much conflict seems implicit in these characteristics. (1975, 21–22)

While many Black interviewees' stereotypes about Koreans belonged to the first type, which could be classified as cultural difference, many Korean interviewees' notions about African Americans belonged to the latter type, notions of innate, biological difference.

A 45-year-old divorced Black male hairstylist (1992) commented on cultural differences of Korean immigrants:

It is like night and day. They think they are superior. Since their culture has been around for so long, they have the right to act the way they do. They bow a lot. Some are nice, but some have attitudes.

Thus, Koreans seemed to African Americans to have a superiority complex; however, the interviewee attributed it to his belief that Koreans have a longer cultural tradition than African Americans and (White) Americans. More importantly, his view indicated that cultural differences are related to power relations. Similarly, many other Black interviewees felt overwhelmed by the high visibility of Korean immigrant entrepreneurship. They speculated about the role of culture—in particular, the connection between prosperity and religion and ritual. Penelope, a hairstylist (1992), was puzzled by the rapidly increasing number of Korean immigrant merchants:

Koreans come here in big numbers. The media shows Koreans as poor people, but I would like to know how they got here without money. Where do they get the money to open businesses, and why do they open businesses in the Black community? They are able to have money and put the money back into their community. Blacks want to know what is happening here.

The economy of South Korea is the 11th largest in the world.[12] However, Americans could have been influenced by the US media's portrayal of war-torn and poverty-stricken Korea in the 1950s. Whatever the case, the perception of Korean immigrants as uprooted peasants turned illegitimate nouveau riche seemed to be prevalent among African Americans, except young Blacks who went to school with Asian Americans.

Like Penelope, other Black interviewees felt that it was unfair for Koreans to own businesses so quickly after immigrating, particularly within Black communities. A 20-year-old unemployed Black man (1993) criticized Korean immigrants for treating Black customers with disrespect while running a successful business:

> They're real business-oriented, but they need to give back to the community. They come to South LA and open a lot of liquor stores, there's a lot of vacant lots, and there are none in White communities. . . . They don't speak good English, but that's not the problem. You still can have some sort of communication. It's about how they treat you and how you treat them. If you come in stealing, they have a reason to follow you.

Some Korean immigrant merchants portrayed themselves as hardworking, family-oriented, and highly ambitious, unlike African Americans, whom they considered easygoing, selfish, and less formal about marriage. For example, a 21-year-old Korean American male (1992), the son of a market owner on Vermont and 51st St., commented on the different work cultures of Koreans and African Americans:

> Koreans are a bit cold, maybe as they are too busy. Because of their history, they are in a rush to establish [themselves] soon: "*anjong ch'atki*," always talking about "*ppalippali*," to be quick. They want to buy a house as soon as possible and so on. It is strange that *hukin*, Blacks, want to work for a few hours only, unlike Koreans who would like to work as long as possible.

Similarly, the Korean American female owner of the Sorbonne Market (1992) depicted African Americans as "shameless":

> Koreans are too smart, and they do not want to work for other Koreans. I had to hire Chinese, Mexican, Salvadoran, and Guatemalan employees. Koreans are well mannered and know shame. On the contrary, African Americans seem to be shameless.[13] For instance, those people who were found to be shoplifting tended to return to my store the next day without shame.

Another Korean American liquor store owner (1992) stated:

> Koreans are egotistical, self-centered, and eager for status-display. For example, although I asked her not to, my mother-in-law still cooks "*kimch'ikuk*," smelly *kimch'i* soup without any concern for others. On the contrary, African Americans are well organized, like Danny Bakewell's boycotting of Korean stores. In addition, while all African Americans are very articulate, Korean Americans are poor speakers, which I felt at the community meeting at the 77th police precinct. However, Blacks are extremely poor, coming to my store with five cents in their hands and often do drugs or are drunk. They are lazy and free riders, perhaps as welfare recipients.

Thus, although this interviewee saw African Americans as articulate, organized, and as having some political power compared to Koreans, he slipped into the prevalent stereotyping of African Americans as lazy and welfare-dependent, even though "the average time on welfare is about two years, not the lifetime of the myth" (Feagin and Vera 1995, 152).

It should be emphasized that shoplifting occurred every day in Korean-run stores. This does not necessarily mean that shoplifting occurred more often in South LA than in other parts of the city, but it was more difficult for small business owners to absorb losses than national retail and grocery chains. To avoid conflict, many Korean merchants let suspicious customers leave the store.[14] But problems would emerge later when suspected shoplifters sometimes attempted to return the stolen goods for cash refunds and deny that the merchandise was stolen. In a few cases, Korean merchants used violence to force the shoplifter to admit that he or she took the merchandise. Some merchants called the police; however, the police often compounded the problem. A common complaint of Korean merchants was that "the police do not give a damn about these (shoplifting) incidents." In some instances, when the police responded to a call, they arrested the merchant if there had been allegations of violence. When Korean merchants were left without protection from the LAPD, they were forced to deal with the shoplifting with very few resources and little training or patience. For many Korean merchants, it was more important for a shoplifter to admit he or she had committed a crime, as morality was more important than the use of violence against the shoplifter. And, as mentioned in chapter 2, in some cases Korean merchants were shot to death while defending their stores.

According to Stevenson (2013), Mrs. Du held racist notions similar to the ones evidenced above concerning the Black people who frequented her Empire Liquor Market: "They look healthy, young . . . big question why they don't work . . . got welfare money and buying alcoholic beverages and consuming them instead of feeding children" (233). Indeed, some Korean merchants tended to express explicit prejudices and racism toward Blacks. Their short immigration history and lack of exposure to multiracial settings and the political correctness of the US have informed their attitudes toward other races and ethnicities in the US. On the other hand, African Americans, with their long history of anti-racist movements and longer socialization process within a racially diverse American society, as well as their very long history of marginalization and oppression, are likely more cautious about making racist remarks.

All Black interviewees mentioned language as a main difference between Koreans and African Americans, which is not surprising. A Black male community organizer (1996) commented on differences in communication style:

"Often their English is stagnant, hard to understand. African Americans use a lot of slang they think the merchant should understand, but that is not always the case." On the other hand, when asked about culture, many Black interviewees were unable to articulate concrete differences. The only cultural specificities mentioned were things like, "They use chopsticks or take off their shoes." Another informant described Koreans as "money grabbers." These responses do not demonstrate much prior thought about cultural differences.

Overall, both Korean and African American perceptions reflected the extent to which both groups had internalized dominant racial ideologies and practices. As discussed earlier, their racist discourse and behavior can be interpreted as "a displacement of the ridicule, rejection, and hatred heaped on themselves by the mainstream culture onto the other people of color similarly ridiculed, rejected, and hated by the racist culture" (Lee 2010, 756). Thus, the other group's behavior and culture were interpreted in terms of the dominant racial discourse in a way that conformed to and reinforced the existing social order. For instance, despite often amicable relationships with African Americans and the explicit recognition of white racism as an oppressive force, many Korean store owners still viewed Blacks as lazy, unreliable, criminals, or welfare queens. These stereotypes, combined with the real and perceived threats to which Korean merchants were exposed in their workplace, strained Black-Korean encounters and led to the overly defensive actions of Soon Ja Du, as discussed in the previous chapter.

Lastly, I should also point out that Korean Americans were not a very well-known immigrant group in the early 1990s. As one Korean American pointed out, "Korean life in America is mostly a caricature, because the host culture doesn't care to know about us. It's myth and misconceptions—Koreans as greedy, gun happy, and exploitative of Blacks" (Kim and Yu 1996, 24). For instance, in the Hollywood film *Falling Down*, released in 1993, Koreans were seen as unscrupulous shopkeepers who would not make change unless something was purchased or who overcharged customers. Following the Hollywood trend of the "white savior," the White protagonist of the film trashed the Korean-owned store (E. Kim 1993, 217). These images of Korean Americans, which Black customers consumed, reinforced the perception of Korean Americans as unscrupulous, callous, and greedy merchants.

## African Americans and Koreans as Ambivalent Other

In addition to positive and negative perceptions held by Black customers and Korean merchants regarding the other group, another common discourse related to feelings of envy and anxiety. Some discussed positive aspects of the culture of other communities, while enumerating negative features of their own community. For instance, a number of Black interviewees made an interesting observation that Korean immigrant merchants tend to treat their regulars better over time.

A 26-year-old Black male UPS carrier (1996) stated, "The Korean merchants tend to watch you, but the ones at the stores that I shop at have 'mellowed out' because I am a regular customer. They are overpriced, but I shop there because it is convenient." Iyanna, a 19-year-old Black female college student (1993), affirmed that Korean merchants treat their acquaintances or friends better. She characterized the business people in her neighborhood as friendly but paranoid. Their treatment "depends on if you know them or if they are familiar with your face." Like other interviewees, she remembered a Korean friend at her high school that was friendly and fond of Black culture. She continued,

> They don't know how to interact with our community. They are smart people to build in the Black community because that's where they get their money. However, they are afraid. They are not accepted by Blacks [or] Whites so they have to look out for themselves.

Similarly, a 19-year-old South LA resident (1993) recalled both pleasant and unpleasant episodes:

> The woman who used to do my nails was Korean. She was real nice, pretty honest. I guess that is because we had that kind of personal relationship. Unpleasant would be one time when I bought a radio at the swap meet, they wouldn't let me return it. I got into an argument with them about that.

In addition, she pointed out that "They would follow the clients around the store and hide prices so they then can convince you that you are getting a bargain."

Most Black interviewees' experiences with Korean merchants were mixed. Some saw Korean merchants' business etiquette as problematic, finding them rude, disrespectful, suspicious, hostile, humiliating, unpleasant, or even paranoid. However, others envied Korean immigrants' social capital (e.g., ethnic and family unity and cohesiveness). A 40-year-old Black paralegal (1992) compared Korean Americans to herself:

> I am a humanitarian and Korean Americans are not. I am sympathetic to the Black community and Korean Americans are not. Korean Americans are also tradition-conscious. Korean Americans come together as a unit when they want something materialistically, but Blacks have been given the idea that they can't

do anything with [one] another. I also note that Korean Americans have not been
oppressed like Blacks.

In the above comments, the woman suggested three things about Koreans:
they were capitalists, they were less oppressed than Blacks, and they were a
unified community.

Similar views were expressed by a 26-year-old Black female graduate
student (1992) who described herself as smart, intelligent, and hardworking,
just like Korean Americans:

> They want the best and go to an extreme to get it. They are more family-
> oriented. They are taught from a young age to succeed. We've gone away from
> that. Blacks are more lackadaisical. I do not like it when rappers use White
> society as an excuse for failure.

A mixed race Black and Mexican American young woman interviewed at the
Slauson Swap Meet (1993) answered similarly: "I guess they're kind of quiet.
They stick with their family. You know that because the stores are usually
run by families. . . . They seem to really stick to their own thing." Nonetheless, she stated that Koreans' fear of inner-city customers caused problems:
"They are just scared of Blacks and Mexicans. They overreact and I think
that causes a whole lot of unnecessary problems." A 32-year-old Black truck
driver (1996) also brought up the unity of the Korean community: "Koreans
are together. They come to the US earning money, with unity. Blacks aren't
together, there is no unity . . . unless they live at the end of a dead-end block
with money, and then there is unity."

African Americans' mirroring of Korean Americans in the early to mid-
1990s can be summarized as follows: Koreans with economic power felt a
sense of superiority to their customers; Koreans viewed African Americans
as criminogenic; Koreans were unfair competitors; Koreans were selfish capitalists; Koreans had more economic, social, and cultural capital than African
Americans; and Koreans were, before coming to the US, poverty-stricken
peasants and a cultured, non-Westernized people. Some Black interviewees emphasized positive qualities, such as Koreans being quiet, friendly,
hardworking, highly motivated, smart, cohesive, and entrepreneurial. These
depictions need to be understood in relation to African Americans' representation of themselves as a hardworking and humanitarian people who were
oppressed, but who also lacked a certain unity.

On the other hand, Korean Americans' mirroring of African Americans emphasized a lack of work ethic, selfishness, laziness, an easygoing
demeanor, and prone to be welfare-dependent, criminogenic, shameless,

and jealous of Koreans' success. Korean Americans viewed themselves as hardworking, family-oriented, highly motivated, and somewhat provincial. However, Koreans also defined themselves as selfish, competitive, tough, materialistic, inarticulate, and hierarchical, while African Americans were viewed as articulate, warm, unified as a community, and democratic. Each group saw the other as unified (i.e., from the outside it looked like unity within the group).

## VARIOUS NOTIONS ABOUT COMMUNITY

As far as my African Americans interviewees are concerned, there are two main factors influencing individuals' ideas about their community. The first is the respondent's age, and the second relates to whether the respondents identified as community leaders. Younger informants (early 20s) were hesitant to confront racial issues, and respondents often circumvented racial tensions by denying the significance of cultural differences. The denial of cultural difference which is actually the denial of racism, reflecting contemporary language politics of "political correctness," leads to the internalization of misunderstandings. Without the verbalization of doubts and feelings, no solution can be reached on either a personal or broader social level.

For example, a 25-year-old Black male student (1996) stated that he did not know much about Koreans. He mentioned friends who were Korean and stated, "My friends and I don't get into cultures; we just hang out." When asked about differences between Koreans and African Americans, he began a story and then abruptly ended it, asking me not to write about it. Increased intercultural contact and teaching cultural relativism in schools, in addition to the dissemination of a color-blind notion of race,[15] has changed perceptions of Koreans among younger generations of African Americans. However, there is a downside: while increased contact facilitates better cultural understanding, cultural relativism can inhibit the acknowledgement of important differences, especially among younger generations.

The second trend I observed concerned the relationship between community leaders and the larger community. Leaders have more education and contact with people outside their community. For example, when asked about improving relations between African Americans and Koreans, one African American community leader suggested greater community involvement as a solution for reducing tension: "They [Koreans] need to learn American culture . . . not just the business aspect of it, like that Blacks like to buy hats, but little league stuff like that. They need to have involvement in the community." Another African American community organizer similarly diagnosed the difficulty as "not so much of a cultural difference in communication but . . . the fact that Koreans don't belong to the community, and they come in and take away resources from the community." He continued:

> I think there has to be a real priority in race relations in this city. Los Angeles hasn't been serious about the racial relations in a city that is the world's most racially diverse city. The resources need to be used to build and nurture relations. Secondly, the community need[s] to demand a better kind of leadership on the level of elected officials, chief of police, mayor, superintendent of schools, all need to play a leadership role in race and human relationships. . . . There has to be attention paid to the economic needs of the people: job creation, job development, job training, all need to be part of the economical [sic] vitalization plan. Education is critical . . . a broader sense of education in which Latinos, African Americans, and Koreans can understand what other communities are all about.

Contact with outside institutions and communities allows leaders to partially identify with perspectives developed outside the South LA community. It means they are more open-minded.

It is important to note that the community I refer to is not necessarily geographic; the individual may live in one community (such as South LA) but become associated with a different group of people who hold distinct beliefs and values. The two are not mutually exclusive; it is probable that an individual identifies with multiple communities simultaneously. I observed that community organizers drew on other groups' ideals and belief systems, in addition to those of South LA, to theorize about their community.


## CULTURE, RACE, AND DIFFERENCE

Among African American interviewees in my study, the term "culture" signified various things, including tradition, magic, or property, and as something foreigners possessed. The first meaning suggested that Koreans cannot change because they are tied to tradition. The second one identified Koreans as successful "owing to their culture"; it is as if they became successful through some sort of magic. The last one implied that, once in the US, Koreans should shed their premodern and un-American culture.[16] Interestingly, both African Americans and Koreans believed that Koreans had "more culture" (or at least a much older one) and that Koreans were not yet Westernized. This perspective revealed Koreans' lack of understanding of Black history. For African Americans, it suggested that the definition of culture in the US tends to stress differences, particularly exotic ones. Perhaps they internalized the hegemonic idea that only non-Western people "have" culture, and they don't include themselves in this group. "Too much" or "a lack of" culture is often used to characterize Third World and immigrant/minority cultures in Western countries. However, I would argue that the invoking of cultural difference in this case was a façade for the more relevant factors of racial and class inequality.

It was not these perceived cultural differences that caused conflict between Korean merchants and Black residents. It was only when the cultural differences were combined with different historical experiences and exacerbated by unequal class and race relations that they became problematic. Therefore, "it is not cultural diversity per se that should interest anthropologists but the political meanings with which specific political contexts and relationships endow cultural difference" (Stolcke 1995, 12). In other words, we need to pay attention to the politics of cultural difference.

For my interviewees, culture largely stood in for race, which corresponds to the ways that contemporary racial discourses are often based on notions of culture. Scholars have noted a movement away from biological theories of racial inferiority to discourses that treat cultural differences as inherently problematic: a culturalization of racism or cultural racism (Verkuyten 1997, 100). In France, Pierre-Andre Taguieff (1987) and Etienne Balibar (1991) discuss differential, cultural, symbolic, or indirect racism as a racism whose dominant theme is not biological heredity but the insurmountability of cultural differences. Meanwhile, in the UK, Martin Barker (1981) describes the rise of a "new racism" focused on preserving a certain way of life under threat from immigrant groups.

In the US, despite histories of racism and anti-racist struggle distinct from those of Europe, the shift from "race" to "culture" has occurred within neoconservative and neoliberal political rhetoric (Prashad 1998, 26). Compared with the European situation, the picture is more complex due to a larger number of native minorities, post-Civil Rights racial politics, and a diverse group of new immigrants. While a certain cultural lack or pathology has long been invoked in relation to inner-city African Americans, Korean culture has often been discussed in terms of cultural "abundance," "backwardness," "abnormality," or "illegitimacy." These are examples of the way racial discourse has been replaced by cultural discourse. Furthermore, discourses around culture relate to economics and differences in class relations, which will be discussed in the next chapter.

All of this is relevant to the Black-Korean conflict in that notions of culture contributed to the politicization of the conflict. Culture, along with the state and capitalism, helped create the meanings of Black-Korean conflict. African American characterizations of Koreans as exotic, strange, and un-American constitutes an example of minorities using nationalist redemptive narratives in an attempt to claim national belonging, dignity, and humanity in a White-dominated country. According to Brackette Williams, particular nationalist ideologies include the quest for homogenized syncretism and their naturalization through the delegitimation of heterogeneous productions and products (1993, 152). She examines the impact of nationalism on the concept of culture in the following way:

> Benefits receivable are hierarchically predicated on a measure of the competing groups' place in the nation consequent to their relative contributions and the suffering these groups may be alleged to have experienced while making their contributions and sacrifices. In the U.S., it is a dialectic that encourages some Jews and some African Americans to compare the relative sufferings attributable to the Holocaust to those consequent to slavery and its aftermath. . . . In these assessments, subordinated groups produce competing set[s] of criteria as they stake their claim to a place in the nation and attempt to keep others from claiming a place they deem inconsistent with the other groups' adjudged sufferings. (Williams 1993, 181)

In this vein, Korean Americans' legitimization as Americans can only occur after Korean immigrants have made sufficient contributions and sacrifices, which is a point many Black interviewees made. Only then can they claim and press for civil rights and economic benefits.

Conversely, pundits advanced a polarizing debate about African American gains (via affirmative action) at the expense of Asian American interests; in other words, they touted the economic gains of Asian Americans as a way to denigrate African Americans. According to Thomas Sowell (2004), affirmative action policies tend to benefit primarily the most fortunate among the preferred group (e.g., upper- and middle-class African Americans), often to the detriment of the least fortunate, for instance the working class, among the non-preferred groups (e.g., poor whites or Asians). Thus, conservative critics added to the interracial tensions between Koreans and African Americans, as well as to the racial and cultural barriers they faced in the larger society, by reinforcing the "othering" of each group. Within the context of the tensions in 1992, members of the two communities identified the other group as the source of the problem rather than focusing on the broader political and economic context. According to Freer (1994, 192), this struggle was the proverbial fight over a slice of pie. Other actors, namely political and economic elites, were therefore relieved of responsibility for the role they played in the evolution of the conflict.

The attitudes of Korean Americans were also based on notions derived from the dominant White majority. In their research on White perceptions of racial groups, Feagin and Vera (1995) reported that many Whites, when asked to explain their position in the multiethnic US, do so in vertical or hierarchical terms, much like the Korean immigrants in my study: "For whites, the category 'black' labels a group as physically (for example, dark skinned or athletic), culturally (for example, promiscuous or lazy), and morally (for example, dangerous criminals or welfare queens) different" (Feagin and Vera 1995, 145).

Manning Marable states that "to be White is not a sign of culture, or a statement of biology or genetics: it is essentially a power relationship, a statement of authority, a social conduct which is perpetuated by systems of privilege, the consolidation of property and status" (1995, 60). To a large extent, Black-Korean discourse reflected the unequal power relationship within the social space of South LA, as well as the unequal relationship of both groups to the dominant White population. In the next chapter, I will examine the intersection of race, culture, and class that contributes to this lack of access.

## NOTES

1. Gramsci famously posited that the cultural arena is a site of struggle: "An integral form of class rule which exists not only in political and economic institutions but also in active forms of experience and consciousness. . . . The overthrow of a specific hegemony can only be done by creating an alternative hegemony" (Williams 1976, 145).

2. Previously Kim worked as an executive director of the Korean Produce Association and later founded the Korean American Small Business Service Center of New York. See Min (1996), K. Park (1997), and Sanjek (1998) for detailed discussion of his activism.

3. I don't think I can claim US English and all its cultural manifestations aren't a culture. Every country has a culture, various cultures even.

4. It should be emphasized that the concept of cultural relativism has been challenged in light of human rights abuses, ethnocide, and genocide. Some countries accused of violating human rights have tried to hide behind cultural relativism and criticized their accusers of being Western moral imperialists. In addition, cultural relativism is often used as an argument to resist changing problematic aspects of a given culture.

5. There were exceptions, such as hip-hop culture and the "culture of poverty" thesis, which only seemed to be applied to African Americans.

6. Although my presence might have affected the way Korean merchants dealt with the customers, they were unfamiliar with what academic researchers would expect of their behavior. For instance, they made insensitive comments about other ethnicities regularly. Thus, I do not believe my presence substantially affected their behavior.

7. As I'll discuss in chapter 6, an increasing number of African Americans were employed at Korean-owned business establishments in South Central after the uprising, often for security purposes.

8. A few Korean men worked as manicurists at nail salons. Before this was considered acceptable, men usually took care of selling beauty supplies and other business matters.

9. In a documentary about the 1992 LA Uprising, *Sa-I-Gu* (4-2-9), one woman grocer was called "Smiley" by her African American customer in South Central for her frequent smiles.

10. Korean interviewees often joked that once Korean immigrants are invited to Black weddings, there will be an end to Black-Korean tensions.

11. I suspect this view reflects Korean immigrants' limited exposure to other lower-middle or working-class communities. Although rare, some Korean immigrants living in suburban, wealthy communities told me that they are impressed with their White parents' dedication to their children's education.

12. South Korea was ranked 11th in the world in nominal GDP and 14th in purchasing power parity (PPP) in 2017 (The International Monetary Fund 2018). South Korea is one of the G20 major economies and is considered to be a high income, developed country.

13. Older Korean immigrant merchants who experienced the Korean War seemed to understand stealing as linked to class, not race, invoking similar cases in the chaotic context of the post-Korean War.

14. In late 1980s Harlem, an urban legend circulated widely in which an obnoxious Korean grocer not only chased a customer who swallowed a grape without paying but also forced the customer to throw up the stolen grape.

15. Color-blind racism refers to "rejecting open assertions of racial superiority or inferiority, but that continues to reproduce a more subtle series of practices that racially differentiate while professing an adherence to the ideal of being color-blind" (Hartigan 2010, 208).

16. The concept of culture in this discourse is analogous to Maykel Verkuyten's (1997) study about Dutch residents' attitudes in multiethnic Rotterdam. The scholar identified three conceptualizations of culture: culture as heritage (cannot be changed), culture as doctrine (is not allowed to be changed), and culture as mentality (people do not want to change). All three have the effect of "blaming the victim," but each attributes a different degree of blame to immigrant groups.

*Chapter Four*

# Triangulating Class at the Crossroads of Race and Ethnicity

From birth, Asian people are structured to be business-minded and to make money. Their main goal is to make money. They don't care if they have to go underground to make the money. Moving into South Central means nothing to them. . . . Since Korean merchants are in the South Central area, they tend to subscribe to negative stereotypes [of African Americans]. Korean merchants do not have a concept of a merchant-customer relationship. They look at Black people as if they were animals. All they care about is the money. You can't walk out of that store with one piece of candy without paying for it because it's about money (a 28-year-old Black female vital statistics clerk 1992).

There is tension between Korean and African Americans because of jealousy. Negroes are jealous because Koreans have more power and power equals money. Negroes are at a lower-class level than Koreans, which means they [Blacks] have less power (a 43-year-old Black welfare recipient 1993).

The Black-Korean conflict cannot be explained by prejudice, cultural differences, or racism alone, but rather as a contested process simultaneously influenced by race/ethnicity, class, and culture. This chapter will examine the intersecting framework of race, culture, and class in the broader historical and political economy context of the United States. Building on previous chapters' focus on cultural differences and racial animosities, I argue that class relations fueled the flames of resentment and hostility during the unrest of the early 1990s in LA. Even a decade earlier in Harlem, in a Black boycott of Korean stores in 1981, Korean Americans were accused of being "vampires" and foreign intruders who were coming in to "suck Black consumers dry" and "take over African American neighborhoods and extract maximum profits" (Waldinger 1996, 278). Korean immigrant merchants were resented for what Blacks felt was class exploitation.

115

The structural violence of racialized capitalism comprises the political unconscious of Black-Asian relations (Sexton 2010, 99). The ability of Korean immigrants to open stores in Black neighborhoods largely depends upon financial resources, and many of the tensions between store-owning Korean immigrants and African American customers are therefore related to class, in addition to being race-based. As Sexton reminds us, "Class difference, pace Marx, itself a euphemism for a permanent state of aggression is the fundamental systematic violence of capitalism" (Zizek 1996, 566, as cited in Sexton 2010, 93).

Both groups occupy vulnerable socioeconomic positions within the context of American capitalism. As Edna Bonacich (1987, 446) emphasizes, minority traders like Korean merchants play a "dual oppressed-oppressor role": they are exploited by big corporations as a cheap labor force, but at the same time exploit other subordinates while operating as agents of the dominant group. Although they are not directly employed by domestic or transnational corporations and thus appear to be independent capitalists, they still serve the interests of corporations as an indirect cheap labor force by penetrating the ghetto market, a poverty-stricken area with a high crime rate, which has been abandoned by large, chain supermarkets (as I addressed in chapter 1). Prashad states, "The Koreans are part of the equation, but not even close to being the agents of bondage" (2001, 112). In the context of 1990s LA, Korean merchants occupied a socioeconomic position as ghetto merchants on the front lines of an exploitative system. They sought to profit off the systematic exploitation of poor people of color living in economically struggling neighborhoods. While most of the surplus profits were reaped by large corporations, such as the producers of food and alcohol, Korean merchants nonetheless functioned as oppressors by appropriating some of the surplus. Because they were on the front lines of an oppressive system, they were perceived as contributing to residents' poverty by draining the community of resources. It was because of this position that Black residents considered them an enemy (Bonacich 1987, 461; 1993, 689–90).

A Marxist, class-based approach has much to offer in examining social conflicts, particularly those involving racial and ethnic differences. Sociologist Edna Bonacich (1972) argues that racial/ethnic tensions can be explained by labor market segmentation rather than individual prejudice or bigotry. In addition, as sociologist Miliann Kang critiques, "While class and economic relations are clearly central to [relations between Asian immigrants and other groups], they are often rendered invisible and rewritten in terms of race, foreign status, or general notion of 'otherness'" (2010, 180). A Marxist approach views racial and ethnic conflict not just through the lens of class, but also the maintenance of ethno-racial tension (as opposed to its origin). Thus, racial and ethnic conflict is perpetuated by the capitalist class in an attempt to divide and conquer the labor force to maximize profits. Bonacich (1972, 1980) offers a traditional class-based approach to ethnic conflicts. Her split labor market model places economic competition, particularly labor, at the center of ethnic antagonism and challenges the idea that it is the sole creation of the dominant bourgeoisie. Capitalists aim to exploit ethnic minorities, while established (White) workers try to prevent capitalists from doing so. Bonacich argues that racial and ethnic antagonism stem from higher-paid White workers' fear of competition from lower-paid workers.

Historian David Roediger (1991) argues that economic competition alone cannot explain ethnic antagonism. He provides a historically grounded analysis of the development of racial identity within the White working class,[1] arguing that people now categorized as "White," for instance, Irish Americans, were not initially viewed as such. By the eighteenth century, he says, "White" had become a well-established racial term, and the notion of free wage labor was born of the need to differentiate White workers from slaves and reconcile the ideological notion of American independence with the realities of a wage-dependent working class. Similarly, Noel Ignatiev (1995) explains how Irish workers in antebellum America earned honorary membership among the established White workforce by differentiating themselves from Black workers through racist violence and the establishment of exclusionist American trade unions. Ignatiev finds that ethno-racial antagonism did not merely stem from moderately paid workers' competitive fears about low-paid minority workers. Irish workers eventually developed solidarity with German workers to promote their class interests, but not those of Black people. What defined life in antebellum America was neither economic competition nor Black slavery, but, Ignatiev argues, "a bipolar system of color caste, in which even the lowliest of 'whites' enjoyed a status superior in crucial respects to that of the most exalted of blacks" (1995, 100).

Roediger and Ignatiev argue that race is central to understanding the American working class and have challenged fellow labor historians who have minimized the importance of race in the hopes of finding a "usable" past of worker solidarity. They also dispute the notion that ethnic tensions can only be studied by *either* race *or* class. My study extends the excellent interrogations of the links between class and race by Bonacich, Roediger, and Ignatiev.

I also draw on sociologist Charles Tilly's "organizational view of inequality-generating mechanisms" (1998, 9), which includes gender, race, occupation, and many other forms of inequalities under a unitary conceptual framework that moves beyond the work of the abovementioned scholars (Wright 2000, 465). Tilly argues that inequalities occur along binary categories, that is, between and because of categories such as "black/white, male/female, citizen/foreigner, or Muslim/Jew" and not because of individual factors such as personal ability (1998, 7). He identifies two fundamental processes through which categorical inequality is generated and perpetuated by organizations. One is the Marxist notion of "exploitation," meaning surplus-value extraction. The other is "opportunity hoarding," which can be applied to the ethnic tension between Korean immigrant business owners and their Black and Latino customers. Opportunity hoarding operates when people within an exclusive community obtain a (renewable) resource that can be monopolized (Tilly 1998, 10). According to Tilly, non-elites like ethnic immigrant groups add to inequality through opportunity hoarding. These groups accumulate their capital through processes such as chain migration and passing skills on to new immigrants of their same ethnic group, both horizontally and across generations. Such groups restrict access to their networks and resources to other ethnic or racial groups.

While there are elements of ethnic antagonism involved in Black-Korean tensions, this does not answer the question of why Latino and Black business owners were also victimized (three quarters of damaged structures were Korean-owned) in the 1992 civil unrest. According to Steven Gold (2004, 315), conflicts between immigrant business owners and their inner-city customers have been common throughout American society. In fact, Jewish merchants in Harlem were the prefiguration of the "trader as stranger," a notion later applied to Korean merchants (Prashad 2001, 98). James Baldwin notes that the "Jew is singled out by Negroes not because he acts differently from other White men, but because. . . . He is playing the role assigned him by Christians long ago, he is doing their dirty work" (1969, 137). In other words, conflicts between business owners and their customers are caused by "broader patterns of inequality, prejudice, and alienation in American society" (Gold 2004, 316). In addition, Chinese and Vietnamese merchants in the South, Arabs in San Francisco and Detroit, and Hasidic Jews in Brooklyn have all experienced antagonism from African Americans comparable to that of Koreans in South LA.

This chapter will examine the issue of class in relation to the Black-Korean tensions of 1992, which is a crucial component of my theoretical construct, racial cartography. I first assess the convergence of race, ethnicity, and class, and then discuss how class operates through the categories of race and ethnicity in interracial conflicts. This requires clarifying the nature of class relations between Black customers and Korean merchants in the early 1990s in terms of domination, surveillance, opportunity hoarding, and exploitation. These class relations will be related to questions of status, and in particular, issues of prestige, honor, and distinction. Class relations and the production of profit remain fundamental to the operation of Korean-owned business establishments and to the reproduction of capitalism itself.

## CONVERGENCES OF RACE, ETHNICITY, AND CLASS

In analyzing cultural models of race, one can identify many elements of ethnicity. The resurgence of ethnic consciousness and racial politics beginning in the 1960s and 1970s, and the application of the term "ethnic group" to African Americans and other minorities helped bring about political power to marginalized groups. However, it would still be erroneous to treat subordinate racial groups in American society as if they were merely ethnic.[2] First, "ethnicity" as the expressive process of cultural identification can be differentiated from "race," the repressive process of social exclusion (Sanjek 1994, 8). However, race and ethnicity are not always easily separated or distinguishable, and the racism expressed in public discourse on issues related to immigration suggests that the boundary between the two is often fluid. For instance, the category of "Latino" is understood by many to be a racial category—designating someone's race—but is actually an ethnic category that designates someone as of Latin American origin.

Race, ethnicity, and class/economic exploitation are permeable categories even in common parlance. A Black female community member who worked as a hairstylist (1992) made a comment on the role of race and economics in the Du-Harlins incident:

> It [race] was the big issue. She was a Black girl and she was a Korean woman in the Black community who was taking people's money and who was not being friendly enough or humble enough.

Thus, she alluded to an exploitative economic relationship between two groups. Her colleague, a Black, male hairstylist (1992), focused on race in discussing Black-Korean tensions, but he also addressed class and ethnicity: "It was racial. It also involved circumstances of money. The Korean businesses take our money and then go back to Korea.[3] We did not ask them to come here anyway." These three Black interviewees clearly saw a relationship of economic exploitation and what they viewed as Korean greed as primary factors of Black-Korean tensions.

An older Black female government worker (1992) expressed an alternative view. Although she spoke about the Du-Harlins case as a racial conflict, she also invoked a class explanation common among more affluent members of the Black community:

> A racial conflict was involved in the Soon Ja Du incident. A racial conflict developed because Soon Ja Du was tired of people from the community stealing from her. She was tired of being victimized and tired of having her livelihood disrupted. If it had been me, I would have done the same thing. They [the African Americans] would steal from anybody. They'd steal from other Blacks.

For her, Black-Korean conflicts demonstrated similar structural dynamics with respect to class relations to the tensions between the Black middle class and the Black urban poor.

These interviewees engaged in what might be called "agenda switching": talking about race in terms of ethnicity, ethnicity in terms of class, and class in terms of race. They're about the relationship between race (which was conflated with ethnicity only in first instance) and economic exploitation. What is significant, though, is that the role of class was mostly obscured by discussions of race and ethnicity. Sherry Ortner notes that in the US, "class is often represented through other categories of social difference: gender, ethnicity, race, and so forth" (1992, 164). Still, people may have perceived themselves to be acting in terms of racial or ethnic allegiance,[4] which does not negate the important role of class structure in understanding manifestations of race and ethnicity.

## THE ROLE OF CLASS IN RACIAL DISCOURSE

Few can deny that class is a real structure in American society. Wealthy people wield an enormous amount of power over other people's lives, especially those who are also marginalized by their race. However, many theorists have failed to address a specific dimension of class: "the power and the pain of class relations" (Ortner 1992, 170). Class is often defined as an economic category, but the central axis of class relations relates to the means of production rather than the market. As first conceptualized by Marx, class includes the consciousness of a group of people regarding their situation and the development of organizations around class distinctions:

> Insofar as millions of families live under economic conditions of existence that separate their mode of life, their interests and their culture from those of the other classes, and put them in hostile opposition to the latter, they form a class. Insofar as there is merely a local interconnection among these small holding peasants, and the identity of their interests begets no community, no national bond and no political organization among them, they do not form a class. (Marx and Engels 1959, 338, 339)

In following this classic Marxist approach to class, we could conceptualize the Black-Korean relationship as a conflict between the urban poor and petty bourgeoisie, while stressing the contradictory division of capital and labor. The LA unrest presented us with a situation where class emerged as a formation: members of a class not only identified themselves with the shared class category, but also took action in terms of class struggle. Under the broad category of the urban poor—people who were either unemployed, underemployed, or not in the workforce—African Americans and Latinos banded together to effectively target the Korean American petty bourgeoisie and other property owners.

In contrast to Marxist analyses that focus on the decline and the vestigial characteristics of the petty bourgeoisie in the precapitalist mode of production, the petty bourgeoisie is a persistent force in modern economies (see Bechhofer and Elliott 1985). While large companies dominated the economy in 1992, especially in manufacturing, small businesses not only survived, but they expanded in the service sectors. Korean immigrant merchants in South LA are a part of this small business owner, petty bourgeoisie class. Roughly 60 to 70 percent of Korean immigrants were involved in small business activities as proprietors or service workers (K. Park 1997). As merchants, they possessed both capital and labor, which was often supplemented by family/kin labor. If Korean American merchants constituted the petty bourgeoisie, then Black and Latino residents formed a critical mass of the working class and urban poor. As discussed in chapter 1, the rise of an "underclass" is often attributed to a culture of poverty and/or a cycle of deprivation rather than to larger structural shifts in the economy. Since 1992, more than half of African Americans and Latinos in South LA belonged to this category. The mass relocation of manufacturing industries in South LA was partially responsible for the marked increase in unemployment, crime, and an emergent gang population in the area.

The literature on class conflict has yet to be applied to the hostilities between Korean business owners and their Black and Latino customers during the Los Angeles unrest. Not only did Korean Americans, African Americans, and Latinos differ regarding rates of business ownership, but they also differed in terms of other socioeconomic indicators, including income, occupation, and educational attainment. Koreans had made some gains in contrast to the other minorities: in the 1990 and the 2000 censuses, Korean Americans' household incomes were higher than those of Blacks and Latinos in Southern California. With the average Korean immigrant having a college education or graduate degree before they came to the US, the community's educational attainment was higher than many other minority groups. However, the class relationship involving Korean immigrants and other minorities was not the traditional conflict between capitalists and the working class. This class conflict manifested itself not in the conventional arena of production, but in distribution and consumption. This difference is partly due to the absence of explicit class-based politics in the US and the decline of union membership in recent decades. In addition, unlike European social democracies with well-developed welfare systems (e.g., Sweden), America provides little help to people not engaged in the formal workforce, leaving them with no social safety net.

## EXPLOITATION, OPPORTUNITY
## HOARDING, AND DOMINATION/SURVEILLANCE

It is important to specify the nature of class relations between Korean and African Americans during the period of the unrest. Under capitalism, industrial capitalists extract surplus value from the working class with the owners of the means of production compensating the workers at a lower rate than the value of the products they produce. According to the neo-Marxist scholar Erik Olin Wright, class in capitalist society should be seen as rooted in the complex intersection of three forms of exploitation: (1) exploitation based on the ownership of capital assets, (2) the control of organizational assets, and (3) the possession of certain skills or credential assets (1985, 283). The first and second classic categories may be applied to class relations between Korean American merchants and Black consumers. Much of African Americans' resentment was related to their economically inferior conditions: "Koreans charge too much for poor quality stuff. I am upset with them not because they are Koreans, but because they are not doing it right. It is not a matter of color, but it is a matter of money." A late-twenties Black male cosmetologist (1992) described the tension as a struggle between the "haves and have-nots": "The violence and conflict is not going to stop, it will only get worse. The problem won't be solved as long as the rich people are controlling the poor."

Class relations between Korean merchants and Black customers can be first identified ethnographically as a matter of exploitation. However, this is not in the classic sense of surplus value's exploitation of labor power, but rather in terms of Korean immigrants' property ownership and parochial, capitalist practices. Complaints by Black customers constituted a super-structural critique of capitalism and exploitative local business practices: marked-up prices, rotten groceries, poor customer service, and hostility toward Black customers. It is worth noting that Watts residents made similar complaints about Jewish and White-owned businesses in their community in 1965.

Some Black interviewees also voiced disapproval over Koreans' takeover of local businesses in their neighborhood: they saw Koreans as outsiders in the same way they had viewed European immigrant merchants in the past. African Americans' experience and history of racism made them hypervigilant regarding racial ownership, and although South LA may have developed as a result of racial segregation, they felt that it belonged solely to them. A common argument was that Koreans shouldn't own businesses in Black neighborhoods, just as African Americans don't own businesses in Koreatown. According to one Black community organizer (1996), "They shouldn't be down here; you don't see any Black stores on Olympic or in Olvera. They shouldn't be here either." The lack of Black business ownership in Koreatown is not due to pushback by the Korean community, however. It is too facile to argue that Koreans were responsible for the absence of Black store ownership in South LA, or on a larger scale, for retail justice and the racial distribution of wealth. In fact, despite this accusation by Black customers, some Korean immigrants in South LA purchased liquor stores from Black owners.

As discussed in the previous chapter, young African Americans generally weren't opposed to Koreans owning businesses in Black neighborhoods. This view was undoubtedly due to their increased interaction with Korean Americans in schools, workplaces, and other venues beyond just stores. They were also less likely to stereotype Korean merchants. One Black female college student (1993) said of a Korean friend in high school[5]: "She was cool. She was herself around Black people, like she wanted to be Black." She also discussed her positive interaction with a Korean liquor store owner: "At the liquor store around the corner from my house, they are very friendly, sincere, and helpful."

Another issue of contention was that Koreans' business ownership facilitated class mobility for many of them, which then translated to African Americans as disempowering them. This perspective can be seen in the quote that opens this chapter, where a 43-year-old Black welfare recipient suggested that African Americans were envious of Koreans' economic success. A related issue was what Tilly called "opportunity hoarding," in which communities hoard information and exclude strangers, thus creating durable categorical inequality in their relations with other groups (Tilly 1998, 152).

Tilly's concept of opportunity hoarding draws upon Max Weber's concept of "social closure," defined as "the process by which social collectivities seek to maximize rewards by restricting access to resources and opportunities to a limited circle of eligibles" (Parkin 1979, 44). To apply the concept of "social closure" to my case study, it makes more sense to see the suburban poor in South LA as excluded rather than exploited, as they suffer deprivation due to being barred from access to resources. The situation of Korean shopkeepers is a classic example of this phenomenon. In 1992, Korean merchants owned 1,600 out of 2,411 stores, or two-thirds of all businesses, in South LA. They excluded non-Koreans from this niche, although they employed mostly Latino labor, a situation that differs from Tilly's case study of Mamaroneck Italians' concentration in landscape gardening. They survived by hoarding opportunities as well as exploiting their workers; however, they did not have "secure control of a productive resource, incorporation of effort by excluded parties, nor appropriation of a substantial surplus" (Tilly 1998, 154). Resources that lend themselves well to opportunity hoarding have certain characteristics: they are renewable, subject to monopoly, supportive of network activities, and enhanced by the network's modus operandi (Tilly 1998, 158).

To make matters worse, many African Americans were falsely led to believe that the US government and banks were backing Korean immigrants to open their businesses; they believed Koreans were given preferential treatment. African Americans also tended to lump Korean immigrants together with Vietnamese and other Southeast Asian refugees, who often received special assistance. Even when they were told that it was Southeast Asian refugees, not Koreans, who received assistance from the government, they were in disbelief. For example, the above Black welfare recipient believed that Korean immigrants received checks from the US government: "When they arrive, they are able to get checks from the county building, but even though I was a Manual Resource Clerk at the DPS [Department of Public Safety] office, I could not get a check." She was offended when Korean merchants did not accept government-issued USDA food stamps from customers. This situation emphasizes the problems with identity labels like "Asian American," as Black customers lumped together Koreans with Southeast Asian refugees, regardless of ethnic differences and very different immigration histories.

Products appeared to be simply "delivered" based on an equal exchange between commodity and money. However, in reality, merchant-customer relations are fundamentally articulated by unequal social relations that make the flow of surplus value possible. The unequal economic and power relations between the Korean merchants and Black customers, which manifested in exploitative business practices and opportunity hoarding, also entailed aspects of domination and surveillance, which were present in many narratives of Black customers. In line with Foucauldian notions of disciplinary power and the panopticon,[6] African Americans believed that Korean merchants were deliberately trying to dominate and humiliate them. Surveillance by CCTV cameras in business establishments in South LA is an example of the ways technology is used to monitor not only African Americans but everyone who frequents these places. Like the institutions explored by Foucault—the family, school, police, hospital, court, prison, and army—Korean-owned stores can also be interpreted as sites of disciplinary power. Inner-city customers were subject to forms of discipline, particularly panopticism, or the constant experience of being watched, usually by a surveillance camera, digital video recorder, or the vigilant eyes of a store owner or employee, often through bullet-proof windows. They felt dominated, humiliated, and mistreated, sensing that Korean merchants viewed them as thieves, gangsters, criminals, or animals. Chapter 5 will discuss this domination via surveillance in more detail.

Black customers complained about Korean merchants following them in the store or rushing them to make a purchase. Korean immigrants, in response, argued that their vulnerability in terms of economic competition with large, chain supermarkets or retail stores justified their practices of "watch-and-follow" and rigid refund and exchange policies. When Korean merchants were robbed or murdered in their stores, these negative perceptions about African Americans were reinforced, further straining Black-Korean relationships. A 22-year-old Black male community college student (1993) recalled his experience with a merchant who mistook him for a gunman: "Sometimes I'm closely watched and followed. One time I went up to the counter of a store and was pulling out my money; the merchant looked scared as if I was going to pull out a gun."

Similarly, a 23-year-old Black male busboy (1993) described his experiences shopping in Korean-owned stores:

Seventy percent of my experiences were pleasant; however, thirty percent of my experiences were unpleasant. For example, I often was subjected to disrespect, rushed to make up [my] mind on purchases, commanded to purchase even though the decision was not made yet and money had been snatched out of my hand.

Another young, unemployed Black male resident recalled (1993):

One time I walked into a store and I was looking for a newspaper. I kept walking up and down the aisles looking because I couldn't find it. At first there was one clerk at the counter, and then there were three. They kept asking, "What do you want? What do you want?" I wanted to find it on my own, but I said, "a newspaper." And they always follow you around the store. Koreans and Whites are scared of Blacks. They expect any Black person to steal and rob them. If they're going to open a store in a Black community, they shouldn't act like that.

A Black male college student (1993) had a similar experience:

I went to a liquor store by La Brea with my friend. They were eyeing us everywhere we went. It was really uncomfortable. I went in to get more than one thing, but I only got a drink because it was so uncomfortable. They were very unfriendly, so we left.

The nature of exploitation between Korean merchants and their inner-city customers did not conform to the classic Marxist sense of the surplus value of worker's labor power, but rather involved purchasing power providing advantages to merchants over their customers. Merchants own businesses (and properties, in some cases); however, they are not capitalists who live off only their rent. Nonetheless, Black customers interpreted the economic hegemony of the Korean merchants in their neighborhood as exploitative and parasitic. They were further disillusioned when Korean merchants failed to meet their moral expectations as positive participants in the community.

## THE MORAL ECONOMY OF SOUTH LA

E.P. Thompson defined "moral economy" in the late eighteenth and nineteenth centuries among Chartists and other critics of capitalism as "confrontations in the market-place over access (or entitlements) to 'necessities,'" in his analysis of small-town food riots (1991, 337, 338). He documented the ways an emerging capitalist market economy violated "customary norms . . . and practices," resulting in violent outbreaks of class conflict (1991, 271). Political scientist James Scott (1985) writes about a similar moral economy with his analysis of rural resistance to super-exploitation by landlords engaging in market speculation in a Malaysian village. These works draw attention to the ways terms of exchange—the price of bread, sharecropping arrangements, rents, access to common land, crop prices—are locally embedded in moral expectations about holding powerful elites accountable to the poor in times of scarcity; I believe they can be applied to equally impoverished consumers in South LA. The subsistence ethic of having just enough to get by is common among people living near the margins of survival. Peasants, according to Scott, strive not to maximize profits, but to reduce the risk of falling below a bare survival income. They judge the fairness of taxes and rents by the degree to which such extractions permit the maintenance of a subsistence level. Like the peasants' unequal relations with landlords and elites, Black (and to a lesser extent, Latino) interviewees argued that merchants should adopt an ethic of reciprocity where reasonable balance exists between the needs of customers and merchants.

   Scott's thesis on the moral economy was inspired partially by Eric Wolf, who found that Mesoamerican communities fended off "capitalist encroachments" by preventing wealth from being mobilized in the community in "capitalist ways" (Wolf, as cited in Greenberg 1995, 79). Similarly, James Greenberg applied Wolf's "closed corporate community" to the Mixe of a village in Oaxaca to explore how elements of capitalist and non-capitalist modes of production are culturally integrated to define a syncretic social formation (1995, 68). He states, "The Mixe merchant is constrained by the norms of reciprocity to respond to his clients in the same way they treat him, that is, with respect, fairness, and even generosity" (1995, 78).

The same type of reciprocity was expected of Korean merchants in South LA by Black customers, who felt that merchants often failed to conform to the community's moral economic concerns. The cost of goods and services in inner cities is often higher due to the presumption of higher rates of shoplifting and robbery, higher rents, higher cost of insurance, and greater difficulty in getting goods delivered (Gold 2010, 75). However, for Black interviewees, a "good" merchant would offset some of these costs by offering a donation to customers preparing for funeral rites, thus canceling out a certain degree of overcharging. We see a commercial transaction balanced against custom and social pressure in these examples.

Despite the complaints of Black customers, some Korean merchants did make efforts to give back to the community, including extending credit to customers, accepting coupons, cashing checks, selling money orders to Black residents, and hiring them as employees. A few participated in their customers' funerals, weddings, birthdays, and other observances; others participated in block parties or exchanged food or gifts with customers on holidays. There was also merchant involvement in Black community organizations and the support of youth or elderly sports teams, other recreational programs, churches, local schools, and the police. In particular, merchants supported local programs such as the Youth Gang Service, Local Explorer Scouts, high school scholarships, the Jesse Jackson campaign, a senior citizen golf tournament, and a local homeless shelter.

These gifts place a future obligation on customers to reciprocate with the things they offer (see chapter 5). In South LA, much like in the Oaxaca village, "running a business is seen as a service to the community, as long as merchants roughly conform to the norms of reciprocity, they may accumulate wealth" (Greenberg 1995, 78). Black community leaders and activists attempted to insert a sense of morality into Korean merchants' capitalism and criticized their failure to employ, invest, and participate in the local community. However, these demands were sometimes contradictory. On one hand, Korean merchants were held to a postcapitalist standard (i.e., socially responsible capitalism). On the other hand, some African Americans wanted merchants to act like "real" capitalists and not small business owners: in their eyes, a reputable merchant would handle shoplifting rationally and write it off as a business expense, rather than reacting emotionally or personally.[7]

In addition, although Black interviewees expected Korean merchants to treat customers with flexibility, leniency, and generosity, as well as respect, fairness, and reciprocity, new immigrant merchants often lack "the skills, contacts, and practices required [for] maintaining a modicum of civility in their relations with customers. These included long-term relations with individual customers, familiarity with their outlooks and forms of sociability, a record of generosity, and willingness to provide jobs" (Gold 2010, 133). The most consistently negative images of Koreans among Black interviewees were of Korean store owners, because they tended to be rigid, not giving customers a break when they were slightly short on change. African Americans interpreted this behavior as Korean merchants unfairly lording their economic power over customers. These criticisms of the Korean immigrant merchants' lack of generosity come close to Thompson's moral economic process, which demands proper resource-sharing from owners who hoard economic resources.

A Black male truck driver interviewed in 1996 recalled what he observed at Korean-owned swap meets and criticized merchants' lack of flexibility:

> You know Koreans own stores in the swap meets. County recipient people go down there. Man, you go down there on a day when you get your welfare checks, they your friends. After the 9th, they short-line [short-change?]. If you're a dollar short, they won't sell it to you, even 50 cents. "No" [attempts to mimic a Korean accent, laughs]. I can't talk their language but they say no. . . . Koreans feel that if you have money to buy, they will be your friend. If you don't have money, they won't give it to you. I don't shop there because the clothes aren't good enough.

Similarly, a 49-year-old Black male security guard (1996) shared a painful experience with Korean merchants:

> They treat Blacks like shit. . . . If something is 49 cents and you have 48 they won't give it to you. This store by my house I told you about, well I had been going there for two years. I was short two pennies. I told her I'll bring it back. She knew where I lived, but she wouldn't sell it to me. I said: "Fine, I no come here." I lived just across the street, she could see my door. There are two markets so I chose [the] other market because of two cents.

A 25-year-old Black man (1996) living on unemployment and disability also recounted unpleasant experiences with Korean store owners. He believed that the merchants exercised a kind of power that was oppressive:

> I purchased something, and they wouldn't let me return it. It happens with other people. . . . I got kind of mad. They called in security and this whole big thing. They didn't have to do that. It's just like if you tell them you're missing something, they won't give it to you, and you have to have the receipt.

A number of Black customers discussed the issue of stealing at Korean-owned businesses, and their perspectives differed extensively from those of Korean interviewees. Each of my Korean interviewees had experienced at least a dozen holdups (many at gunpoint), and some did business from behind thick bulletproof glass. Nonetheless, Black customers resented being stereotyped as thieves. A 42-year-old Black female service worker (1992) stopped patronizing a store after being suspected of stealing countless times:

> At swap meets, I have had some unpleasant experiences. When I am looking around for something, the Korean merchants walk around with me. They are very watchful. You can't turn around without bumping in with them. They have many mirrors, and at one store, the Korean merchant stands upon a platform in order to watch people better. I could see this type of behavior at the May Co. [now a defunct department store chain], but not at a swap meet. I try to avoid this type of treatment by not shopping at Korean merchants. I do not like them to think that I am stealing, so I try to avoid confrontations.

Other customers also felt similarly disrespected. A 21-year-old Black male college student (1993) stated: "Last time in a store, the merchant looked suspiciously over my shoulder as if I was going to steal. They seemed to think they were better." A Black grocery owner contextualized Korean merchants' accusations of stealing by African Americans:

> [L]et me add the Korean perception of Black and White—White is good and Black is no good. So when we have somebody picking up milk it translates to, "All Blacks Are Thieves" which, of course, is untrue. A very small minority of any ethnic group are really thieves. The irony is that the same person who is calling that African American a "thief" will turn around and pay under the table for a case of merchandise so that he can save a little money here and make a little money there. What's the difference in the thievery? Both are trying to make it. I am talking about vendors in the community who will do anything to get a cut price. So in each case, we are taking. But my take is okay because he is taking from me! (Ussery 1994, 91)

As with this perspective, some Black interviewees contested the meaning of "stealing." While Korean merchants regarded it as evidence of shameless behavior, some Black interviewees considered it to be a question of poverty or a Scottian form of indirect everyday resistance (e.g., foot dragging, feigned ignorance, and sabotage).

Psychologist Halford Fairchild, who is half Japanese and half Black, also explains stealing among poor African Americans as a function of poverty:

> The terrible peril of African people places us in a position of having to do whatever we can do to survive, and a lot of times that means to steal. . . . We have an interesting situation, where Korean Americans are coming in as capitalists, as merchants, as individuals who are selling goods for a profit in convenience stores and liquor stores, and I'm sure they experience theft on a regular basis.

People steal because they don't have money to buy. (As cited in George 1992, 78)

Similarly, Jan Sunoo, a mediator with the federal Mediation and Conciliation Service and an LA City Human Relations Commissioner, noted that the tensions were mostly between Korean shopkeepers and poor (not middle-class) African Americans:

> The tension has to do with class and discrimination. . . . I don't think you see Korean merchants shooting Blacks in middle-class neighborhoods. I think what we're seeing is a very specific problem that happens in poverty. . . . The violence has gotten worse. I think that they are scapegoating these Korean grocers, who are not really the major problem. It's very hard to attack the establishment, or to attack the educational system, or to change the political economic structure for someone on the street. So he'll say, "Well, maybe I can't change the world, but at least I can get this damn grocer to respect me." (As cited in George 1992, 83, 84)

Some customers offered concrete suggestions regarding how to improve relations between Korean merchants and Black customers. A 40-year-old Black female manager at a law firm (1992) stated:

> Merchants should become familiar with the community and the community's culture in which they conduct their business. Merchants should try to avoid a "9-5 business relationship" with the community. When they open their businesses, they should get to know their customers and educate themselves about their consumers. . . . The merchants should attempt to practice what large department stores practice by stocking the items that the community frequently buys. *They should not just take a capitalistic approach* [my emphasis].

A 35-year-old Black female teacher (1992) advised store owners: "The merchants should be more polite and courteous to everyone. Don't judge people by the way they look or dress. Don't treat them as unintelligent or ignorant." Similarly, a 33-year-old Black female cosmetologist (1992) stated: "They should try to be more open-minded and friendly. They should do away with their superior attitudes. People should not have superior attitudes because they own a business or make more money. Everyone is working."

A Black male college student (1993) was more extreme in his views and believed the only way to resolve the problem was to remove Korean merchants from local neighborhoods:

> Problems can't be resolved in a constitutional way unless the Koreans are moved out. One can't say that the Koreans can't be there, it is their right, but as long as they are there, there will be conflict. The tension, however, can be

lessened by negotiations with interest groups to make more peace. It may not resolve the conflict, but it can release some of the tension.

This interviewee later changed his views and ended up encouraging Korean merchants to negotiate their relationship with African Americans, ultimately demonstrating that there is room for compromise. It should also be noted, however, that this interviewee's and others' comments displayed a somewhat misplaced antagonism toward the petty bourgeois Korean merchants, instead of directing their anger at the real source of economic power—the elite.

## CLASS AND STATUS

The centrality of domination and surveillance within Korean-Black relations raises the issues of prestige, honor, and dignity. Weber (1961/1946) devoted more attention to the role of politics and power in his analysis of social life than did Marx, who focused on economic domination. In contrast to Marx's economic determinist view of the "class situation," Weber's notion of "status situation" was determined by a specific positive or negative social estimation of honor (1946, 186–87). Weber's "classes" were stratified according to their relations of production and acquisition of goods, whereas "status groups" were stratified according to their consumption of goods as represented by special "styles of life" (Weber 1946, 193). Although Weber separated class from status in his study of domination, he clearly saw that status relations overlap with class relations. Most importantly, Weber viewed ethnicity as an extreme case of "status group."

Following this approach, Bryan Turner (1988) draws attention to two related conceptions of status; namely, tatus as lifestyle (cultural status) and status as politico-legal entitlement (the citizenship component)[8]:

> A status group is therefore a collection of individuals who are organized to maintain or expand their social privileges by a mechanism of social closure to protect existing monopolies of privilege against outsiders, and by usurpation to expand the benefits by reference to proximate or superior status groups. The existence of status groups inevitably involves social conflict and social struggle, although these forms of social struggle may be frequently disguised or hidden. (1988, 8)

Along with this inevitable conflict, social status also involves practices that exhibit cultural distinctions imperative to all social stratification (Bourdieu 1977). Status may be conceptualized as the totality of cultural practices, like dress, speech, outlook, and bodily disposition. The social location of a group within a system is expressed by their taste and aspects of their lifestyle. Social groups distinguish themselves from others through self-determined superior dispositions, bodily gestures, speech, and deportment.

For the Black community, class distinction has been more nuanced than for Whites. As Sides (2003, 123) notes, during the Jim Crow era, many African Americans conceived of class as a social distinction involving values/ morality, lifestyle, and aspirations (e.g., genteel behavior, impeccable church attendance, and a predilection for fine clothing) rather than an economic one (wealth, occupational status, or relationship to the means of production). As barriers to employment and residential segregation were reduced in the 1960s, economic distinction between African Americans became more significant.

Class distinction within the Black community of LA is spatialized. The area that came to be known as South Central was traditionally split between East and West, with Crenshaw Boulevard as the dividing line. "East" (East South Central) which includes Watts, was the distinctly poorer, more working-class part of the community, and this was my research area. As Tom Bradley, the city's first African American mayor, noted, residents in the West (West South Central) were:

> The least poor among us. . . . The wealthier people include churchgoing folks who believed in education and hard work, or middle-class values, even if they didn't have middle-class money, whereas the further south and east you went in Los Angeles, the less of that people you had. (Simon 2011, 63).

As Khalil Edwards, organizing director of the Los Angeles Black Worker Center, similarly pointed out,

> Among this Black community, you have different class statuses. You have folks who have higher income, [are] middle class and are homeowners that are able to stay, and then you have folks that are making a living wage and are worried if they are going to be able to afford their rent in a few months. (*LAT* Sept. 17, 2017).

Mary, a 26-year-old Black female dental office aide (1993), felt slighted when a merchant told her not to touch the merchandise if she couldn't afford it:

> In a shopping mall, a store was leased by a Korean store. The lady shouted out prices rudely as my friend and I walked down the aisle as [if] to say that we couldn't afford the merchandise and not to touch it. . . . Korean merchants treat African Americans with less dignity. They have screamed at my girl and other kids when they are annoyed at them. They believe they are doing us a favor by selling items to us instead of the reverse.

At another store, I noticed a Black customer call the Korean shopkeeper "Mr. King." I later found out that the merchant wanted to be addressed this way. Although the merchant and his customer burst into laughter and thus deflected the formality and potential hierarchy this label suggested, Bourdieu's idea that distinction in taste matters in the forming of status boundaries is useful here. In this simple act of self-renaming, the merchant enacted a strategy of promoting and differentiating himself from his Black customers. Bourdieu pointed out similar behavior among the petit bourgeoisie, typically the small shopkeeper, clerk, or salesman, who used strategies of pretension to further their own ends: "He [the petit bourgeoisie] is as insecure as the bourgeois is self-assured, incapable of playing 'the game of culture as a game,' anxious about the right classifications and about knowing the right things" (Hoffmann 1986, 46). Accordingly, some Korean immigrant store owners found it necessary to make status assertions by distancing themselves from, or degrading, their customers.

Status differentiation is also related to issues of social or political rights. Stereotypical attributes are used for status distinction and determine the behavior that different groups believe they are owed (Williams 1991, 77). Status struggles related to differences in social honor between African Americans and Koreans were bound up with claims that each group wanted to be treated equally as citizens. African Americans contested both Koreans' and the larger society's domination and surveillance over them, and in doing so, made claims for their full social citizenship. Class contestation, then, should be differentiated from status struggle. However, they are not mutually exclusive and should be together.[9] We can best understand how status and class operate in the cultural distribution of prestige, honor, and respect through such institutions as the school, university, hospital, prison, or, in this case, small businesses.

## CONCLUSION

This chapter has examined the question of class relations in the Black-Korean tensions of 1992. It became apparent from my interviewees' responses that discussions of class were viewed through the categories of race and ethnicity in this conflict; however, they commented explicitly on economic relations. So they were keenly aware of class issues. Class relations entail more than differences in income, occupation, and wealth. Although Korean immigrant merchants are self-employed and are not capitalists in the traditional sense, they often occupy an exploitative position. Black customers complained of

experiencing opportunity hoarding, exploitation, surveillance, and poor treatment from the merchants. While Korean immigrants may have appealed to
a merchant logic rooted in a capitalist mode of production, Black customers
turned to a moral economy, protesting the exploitation and a violation of the
moral order by merchants accumulating profits.

Many Black interviewees disapproved of Korean immigrant-owned businesses and their perceived exploitation of the community. The nature of this
exploitation between Korean merchants and their inner-city customers was
hierarchical, with the purchasing power of merchants giving them an advantage over inner-city customers who resented the economic hegemony of the
Korean merchants. Korean immigrant merchants in South LA were primarily
distributors, selling the products of large corporations to minority customers
in ghetto areas that corporations were neglecting. However, one wonders
why minority distributors such as Korean immigrants attracted such a large
amount of antagonism, which was not directed at majority (White) distributors? These dynamics call for examining other dimensions of social inequality, such as race and the politics of citizenship, beyond simply interpreting it
in terms of class exploitation.

At the same time, a common explanation for conflict between immigrant
entrepreneurs and native minority customers is African Americans' low rates
of self-employment. A group of pundits, politicians, and researchers emphasized the low rates of Black business ownership and vindictive conflicts with
immigrant merchants as evidence of African Americans' dysfunctional behavior and retrograde values, rather than as due to poor economic conditions,
lack of resources, and discrimination (Gold 2010, 233, 236). However, "from
the antebellum era until the Great Depression, African Americans did have
a small yet [accomplished] business class" (Gold 2004, 319). As discussed
in chapter 1, after the 1880s, increases in residential segregation due to Jim
Crow laws and competition from European immigrants resulted in a significant reduction in Black entrepreneurship (Gold 2004, 318).

The sociological literature also reflects the dominant discourse that some
ethnic groups have had higher rates of participation in small business ownership than others. A decade after the riots, the 2000 Census data indicated
that almost 37 percent of Koreans operated small businesses with employees,
while only 11 percent of African Americans and 18 percent of Latinos did
(Yu, as cited in N. Kim 2008, 141). While on the surface these data support
the dominant discourse, these interpretations deflect attention away from
institutionalized racism: "Because of the focus of the literature, the issue of
Black unemployment in the U.S., for example, is implicitly characterized as a
problem of the Black population, rather than of institutionalized racism" (N.
Kim 2008, 164). It should be noted that Black interviewees were well aware

that one of the sources of Black-Korean tensions was the dearth of Black business ownership. Black community activists have long regarded political and economic obstacles—including the lack of Black-owned businesses and the presence of immigrant entrepreneurs in low-income areas—as symptomatic of the more generalized oppression of Black people.

The economic hegemony of Korean immigrants and class conflicts between them and inner-city customers were often effaced within the dominant discourse surrounding Black-Korean tensions during the unrest. Nonetheless, I argue that this racialized class conflict developed in part as a way of reproducing the American capitalist state. I would suggest modifying the Marxist framework so that certain class conflicts are interpreted as conflicts between an immigrant petty bourgeoisie and the urban poor, especially during times of crisis. The economic dispossession of Black people and the diaspora of Koreans were associated with the creation of a new kind of proletariat, one that was dispersed throughout the world and was found in an enormous growth of low-wage service jobs that undermined generational upward mobility and undercut the formation of communities. In the severely segregated society that is Los Angeles, the petty bourgeoisie, including Korean shopkeepers, symbolized the system of exploitation of the urban poor. Merchants were on the front lines of class struggle, while "financial houses were protected by their spatial invisibility and by their crafty mechanisms that create economic distance" (Prashad 2001, 104).

The unequal class and power relations between Korean merchants and Black customers entailed aspects of domination and surveillance as well as exploitation. Much like Foucault's concepts of disciplinary power and the panopticon, African Americans felt surveilled and humiliated by Korean merchants. Accordingly, in the next chapter, I will scrutinize various interactions between a Korean merchant and his Latino and Black customers in order to understand how and why disputes occurred, and discuss the implications for property ownership and civil rights.

## NOTES

1. Saxton (1990) is equally relevant as a case study involving Irish and Chinese workers.

2. For more on this fallacy, see Omi and Winant (1994), especially chapter 1, "Ethnicity."

3. Although it is not true that Korean merchants regularly return to Korea with the money they made in South LA, this statement conveys feelings that Korean merchants are siphoning away residents' money instead of spending it in the community.

4. The last interviewee was clearly on the side of Korean merchants in her disdain for the Black underclass.

5. She was interviewed by an African American research assistant. Thus, I can discount the possibility that she was trying to say something positive about the interviewer's culture or ethnicity.

6. Foucault's notion of the panopticon relates to a high surveillance prison as a metaphor for modern "disciplinary" societies and their pervasive inclination to observe and normalize. See chapter 5 for more on this concept.

7. This is not to say that large outlets never prosecute shoplifters or always write these losses off as a business expense.

8. Turner derives his notion of status from Bourdieu's conception of distinction and Marshall's discussion of citizenship.

9. US sociologists tend to conflate class with status (Atkinson 2009, 899).

*Part III*

# BLACK, LATINO, AND KOREAN RELATIONS AFTER THE UNREST

*How Race and Ethnicity Have Become the Expresser of Changing Class Relations*

*Chapter Five*

# Class Relations of Surveillance

Despite much literature on Black-Korean tensions in 1990s Los Angeles (Min 1996; C. Kim 1999; Lee 2002), there have been few attempts at a detailed analysis of actual interactions between the two groups. Notable exceptions are Stewart (1989), Bailey (1996), and Ryoo (2005), who have written thoughtfully about cultural differences and language barriers between Korean merchants and Black customers, which tends to inhibit friendly small talk. As discussed in previous chapters, Black customers often view Koreans as sullen, unfriendly, and/or racist, and the fatal altercation between Du and Harlins, discussed in chapter 2, was inseparable from the accumulation of everyday tensions and sedimentation of stereotypes.

Notwithstanding these contributions to the literature, these authors' examinations of inner-city store disputes are limited to questions of retail propriety. Moreover, linguistic and cultural differences alone do not automatically produce interethnic tension. The presumption of suspicious conduct by Koreans and a sense by African Americans that they are chronically disrespected, for example, are tendencies develop within larger sociohistorical relationships (C. Kim 2010, 538). In other words, inner-city store disputes are part and parcel of deindustrialization, segregation, and neglect (Karandinos, Hart, Montero Castrillo, and Bourgois 2014, 3). Utilizing Bourdieu's concept of habitus, theater scholar Ju Yon Kim notes that the economics of these encounters are *embodied*, mediated, and complicated by the behavioral and perceptual habits of those involved (2010, 545). To better understand how, why, and over what issues disputes develop, a processual analysis is necessary: what is going on during actual face-to-face interactions between Korean shopkeepers and inner-city customers?

As Ryoo urged, we need to reconsider taken-for-granted notions that "interaction between Korean immigrants and African Americans are inherently

139

problematic and full of conflict" (2005, 82). Sociologist Jennifer Lee (2002) has pointed out that contrary to popular misconceptions, most merchant-customer interactions are positive, civil, and routine, including those between Korean immigrant merchants and their Black customers. However, it should be noted that as an idea, "civil" interaction is not without problems. Lee's study does not offer an explanation as to why seemingly civil interactions sometimes erupt into large-scale conflicts. Furthermore, it is notable that after the unrest, Korean merchants (and their customers) attempted to maintain civil and friendly interactions with each other (see next chapter). Based on videotaped and audiotaped interactions at a beauty supply store and jewelry store in a Midwestern city, Ryoo (2005) also reported positive interactions between Korean shopkeepers and African American customers, which has been obscured by prevailing research.

In this chapter, I explore how shopping at Korean immigrant liquor stores shaped customer subjectivity. Many of the interactions discussed in my study constituted simple business transactions (e.g., inquiring about the availability or prices of merchandise), while other interactions went beyond simple exchanges. The store encounters took place in the context of a proliferation of techniques through which customers' behavior was closely monitored, controlled, and regulated. I suggest that these disciplinary measures and surveillance backfired, as customers felt they curtailed their freedom of movement: As Scott asserted, some of the most explosive acts of resistance are sparked by an indignity, an injustice, or a refusal to reproduce hegemonic relations in which subordinates show deference in the presence of the powerful (1990, 203). Expanding Scott's notion of resistance, we need to examine the subtler forms of power: discipline, opposition, and accommodation.

Violence must be understood functionally—as a constitutive element of a social situation marked by the distributive effects of market and state forces—rather than as a deviance from the norm or a specific cultural trait of certain groups (Karandinos et al. 2014). While fully recognizing the political and economic factors that contributed to the development of interracial tensions, this chapter visits a Korean-owned liquor store in 2002, examines the operation of power in everyday interactions, and analyzes which factors contributed to disputes, including under what circumstances these disputes escalated into violence, including murder.[1] I interpret customer-merchant relationships in terms of the patterns of surveillance and power that defined day-to-day interactions in the public and commercial spaces of the post-industrial city.[2] It is also crucial to recognize that inner-city merchant-customer encounters were constantly being shaped by media, extra-local politics, economic conditions, and social movements.

My analysis of surveillance, control, and discipline at the inner-city liquor stores and markets shows a clear influence from the work of Foucault. He viewed many societal institutions, such as prisons, courts, hospitals, barracks, schools, and factories, as practicing techniques associated with eighteenth-century humanist Jeremy Bentham's notion of the panopticon:

> that the inmates should be caught up in a power situation of which they are themselves the bearers. . . . The Panopticon is a machine for dissociating the see/being seen dyad: in the peripheric ring, one is totally seen, without ever seeing; in the central tower, one sees everything without being seen. (Foucault 1977, 201–2)

As a means of surveillance, the panopticon facilitates the collection and storage of information, and provides the means of monitoring behavior and complying with instructions through a physical structure of control based on visibility. Meanwhile, the subject population's compliance is achieved by economic, coercive, or normative sanctions. Thus, the ability to detect criminality—in this case, Korean merchants' surveillance and incessant interrogation of customers' movements—is the technique for regulating and disciplining the marginalized poor, and thus becomes an instrument of power. In addition, crime is gauged by degrees of (ab)normality.

Critics have increasingly pointed out that the ubiquitous nature of the Foucauldian notion of discipline leaves little room for social change and, in particular, the role of resistance. "If it is true that the grid of 'discipline' is becoming clearer and more extensive," philosopher Michel de Certeau asks, "is it not—then—all the more urgent to discover how an entire society resists being reduced to it?" (1984, xiv). De Certeau's goal was to examine the small but multifaceted acts of resistance to discipline that abound in everyday life. He also made an important distinction between strategies and tactics: a strategy is "the calculation (or manipulation) of power relationships that becomes possible as soon as a subject with will and power (a business, an army, a city, a scientific institution) can be isolated," while a tactic is "an art of the weak," the less powerful actors in society (1984, 35–37). Everyday activities such as dwelling, moving about, speaking, reading, shopping, and cooking seem to correspond to the characteristics of tactical ruses and surprises: clever tricks of the "weak" within a social order established by the "strong," such as outwitting the adversary on their own turf (1984, 39–40).

De Certeau was able to point out the limits of Foucault's analysis, such as ignoring the fact that human actors are not always completely dominated; people do not always respond to or resist institutional control. After all, in this case study, neither merchants nor customers paid much attention to the surveillance camera; only the police would consult it if a crime occurred.[3] De Certeau attempted to correct what he saw as an "exclusive and obsessive" concern with mechanisms of repression by paying attention to various ways in which ordinary people subvert, evade, and redefine the disciplinary apparatus. Notwithstanding this important theoretical intervention, he was also a conservative defender of the status quo: he failed to go beyond endless diverse pedestrian or consumer behavior, or the experiential maps of individual actors, and his theory was devoid of materialist analysis.[4] It is important to ask what is going on, who engages in it, with whom, when, and how. Wolf urges us to ask, "For what and for whom is all this going on and—indeed—against whom?" (1990, 591). This point is especially important because store disputes in early 1990s LA were often about class relations and did not develop in a vacuum. Finally, de Certeau's analysis is blind to considerations of race and gender, which glosses the relations of domination and subordination within these categories.

With these caveats, this chapter examines the causes, developments, and consequences of escalating violence within customer-merchant relations that involved shoplifting, hold ups, and other incidents. I focus on the micro-techniques of surveillance and social control that targeted the body as an object to be watched and manipulated. Merchant-customer interactions within the inner-city liquor store are analyzed as a site of de Certeau's everyday life in which the "tactics" of the weak can outwit the "strategy" of the strong. In this case, the strong were the liquor store owners, whose strategy was surveillance, and the weak were the customers, whose strategies included defiance and confrontation. Thus, my analysis also draws upon Scott's (1985) notion of everyday forms of resistance against the rich and powerful.[5] This chapter is also predicated on the understanding that both merchants and customers were able to coerce, contest, or manipulate each other, although they did not hold equally powerful social positions. Merchants and customers were not equal players, but rather participants in a power dynamic that was predefined by broader racial, gender, and class relations.

Stores in South LA were often equipped with security cameras: owners and employees keep an eye on their customers, owners watch their employees, and multiple surveillance cameras watch everyone. Given this culture of surveillance, participant observation[6] may seem to be just another "eye" of the panopticon; however, in order to conduct a processual analysis of how, why, and over what issues disputes develop, this chapter draws on approximately 200 hours of direct observation of interactions between Korean merchants, inner-city customers, and employees at a Korean liquor store in South LA from January to August of 2002. I did not rely on a surveillance camera installed in the store. My research assistant Dave Kim, who worked at his father's stores from 1994 to 2002, recorded observations two to three times a week and also videotaped the interactions; he had permission from his father to do this. Kim's observations were mostly in the form of taking notes while working at the cash register or bagging groceries at Kimbo Liquor Store. This provided an excellent opportunity for Kim to observe the entire store, a vantage point that could not be captured by a security camera, while giving him firsthand experience with interracial merchant-customer interactions.

## KIMBO LIQUOR STORE

Kimbo Liquor Store was located off Vernon and Central Avenues in Historic South Central LA, in a small shopping plaza.[7] Since Vernon Avenue is a busy street, it was convenient for passersby to drop in. The store's appearance was reminiscent of many other post-unrest liquor stores, with a prison-like, concrete, boxy structure. The majority of the regulars were neighborhood residents, and there was an apartment complex nearby. For the most part, people in the neighborhood seemed to know and take care of one another. In the 1980s and before, the neighborhood surrounding the store was predominantly African American. However, by the mid-1990s, it was about 50 percent African American and 50 percent Latino. When Scott, the Korean American storekeeper, bought Kimbo Liquor Store in 1994, the proportion of Latinos was clearly increasing.

Kimbo Liquor Store was formerly called Star Liquor and Junior Market, and had been run by a Korean couple before Scott bought it; before that, the store was called Fred's Liquor. Under Scott's management, this store had been caught twice selling alcohol to minors, which may have earned it a reputation with the local anti-liquor store campaign group as a "public nuisance." In both instances, Scott was heavily fined.[8] Other difficulties running the store included persistent danger,[9] high employee turnover,[10] and rising rent. Generally speaking, the store did better on hot days, and spring and summer generated more sales than fall and winter. However, there was also increased verbal and physical conflict between Scott and the customers and among customers, and there was more petty theft on hot days.[11] Welfare (Aid to Families with Dependent Children or AFDC) checks and most wage earners' checks arrived at the beginning of the month, so the end of the month was also a particularly "dangerous" time, since many customers' money had run out. It is worth noting that the 1992 unrest occurred near the end of the month.

Unlike other businesses in South LA, no bulletproof glass window—often costing $10,000 or more—separated Scott from customers at Kimbo Liquor Store, and thus, transactions took place face-to-face. Scott came to recognize the importance of having this barrier removed,[12] especially because without it, Scott could easily chase any customer making a beer run.[13] He was also able to shake customers' hands, emphasize his jokes with hand gestures, and interact more personally with his customers. In return, they had a clearer view of his face and vice versa.

Like other Korean merchants, Scott was college educated and a self-described workaholic. Unlike other Korean merchants, however, Scott ran the store by himself with minimal help from his son and one part-time Black or Latino employee.[14] Scott once worked two years without taking a day off, and he sometimes slept inside the store six days a week because of the long commute home. Scott's family members were concerned about his safety because of potential danger and conflicts with customers, but they were more worried about his health than anything else; the effects of running the liquor store took a major toll on his body. Compared with other Korean merchants, Scott was considered an old-timer. He arrived in the US in 1974 when he was 27 years old. He had been a college student, but he was then required to fulfil his military service in the South Korean army before he came to the States. He worked the graveyard shift as a janitor, eventually moving on to work as an electrician. Eventually, he and his wife went on to own a sandwich store in Santa Ana and a doughnut shop in Cyprus. Since then, his wife has worked in a factory, which has provided good benefits for the family. Scott also worked as a liquor salesman in the South LA area for a few years prior to running the liquor store.

Although Scott still spoke English with an accent, he had a large vocabulary that included American slang, unlike other Korean merchants; he commonly used phrases such as "don't spill the beans," "let bygones be bygones," and "kick the bucket." He was also knowledgeable about American politics and popular culture, such as the 1960s social movements, the movies of John Wayne and Frank Sinatra, and baseball. This knowledge helped him converse and communicate with his customers at all of his businesses. He was often affectionately called "papa" or "papa san" by his customers, and his son was known as "junior." Nonetheless, Scott and his son Daniel did not expect to be fully accepted by the surrounding community, no matter how much they tried. When he walked outside to go to the post office, McDonald's, a check-cashing place, or any other business, Daniel was often the only person who was not Black or Latino. He was often reminded that he was an outsider. For example, once while driving to his father's store, Daniel pulled up next to a group of Latino teenagers, and they opened their car window and spat on the hood of Daniel's car. Another time, while waiting at a stoplight, he made eye contact with a Black teenager at the bus stop who immediately said, "What the fuck are you looking at? You ching-chong," and continued to curse as Daniel drove away. Even inside their store, customers have told Scott and Daniel to "go back to China, Japan, or wherever the fuck you came from."

Despite these verbal conflicts, the store provided a stable source of income and was Scott's most successful business. He took pride in the vast improvements he made in the store's infrastructure of the store, including upgrading the plumbing and roofing and painting the store. Most importantly, Scott enjoyed working at the store, feeling that not all the customers were bad or disrespectful. He expressed that he had met many interesting "characters," and that there was rarely a dull moment.

## Store Owner's Strategy

For the most part, my observations led me to infer that most interactions between Scott and his customers were civil, but somewhat constrained and wary; that is, there were sometimes undercurrents of humiliation, insult, or subtle discipline. Scott employed several strategies to maintain civil encounters with his customers. First, he cultivated friendships with customers, with a focus on the "interactional" rather than "transactional" aspects of service encounters. Thus, he greeted his regular Latino customers with "¿Qué pasa?" (meaning "How are you?"). Some customers greeted him by saying "*annyonghaseyo?*" (meaning "How are you?" in Korean). When Latino customers bought 12 or more cans of beer on busy Friday or Saturday nights, he would jokingly yell, "¡Apúrate!" or "¡Ándele!" ("Hurry up" in Spanish). Jokes, laughter, personal communication, shared attitudes, and words of support were used to evoke personal and friendly relations with customers. Sharing attitudes entails showing agreement and support about the objects or reality they both possessed or experienced, or showing support for the other party's state or experience.

Contrary to most studies of interactions between Korean merchants and their inner-city customers, small talk (about the weather, sports, music, or pop culture) and personal communication were quite common between Scott and customers, [15] and often initiated by Scott.[16] Joking and laughing, producing a lighthearted climate and temporary sense of bonding, were crucial elements of a positive, rapport-building interaction between shopkeeper and customers in the present study.[17] Scott was aware that being humorous and funny with his customers was good for business and encouraged customers to give him repeat and regular patronage. Scott's strategy was the exception.

Notwithstanding this generally successful strategy, there was also the danger that his use of "confrontation" and humor might unwittingly humiliate or offend a customer. At 10:05 p.m. on January 25, 2002, Daniel walked into the store and saw a regular customer, a Black man in his fifties, talking to Scott.[18]

*C:* Your daddy, he crazy man! Hey, your son oughta whoop your ass!

*S:* Get out! You know, Carl's Jr. commercial, don't bothering me!

*C:* Shut up! [Walks out]

The customer's final "shut up" can be construed as a defensive remark or as half teasing, indicating the importance of context and connotation. Some might note the frequent usage of "profane" language and "aggravated" teasing, but Scott's humorous interaction encouraged customers to return to his store. Scott even invented some of his own sayings, such as, "I'm sick and tired of your face"[19] or "O.J. Simpson say don't bother me," or "Carl's Jr. commercial say don't bother me." It seems that his accent and ironic smile made these phrases funnier and less threatening; some customers even suggested he should have become a comedian.

Despite these friendly exchanges, communication barriers were not uncommon between Scott and his customers. Some Latinos took Scott's teasing and mock threats as actual hostility. For instance, once Scott greeted a customer with "¿Qué pasa, cabrón?"[20] The customer was insulted and asked Scott why he used the term. Scott apologized, realizing that the customer was not in the mood to joke or did not like Scott cursing in Spanish.[21] In situations when a customer was unable to understand Scott, his son observed that both parties spoke in a condescending manner toward each other. For example, a customer spoke more slowly and/or in broken English to Scott when Scott did not understand what the customer was saying. Likewise, Scott responded condescendingly or sarcastically to a customer who did not understand him.

A second strategy Scott often used was to "go native." He had become acculturated to local South LA culture and to American business practices, and he had become a part of the community which was a testimony to his symbiotic existence with his customers and other local residents. In a way, his customers had exposed him to their lifestyle—teaching him their characteristic body gestures, movements, and attitudes—and he had been receptive to this.[22] His workplace became his second home. Nonetheless, the power structures that privileged Korean immigrant merchants also reinforced the hierarchy that subordinated inner-city customers: shopkeepers generally had the power to access and appropriate cultures of the inner city whenever, wherever, and for however long they wished. Thus, Scott had the freedom to become a man of "South LA," acquiring its slang and adopting African American Vernacular English and simple Spanish phrases. In addition, he ate at local establishments several times a week: fast food restaurants, local taco stands, hamburger shops, and pastry stores. He also conducted his banking and postal business in or around South LA. He even paid one of the employees of the laundromat to do his laundry once a week. Finally, he found local mechanics and repairmen to be more trustworthy, efficient, and cheaper.

Scott enjoyed bartering all kinds of goods and services with his customers. For instance, a customer who worked at a seafood store brought him jumbo shrimp or fish, and in return, Scott gave him beer. Another customer who worked at a chicken store brought him chicken in return for groceries. Yet another worked for a bakery, and Scott exchanged bagels, bread, and cake for beer. Once, he ran into one of his customers working a hot dog stand at Dodgers Stadium, and the customer offered Scott free popcorn and peanuts. Interestingly, unlike other Korean merchants, Scott did not make donations to local institutions. Instead, he literally ate, slept, and lived in South LA. He spent his money and used the goods and services of South LA. In a strange yet startling way, Daniel saw his father becoming more and more like his customers. Although I can't make any assumptions about his intentions, Scott made a conscious decision to do it. When he went to run an errand, it was not uncommon for residents to greet, honk, or acknowledge him. Some of his customers brought him desserts and barbecue, especially during the holidays. One Thanksgiving, he received three full plates of turkey, mashed potatoes, and other fixings from his customers. In return, he gave out posters, T-shirts, shot glasses, and key chains to his customers during holidays. He was even invited to go golfing and fishing in Las Vegas with some of his customers. Scott was on such good terms with some of his regular "good" customers that they invited him to family funerals.

As a third strategy, Scott made it a habit to get to know his customers, collecting data on their purchases and preferences. He learned, for example, what brand of beer they drank, what type of cigarettes they smoked, where they worked, and their hobbies. He also knew that customers who bought malt liquor tended not to have much money and were likely to be alcoholics and/or unemployed. Customers who bought more expensive beer or wine coolers tended to be younger, in their twenties. For Scott, the amount of beer purchased at one time also served as an indicator about the customer's economic and/or family status.[23] Scott kept close tabs on his customers' movements, activities, employment status, criminal history (if applicable), family dynamics, friendships and romantic relationships, living situation, religion, attitudes, and beliefs. He studied the words, gestures, attitudes, and values displayed by each customer.

Scott also exercised certain practices that could be interpreted as spatial governmentality, or "new mechanisms of social ordering based on spatial regulations" (Merry 2001, 16).[24] To prevent theft, Scott stocked the expensive laundry detergent away from the door and limited shelf displays to no more than three or four boxes of that brand of detergent. Also, cigarettes were placed away from the first row on shelves above the counter, which was a result of customers reaching over the top overhead drawers to steal packs of cigarettes. Spatial regulation often entailed a temporary "time-out" for problematic customers. In other words, customers who had verbal or physical fights with Scott were put on "probation," and only after weeks or sometimes months did Scott allow them back into the store. After the probation period, the customers usually behaved, whether out of fear or resignation.

## Surveillance

Legal scholar Anne-Marie Harris and her colleagues define consumer retail profiling as "a type of differential treatment of consumers in the marketplace based on race/ethnicity that constitutes denial of or degradation in the products and/or services that are offered to the consumer" (2005, 163). Allegations of racial profiling, especially in retail settings, are not new. Many African Americans and other racial minorities, whether they are wealthy or not, are said to experience "shopping while black" or even "shop and frisk" (being detained and questioned after paying for items or simply leaving a store). Numerous qualitative researchers who have interviewed Black shoppers have concluded that African Americans are treated differently than Whites in retail encounters and that consumer racial profiling may be even more pervasive than the type of profiling associated with "driving while Black" (Harris et al. 2005). Black customers from Philadelphia and New York City, interviewed about their shopping experiences in predominantly White communities, complained of being ignored, treated rudely, or followed by merchants (Lee 2000, 361). Other studies have shown that over-surveillance of African Americans is a common occurrence, although other minority groups experience similar levels of perceived discrimination. People tend to think of the typical shoplifter as a young, Black male, even though law enforcement statistics actually show that the most common offender is a White female (Schreer et al. 2009, 1433).

In 2014, two high-profile retailers in New York, Macy's and Barneys, each paid more than a half million dollars to settle racial profiling claims after investigations by the state's Civil Rights Bureau. Employees of CVS, one of the largest pharmacy chains in the nation, filed a class-action lawsuit in 2015, alleging that their supervisors instructed them to profile and follow Black and Latino customers to prevent shoplifting, because "black people always are the ones that are the thieves" and "lots of Hispanic people steal."[25] The former employees—who are Black and Latino—also allege they endured racial discrimination and were subjected to racist slurs by their managers.

Surveillance techniques position inner-city customers as delinquent, poor, and untrustworthy, and Korean merchants as suspicious, racist, and greedy. Some merchants did equate inner-city customers with crime and substituted stereotypes for probable cause. Scott, in contrast, did not follow customers around the store and did his best to keep things legal and pleasant. However, this does not mean he did not engage in common surveillance techniques among Korean merchants in South LA. He would often rely on class-based criteria (customers' clothing) to identify potential troublemakers. He subjected his predominantly Black and Latino customers to surveillance and sometimes body searches based on their behavioral cues. However, customers don't have to subject themselves to body searches or they can refuse. This type of surveillance is a common complaint in many federal court decisions involving customer allegations of racial profiling in the marketplace (Harris et al. 2005). Typically, merchants justify these civil rights violations against Black and Latino customers by stating that they constitute a necessary precaution against shoplifting or armed robbery.

These surveillance techniques could be interpreted as controlling or coercive. In the absence of the presence of law enforcement, such merchant-customer interactions illustrate how private citizens can become agents of coercion in civil society, in addition to the state. Feeling vulnerable to criminal activity, merchants often take justice into their own hands because they perceive the authorities to be neglectful of their needs. In other words, merchants believe it is legitimate to harass suspicious customers, catch shoplifters, or even use violence in order to manage their insecurity and fear. Scott also felt that confrontation was a successful deterrent to bad behavior. When handling a customer who regularly stole or created other problems in the store, Scott would yell or curse at, harass or threaten, or kick the customer out. He was relentless and stubborn because some customers perceived such interactions as a game. As Scott noted, "Some will try to steal, and if they get caught, they will simply put the beer back, with no sign of remorse." In instances where customers complained, resisted, or exhibited undesirable behaviors, they were met with threats from Scott, who would reprimand or call the police.

Like most Korean merchants in South LA, Scott sorted and classified customers, using differential treatment by creating profiles: tough customers and ordinary customers. Based on this emic categorization, he aimed to exert control over "tough" customers by showing he was in control over any conflict that may arise. When a customer entered the store with an aggressive attitude, Scott reciprocated the aggression; he overplayed his masculinity with tough customers. For instance, if a young, tall, muscular male customer came in and yelled "What's up?" Scott usually responded with a louder, deeper voice than usual, and sometimes with a curse word as well.[26] Over the years, Scott developed an intuition that could be used for discerning which customers may be a nuisance or threat to the store. If the customer seemed intimidating, Scott became more aggressive verbally and physically. He used his "game face," trying hard not to show any hint of fear.

For heuristic purposes, I will now examine in some detail disputes and possible confrontations between Scott and his customers. Most customers in these interactions were male, and the involvement of alcohol always increased the possibility of a violent confrontation. In these interactions, Scott attempted to control and discipline customers through an objectification of the subjects. Scott tended to reprimand his customers if they were young or female and showed signs that they might drink too much. For instance, at 9:36 p.m. on January 30, 2002, a regular customer, a Black woman in her forties, walked in.

*S:* Today, second time, third time coming. You do it yourself? [He is asking whether she is drinking all those beers herself]

*C:* No, me and my friend.

*S:* You strong stomach. Magnum, mucho strong.

*C:* Ha ha, Scott.

*S:* All right.

Similarly, at 6:25 p.m. on February 11, 2002, a Latino customer in his late twenties walked into the store. Daniel did not recognize him, but Scott did. The overweight customer bought two 40-ounce bottles of Budweiser.

*C:* ¿Que pasa, cabrón?

*S:* You cabrón. You codo [Spanish word for elbow, and the gesture of pointing to an elbow signifies someone who is cheap][27]

*C:* Free beer?

*S:* Feliz Navidad! I give you free beer. . . . You drink all [referring to the two 40-ounce beers].

*C:* Yeah.

*S:* Too much drinking, mucho problem. Stomach problem. You need one day off [points to his belly]. . . . Me, Bud Light bottle.

*C:* [Lifts up his shirt, shows Scott his belly]

*S:* You mucho strong.

*C:* [Flexes his arms]

*S:* Okay, amigo.

Scott gently reprimanded his young Latino male customer who demanded free beer, saying that he should moderate his drinking. This customer did not take it badly, responding that he is healthy and strong enough to handle some drinking.

To prevent shoplifting, Scott let his customers know that he was keenly aware of their potential attempts to steal. He followed shoppers who had ways to conceal merchandise (e.g., baggy clothes or a purse/bag) or who exhibited common behavioral cues for an intention to steal (e.g., looking around, looking for anti-shoplifting measures, etc.). Scott would usually approach such customers repeatedly or bluntly accuse them of theft. In addition, surveillance sometimes led to body searches. On August 9, 2002, at 10:28 p.m., two Latino customers, both in their mid- to late twenties, entered the store. Daniel recognized one as a regular customer. Vin, a Black employee, told Daniel that they were stealing beer. Daniel then told Scott, who ran around the counter. The two customers were at the register, paying for a 40-ounce bottle of Miller High Life.

*S:* Okay no steal!

*C1:* What's up, Pops?

*S:* [Reaches behind his [the customer's] pants and pulls out a bottle of wine cooler from the customer's bulging pants]

*C1:* Oh, come on, Pops!

*D:* Check in the front.

*S:* [Pulls out a 40-ounce Miller High Life from the front of his pants] Okay, why you steal?

*C2:* [Laughs]

*C1:* Okay, put this one [the wine cooler] back. I just want the Millers.

*S:* Okay, you are not kid anymore.

*C1:* Yeah, okay, Pops. Hey, this is South Central though, man. There's always crazy shit going down here.

*C2:* [Still laughing]

*C1:* [Pays and leaves]

Scott and Melinda, a Black woman in her forties, did not get along at first. Melinda had stolen from Scott previously, but she had not done so again. She and Scott often yelled and cursed at each other, though they were able to part with no hard feelings. On February 6, 2002, at 9:43 p.m., Melinda carried a small radio into the store and brought two cans of malt liquor to the counter.

*S:* Cut it out! [Referring to the music, but Melinda ignores him] What is your thinking of me? I'm tough guy?

*C:* You all right, Scott.

*S:* Okay. I still loving you.

*C:* All right.

A couple of weeks later, at 2:35 p.m. on February 18, 2002, Melinda re-appeared.

*S:* You stealing 20 dollars. I know.

*C:* No, no, I didn't, Scott.

*S:* You genius, okay. Genius!

*C:* I told you before, Scott, I don't steal.

*S:* You one of a kind steal. You touch my banana [groin area], and you steal.

*C:* I may be on drugs, but I don't steal.

*S:* I pray for you!

*C:* Thank you.

*S:* [Smiles at Daniel because Melinda thanked him].

Scott was referring to an incident a few months earlier, in which Melinda distracted him by touching his groin area. As he was trying to ward her off, she took a $20 bill from his pocket. He found the bill missing after she had left the store. In all these cases, both the storekeeper and customer confronted each other over accusations of theft and subjected each other's bodies to surveillance and coercion. To be accurate, while Scott's behavior was fairly consistent in all of them, the customers had different types of reactions.

Sometimes regular customers informed Scott of wrongdoings by other customers. Once, a customer tried to use a fake $100 bill and argued with Scott. Robin, a regular customer, told the customer to stop, leading to a fistfight outside the store between Robin and this customer. Robin reported, "I tore his ass up!" As seen in this example, some of the customers acted as agents of surveillance for Scott, as they participated in surveillance, which is a part of the peculiar power of disciplinary processes where awareness of the power works in advance of its exercise.

## Resistance to Surveillance

Foucault calls our attention to the shifting ways that bodies and social institutions have entered into political relations, such as those between Korean merchants and their non-Korean clientele. In this case, powerless customers could be seen as victims subjected to processes of objectification and constraint. Merchants trusted their own eyes and surveillance cameras in mapping out consumer behavior or profiling specific subpopulations to discourage crime and detect criminals, much like Foucault's panopticon. In accordance with what de Certeau and Scott have argued, however, customers were not entirely passive; they reciprocated or contested the treatment from merchants and employees, while also playing games or escalating levels of confrontation. Acts of resistance (e.g., stealing) were sometimes justified on the grounds of subsistence (among other reasons).[28] De Certeau's interest in creative diversions as well as passive resistance, as with Scott's Malay peasants (discussed in chapter 4), is pertinent to this case study. When customers at Scott's store were stared at or followed, they withdrew or left the store, responded both verbally and physically, manipulated, confronted, or even killed the merchant (in my study), and threatened boycotts. A Black customer was more likely, because of past experience and expectations, to interpret the same behavior as prejudice-driven, suspicious, or discriminatory behavior (Schreer et al. 2009, 1440).

Customers were not entirely passive in the merchant-customer relationship at Scott's store, either. Many succeeded in convincing Scott to go along with food stamp fraud. For instance, on July 24, 2002, at 8:30 p.m., a Black woman in her thirties, a regular customer, put a pack of gum on the counter and paid with a food stamp. She placed the 75 cents she received in change into a plastic bag full of coins. She then walked around the store for a while and then asked for a pack of cigarettes. Sometimes a regular customer asked merchants to sign a document that stated that he or she was seeking employment at the store. The form was from the welfare agency and was intended to verify that the recipient was looking for work. In addition, knowing that it was a crime to sell alcohol to minors, some underage customers asked other adults to purchase alcohol for them, which was a practice known as "shoulder tapping." On July 22, 2002, a group of four or five teenagers walked into Kimbo Liquor Store, followed by a regular customer in a wheelchair. The adult customer took four 40-ounce beer bottles and the teenagers slowly walked out of the store. Scott refused to sell the customer the beer, apparently aware that it was for the teenagers. The customer argued and pleaded but finally gave up and left the store.

Customers were not afraid to express how they felt about Scott. They often complained about how cheap he was, how expensive his products were ("highway robbery"), and that Scott made a fortune off of them. He usually responded, "Too much think price, then taste go away!" Some Latino customers started to jokingly use the elbow gesture and say "codo" in response to what they felt were high prices for beer. When Latino customers jokingly asked for a free case of beer or a bottle of hard liquor, Scott responded, "cabrón!" Frequent confrontations occurred over accusations of overcharging, shortchanging, requests for discounts, unpaid credit, shoplifting, or stealing. Even in a dispute over one cigarette, Scott was ready to defend his property in a way that offended his customer. At 9:40 p.m. on February 18, 2002, two Black men entered the store.

*C1:* [Looking at the glass wall] Where's my picture?[29]

*S:* You want your picture up?

*C1:* [Ignores the question] Give me some singles, man.

*C2:* He put somebody else's pictures up.

*C1:* Four [cigarettes] for one dollar?

*S:* You wanna see me die?

*C2:* Off of one cigarette? Ah, come on man.

*C1:* Let me have some matches.

*S:* Don't bother me this year. . . . Leave me alone.

*C2:* [Walking out with C1] Leave me alone? What kind of shit is that? [Mutters something else]

Even though customer 1 started with a friendly question at the beginning, soon his accusations escalated and Scott responded in an overly defensive attitude, refusing to offer matches.

At 2:37 p.m. on February 18, 2002, Robin, a Black regular customer in his late forties, entered the store. He was generally kind to Scott and Daniel; however, they were cautious around him. Robin had gotten into fistfights in the store with other customers, mainly Latinos. Every time he came into the store, he bought the same thing: Taaka Vodka, the cheapest vodka they sold. On that day he arrived with his three children, and his wife was by the door with another baby in a stroller. His children grabbed chips and cookies while Robin tried to stop them from buying items that were too expensive. His son brought a Hi-C juice bottle to the counter.

*C:* How much is that shit?

*S:* 50 cents.

*C:* No. Put it back. Get me those chips . . . and give me a Taaka, Scott.

*S:* Big one?

*C:* [Gives Scott an annoyed look] You know I can't afford that.

*S:* When you gonna pay credit?

*C:* When I get the money.

*S:* Where's your wife?

*C:* I don't go over $10. Give some time.

*S:* You pray for Jesus Christ.

*C:* I do. My kids go to church every Sunday.

*S:* What a shame. You no pay credit almost one month.[30]

*C:* I lost my job. Scott, I got five more children. Six more children. [Starts to list the ages of his children who are not at the store]

In this situation, Scott could be interpreted as taunting the customer by showing him the larger bottle. He was, in Bourdieu's terms, distinguishing his own status from that of his customers by emphasizing who owned the property. Moreover, Scott invoked Christianity in order to remind his customer of his outstanding balance. In return, the customer admitted that his overstretched credit at the store was a result of his unemployment.

On July 22, 2002, at 4:00 p.m., one of Scott's daily customers arrived. This customer's wife often gave Scott trouble. Both customers often deliberately remarked or commented on Scott's material comfort in order to irritate him. This time, Daniel was working the cash register when the customer placed two cans of beer on the counter. The customer then took off his shoe and pulled out some dollar bills.

*C:* You probably live in Beverly Hills, right?

*D:* [Feels that they have had this conversation before and is irritated by his comment. Doesn't respond]

*C:* In South Central, they'll kill you for a dollar. . . . Where your dad at?

*D:* He's sleeping.

*C:* All right.

Here, the customer definitely pointed out the class difference by referring to their economic privilege relative to that of their customers, hinting that their wealth was earned by exploiting people in South LA.

Some customers didn't mind showing signs of disapproval feeling that Scott was a bigot. At 9:39 p.m. on August 16, 2002, two of the four or five men who always loitered around the store entered. One man brought two cans of malt liquor to the counter. Daniel was working the register with his father nearby.

C1: [To his friend] I don't like them. They're prejudiced motherfuckers.

C2: No, he's alright [referring to Daniel].

C1: Well, I don't like both of them.

A similar confrontation took place at 6:05 p.m. on March 1, 2002, when a Black man in his fifties who had given Scott many problems in the past came into the store. He bought a can of malt liquor but did not leave and instead stood in the store staring at Scott. Scott told him to leave, but he did not move. Daniel started to yell at the customer and again told him to leave; he could tell that the man was drunk.

C: Don't yell at me!

S: Please go!

C: Don't fuck with me!

D: Hey, man, just get out of here. Just leave.

C: Don't mess with me, cuz I'll take any one of you out! [Starts to walk slowly toward the exit while mumbling]

He was drunk, so of course he was more confrontational and threatened to put Kimbo Liquor Store out of business.

## NEGOTIATING SURVEILLANCE

Scholars generally concur that there is more than cultural difference at work in the kinds of tensions displayed between Korean merchants and inner-city customers (Abelmann and Lie 1995; C. Kim 2000). Nonetheless, it is still important to assess in what ways cultural difference contributed to escalating these hostilities, which often incited organized protest. Some studies on Black-Korean tensions narrowly focus on the way that communication barriers contribute to the tense dynamics. Nonetheless, they are often inadequate analyses because they tend to encourage ahistorical notions of difference and obscure material factors at play (K. Park 1996, 69); they fail to explain why disputes occur even in the absence of noticeable communication differences. Thus, for example, Scott had lived in the US for thirty years and had only minor language barriers with his customers; he even felt comfortable enough in his language skills to use American and Spanish slang in order to develop friendlier relations. However, he still had conflict with customers.

It is overly simplistic to characterize an unfriendly, abrupt, or curt way of communicating as the "Korean" way (Stewart 1989, Bailey 1996), as this mode of communication is used by Korean as well as non-Korean customers. In other arenas, the Korean mode of communication is characterized by a contrasting style, such as the friendly and dynamic style within Korean American Christianity (S. Kim 2010). In addition, before the entry of Korean immigrant merchants into South LA, Jewish and other White merchants had similar disputes with their customers despite a perceived lack of communication gap. In fact, the White American couple that previously owned Kimbo Liquor Store accidentally killed a Black woman in an altercation over shoplifting. Thus, attributing Black-Korean tensions to communication and cultural differences is too simplistic. This case study has shown a fairly large range of communication styles between merchant and customer. In the cases like Scott's where merchants have been more open, adopting communication styles of their customers, sometimes this tactic has backfired and offended the customer. At times, Scott was interpreted as being abrupt, rude, and insensitive in his dealings with his customers. In reviewing field notes, I perceived that Scott generally expressed his emotions immediately instead of keeping silent. Although he tried to keep his emotions in check, yelling and shouting were a part of his everyday interactions with customers. I noticed that this was more common among other Korean merchants in South LA. Scott had a short temper when he was tired, in the middle of the day, or when business was extremely slow.

My focus on subtler forms of power, in particular to the dramaturgical nature of the transactions from a different theoretical angle, brings us to Erving Goffman's basic idea (1956) that in interacting, people put on a "show" for each other, stage-managing the impression that others receive. People project images of themselves in ways that serve their own ends, because such information helps to define the situation and create appropriate expectations. Similarly, in anthropology, advocates of transactional analysis (Barth 1959) maintain that within the "rules of the game," individual actors make strategic choices that maximize their interests and that these choices have an impact on the overall system. Thus, merchants make clear to customers that they are being judged in order to protect his or her merchandise.

Notions of interactionalism, transactionalism, and ethnomethodology are less prominent now and have been criticized for failing to give sufficient weight to objective restraints on social action, not to mention relations of power. As Pierre Bourdieu (1990) wrote, "Interpersonal relations are only apparently person-to-person relations and that the truth of the interaction never lies entirely in the interaction" (291). In other words, it is a mistake to limit the analysis of interactions to merely person-to-person relations. Merchant-customer interactions do not explain everything about Black- and Latino-Korean relations.

Here most of my chapter is focused on Scott and how he uses different strategies, both friendly and not, to control interactions and customers resistance to surveillance. What we have seen indicates a linkage between everyday forms of resistance and the potential to bring about socioeconomic and political change via boycotts and race riots. (See chapters 2, 7, and 8). However, the key word here is potential. Clearly, individual resistance by a customer does not always lead to a collective response. Unlike more organized forms of resistance, these actions do not change the system as a whole, nor do they use the language of rights to describe the realities of their surveilled lives. Instead, they focus on an ethic of moral economy, as discussed in the previous chapter. However, individual and collective responses are sometimes linked, as when protest movements grow out of or encourage individual resistance (see chapters 2 and 7).

For the most part, transactions between Scott and his customers were characterized by mundane daily contact, and did not lead to confrontations or disputes, and most encounters were friendly and harmonious. However, these same transactions served to acknowledge the property rights of the merchant and his right to monitor the customers' conduct and hold them accountable. Both parties practiced disciplinary power on themselves and each other; however, the power relations were clearly asymmetrical. All customers were subject to the merchant's discipline and surveillance, and "tough" customers sometimes confronted the merchant with threats of physical retaliation, and, more occasionally, a boycott or riot. These customers used the tactics of confrontation or even shoplifting to defiantly express their freedom and negotiate their powerlessness. Korean American store owners operating businesses in low-income, high-risk neighborhoods are confronted with a range of customer problems which, unfortunately, often reinforce their prejudicial attitudes towards customers. Thus, Korean shopkeepers are sometimes at the mercy and suffer violence at the hands of their customers. In this way, surveillance and resistance work in a back-and-forth cycle, as resistance is always coextensive with relations of domination.

In addition to the potential for engendering protest, strategies of surveillance do not always succeed. A liquor store is not a controlled environment like a prison, and storekeepers like Scott do not have full authority over the venue: they lack the backup of state power to guarantee security. Furthermore, their surveillance does not always lead to oppressive conditions. In 2005, Scott was murdered by one of his regular customers—a Black resident who retaliated after Scott refused to give him free food and beer a day earlier. This customer beat Scott, strangled him with his own belt, dragged him around the store, and poured bleach on him while he was still alive. Scott died of blunt force trauma and asphyxiation. The killer then left the store to gamble and get high. He had been out on parole for less than two and a half months when he killed Scott. The man was convicted and sentenced to state prison for a term of life without parole on first-degree murder charges and second-degree robbery and commercial burglary, in addition to a consecutive term of 25 years to life on unlawful vehicle taking.

It seems particularly tragic that it was Scott who was murdered by a customer given that he did seem to take more care than other merchants to relate to his customers. It was one of those horrible events that cannot be attributed to just one thing. Scott had a relatively good reputation among customers, so there's no reason why he would be targeted so viciously.

Foucault's theories provided important insight into the institutions and practices that distribute power throughout societies, but gave little guidance about how they might be changed. I depart from Foucault in the sense that my final analysis contradicts the idea that disciplinary effects are at the heart of repression. Discipline does not preclude contestation by the subject being disciplined, nor does it always subjugate their bodies. Scott's death testifies to the failure of his strategy, and Foucault's theory can't be applied wholesale to all cases.[31] Scott's strategy of surveillance did not lead to oppression, but to opposition, retaliation, and his own death. The reason for the murder wasn't surveillance per se, but retaliation—Scott wouldn't give the man free food/ beer. And why should he? He has a business to run. What this man did is not an appropriate reaction to what Scott did. Scott was unlucky enough to have crossed paths with a dangerous criminal.

Wolf (1990) differentiated Foucault's notion of power from that of Marx, which entailed the power of capital to harness and allocate labor. Foucault's power, in contrast, is organizational power, which is the ability "to structure the possible field of action of others" (Wolf 1990, 586). Korean merchants are not the primary cause of poverty in South LA—unlike James Scott's (1985) Malay landlords or slave owners—but they do take advantage of "captive" consumers who have few other choices of venue to purchase groceries. Still, control over a sector of small businesses is not the same as control over resources. In Scott's case, the merchant's strategies and techniques, based on rational choice psychology,[32] backfired: surveillance did not lead to oppression, but to opposition, retaliation, and ultimately murder. Customers refused to submit to the rhetoric of the public transcript of power, and behind the eyes and ears—or sometimes in front—of the merchants, created a discourse of resistance and "hidden transcripts": "politics that might make use of disguise, deception, and indirections while maintaining an outward impression, in power-laden situations, of willing, even enthusiastic content" (Scott 1990, 17). Customers responded, resisted, and reacted to the oppressive scenarios within which they found themselves, ranging from a very extreme response to Scott's techniques (murder) to what other customers did: identifiable yet spontaneous gestures, activities, practices, and speech acts such as laughing, grumbling, anger, ridiculing, criticism, whispering, rumor, or gossip. As Scott enforced his rules, customers griped about it, but not really resisting in any organized way, though. When pressures to meet expectations were performed, a "sly civility" of simple facades and superficial niceties became encrypted expectations that reflect distinctions of power and status (Sonu 2012, 255). From this perspective, civility could be interpreted as a conflict management strategy employed by store owner or customers.

## CONCLUSION

In general, the customers who gave Scott the most trouble were alcoholics, drug abusers, gang members, transients, and teenagers: in short, the customers who tended to have less money. These "tough" customers, as Scott referred to them, also frequented the store anywhere from once to 20 times a day, regularly loitered, or came in because they had nothing else to do or nowhere to go; some came in repeatedly asking for a discount and paying with pennies. A high proportion of these customers were Black. Problems of joblessness, alcoholism, and drug abuse are clearly tied to poverty. Scholars maintain that the economic transformation of American society has had a particularly potent impact on urban areas, and that the Reagan-Bush era policies of the 1980s and early 1990s resulted in severe economic crisis in urban Black communities (see chapter 1). Deindustrialization and the exodus of corporations from the city fostered a set of interconnected social problems. The resulting unemployment had devastating effects: an expanding drug economy, heavy reliance on public assistance, an increase in single female-headed households, and deteriorating work environments.

Although substance abuse was not limited to inner-city neighborhoods, poverty, unemployment, joblessness, gang violence, hopelessness, state neglect, and lack of resources compounded the urban problems. In Scott's own analysis, the root cause of many of the problems in South LA was the lack of jobs: "If you do not own a business in South Central, you are limited to mostly low-wage, labor-intensive jobs, usually in the service sector." Many people who worked full-time jobs were not above the poverty line, either. However, poverty did not automatically produce tension between Scott and his customers, and disputes rarely developed over communication difference or language barriers. The subtler forms of power (e.g., discipline, surveillance, etc.) did contribute to disputes.

Unlike in middle- and upper-class neighborhoods, there are no institution-alized ways to address shoplifting (such as employing security guards) in South LA. Thus, local store owners actively sought to protect their property and seek physical safety by adopting both legitimate and questionable tech-niques to manage theft and other problematic issues: coercing, confronting, controlling, manipulating, humiliating, teasing, disciplining, or criminalizing their often powerless and poor inner-city customers. Vendors also used a range of strategies for tough customers. Although merchants did not control the means of production, they had power over poorer neighborhood residents and impacted their life conditions. Vendors differentiated between customers, recognizing that positive reinforcement of and interactions with good custom-ers made their work easier.[33] They were then able to devote more attention to tough customers.

At Kimbo Liquor Store, although both Scott and his customers attempted to control, contest, and/or manipulate each other, the dynamics were still structured largely by the contradictions of capitalist social relationships; in short, Korean shopkeepers had an advantage, class power, over their custom-ers. South LA conflicts were not the outcome of independent actors making free choices, but of cumulative historical processes that led to a particular class structure. Instead, race or ethnicity—in contrast to class interests or civil rights issues—was attributed to be the cause of violent encounters. The hyper-visibility of minority merchants and customers obfuscates the influ-ence of institutions and peoples, for instance, distinct patterns of immigration, segregation, and racialization, less visibly implicated in their interactions. There is a long history of interracial/ethnic hostilities in the US, including Jewish-Black tensions in the 1960s, Korean-Black tensions in the 1990s, and Latino-Latino tensions in the new millennium. Despite a dramatic national decrease in violent crime rates since the mid-1990s, shootings, stabbings, and assaults continue to occur at high rates in inner cities (Karandinos et al. 2014, 10). Experiences of subordination via commercial surveillance, together with a history of exploitation, were the primary cause of antagonism between Korean merchants and Black/Latino customers. This fragile co-existence became more inflammatory when internal and external social forces erupted without warning, as is the case of Los Angeles in 1992. The moral economy of violence in the inner city, in the context of extreme spatial class segregation and disenfranchisement from integration in the legal labor force, profoundly depoliticizes the poor, turning violence inward, to neighbor on neighbor. However, like the incipient class solidarity identified by Thompson in the eighteenth century's moral economy of grain riots, moral economy practices provided the basis for an emergent class consciousness during the 1992 civil unrest. The next chapter will examine how Korean merchants experienced the 1992 unrest, came to perceive customers of other races and ethnicities, and replaced Latino employees with African Americans in its immediate aftermath.

## NOTES

1. There was a murder at this specific store.
2. Surveillance refers to the process of watching, monitoring, recording, and processing the behavior of people, objects, and events in order to govern activity.
3. The surveillance cameras are there so that customers will discipline themselves.
4. He only analyzed consumerist behavior. Or, he said nothing about class domination or relations.
5. Korean merchants are not rich and powerful in the big scheme of US society, but they have some access to means of production as petty capitalists.
6. Anthropological observation often means "participant observation" that involves what is going on inside the entire community; however, in this case, "participant observation" is a form of micro, direct observation of a store.
7. It was closed since the owner was murdered.
8. According to California State law, when a liquor store or market owner violates regulations regarding alcohol sales, they are heavily fined up to 50 percent of the amount of sales—as much as $3,000. For a second violation, the store's liquor license is revoked for 25 days. For a third violation, the store permanently loses its liquor license.
9. In April 1999, two armed robbers came into the store and put a gun to Scott's head, hit him with the pistol butt, and fled with a bag of money. Scott was hospitalized but returned to work the next day. From 2002 to 2003, the store was burglarized twice. Daniel was working at the cash register and his father was taking a break when one of the burglaries occurred. The burglar, a local drug dealer, was also one of their regular customers. Scott and Daniel called the police but dropped the charges after receiving a death threat from a friend of the burglar. However, the District Attorney's Office still pursued the case.
10. Many of Scott's former employees, mostly local residents, left after a few weeks, never came back after their first paycheck, or got fired for stealing beer or money. Having employees who lived outside South LA did not solve these problems. Scott had three Korean employees, all of whom were hesitant to work nights, weekends, and holidays. In addition, they demanded higher wages than the Black and Latino workers. Female employees were less willing to do the labor-intensive duties, such as stocking and cleaning (mopping, sweeping, throwing trash into the dumpster, and cleaning the toilet).
11. Mostly malt liquor was stolen.
12. It was put up initially.

13. A "beer run" is local slang for running out of the liquor store with a pack or packs of beer without paying.

14. Most Korean merchants have at least one employee. Large liquor stores or markets tend to hire up to 10 employees.

15. Mostly I've discussed how interactions are not very friendly and that Scott is an exception.

16. Bailey (1996) reported that while African American customers tended to initiate topics of personal communication, such as jokes and storytelling, Korean merchants tended to use business-oriented attitudes in their interactions, which was perceived by customers as disrespectful and rude.

17. Most interactions I've discussed have been business-like or hostile, not friendly.

18. In the following transcripts, S indicates Scott; D is used for Daniel; C denotes a customer; C1 signifies customer 1; and C2 is customer 2.

19. Scott said this phrase sarcastically and/or with a slight smile.

20. When dealing with the word "cabrón," context is everything. Its meaning depends on who is saying it and to whom it is being directed. The word cabrón derives from the Spanish word "cabra," meaning "goat." In traditional Mexican culture, the word cabrón is used in the derogatory sense and signifies "asshole." When the word "pinche" is used before "cabrón," the offensive significance of the word doubles. Again, context determines the meaning. When the word "cabrón" is used among friends or relatives who share a joking relationship, it is not found offensive at all. It may also be used to reduce tension. When used jokingly, the word cabrón is rarely used with pinche (personal communication with Maria C. Maldonado July 31, 2002).

21. Another issue that this brings up is the one usually related to non-Blacks using the "N" word: if you're not Black, you shouldn't ever use it. (Same with other marginalized communities and historically derogatory terms, like "dyke," "fag," etc.) So perhaps the customer felt only other Latinos/Mexicans could use the term in a joking manner.

22. All Korean merchants have the opportunity to learn culture from customers, but not all are willing to adopt these elements.

23. For example, if a customer bought a 12-pack of regular beer, Scott could infer that he or she: 1) had disposable income, 2) was employed, 3) lived in a multi-member household, and/or 4) was more likely to be Latino. Conversely, those who bought a single can of regular beer might be: 1) single, 2) on a lunch break from work, or 3) could be an alcoholic, albeit not as likely as the customer who bought a can of malt liquor.

24. Many cities define spatial areas that are off limit to certain social groups in order to control types of undesirable behavior. Similarly, Scott, like law enforcement, attempted to regulate store spaces by keeping out criminals altogether, rather than preventing and/or punishing criminal activity in those spaces, while shifting more to risk management practices.

25. "Shopping while black" lawsuit—a first by employees—targets CVS (+video) by Harry Bruinius (*Christian Science Monitor* JUNE 4, 2015): http://www.csmonitor.

com/USA/Justice/2015/0604/Shopping-while-black-lawsuit-a-first-by-employees-targets-CVS-video

26. He often said, "Whassup, motherfucking guy?"

27. This gesture would be unintelligible to most Korean immigrants.

28. Stolen items tend to be expensive ones such as liquor, not food.

29. Daniel had taken pictures of their regular customers and put them up on the store wall. This is common practice for Korean liquor store owners. Despite good intentions, many joked about the similarity between the store wall and the pictures of criminals wanted for arrest due to outstanding warrants.

30. It is common practice for store owners to allow regular customers to purchase items on credit. Once a month or so, customers are expected to clear their debts.

31. Foucault couldn't account for all instances of discipline, and his focus was on particular institutions at particular time periods.

32. In criminology, rational choice theory (Clarke 1997) adopts a utilitarian belief that man is a reasoning actor who weighs means and ends, costs and benefits, and makes a rational choice. Scott's strategy and technique may be considered part of various situational crime prevention measures: opportunity-reducing measures, management, design or manipulation of the immediate environment, etc.

33. We don't know if other vendors distinguished between different customers.

*Chapter Six*

# Changing the Business Plan

## *Korean Merchants Try to Reintegrate into the South LA Community*

Mainstream media often portrayed the 1992 crisis as an "ethnic" conflict between African American and Korean Americans, but it was, and is, much more complex. From the long-standing racial economic oppression and social discrimination experienced in African American communities, to the exclusion and exploitation of Korean and Latinx immigrant workers and their families, to the economic conditions requiring struggling immigrant storeowners to work 70- and 80-hour weeks, to failed planning investment policies in our cities, to the failure to convict the police officers who beat Rodney King, to the LAPD's decision to protect Beverly Hills while Koreatown, Central L.A., and South L.A. burned—Sa-I-Gu was a moment of convergence of so many of our city's and our country's social, political, and economic ills. The violence and pain of those days was a distillation of the violence and pain of our times.

—Alexandra Suh, Executive Director,
Koreatown Immigrant Workers Alliance

Unfortunately, the above quote by Suh didn't make the dominant discourse on the 1992 Los Angeles civil unrest.[1] The film *Menace II Society* is a perfect reflection of the dominant discourse: it frames the 1992 Los Angeles civil unrest as the result of "Black-Korean tension." However, Latinos were the largest segment of the population to be arrested during the unrest. It is not possible to discuss the unrest without considering either Latinos or Latino-Korean relations. Chapters 6 through 9 (also chapter 5) aim to discuss the presence of Latinos in South LA and Latino-Korean relations, and then to demystify the oversimplified narrative of racial and ethnic relations (see figure 6.1).

165

Figure 6.1.   As seen in this graffiti, many undocumented workers live in South Central LA (photo by Kyeyoung Park).

These chapters will offer a new understanding of the way Korean immigrant merchants developed new business practices in the aftermath of the unrest, and how this reflected a broader understanding of race relations that go beyond the Black-White binary.

The unrest raised fundamental questions about the current and future state of race relations in Los Angeles, the nation's most diverse metropolis (Bobo et al. 1994). Unfortunately, even after the unrest, the dominant discourse defined race narrowly and failed to go beyond the conventional "Black-White" racial framework. A debate between John Hope Franklin and Angela Oh illustrates this binary racial framework. Franklin, a distinguished Black historian, was chair of the Advisory Board of President Bill Clinton's Initiative on Race and Reconciliation. Oh, a Korean American criminal lawyer, was a fellow member of this Board. Oh called on the US to go beyond a "Black-White paradigm" and was rebuked by Franklin, who repeated his belief that "this country cut its eyeteeth on racism with Black-White relations" (*New York Post* September 30, 1997). Franklin declined to broaden the panel's focus to include all races and claimed that the primary issue was still between Blacks and Whites. To believe, as Franklin did, that Asian Americans and Latinos do not really count is to miss how race relations have been evolving for decades; the unrest, with its multiracial cast of characters, illustrated this fact.[2]

The Franklin-Oh debate reflects a larger debate on racism. Traditional narratives tend to reinforce the idea that racism is "singular and monolithic" and will last forever without changing (Goldberg 1990, xii). This prevailing, reductionist approach takes racism to be sexually or economically determined or the result of an "authoritarian psychotic-group personality type" (Goldberg 1990, xxii). However, manifestations of racism have evolved and are multiple, instead of remaining static and singular. Decades of scholarship, beginning with Omi and Winant's important intervention (1994), have argued that race is not fixed, but it is rather a contested and negotiated process. However, researchers thus far have focused primarily on majority-minority relations, particularly White-Black relations. Scholars have also ignored the structural processes in which racial ideology and practice are constantly being rearticulated. Paying attention to power relations and the structural process allows for a non-positivist approach to understanding the relationships among ethnicity, ideology, and other social constructions. As Frederik Barth (1969) insisted, ethnicity can only be understood as a process. This understanding must come from a close examination of the history of intergroup relations and the ways in which ethnic boundaries arise historically from these relations. Moreover, there is much to be gained from John Comaroff and Jean Comaroff's idea that ethnic genesis is always rooted in simultaneously structural and cultural-historical forces, and that ethnicity cannot be understood unless the social and historical situations for its persistence are also revealed (1992, 50).

Although ethnicity came to assume a new meaning in anthropology with the publication of Barth's *Ethnic Groups and Boundaries* (1969), its structural functionalist limitation must be noted. Barth (1969) rejected the idea that ethnic groups are definable by some total inventory of cultural traits that their members share. Rather, the group is always in the process of creating itself, with "criteria of membership" that it produces in order to mark its boundaries (38). Jenkins (2001) criticized Barth for discussing the fluid nature of ethnicity but not "taking on board the more difficult questions about the nature of collective social forms in which [he] is interested" (2001, 4825). Indeed, Barth's analysis has proven inadequate for understanding the ethnic confrontations, conflicts, and violence that have become so common in the late twentieth century (Wolf 1994). Whereas the persistence of ethnic identity was interpreted some time ago as atavistic, ethnicity has become a much more significant factor in social relations since the emergence of the nation-state

(Williams 1989). In addition, as explained in chapter 2, various state agents play a critical role in the development of interethnic tension.

An ethnographic perspective on the processes through which racial ideologies are contested and rearticulated can contribute to our understanding of race (Gregory 1994, 25). This chapter examines the articulation of race and ethnicity in the context of both ideology and practice through an examination of Korean immigrant merchants who were directly affected by the "first multi-ethnic unrest" in twentieth century urban America and Korean-Latino relations. My interviews also touch upon social and historical information that helps define the shift in racial perception. My observations are based on in-depth interviews with 71 Korean American merchants that were completed during 1992 and 1994 (19 before and 52 after the 1992 unrest).

## RODNEY KING BEATING AND
## THE 1992 LOS ANGELES CIVIL UNREST

On March 3, 1991, Rodney King and two passengers were driving west on the Foothill Freeway (I-210) through the Lake View Terrace neighborhood of Los Angeles. The California Highway Patrol (CHP) attempted to initiate a traffic stop. A high-speed pursuit ensued with speeds estimated at up to 115 mph, first over freeways, and then through residential neighborhoods. When King came to a stop, CHP Officers ordered the occupants under arrest. King was tasered, struck with side-handled batons, then tackled to the ground and cuffed. In the videotape, King continues to try to stand up as the police officers hit his joints, wrists, elbows, knees, and ankles. Officers attempted numerous baton strikes on King, with 33–50 blows hitting King, plus six kicks.[3] The officers claimed that King was under the influence of the dissociative drug phencyclidine (PCP) at the time of arrest, which caused him to be aggressive and violent.[4] Nonetheless, a subsequent test for the presence of PCP in King's system several days later turned up negative.

The footage of an unarmed Black man being mercilessly beaten by White officers resurrected "the long, black memory of whippings, lynchings, dismemberment, rapes, and burnings," and became a rallying point for activists in Los Angeles and around the country (Stevenson 2013, 287). The LA District Attorney subsequently charged four police officers with assault and use of excessive force (*NYT* March 6, 1992).

A year later, on April 29, 1992, on the seventh day of deliberations, the jury acquitted all four officers of assault and acquitted three of the four of using excessive force. The verdicts were based in part on the first three seconds of a blurry, 13-second segment of the video tape that was edited out by television news stations in their broadcasts. During the first two seconds of videotape, the video showed King attempting to flee past one of the police offers. During the next minute and 19 seconds, King was beaten continuously by the officers. The officers testified that they tried to restrain King prior to the starting point of the videotape, but that King was able to fend them.[5] However, the verdict also epitomized "the systematic bias of American legal and political structures against Black people," against the backdrop of decades of socio-economic decline, disenfranchisement, and despair in Black communities (Economic and Political Weekly July 25, 1992).

The unrest started the same day of the acquittal in South LA and then spread to other areas in LA over a six-day period. By 3:45 p.m. on April 29, a crowd of more than 300 people had appeared at the Los Angeles County Courthouse protesting the verdicts passed down a half hour earlier. The first recorded attack involved theft and assault on Korean property. About an hour after the acquittals were announced, mostly older teenagers ("most likely gang members, judging from their style of dress and the constant 'throwing' of gang signs during the evening"), went to the Pay-Less Liquor and Deli on Florence just west of Normandie (Hayes-Bautista et al. 1993, 441). They were stopped at the door, and at that point, the store owner's son was hit in the head with a bottle of beer. Two other youths threw beer bottles at the store's glass front door, shattering it. "This is for Rodney King," one of them yelled.[6]

There was another disturbance at Florence and Halldale, a block to the east. A young Black man, cheered on by several others, used an aluminum baseball bat to break the windshield of a Cadillac with two White men inside. The man with the bat was arrested, but police officers who responded to the call came under a barrage of rocks, bottles, and anything else that could be picked up and thrown. After handcuffing the rock thrower, the officers confronted a group of gang members who attempted to wrest him away from their custody. Lieutenant Michael Moulin was at the scene and, seeing that his officers were greatly outnumbered and that most were not wearing helmets to protect them against the objects being hurled at them, ordered them to leave the area in the apparent hope that the situation would de-escalate on its own.[7] The crowd did not disperse, but instead grew larger and more violent. The absence of the police for nearly three hours allowed the crowd to grow and culminated in the looting of stores and the arson of various buildings (Hayes-Bautista et al. 1993, 442).

By midmorning on the second day, the violence appeared to be widespread and unchecked as heavy looting and fires were witnessed across LA County. Stores owned by Koreans were widely targeted.[8] Of the 4,500 stores destroyed during the unrest, more than 2,300 were Korean-owned, and nearly every building in Koreatown was damaged. Korean Americans, who made up only 1.6 percent of the city's population at the time, were disproportionately affected: approximately half the businesses destroyed belonged to Korean immigrants, and another one-third of those damaged were Korean-owned (see figure 6.2).

According to several sources (the FBI, newspaper accounts, and interviews), Black people deliberately targeted Korean-owned stores (Kim 2007).

A dusk-to-dawn curfew was established in some areas. The Southern California Rapid Transit District (now Los Angeles County Metropolitan Transportation Authority) suspended all bus service throughout the LA area, and some major freeways were closed down. In addition, hundreds of thousands of residents lost electric, water, and phone service. All local schools, including some colleges, and LAX were closed (Stevenson 2013, 280). Widespread looting, assault, arson, and killings occurred during the riots. Approximately 3,600 fires were set, destroying 1,100 buildings (*Christian Science Monitor* April 29, 2002).

A total of 53 people died during the riots (*LA Weekly* April 24, 2002). Black people constituted 44 percent of those killed in all related deaths, while Latinos made up 31 percent, Whites made up 22 percent, and only one Korean American was among the victims (Stevenson 2013, 288). As many as 2,383 people were reported injured, and more than 12,000 people were arrested (Stevenson 2013, 280). The rioters were comprised of "an assortment of people—mostly young and male, some who were petty criminals and gang affiliated, and protesters" (Stevenson 2013, 298). Estimates of material losses vary between about $800 million and $1 billion (*Time* April 25, 2007). Of these losses, damage to Korean-owned property was between $350 and $400 million. The establishments affected were diverse, including grocery stores, swap meet shops, clothing shops, liquor stores, dry cleaners, electronics shops, gas stations, jewelry shops, restaurants, beauty salons, auto shops, furniture shops, and video shops. Mayor Bradley lifted the curfew on May 4, signaling the official end of the riots. By then, the rioting had extended across the nation to New York, Chicago, and Atlanta. Korean business owners faced a daunting, and for many impossible, recovery. Most received very little, if any, aid or protection from the authorities. Police Chief Daryl Gates left police headquarters to attend a political fundraising event in West LA, even though at that very time, rioting and arson were escalating. He attempted to justify his action, stating, "There are going to be situations where people are going to go without assistance. . . . That's just the facts of life. There are not enough of us to be everywhere" (*LAT* May 5, 1992). Sensing that the police had abandoned Koreatown and realizing they were being targeted; a number of Koreans took security into their own hands, taking up arms and improvising security forces. Store owners called in to Radio Korea, a local

Figure 6.2.   Many Korean-run stores were looted or burned (photo by Kyeyoung Park).

Korean-language radio station, and reported that they were being attacked and called for help from other Korean immigrants. The community organized the Korean American Young Adult Team, squads of ten men each who would be deployed to protect Korean properties from looters, armed with a variety of improvised weapons, shotguns, and semiautomatic rifles. Jong Min Kang, President of the Korean American Business Association and Leader of the Korean Young Adult Team, was proud that the Korean American community was able to rebuild:

> When the police were missing in action, the young Adult Team that I mobilized helped to defend the store owners and our community. The lack of assistance was again true when the Federal Emergency Management Agency (FEMA) came into LA. Victims could not get the help of elected officials to access these funds. However, through advocacy, we were able to negotiate with (now a defunct) Community Redevelopment Agency of the City of Los Angeles (CRA), FEMA, Red Cross, Employment Development Department (EDD), and Los Angeles County Department of Public Social Services (DPSS)—altogether about 12 governmental organizations. I was also part of advocating to President Bush for establishment of the CRA to help victims.

Armed confrontations involving Korean merchants were televised, as in one well-publicized incident where shopkeepers armed with M1 carbines, pump action shotguns, and handguns exchanged gunfire with a group of armed looters, forcing them to retreat. One of the most iconic television images of the riots involved Korean merchants firing pistols repeatedly at roving looters. These merchants—jewelry store and gun shop owner Richard Park and his gun store manager, David Joo—were reacting to the shooting of the owner's wife and her sister by looters who had converged on the shopping center where the shops were located. David Joo said, "I want to make it clear that we didn't open fire first. At that time, four police cars were there. Somebody started to shoot at us. The LAPD ran away in half a second. I never saw such a fast escape. I was pretty disappointed" (*NYT* May 3, 1992). Carl Rhyu, a participant in the Korean immigrants' armed response to the rioting, was in the same situation: "When our shops were burning we called the police every five minutes; no response" (*NYT* May 3, 1992).

After the acquittals and the riots, the United States Department of Justice sought indictments against police officers who violated King's civil rights. Before a verdict was issued, Korean shop owners again prepared for the worst; as fear ran rampant throughout the city, gun sales went up. Some merchants at flea markets removed their merchandise from their shelves, and storefronts were fortified with extra Plexiglas and bars. The media reported that once again Korean Americans were arming themselves to prepare for the worst, noting that a licensed gun seller in Koreatown, Western Guns, was selling a dozen or more weapons a day. As John Lee, then Los Angeles Times reporter, pointed out, however, the media failed to note that a gun shop on the Westside was selling more than 150 weapons a day.[9]

The media applied a double standard, scrutinizing Korean merchants' gun purchasing, but not White Americans' fanatical gun purchasing that occurred simultaneously. Lee, deployed to Koreatown during the unrest, also noted that the media coverage was distorted: "They [Korean merchants] had itchy trigger fingers and would shoot those who trespassed . . . however, rioters would drive up to Korean American stores and open fire with automatic weapons. . . . There were Koreans who laid down their weapons, locked up their stores, and tried to avoid violence" (*LA Weekly* April 26, 2012).

In 1993, the shock of the unrest was still fresh in the minds of the Korean American community. The average financial loss for storekeepers was $179,045, with individual losses ranging from $2,000 to $1,750,000 (Kim-Goh et al. 1995, 141). Only 35 percent of Korean American owners had been insured, and of those, many policies offered limited to no riot coverage. The Korean American Inter-Agency Council (KAIAC) reported that 75 percent of Korean American victims had not recovered from the unrest one year later. Of the affected businesses, only 27.8 percent reopened within a year. Some turned to high-interest loans to pay for their expenses and subsequently fell behind in their mortgages, leading to the loss of their homes. The KAIAC report also indicated that 15 percent of college-age Korean American youth whose families owned stores in the areas of the riots dropped out of school because the stores were unable to recuperate. According to a *Los Angeles Times* survey conducted eleven months after the riots, almost 40 percent of Korean Americans said they were thinking of leaving LA (*LAT* March 19, 1993). A second study about the psychological impact of the unrest on a sample of 202 Korean American victims who sustained financial loss or physical injury indicated that the majority of victims suffered from symptoms of post-traumatic stress disorder. It was not surprising, then, that following the riots, the Asian Pacific Counseling and Treatment Center in LA treated 730 Korean American victims for severe anxiety and depression, somatic complaints, and psychotic symptoms (Kim-Goh et al. 1995, 139).

The unrest left a deep impression on the Korean American community, particularly with regards to the way they viewed and interacted with the Black community. This chapter will examine Korean store owners' perceptions of Black and Latino customers, who, despite common narratives about the unrest, were just as involved as African Americans. Since Korean-Latino relations have received little attention compared to Korean-Black relations, the following section hones in on Korean-Latino encounters (see also chapter 8).

## KOREAN-LATINO ENCOUNTERS

Despite the media's primary focus on the Black-Korean conflict, the 1992 unrest was a multiethnic event. It initially began as a political expression of pent-up frustration and anger by African Americans, but both its nature and demographic profile shifted as the protest at Parker Center, located in downtown, led to the fulfillment of socioeconomic needs, especially by low-income Latinos. The violence and looting shifted from South LA north toward the racially mixed neighborhoods of West Adams, between the Santa Monica Freeway and Pico Boulevard; by the second day, rioters had invaded stores in Koreatown as far north as Santa Monica Boulevard (Morrison and Lowry 1994).

Although the Latino population had risen to about half of South LA, few Latino elected officials represented the riot-torn areas in the early 1990s. There were also sharp class distinctions among Latinos: those who lived around Koreatown were mostly poor, recent immigrants who did not speak English. Of these, a good proportion of Mexicans were undocumented, while those from war-torn El Salvador and Nicaragua were legal immigrants who possessed only temporary status (Kwong 1992, 89).

Koreans referred to Latinos in many different ways, including "Seupae-niswi" (Korean pronunciation of "Spanish"); "Seobaneoin" (meaning Spanish speakers in Korean, and used only among older people), "Hispanic" (the most popular term), "Latino," "Mexican," "Maekjak" (meaning Mexican worker; this alluded to the perception of Latinos as steady and loyal workers for Korean employers), "Amigo" (friend in Spanish), "Hermano" (brother in Spanish), and "JJanggu" (meaning blockhead or someone with tunnel vision, but in an affectionately teasing way). The shift away from a more functionalist term, "Maekjak," to a friendlier term, "JJanggu," indicated a closer relationship between these two groups, at least from the Korean immigrants' perspectives. While these terms were used among Korean immigrants to refer to Latinos, the terms "amigo" and "hermano" were often used to address them. One interviewee reported that when he wanted to hire 10 Latino workers, he said, "I need Amigo 10," calling Latinos "friends" for instrumental reasons. "Hermano" was used in more informal settings. The use of Spanish terms reflected the fact that Latinos were the majority of the workforce at Korean business establishments.

In terms of the ways Latinos referred to Korean immigrant merchants, the most common terms were "chino" (Spanish for Chinese), "coreano" (Spanish for Korean), "cochino" (Spanish for dirty), or "ppali ppali people" (literally, those who ask you to work as fast as possible). "Chino" implied a certain amount of contempt, reflecting Latin Americans' first contact with Chinese merchants in the nineteenth century.[10] Just as Korean immigrants were somewhat ignorant about the heterogeneity within the Latino community, Latinos often failed to distinguish Koreans from other East Asian immigrants; thus, the common use of "chino." Nonetheless, some Latinos did recognize a specific Korean ethnicity and used "coreano." "Ppali ppali people" connoted Koreans' fast-paced work ethic, middle-class position, employer status, and frequent commands to hurry up.

While Black-Korean tensions were primarily based on a merchant-customer relationship, Latino and Korean immigrants related to each other in myriad ways, including employer-employee relations, fellow worker relations, landlord-tenant relations, neighbors, or merchant-customers. Even before the unrest, Korean-Latino relations were sometimes antagonistic, though such tensions often went unarticulated. In the 2000 Koreatown Immigrant Workers Alliance (KIWA) survey of restaurant workers, 30 out of the 52 Latino workers had specific complaints about their treatment by Korean owners, including low wages, unreasonable hours, no lunch breaks, and insults from their supervisors.[11] Korean employers tend to believe they treat Latino employees with respect and fairness, but they often "reproduce the subordination of Latinos" and safeguard Korean advantage in workplaces, albeit to a lesser extent than White and Latino agricultural employers (Maldonado 2009, 1032). They also use race/ethnicity, citizenship, or legal status as proxies for worker quality and as markers for the desirability of workers. This racialized assessment reflects their hiring and recruitment practices of targeting Latino worker networks to fill low-wage jobs. The invocation of ethnic/cultural difference by Korean employers tends to normalize and fails to problematize the ethnic segmentation of jobs and racial hierarchies at Korean-owned business establishments.

Therefore, while African Americans encountered Koreans primarily as merchants, Latino-Korean encounters took place in a wider range of situations, partly because of the predominantly Latino employees at Korean business establishments. The situations were "not a blatant conflict like Blacks and Koreans. [Latinos and Koreans] are both immigrant, politically marginalized communities" (*LAT* September 21, 1998). I was surprised when I heard a Korean customer complimenting Latino employees' Korean language skills at a Korean-run supermarket in Gardena. In another case, a Nicaraguan church minister was invited to an after-lunch service for a Korean employer, as well as other Nicaraguan and Latino employees. At the service, the minister asked Latino garment workers to express thanks for the chance to work in the US. Specifically, he reminded his fellow Nicaraguans of the nearly 80 percent unemployment rate back home.

Despite a certain degree of interethnic tension, young Latinos and Korean Americans seemed to socialize in increasing numbers during my period of research. Miguel, a 33-year-old Salvadoran car mechanic who worked for a Korean employer for more than a decade, told me, "I would like to marry a Korean woman. That would be nice. You know anybody you can introduce to me?" Both the *Los Angeles Times* and *Korea Times* featured stories of interracial marriages between Latinos and Koreans, which partially reflects an overall rise in interracial marriage more broadly in the US. Koreatown youth were also influenced by other inner-city youth, including Latinos, in their conception of gender and sexuality. I observed young Korean American women applying makeup or wearing clothing in similar ways to Latinas, and some Latinas frequented Korean cosmetics stores. Some US-born Korean American children also complained that their parents speak Korean and Spanish to them, but not English. On the other hand, some Korean immigrant parents complained that their children speak Spanish, Portuguese, and English, but not Korean. Despite a certain degree of interethnic harmony, I found that language barriers, cultural differences, and prejudices still prevented many Korean and Latino workers, employers, and schoolmates from developing close relationships.

## FOUR KOREAN PERSPECTIVES ON BLACKS AND LATINOS

After the unrest, the Korean immigrant small business proprietors I interviewed articulated four different constructions of race and ethnicity concerning African Americans and Latinos. In the first, Latinos were thought of more positively than African Americans, a view that developed before the 1992 riots. The second contradicts the first one, in that African Americans were viewed more positively than Latinos. The third construction portrayed both Latinos and African Americans negatively. Finally, there were the interviewees who adopted a "big picture" perspective: the participation of both African Americans and Latinos in the rioting made them more cognizant of the class-based nature of the unrest, and they tended to blame the "system." I now discuss these four perspectives in detail.

### More Positive Views toward Latinos than African Americans

The 1992 LA unrest reinforced some Korean interviewees' notions of African Americans as poor, uneducated, violent criminals, partly because media coverage focused on Black mobs burning down Korean stores (Cho 1993). Many Koreans accused Blacks of exploiting their more "authentic" Americanness and greater political power to hurt Korean economic interests. One-third of interviewees (N=52) held this view. Perhaps it was because "although at times [Koreans] have not helped to improve the situation of Blacks in this country, they certainly didn't create the inequality either" (Lee, cited in Choi 1992, 95). However, while Korean merchants did have a choice and contributed to the inequality that Black customers faced, it was that perpetuation of inequality that African Americans were protesting when they targeted Korean businesses.

A positive view of Latinos and negative view of African Americans was articulated by the owner of Jean's Liquor Store (1992) (see figure 6.3).

Upon first immigrating to the US, he wanted to work in the field of computer manufacturing. He had received his engineering degree in Korea, but the credentials did not transfer to the US. Limited by his financial resources, he bought a business in South LA. In justifying his negative view of African Americans, he said that unlike Koreans, they lacked concern for their children:

> For instance, once they receive their welfare checks, selfish mothers tend to buy beer for themselves instead of things needed for their children. I know that I have no right to judge others. Look at Mexicans living in this neighborhood. They always work very hard, and yet they are often robbed by Blacks.

It was not apparent whether this merchant believed that the class of "selfish mothers" was limited to inner-city Black women, but his observation spoke

Figure 6.3.  Liquor stores are corner stores for everything (photo by Kyeyoung Park).

to interracial crime in the neighborhood. He asserted that after *Sa-I-Gu,*[12] his view of African Americans deteriorated, while his view of "Mexicans" (a term he used to refer to Salvadorans as well) remained positive. When I mentioned that the looters were not only African Americans, he responded: "In the middle of *Sa-I-Gu,* once Blacks unlocked the stores, then other people such as Latinos joined the looting. Well, the reason why more Latinos than Blacks were arrested was due to the fact that police arrested them, not Blacks."[13] It was not possible to verify whether his statement was true.

The owner of Right on Market on Arlington Blvd. (1993), whose entire store was looted, lost $60,000 worth of property during the unrest (see figure 6.4).

He also expressed a deeper affinity with Latinos than with African Americans.

"Spanish," like the African Americans, are very naive. However, because they think a little bit more like Asians, it is easier to understand and befriend them. Blacks are very naive and simpleminded. They have no sense of right and wrong, so I do not blame them and I have no hatred for them.

He's clearly reinforcing racist notions about Blacks, but he's also infantilizing them. It's not the same as what the previous interviewee said.

**Figure 6.4.** A looted Korean-run store shows the damage some merchants had to confront (photo by Kyeyoung Park).

Similarly, the son of Moon's Market's owner (1993), a 26-year-old 1.5-generation immigrant, spoke positively about Latinos: "'Spanish' are more afraid of going to jail. They are more family-oriented. They are not real Americans. They came here for a better life like us." My interviewees repeatedly commented on how similar immigrant experiences and mentalities of Koreans and Latinos contributes to a greater affinity for each other, namely greater degree of shared work ethic, both don't have as much historical baggage in the US as African Americans, etc. (though Latinos have a much longer history than Koreans).

On the other hand, he stated of African Americans:

> Blacks are the most racist people alive. Why do they pick on the Korean community because Rodney King got beat up? Why didn't they burn down Beverly Hills first! If Koreans were to be picked on, then this whole thing should have blown up after the Soon Ja Du incident, but it did not. Of course, we can't forget that media had a lot to with venting hatred among Blacks and Koreans, but they didn't make up something that was never there.

He seemingly disagreed with the parallels made by the African American community with regards to the acquittal of four LAPD officers in the Rodney King trial and the aftermath of the Soon Ja Du trial. In other words, for Blacks, both incidents indicated the devaluing of Black lives by the judicial system and justified the anger directed at Koreans during the unrest (Stevenson 2013). Finally, the owner of B&W Market (1993), whose store was also looted and destroyed, expressed his affinity for Mexican immigrants, while noting diversity within the Latino community: "There are indeed so many different nationalities within the Hispanics, so it is hard to generalize about them. But the Mexicans are much nicer, and I feel that they are culturally similar to Koreans. For example, look at their food . . . they eat spicy things just like we do."

What is apparent within this first perspective is that Korean immigrant shopkeepers seemed oblivious to African Americans' long history of struggle for equality, including the Civil Rights Movement, and the histories of the neighborhood in which they had established businesses. This is in line with common views before the unrest, reflecting Korean immigrant merchants' defensiveness in the wake of much-publicized Black boycotts of Korean stores. It is also relevant that these interviewees, as direct victims of the unrest, were still traumatized from the violent racial conflicts and considered their Black customers a potential threat. Finally, this view perceived Black and Latino participation in the unrest in contrasting ways, believing that while African Americans instigated looting and burning out of racial antagonism, Latinos joined the rioting passively, due to poverty and mob psychology. It is worth noting that this view corresponded to the dominant public discourse on the subject.

## More Positive Views toward African Americans than Latinos

The second perspective viewed African Americans positively and Latinos negatively. Many interviewees seemed shocked by the large number of Latinos who participated in the looting, because they had held positive views of Latinos before the unrest. There was a 50-year-old widowed mother of four (1993) who had immigrated to the States in 1971 and run a market in Compton for the past 13 years. Her market was completely destroyed during the unrest, and she lost nearly $500,000 in addition to experiencing emotional trauma. However, her view of African Americans was positive:

> Those Blacks who are educated are wonderful. The good ones always say "thank you" and "please." The nice Blacks are very nice. When I went back to my store, several of my customers came, hugged me, and asked why something like this should happen to such nice people like us. They were genuinely sorry for what happened to us, and I know that they meant it. . . . The Blacks are more honest and say sorry for what happened to us.

Hope (1993), a 33-year-old woman who immigrated to the US in 1960, owned New Star Market on Normandie Avenue and had similarly positive experiences with Black customers. On the first night of the riots, she got a call from her Black neighbor telling her not to go to the store because the rioters would kill her. Her Black neighbors also saved her store from burning down. When asked how and why she thought the unrest happened, she responded:

> The main reason why this happened is [because] there was an [explosion] of feelings of hopelessness among the Black community members. The verdict was an excuse for the rioting. The primary reason for the riot was poverty and low standards of living. . . . Elderly Black customers came into the store after the riots, crying and asking how something like this could have happened. In America, there is no fear of God. People need to come back to a real relationship with God in order to get their lives straight.

Her view of African Americans was atypical among Koreans:

> I don't have any difficulty with Blacks. When I was younger, my mother and father ran a grocery store in South Central LA, and all of their Black customers used to call my mother "mama" or "umma." Blacks are warmer people who show gratitude willingly. I really like them. I miss many of my customers. They do treat me well. They saw me pregnant with both of my boys and always ask

about them. Whenever I go into the store, I hug and greet them. I realize that other Koreans cannot do this because they are not as physically affectionate. I can relate better with some Blacks than Koreans. There are bad Blacks just like there are bad Koreans. I try to see people as individuals, and I firmly believe that with most people, if you are nice to them, they will respond.

Daisy (1993) was a 1.5-generation immigrant, 38-year-old lawyer, and mother of two children who had a law office on Wilshire Blvd. She witnessed the fires and chaos breaking out from her office window. While her view of African Americans did not change after the riots, her view of Latinos deteriorated:

I used to think positively about Latinos and their contributions to this city. I was happy to have them in LA and saw them as hard workers. However, after I saw them looting the stores and trying to justify their actions by saying that it is OK to steal, I [had] a big change in my attitude about illegal immigration. I am now totally against it and believe that we need to monitor the immigration system more thoroughly. I am against them crossing the border.

She assumed the looters were undocumented and not here legally or citizens. Her views of Latinos resonated with studies showing that Mexican immigrants are stereotypically identified as undocumented and dangerous criminals (Gomberg-Muñoz 2010, 301).

Jane (1993), a 36-year-old woman who immigrated to the US in 1985, owned a music store located within an indoor swap meet on Slauson Avenue that was looted and burned. For many days, she could not sleep because of nightmares and held tremendous anger against both African Americans and Mexicans. However, she seemed to justify African Americans behavior, but she did not attempt to understand Latinos:

Before, I thought that the majority of Blacks were lazy and undisciplined. Now, I see that there may be other outside forces, which shape their attitudes and actions. They [Latinos] don't have a sense of wrong or right. I think they have low morals. I heard that Mexican men are very girl crazy and cheat on their wives. They whistle [at] another woman when their wives are standing right next to them.

Finally, the owner of King's Market (1994), a business that suffered $150,000 in damage, held more negative views about Latinos than Blacks, especially those in Latino gangs:

They [Mexicans and other Latinos] are equally wicked like Blacks. Whereas Blacks do robbery only, Mexicans are crueler to the extent that they just shoot at you even after taking money and other things.

Compared with the first, more positive view of Latinos, this more negative perspective was not widespread: it corresponded to only 25 percent of interviewees.

## Negative Perspectives on both African Americans and Latinos

A substantial number of interviewees expressed negative views of both African Americans and Latinos, with feelings corresponding more to fear than resentment and anger. One of my students whose family's shoe store had burned down in 1992 recollected:

> As my parents were coming home, they heard on the radio that a shoe store on Olympic and Alvarado was being looted. They were not on the freeway for more than a few minutes, so they turned around and went back to the store. As they drove up to the parking lot, they could see people running out of the store with our shoes. According to the shopping center security guard, 15 to 20 African Americans armed with shotguns, pipes, hammers, and other threatening objects came and broke into the store. . . . Instead of going to school the next day, and our whole family went to see our shoe store. Nothing was left. The whole complex was burned down. All we could see was the shelf of the building and a little fire still burning in the back. That was my birthday.

Having experienced the ordeal firsthand and hearing about the experiences of other Koreans, she became very angry: "I hated all Blacks and Mexicans. These are not politically correct terms, but that is how I felt. I felt the Korean community was targeted by the Black community." Although she personally thought the Korean merchant Soon Ja Du had gotten off too easily and the verdict in the Rodney King case was unexpected, she was upset that racial tensions led minorities to destroy their own community.

A 51-year-old Korean immigrant, owner of Park's Super Market (1993), lost $450,000. He had owned his business since 1985, and all of his employees were African Americans. His view of African Americans and Latinos deteriorated in the aftermath:

> There is racial preference in the US. After the riots, our perception of African Americans changed drastically. Initially, we wanted to be friends with them. But both parties have built up now the wall between us even higher. The Hispanics looted even more than the Blacks. Out of the 700 people that looted our store, more than half of them were Hispanics. We also grew to hate Whites, even more so than before. They are selfish and concerned solely with their own agendas.

After the interview ended, this man's wife explained how she and her husband had tried to live peacefully in South LA: "We did all we could. We got along really well with our customers. In fact, we thought they were our friends." She broke down in tears as she explained the situation: "During the riots, even our friends joined in the free-for-all. If God grants us, we will pack up and leave the second we can. . . . But I can't because I'd be buried in debt."

A similar perspective was offered by the owner of L.A. Frank's Liquor store (1993). When I interviewed him, he was seated in an oversized director's chair elevated a foot off the ground and encircled by a large counter, looking more like a sheriff in a Western film than a merchant in his fifties from South LA. In April 1992, he suffered not only economic losses of $100,000, but also physical, psychological, and emotional damage. He expressed disappointment in Latinos as well as African Americans:

These [Black] people are generally good . . . but ignorant. They need to work instead of relying on welfare. To the contrary, the Hispanics work, and still they looted! Their history is actually longer than African Americans. Therefore, they live better than African Americans. But they are still the same [as Blacks]!

Wealthy property owners who owned numerous commercial buildings had similar views on African Americans and Latinos. Yolanda (1993), a 51-year-old woman, and her husband own five commercial buildings, including one in Inglewood. One-third of a building they own in Long Beach was burned, and all of their stores were looted. She experienced stress and insomnia, expressing fear of African Americans and a stereotyped view of Latinos:

I have an intense fear of Blacks. After the riots, I have been trying extra hard to be nicer to them so that they will not destroy our stores again. When I am nice to them, I hope I am giving them a good impression of Korean people. Although I am nice to them outwardly, I am truly scared and do not like them deep inside.

I feel very sorry for [Latinos]. They have to take all of the menial jobs, such as janitors and house cleaners. They are below everyone else. They are probably the lowest status group in America, below Blacks. It's because they are illegal aliens and can't speak English.

Similarly, Melody (1993), a 49-year-old woman who has lived in the States since 1980, was the owner of Young's Fashion, a women's clothing store at an indoor swap meet in South Gate. She described how worried she was during the unrest:

I cried every day whenever I thought about what happened. I would be driving, and when I [thought] about it, I [started] weeping. When I [watched] TV or when anyone talked about it, I cried. My eyes were filled with tears. I felt that under my skin was just water waiting to spill forth gallons of tears. I have an intense fear of Black people now. I felt like I was going crazy, and I had extreme paranoia.

> When three Hispanic men walk in together into the swap meet, I get incredible fear and panic. I am very suspicious of everyone. Everyone seems like a thief or criminal to me these days. I fear Blacks a lot, but there aren't too many around where I do business. So I am more afraid of Mexican cholos [Mexican gangsters].

She generalized negatively about her Black customers as well:

> I don't hate Blacks. I feel sorry for them because they have no education. They are lazy and dirty, and there is nothing that the government can really do about that. In Korea, the poor people raise their children better than the rich people. So, the Blacks have no excuse as to why their children are so corrupt and without any morals. You cannot blame everything on poverty. . . . When Blacks come into my store, all they think about is stealing. When I see a Black girl in my store, I tell my employee to keep an eye on her. One hundred percent of the time, they are caught stealing—100 percent. Even when I am nice to them, they steal. So whether I am polite or suspicious, they steal. They also come into my store and make a big scene. They are so loud. When I see them like this, I feel very sorry for them. They seem so ignorant and uneducated. I know [Latinos] well because they worked for me for so long. . . . When they are amongst themselves, they make fun of us Koreans. They gossip about us a lot. I know this because my employee tells me. They look docile, but they are tougher and stronger than us. I noticed that they help each other out a lot. They are what we Koreans were 30 years ago in Korea.

The above quote is fairly extreme, as it reinforces racist stereotypes. Nonetheless, she tends to racialize a significant amount of work-related stress, which is caused by high levels of criminal victimization, a variety of face-to-face interactions with culturally unfamiliar and heterogeneous customers, and the financial precariousness of small business ownership, as riot victim.

The owner of Century Liquor Store (1992) also perpetuated racist stereotypes:

> In a way, [Latinos] are similar to Blacks. From our perspective, they are mostly thieves. . . . I wonder whether they [Latinos] have any conscience at all. The only difference is the fact that they do not file lawsuits against the store owners after shoplifting or robbery and that their leaders do not demand *t'ose*, site tax [claims on a certain territory], particularly toward newcomers.

Even a decade after the unrest, there remained a general tendency in our dominant discourse to view Latinos close to African Americans in a new racial hierarchy that placed Whites (and to a lesser extent Asians) at the top. The negative feelings expressed by Korean store owners coincided with this tendency of the dominant discourse.

## Class-Based Perceptions of African Americans and Latinos

Nopper (2006) noted a striking similarity of the criticism lobbied at both Black rioters and public officials in the 1960s to that expressed by various Korean/Asian American commentators toward the police and government regarding their responses to the 1992 L.A. Riots. Nopper asserts that perhaps the criticism lobbied at the police and public officials is a structural perspective dictated not just by one's racial position, but also by one's economic relationship to African American consumers (Nopper 2006, 84).

Some Korean interviewees recognized the importance of class as a way of distinguishing people of different races and ethnicities in US society, even if it was not a fully developed analysis or they did not attribute the situation directly to class. For instance, a substantial number of interviewees seemed to distinguish between local Black customers and Black community leaders, indicating their awareness of class status differences within the African American community.

The interviewees also identified outside gang members (who were a class of their own) as instigators of the looting and arson during the 1992 unrest and differentiated them from their local customers. In this way, the interviewees justified continuing to conduct business with local customers, deliberately trying to forget the fact that they witnessed their looting. In the aftermath of the unrest, Korean immigrant merchants seemed to be more aware of class differentiation, in particular different levels of education and age differences within the Black community.

The Latinos who looted also challenged most Korean merchants' construction of race and ethnicity. Korean Americans interpreted African Americans' participation in looting as connected to their lack of family ties or a "culture of poverty," but could not attribute similar causes to Latinos. In their opinion, Latinos, like Korean immigrants, worked hard and were family-oriented; and yet, they still participated in the looting. Some merchants blamed Latino looting on other Korean merchants' bad treatment of Latino employees. Others distinguished between different kinds of Latinos in terms of ethnicity, national origin, legal status, and/or class position.

Despite the overall perceptions of class as related to African Americans, some merchants recognized that it was Black customers who saved their businesses during the riots. The owner of Benji Liquor Market on Vermont Ave (1993), a 54-year-old man, immigrated to the US in 1977. He incurred $100,000 in damages, although he was able to put out the fire just in time due to his Black customers' warning. When he was asked how and why the riots happened, he responded: "It was not a racial issue; it was more an excuse for what I believe to have been a class issue." He continued:

> I have no special feelings for them [Blacks]; they are just like everyone else. . . . It was an African American who helped salvage my store. Before the riots began, he warned me so I was able to get prepared. When I asked him why he did that, he told me that it was because I was so nice to his kids. This person has a son that is very cute, so I used to give him candy and tell him that I would like to make him my own son. By simply being nice, I was able to build a friendship that helped save my store.

Some Korean merchants attributed the unrest to systematic inequality, and not to individual Black or Latino customers. A 52-year-old man (1993), the owner of B+W Market on Vermont Ave., immigrated to the US in 1989. He lost about $25,000 in merchandise and planned on leaving at the end of that year. However, he did not blame African Americans: "It's the US political system's fault. The Whites are suppressing the Blacks from going up. It's the top people trying to keep down those on the bottom. Cultural differences are here and will be here always. But that is not the cause." Similarly, some Korean store owners, like the owner of Western Grocery (1992), rationalized African Americans' behaviors by citing poverty and drug abuse in the Black community:

> I do not think I ever discriminated toward any other people, including Blacks. In my opinion, Black problems are due to their extreme poverty, something like moon village, *taldongne*, in Korea.[14] They are poverty-stricken beyond our imagination. I have seen three African American households living in a one bedroom apartment upstairs.

The owner of ABIC Liquor Store (1992) also focused on the poverty of his customers:

> In principle, Blacks are simple and good-natured, but need education. During the riot, I have seen Black gang members from outside our community, *kkeom-dungyi*, ["dark-faced Black folk"] load my stuff onto their truck and set fire to my store, which was put out by my customers. Nevertheless, I interpret that they [the gang members] did it not because of their hatred toward Korean Americans, but because they wanted to express their dissatisfaction with the current system that keeps them poor. According to our Korean proverb, "Without food for three days, anybody can climb the wall in search of food."

The owner of Pay-Less Liquor Store (1992) felt discouraged about the possibility of improving relations with African Americans. Despite his negative perceptions, he stated that during the riots, he shouted out "We are also

Blacks," a line from the acclaimed Spike Lee movie *Do the Right Thing*. He thought his store would be saved from destruction if he pretended it was Black-owned (see figure 6.5).

When I asked him about Latinos, he likened them to his Black customers:

> Sometimes they [Latinos] bring fake checks to cash. They seem to be a neighbor to Blacks. Despite their Catholic tradition, they were involved in [the] looting and destruction. From their participation, I could understand that this riot originated from poverty. This reminded me of the Korean War [1950–1953], *Yuk-I-O*.[15] We all starved those days.

Indeed, older Korean immigrants who had experienced the Korean War were more able to sympathize with poor people of other races or ethnicities, indicating the role of intertextual memory in forming opinions and class-based sympathies toward other ethnic groups.

Mrs. Kwon (1993), a 50-year-old woman who immigrated to the US in 1980, had been running a One Hour Photo Shop on Crenshaw Blvd since 1990. All the machines and camera equipment were damaged and the front

Figure 6.5.   After the 1992 uprising, many signs indicating Black ownership appeared on storefronts (photo by Kyeyoung Park).

windows smashed during the unrest. Nonetheless, although she and her husband were also physically attacked, she was able to differentiate looters from her own customers, stating:

> Our customers are nice people. I don't think of them as necessarily bad. But some Blacks lack education (of life, of manners) and behave in less sophisticated ways . . . the [Rodney] King verdict may have started this, but when we look at the whole scheme of things, the Blacks have been ignored by White society and the tension from that; Koreans got caught in the middle.

Mrs. Lee (1993), a 56-year-old mother of three, immigrated to the States in 1979, and had run a book and gift store since 1987. She felt that Koreans had mistreated African Americans, and that was why they were targeted. Immediately after the riots, she felt fear and suspicion about every Black person she saw. However, as a Christian, she tried to practice generosity:

> Many Blacks come into our store to ask for money. Oftentimes, I try to smile at them and give them either money or small gifts. At least once a day, a Black person comes into our store. I find myself trying to prepare something to give them every day. If they come during lunchtime, I usually share my lunch with them.

Mrs. Kim (1993), a 54-year-old mother of one, immigrated to the States in 1971, and had run a gas station in Compton since 1979. The looters came to their store with a pickup truck and took everything. However, the looting did not affect the way she felt about African Americans and Latinos:

> I really like Blacks. Although there are many who deal in drugs, I love them too. I feel very sorry for them. I have been working in the Black community for so many years now that I feel very close to them. Whenever my regular customers meet me, they always say, "Hi, Mom." I really feel that people are much nicer after the riots. I really appreciate the Black people making an extra effort to be more polite and nice to me. If we were in [the Latinos'] situation, we would have done the same thing. If we could understand the misery and poverty that they live in, we cannot point fingers and judge them.

Like Mrs. Kim, a former nurse had nothing but compliments for African Americans and Latinos in the aftermath of the unrest. Mrs. Ho (1993), 53 years old and widowed, immigrated to the US in 1969. She has run a liquor and deli store on Vernon for the past four years. She lost nearly half a million dollars in damages, as her business was burned and destroyed; she was left with almost nothing after over twenty years in America.[16] In spite of this, her positive perception of other minorities didn't change in the aftermath: "I felt no animosity towards Blacks before or after the riots. . . . I have worked with a lot of Blacks as a nurse and as a business owner. I was very comfortable with them. I didn't have any troubles with them. . . . I like Latinos, especially Mexicans. I have nothing against them."

The following exchange is excerpted from a discussion about Latinos among three Korean immigrants (1994)—a painter with his own firm (P), a pharmacist and drug store owner (Ph), (and a missionary)—who were taking Spanish lessons from a teacher (T) at the Koreatown YMCA. They came to feel sympathetic towards Latinos, as they realized that they racialized and ethnicized Latino working-class lives, overlooking the effects of poverty:

*Ph:* We tend to look down upon them for various reasons—lack of education, having many children, particularly teenage pregnancy, dependency on welfare, etc. However, their close family ties seem to be similar to ours.

*P:* Yes, you are right. Their lifestyle is strikingly similar to us. For instance, when I offered Korean hot and spicy food such as *Kimch'i-kuk* [soup made of *kimch'i*], *sundae-kuk* [soup made of Korean sausages], and fish stew, they were able to enjoy it so well.

*Ph:* They seem to care about *jeong* [a Korean concept meaning warmth, affection, or love] like us. Friendship seems to matter a lot to them, even in business transactions.

*P:* I have hired many of them for my painting business. They work well and their wage is inexpensive. . . . I would give orders to my Hispanic employees in Korean in my painting work. . . . They often ask for workers' compensation or sue Korean employers for that reason. Nevertheless, I say that they work better than Koreans. They are handy men. Once they start to work, they work hard. They know how to fix various things, even automobiles.

*Ph:* I also see them work hard when they need money. Otherwise they would like to have fun without work. They often come late for work, as they often stay late drinking beers.

*T:* Now, our generations know how to fix only one thing, not everything, but our parents used to do that, didn't they? [All agreed.] Why do you think that they often drink a lot?

*P:* Perhaps they are lonely as they left their family members in Mexico.

*Ph:* There is a great heterogeneity within their community. For instance, Mexicans living in Northridge belong to the middle class, unlike those living around Olvera Street. One day a job candidate for my drug store told me that her father doesn't want her to work in dangerous places like Koreatown. I was surprised to hear that.

*P:* Yeah, I find people from Peru to be responsible and to have close ties to each other. I also like people from El Salvador, toward whom I feel friendly.

*Ph:* I was really impressed with the fact that they really help each other. Once, one of my Latino employees asked me to sponsor him in purchasing the house. He bought it based on ten or twelve of his family members collectively. He reminded me of the extended big family in Korea.

Early in the discussion, these Korean, immigrant, small-business owners and professionals presented somewhat negative perceptions of Latino immigrants. As they discussed their everyday experiences with Latinos at their workplaces, however, they came to realize that poverty was prevalent among Latinos. They were also able to distinguish between different Latinos, speaking about Latino culture and some similarities to Korean culture. As a result, they began to feel sympathetic towards Latinos, affirming the influence of perceptions of poverty in cultural processes.

## POST-UNREST HIRING PRACTICES IN SOUTH CENTRAL

How did the traumatic effects of the unrest affect Korean immigrant merchants' conception of race and ethnicity in their everyday lives? Hiring practices are one angle through which to understand this issue. Before the unrest, many Korean storeowners utilized a family and wage labor system, using both Korean and non-Korean labor for the latter. Since the African American community demanded the hiring of local residents before the unrest, I wanted to explore whether there were any changes in the hiring practices of Korean immigrant merchants after the 1992 unrest. Before the unrest, 39 percent of paid non-family employees (N=64) in Korean-owned stores were Mexicans/ Latinos and 31 percent were Black employees, showing a slight preference for Latinos rather than African Americans (see Table 7.1). In contrast, after the unrest, 52 percent of paid non-family employees (N = 52) were Black employees and 21 percent were Latino employees.[17]

Jennifer Lee (2002) found, Jewish and Korean merchants in New York and Philadelphia hired Black employees and managers to act as "cultural brokers" between Korean store owners and their predominantly Black clientele in order to minimize arguments with their customers. Similarly, in my study, the newly built C+ C Market on Vermont Ave hired an African American man from the neighborhood as a guard. He did not wear a uniform or carry any kind of weapon; his only task was to follow the customers who came in and make sure no one caused any trouble. Because he was Black, African American customers took it much better when they were told certain things. For example, in one incident, the Korean business owner said something in English to a customer, and they claimed not to understand. However, when the Black employee stepped in and translated

**Table 6.1.** Racial Makeup of Non-Family Employees at Korean Stores in South LA before April 29, 1992

| No. of employees per store | Latino | Korean | Black | Other* | |
|---|---|---|---|---|---|
| 0 (2 stores) | | | | | |
| 1 (2) | 1 | 1 | 1 | | |
| 2 (3) | 3 | 0 | 3 | | |
| 3 (3) | 1 | 4 | 4 | | |
| 4 (4) | 7 | 2 | 5 | 2 | |
| 5 (2) | 1 | 4 | 5 | | |
| 6 (2) | 5 | 3 | 2 | 2 | |
| 7 | | | | | |
| 8 (1) | 7 | 0 | 0 | 1 | |
| total | 25 | 13 | 20 | 6[a] | 64[b] |
| % | 39.1 | 20.3 | 31.3 | 9.4 | 100 |

[a]Includes non-Korean Asian Americans, such as Chinese, Japanese, and Filipino Americans.
[b]64 non-family employees for 19 stores (median number of employees: 3.4)
*Source:* Kyeyoung Park

what she had said, the customer could no longer accuse the merchant of being unintelligible. Essentially, the guard was there to deter shoplifters and to intervene in any possible dispute between customers and the merchant. Nonetheless, the use of Black security guards remains controversial among African American customers, and this guard at C+ C Market was harassed and called a traitor so often that he quit. Just like Black residents don't appreciate Black cops restricting their freedom of movement, I doubt they

**Table 6.2.** Racial Makeup of Non-Family Employees at Korean Stores in South LA after April 29, 1992*

| No. of employees per store | Latino | Korean | Black | Other | |
|---|---|---|---|---|---|
| 0 (4 stores) | | | | | |
| 1 (2) | | | 2 | | |
| 2 (3) | 1 | 1 | 4 | | |
| 3 (3) | 2 | 1 | 6 | | |
| 4 (4) | 1 | 6 | 8 | 1 | |
| 5 (1) | | | 5 | | |
| 6 (1) | 3 | 2 | 1 | | |
| 7 (0) | | | | | |
| 8 (1) | 4 | 3 | 1 | | |
| total | 11 | 13 | 27 | 1[a] | 52[b] |
| % | 21.2 | 25.0 | 51.9 | 1.9 | 100 |

*Note:* Represents a different set of businesses than those present in Table 1, since not all merchants reopened their businesses after April 29, 1992.
[a]One was a Chinese American.
[b]52 non-family employees at 19 stores (median number of employees: 2.7)
*Source:* Kyeyoung Park

would look kindly upon security guards following them around. After all, the guard is just another surveillance technique.

Although the hiring of Black employees requires a more in-depth investigation, it should be noted that in South LA, Korean immigrant merchants began to hire African Americans in significant numbers only after the 1992 unrest, perhaps because the community demanded such change. They were unconsciously trying to appease Black customers. This wasn't completely successful as it wasn't really addressing the underlying issue: Black disempowerment, poverty, racism, etc. However, if they employed Black employees before the unrest, it could have reduced the tension.[18]

The racial makeup of employees changed as employers halved the number of Mexicans and Latinos they had hired, while increasing the number of Blacks employees from 31 percent to 52 percent. Thus, the specific attitudes held by merchants on race and ethnicity conflicted with their hiring practices. Hiring more African Americans did not fully translate into new perceptions of African Americans.

As we saw in the previous sections, in the aftermath of the unrest, Korean immigrant merchants' constructions of race and ethnicity reflected varied feelings, not only toward Latinos and African Americans, but also toward Whites, indicating victimhood and a sense of betrayal.

## POST-UNREST KOREAN IMMIGRANT MERCHANTS' CONSTRUCTIONS OF RACE AND ETHNICITY

As I discussed in previous chapters, the state's response to Korean-Black tensions in the 1980s was ad hoc and used stopgap measures rather than broader policies. Before the unrest, the state only intervened to manage interracial relations. Their policy included efforts to incorporate and mobilize the leaders of each community and focused on interpersonal conflicts rather than assessing the structural causes (Ong, Park, and Tong 1994b, 282). The 1992 unrest instantly transformed the political climate and actions of local government, raising new concerns about urban poverty and racial injustice. However, the LA mayor's solution relied on the privatization of rebuilding efforts,[19] and new policies placed Korean merchants at a disadvantage with little consideration or compensation. For example, the policy favored a campaign to "rebuild LA" without liquor stores, barring Korean Americans' efforts to rebuild many of their businesses (see chapter 7).

In the mainstream, state-connected media, armed Korean men were portrayed as lawless vigilantes shooting at looters randomly, while women were shown screaming hysterically or begging and crying in front of their ruined stores (Choy et al., 1993). The tape showing Soon Ja Du shooting Latasha Harlins, discussed in chapter 2, was the second most played video during the week of the 1992 riots. African Americans were criticized for blaming others for their poverty, while Korean store owners were reprimanded for neither investing in the Black community nor treating customers with respect.

Right-wing commentators denied that anti-Black racism played any role in either the unrest or the King verdict. President George H. W. Bush addressed the country on May 1, 1992, denouncing "random terror and lawlessness," summarizing his discussions with Mayor Bradley and Governor Wilson, and outlining the federal assistance he was making available to local authorities. Citing the "urgent need to restore order," he warned that the "brutality of a mob" would not be tolerated and that he would "use whatever force is necessary." Furthermore, Bush and other commentators indicted the programs of the Great Society for creating the conditions that led to the unrest.[20] Thus, they argued for even more militarization and policing in the daily lives of poor minorities deemed threatening to the public welfare, not to mention of shedding "the pathologies of the decimated Black family" (*National Review* June 8, 1992).

Left-wing commentators, in contrast, interpreted the 1992 riots as an uprising and massive protest, and not a random, senseless outbreak of mob violence. As discussed in chapter 1, South LA's longtime major employers in heavy industry had been leaving the area since the 1960s and were virtually wiped out during the economic recession of 1979–1982. Furthermore, the War on Poverty and its programs, which had been lifelines in this community, had been either curtailed or eliminated, with devastating social and economic effects. By the 1980s, Los Angeles embodied a remarkable paradox in which an "accumulation of misery" existed alongside "spectacular displays of wealth" (*Economic and Political Weekly* July 25, 1992).

Sociologist Rose Kim aptly writes that it was the overarching society's neglect of the Black community and urban poverty that created the social environment in which Korean Americans could be scapegoated for the riots (2007, 348). Angela Oh, in her interview with *The New York Times* (May 2, 1993), expressed similar sentiments:

> The place of Koreans in American society is lonely and precarious and has served as a convenient buffer between the racism of the White majority and the anger of the Black minority. Just as Korean-owned businesses, which suffered nearly half the looting and vandalism in last year's violence, became an outlet for the rage of many rioters, Korean Americans here now view themselves as "human shields" in a complicated racial hierarchy. . . . We are perceived as being, as a people, greedy, selfish, insulated, and unwilling to become a part of America.

Worse, Korean Americans lacked political clout to appeal to the public, especially since, for the most part, their perspective had been shut out of local and national media coverage of the unrest. Within hours of the King verdict, most media coverage had shifted their focus to rudimentary depictions of the "Black-Korean" or "Black-Asian" conflict. What was missing from media coverage was in-depth analysis of why. While describing Korean merchants as "vigilantes" and as running businesses that exploited the Black community, the popular ABC news show *Nightline* invited prominent Black leaders to air their views on Black-Korean tensions, but they initially did not invite their Korean American counterparts. Prompted by protests from Korean Americans, *Nightline* host Ted Koppel later invited Angela Oh to provide another perspective.

Television screens also bombarded viewers with images of desperate merchants firing from the rooftops of their shops, but they failed to show that these store owners, abandoned by police and other law enforcement authorities, were returning gunfire initiated by others (E. Park 1998, 51). K. W. Lee (1999), then editor of the *Korea Times* English edition, wrote of the 1992 riots: "It was our Warsaw. Of all places on earth, we have met our own latter-day pogrom in the City of Los Angeles. . . . .[21] It's a textbook case history of media scapegoating in these hard times, pitting a politically powerful but economically frustrated minority against a seemingly thriving tribe of strangers." Similarly, filmmaker Kim Gibson commented: "I was angry, furious and enraged by the way mainstream media covered the losses of Korean American victims . . . it appeared as if we were the issue, we were the problem. We were never represented as if we were . . . human beings" (Gateward 2003). The Korean American community also complained that the media spotlight focused on poor African Americans who deserved pity and excluded the impoverished Korean merchants who seldom had the insurance necessary to rebuild their businesses; in other words, the media had reduced them to voiceless foreigners and greedy, vigilante storekeepers. Korean Americans also contested the way mainstream media framed the riots as an event played out among minority groups—Blacks, Latinos, and Asians. Instead, they stressed the role of the dominant White society plagued by racism and stratification and reflected in the various state apparatus: the politicians who ignored them, the police who failed to protect them. Other Korean Americans blamed themselves, as if they somehow deserved what they got.

Based on this new critical understanding of American society, many in the Korean American community learned the importance of participation in political and social processes. Political empowerment became an urgent and immediate goal. A number of US-educated 1.5- and 2nd-generation Korean Americans recognized this gap and began to pursue representation in mainstream politics. It was no coincidence that six Korean Americans were elected to local, state, and federal political offices during the 1992 November elections.[22] In addition to attributing the predicament of Korean Americans during the unrest to political exclusion, progressive political leaders also linked the events to Republican neglect of the inner cities and racial inequality in mainstream political institutions, including the criminal justice system. Some sought to build interracial coalitions (Regalado 1995), such as the Multicultural Collaborative (MCC), Asian Pacific Americans for a New Los Angeles (APANLA), and the Asian Pacific Planning Council (APPCON). These organizations demanded interracial and interethnic coalition-building in exchange for their participation in the rebuilding process.[23]

To a certain extent, the unrest made Korean immigrants aware of institutional racism, social and economic injustice, and the myth of the American dream of meritocracy and hard work. Nopper (2006) urges readers to acknowledge that the suffering endured by Korean American merchants should be framed in the context of relative privilege:

> The collective experience of loss, both materially and psychically, involves the mourning of conservative ideological commitments and the divestment of ill-gotten (as the realization of value under capitalism is premised on exploitation) value. It is, moreover, the resentment of frustrated bourgeois aspirations by the relative loss of status and working proximity to . . . the most despised classes of the most despised racial group in the USA. (98)

As part of the immigrant bourgeoisie, Korean merchants' racial discourse reflected dominant American views. For instance, Kapson Yim Lee (1997), an editor of the English edition of the *Korea Times*, asserted that Sa-I-Gu was a riot, not a "civil unrest," arguing that those who looted and burned down Korean immigrants' livelihoods were hoodlums and vandals, not average citizens rebelling against social injustice.[24]

Nevertheless, Korean merchants' reconstructions of race and ethnicity also conveyed aspects of oppositional ideologies, particularly as they recognized the structural causes and the multiracial dimensions of the 1992 unrest. On May 2, nearly a week after the violence erupted, about 30,000 mostly Korean Americans rallied in Koreatown to offer a unified demonstration of support to those who had been victimized, calling for peace and denouncing police violence. The protest turned out to be the largest Asian American demonstration ever held in the city. Notably, the Korean American leadership did not blame Black and Latino communities writ large for the looting and burning, although a few demanded an apology from Black community leaders. Instead, they critiqued American institutions—the media, police, and government— "for inciting tensions, reinforcing economic and political inequalities, and indirectly instigating urban violence" (Gold 2010, 146). Jin H. Lee, owner of a Compton store that burned down to the ground, stated: "I do not hate the people who burned my store. I hate the government that did not do its job because we are a minority" (*LAT* October 27, 1992). Moreover, many Koreans attributed the causes of this urban violence to oppressive federal and state policies (E. Park 1998, 48–49). What we can observe in my interviewees' responses is the coexistence of both race-based, rather prejudiced interpretations—perspectives that view African Americans and Latinos as racialized others—and class-based explanations for the unrest.

Korean immigrant merchants' four different perspectives about other minorities, as discussed above, illustrate how social inequality is often viewed in terms of race or ethnicity instead of class. Stephen Steinberg (1989) rejected the prevailing notion that cultural values and ethnic traits are the primary determinants of the economic states of racial and ethnic groups in America. He argued that locality, class conflict, selective migration, and other historical and economic factors play a far larger role not only in producing inequality but in maintaining it as well. Comaroff and Comaroff (1992) are also correct when they invoke Marx's image of the camera obscura and write: "once objectified as a 'principle' by which the division of labor is organized, ethnicity assumes the autonomous character of a prime mover in the unequal destinies of persons and populations" (59). One can see this in the aftermath of the unrest, as Koreans initiated new hiring practices and took on more Black employees (K. Park 1995). However, this strategy had other consequences, such as the pitting of African American workers against Latino workers. The identification of African American workers as an alternative to Latino labor points to "how the positioning of ethno-racial groups within the US labor queue is relational and dynamic" and responds to historically specific articulations of race, gender, class, and state formation processes (Maldonado 2009, 1033). As the ethno-racial composition of jobs change, we might expect the ideological terrain to change as well, though.

It seems that the Korean American community at large was not fully aware of the implications of their post-unrest hiring and business practices. A Korean television news crew who accompanied me to South LA Korean-immigrant businesses in the aftermath appeared to be uncomfortable with the racial makeup of the new business scene: they did not know how to make sense of Korean woman merchants continually complimenting their new Black female employees on their hairstyles and work ethic. Korean merchants also changed other business practices following the unrest, such as attempting to treat their customers with more respect and kindness to show that "the customer is king"; it should be noted that this was partly in response to the fact that many Black customers treated the merchants with apologetic politeness in the aftermath. These attempts to rethink their behavior demonstrate that these merchants did not rely exclusively on prejudice to interpret questions of race and ethnicity. Moreover, seeing Black-Korean tension as a matter of Korean prejudice toward African Americans or vice versa does not explain the shift in hiring practices. Merchants made a calculated decision to make hiring changes, but this doesn't necessarily mean they abandoned their prejudices.

Korean immigrants' reconstruction of race and ethnicity raises several important issues.[25] First, there is a disparity between ideology/culture and practice/experience (i.e., political, economic, and social realities), although both factors influence each other. We have seen contradictions between Korean immigrants' racialized business practices and their perceptions of other ethnicities, which are contradictions that neither ideology nor materialism alone can explain. For example, hiring more African Americans did not fully translate into new perceptions of African Americans. The trends reported and witnessed in the aftermath of the riots lasted for several years. However, by the late 1990s, Korean business owners had reverted to relying on Latino employees, reflecting the increasing dominance of the Latino population in South LA. Nonetheless, Korean immigrants learned a valuable lesson from the unrest: hire local people. Before the unrest, their employees were mostly Latinos, who were not necessarily local residents, supplemented by African Americans and Koreans. In the aftermath, partially as a response to the demands made by Black community leaders and partially as a reaction to Latino participation in looting, Korean merchants increased the number of Black employees and decreased the number of Latinos, which led some Korean merchants to actively pursue hiring local people. However, as increasing numbers of African Americans moved out of South LA, Korean merchants continued to hire local people, this time Latinos.

This analysis of racial/ethnic perspectives by Korean merchants reveals the circularity of the discourse surrounding the ethnically segmented labor market. Some Koreans blamed the unrest on Latinos, suspecting their Latino employees had helped Latino looters target stores. Others failed to see the systematic racism and classism at the root of the 1992 unrest. Still others saw class as the most fundamental factor in the social and cultural construction of race and ethnicity. Race scholars often think of Black-Korean or Latino-Korean relations as always polarized; however, they are much more complex. Perhaps the best we can say is that prejudices are not deep-seated, and that with personal interaction, people's attitudes towards other races and ethnicities may change over time. The next chapter takes us into the streets of South LA and examines how immigrants and native minorities interacted with each other and with mainstream institutions in the aftermath of the unrest.

# NOTES

1. This chapter was originally published, in slightly different form, in *Urban Anthropology* 24 (1995): 59–92. Reprinted with permission.

2. In addition, as many Ethnic Studies scholars have pointed out, there are places in the country where it's never simply been about Black and white. California is a prime example—where primary tensions always involved Chinese/Asians and Latinos.

3. "LAPPL–Los Angeles Police Protective League: Controversy over Rodney King beating and L.A. riots reignites," http://lapd.com/news/headlines/controversy_over_rodney_king_beating_and_la_riots_reignites/lapd.com. Accessed: October 2, 2015.

4. King knew that an arrest for a DUI would violate the terms of his parole.

5. The National Geographic Channel "The Final Report: The L.A. Riots" aired on October 4, 2006, 10 pm EDT.

6. "LAPPL–Los Angeles Police Protective League: Controversy over Rodney King beating and L.A. riots reignites," http://lapd.com/news/headlines/controversy_over_rodney_king_beating_and_la_riots_reignites/lapd.com. Accessed: October 2, 2015.

7. "LAPPL—Los Angeles Police Protective League: Controversy over Rodney King beating and L.A. riots reignites," http://lapd.com/news/headlines/controversy_over_rodney_king_beating_and_la_riots_reignites/lapd.com. Accessed: October 2, 2015.

8. In 1990, two years before the unrest, Koreans owned 1,600 out of a total 2,411, or two-thirds of all businesses in South Central.

9. The Westside or West LA is known for its affluent neighborhood, the majority population being White Americans. Koreatown is centrally located between East and West LA.

10. It's generally ignorance about the differences between Asian ethnicities. It doesn't always imply contempt, though.

11. Please refer to the "Survey of working conditions in Koreatown restaurants" at www.kiwa.org.

12. Koreans call what happened in 1992 in Los Angeles "Sa-I-Gu," literally April 29, following the Korean tradition of using a date to refer to major political and/or violent events in their history.

13. During the unrest, the LAPD shifted its longstanding policy of apprehending undocumented immigrants and turning them over to the Immigration and Naturalization Service (INS)—which is now Immigration and Customs Enforcement or ICE—for possible deportation. According to INS officials, undocumented immigrants accounted for more than 1,200 of the 15,000 people arrested. Many came from Mexico, El Salvador, Guatemala, Honduras, and Jamaica (Navarro 1993, 73).

14. Squatter settlements on hills are somewhat romantically called moon villages in Korea. They are often populated with poor people from rural areas who migrated to urban ones in the 1970s and 1980s, and are notorious for low-quality living conditions.

15. For the best study on the Korean War, see Cumings (1981).

16. She became a sort of spokesperson for the Korean merchant community, talking to the media on behalf of victims of the unrest.

17. Although 71 businesses owners were interviewed, for the purpose of the data on hiring practices, I included the same number of businesses that were present before the unrest.

18. It is just a hypothesis.

19. See *Rebuilding L.A.'s Urban Communities: A Final Report from RLA*, published by Milken Institute (1997): "Business, government, and the community (a 'three-legged stool') together would bring prosperity to neglected communities by securing substantial outside private- and public-sector investments in large part by major corporations; by cutting red tape; and through volunteerism" (1997, 11).

20. The Great Society refers to a set of domestic programs in the United States launched by President Lyndon B. Johnson in 1964–1965. The new major spending programs that addressed education, medical care, urban problems, rural poverty, and transportation were launched during this period.

21. Pogroms were tactics of state-sponsored repression of a minority group; this situation is not analogous to that.

22. I was unable to verify how many Korean American candidates ran.

23. Angela Oh and Bong Hwan Kim played integral roles in the formation of MCC and APANLA. Cindy Choi was the founding director of MCC. In addition, the Los Angeles Times hired K. Connie Kang as a writer and the Department of Commerce hired T.S. Chung. They did this specifically to address lack of Korean representation.

24. Korean immigrant merchant interviewees used the term "riot" interchangeably with "Sa-I-Gu," but their explanation of what happened indicated their understanding of the structural causes of the unrest.

25. I am not suggesting they had a complete change of heart about this.

## Chapter Seven

# Ethnic Tension in the Aftermath
## *"Rebuilding LA without Liquor Stores"*

While the previous chapter addressed the reactions of Korean immigrant business owners to the 1992 unrest, this chapter highlights collective action among people in South LA.[1] It examines how a coalition of immigrants and minorities were able to mobilize and challenge a powerful and well-connected liquor industry, and how they successfully changed the way the American liquor industry operated in their community. Social movements include various forms of collective action aimed at social change, and they sometimes arise from spontaneous protest. If social movements are viewed as processes rather than entities, this anti-liquor store campaign in South LA can reasonably be interpreted as one. As Nancy Abelmann (1996, 3) maintains, social movements are emergent phenomena that are never entirely prefigured or scripted by their agendas; consequently, they are constituted in particular historical moments and on particular discursive terrains.

Literature on social movements has generally attempted to capture the changing sociocultural contexts and their accompanying adaptive strategies. Often, the rise of the postindustrial or postmodern condition is closely linked to the necessity of understanding new social movements (NSMs) since World War II, such as the Civil Rights Movement and the radical student movements of the 1960s. NSMs designate a broad range of contemporary social movements, including feminist, queer, anti-racist, and national minority organizing (Cohen 1985; Weir 1993).[2]

Post-Marxist thinkers such as Ernesto Laclau and Chantal Mouffe argue that theories stressing the primacy of structural contradictions, economic classes, and crises in determining collective identity are inapplicable to contemporary contexts; this argument is largely based on criticism of both classic theoretical paradigms of collective behavior theory[3] and "resource mobilization" theory,[4] as well as awareness of the inadequacies of Marxist analyses

201

of social movements. Laclau and Mouffe also maintain that one cannot apply neo-utilitarian, rational actor models to collective actors whose conflictive interaction is not restricted to political exchanges, negotiations, and/or strategic calculations between adversaries (Cohen 1985, 691). Accordingly, I conceptualize this anti-liquor store movement as a new social movement.

This chapter challenges three deeply ingrained ideas related to this movement: 1) that inner-city minorities are so mired in poverty and substance abuse that they are apathetic about their surroundings and uninterested in creating change; 2) that inner cities are deeply segregated and characterized by interracial tensions; and 3) that Korean immigrants were the only victims of the 1992 LA unrest. To examine this conflict, I initiated a critical dialogue with interviewees about how Korean immigrants and their business practices were understood by their inner-city customers and vice versa. I closely followed events, activities, and gatherings organized by the Community Coalition for Substance Abuse Prevention and Treatment (henceforth referred to as the Community Coalition and detailed below), the organization that led the effort to reduce the number of liquor stores in South LA. At many public hearings, I was viewed by the Community Coalition as a concerned citizen or activist and was often the only Asian American present among mostly Black members. Some Korean Americans assumed I was an advocate for targeted Korean immigrant liquor stores. These contradictory assumptions illustrate the polarizing nature of the liquor store controversy.

Over 2,280 Korean-owned businesses were damaged during the unrest, resulting in a loss of nearly $400 million. Liquor stores comprised 10 percent of the total property damage,[5] and Korean Americans owned an estimated 75 percent of looted, damaged, or completely destroyed liquor stores.[6] Community opposition to liquor stores plagued the rebuilding process, as a coalition of Black and Latino residents in South LA rallied against it, and media coverage heightened already tense relations between Black and Korean immigrant communities.

The controversy over liquor stores in South LA was the focus of the campaign "Rebuilding LA without Liquor Stores," which started in 1990 and continues today. Anti-liquor movements had traditionally been organized in middle-class neighborhoods, as inner-city minorities were often seen as alcoholics indifferent to any form of prohibition. Jewish and Korean immigrants were also stereotyped and perceived to be preoccupied with monopolizing the inner-city liquor sector in the name of self-enrichment, without serving the community's best interests. Accordingly, "when these symbols of diminished control and limited retail options went up in smoke in the spring of 1992, few mourned" (Simon 2011, 45). At the same time, African Americans involved in the anti-liquor store movement were portrayed as attacking Koreans. For the most part, Blackness and Korean-ness were constructed as inhabiting conflicting positions with regards to this issue: African Americans in support, Koreans in opposition.

## THE STRUCTURE OF THE
## LIQUOR INDUSTRY IN LOS ANGELES

Since the repeal of Prohibition in 1933, federal and state government agencies have required liquor manufacturers to sell to distributors that maintain rigidly controlled geographical territories. Distributors can sell only to retailers—such as bars, restaurants, and liquor stores—which in turn sell to individual consumers.[7] For the most part, this three-tiered system has kept organized crime out of the liquor business and ensured the effective collection of taxes. It has also stifled the liquor industry by imposing and maintaining a distribution chain that relies on middlemen.

Stores in South LA are a crucial nexus of the multibillion dollar liquor industry, in large part because inner cities are the biggest markets for potent but inexpensive drinks like malt liquor and fortified wine. The liquor industry makes profits when the consumer demographic correlates with low educational attainment, high rates of alcoholism, and poverty. During my fieldwork in South LA, a sales representative from a wholesale liquor company admitted that they sold more liquor in South LA than in the combined area of Pennsylvania and Massachusetts. The liquor industry is second only to the tobacco industry in sponsoring community organizations, events, and scholarships, undoubtedly as a public relations tactic to deflect debate on the harmful effects of alcoholism. The liquor industry is also known for its powerful lobbying efforts, including making soft money contributions to members of Congress and influencing both state and federal elected officials.[8]

As with other mind-altering substances, cultural attitudes toward drinking range from veneration to scorn. According to Joseph Gusfield (1987), alcohol is a point of tension, ambivalence, and conflict in American life. Only Finland, Norway, and Sweden have had anti-alcohol movements as politically salient as in the United States. Political battles have been fought over the regulation of when and to whom liquor may be sold, and even after the Prohibition amendment was repealed, alcohol continued to be a restricted commodity. A number of scientific studies have put the liquor industry on the defensive. A key study of excessive drinking, published in the *Journal of the American Medical Association* (2003), sparked a dispute between the article's authors and liquor industry leaders, with each side accusing the other of manipulating figures. The study, conducted by an institute affiliated with

Columbia University, reported that half the alcohol purchased in the United States was sold to teenagers or alcoholics.

## The State's Role in Liquor Sales

Paradoxically, the California government has exploited American regulatory policies on liquor and created a substantial revenue stream from state-issued liquor licenses (K. Park 1995/1996). In this particular controversy, the politico-juridical state served to regulate private individuals and their choice of businesses. Indeed, state institutions were implicated in this liquor store controversy and should also be subject to reform and transformation. The California Department of Alcohol Beverage Control (ABC) employed so few agents across the state that comprehensive enforcement was almost impossible. [9] Even when the agency's budget remained stable in 1991,[10] its enforcement dropped sharply when Governor Pete Wilson ordered all agents to process license applications, which generate revenue, rather than go after violators.

In addition, there were loopholes in state regulatory policy regarding the number of liquor outlets in South LA. The *Los Angeles Times* reported that "this situation is the result of a loophole created by the ABC formula, which sets the density limit by dividing a county's population by the total number of outlets in the county" (*LAT* June 2, 1992). Critics also pointed out that the threat of ABC penalties were not severe enough to counter profits made on sales to minors, particularly in the case of convenience stores that could continue to sell food and other merchandise during a one- or two-week suspension from alcohol sales. Businesses that sell liquor to minors would get a $5,000 fine but risked losing their liquor licenses if they received three violations within three years. ABC records showed that first-time offenders seldom lost their licenses for selling alcohol to minors. Repeat offenders often faced only incremental fines as violations piled up. On the second offense, the penalty for sales to a minor decoy rose to an average suspension of 11.7 days, and for the third to 15.1 days.[11] Only 4.7 percent of the 49 third-time offenders in a 13-month period lost their licenses between 1991 and 1992 (*LAT* June 2, 1992). The state, as well as local, government became directly involved in regulating liquor selling by revoking liquor licenses after the unrest. Korean merchants were confused and frustrated with the way the government handled the issuing of liquor licenses. One store owner stated, "It was the government who issued costly liquor licenses, and now they tell us to give up our life savings."

## Liquor Stores in South LA

As many Korean Americans who opposed the Community Coalition pointed out, the liquor industry profits the most by distributing liquor. Unlike highly visible Korean American minority middlemen, mainstream corporations profited from the goods sold in these markets and yet did not have to bear the burden of anger at the continuous flow of money out of these neighborhoods. Korean merchants accused the Community Coalition of focusing on individual small business owners rather than the more powerful liquor industry. Liquor stores, they said, were a symptom of larger problems in their neighborhood, not the cause. Indeed, ridding the area of Korean-run liquor stores would do nothing to address the fundamental problems confronting South LA, such as deindustrialization, job loss, unemployment, poverty, and social inequality.

Korean liquor store owners, who often did not live in South LA, developed a reputation for being eager to profit without considering the community's well-being. For Korean immigrant merchants, liquor held an important source of exchange value in terms of profit-making and life-savings investment (K. Park 1995/1996). Although the presence of Koreans did not increase the number of liquor stores in South LA, nor did merchants specifically target local customers, they were implicated in victimizing neighborhood residents (K. Park 2004). In addition, the unwillingness of large supermarket chains to open stores in South LA made selling groceries and liquor profitable for liquor store owners. Studies have shown that alcohol sales, consumption, and various alcohol-related problems in the US are all correlated with the physical availability of alcohol (LaVest and Wallace 2000, 614). Thus, the disproportionate concentration of off-premise establishments like package liquor stores in South LA is significant because these outlets typically sell chilled alcohol in larger quantities than in taverns or restaurants (e.g., 40- and 64-ounce bottles) and ready for immediate consumption (LaVeist and Wallace 2000, 614). This availability is more likely to result in excessive drinking, public drunkenness, automobile crashes, and physical altercations that lead to injury or death.

Alcohol-related problems have had a substantial impact on Black communities. La Veist and Wallace (2000) reported that census tracts that were both low-income and predominantly Black had substantially more liquor stores per capita than other census tracts. There were 728 liquor stores in South LA before the unrest: 13 per square mile, which is more than 2.5 times as many as in the state of Rhode Island. Moreover, the South LA stores cater to a population of 500,000; in comparison, Rhode Island has a population of one million. Roughly half these businesses were convenience stores that sold beer and wine; the rest also sold hard liquor. Similarly, Mayor Tom Bradley's *South*

*LA Community/Merchant Liquor Task Force Report* (City of Los Angeles 1992) reported that there were 682 alcohol licenses issued in South LA before the unrest.[12] There were 17 licenses issued per square mile, as compared with 1.6 liquor store licenses per square mile in the remainder of LA County.

The situation of liquor stores in South LA is quite distinct from that of the other major American metropolis, New York City, where stores can only sell liquor and are only open during restricted business hours.[13] The liquor stores in South LA are often open from 6:00 am to 2:00 am, seven days a week.[14] Additionally, the term "liquor store" is a misnomer that does not encompass the variety of services the businesses in South LA provide. Like Scott's store, discussed in chapter 5, South LA liquor stores stock a variety of groceries, including produce and meat, milk, processed foods, snacks, pantyhose, and diapers, in addition to beer, wine, and hard liquor. Customers can cash checks and welfare stipends,[15] buy money orders, and pay for purchases with food stamps at liquor stores.[16]

In many of these stores, liquor accounts for less than one-quarter of the total inventory but generates the largest profit margins. Not surprisingly, then, these local businesses depend on liquor sales to survive. Shin, a Korean merchant whose store in Compton was destroyed during the 1992 unrest, said she would be ruined financially if she could not sell alcohol along with groceries in her tiny liquor store. When Shin bought the store in 1988, its liquor license was worth $100,000. She stated, "On bread and milk, we don't make money, because of the low profit margin. On liquor, beer and wine, we get 25 percent" (*LAT* July 22, 1992).

## ALCOHOL ABUSE IN SOUTH LA AND
## THE FORMATION OF THE COMMUNITY COALITION

Liquor stores are one of the few public spaces in which people can gather socially in South LA. There are few signs of middle-class neighborhood life, as the area lacks supermarkets, stationery stores, discount stores, banks, bars, restaurants, coffee shops, public parks, pharmacies, bakeries, hardware stores, or libraries. The few businesses in South LA appear to be fronts for drug dealers, and liquor stores and churches often stand side by side. Nonetheless, despite the social function of liquor stores in South LA as public meeting places, in the 1980s these businesses began to be targeted as "public nuisances" that negatively impacted the neighborhood. For South LA residents, the overconcentration of liquor stores was interpreted as a blight on their communities, an "easily accessible avenue for alcohol abuse . . . a destructive means of escape from hopelessness, and potential magnets for criminal and other negative activities" (APPCON/APANLA Proposal 1992).

Alcohol abuse has long plagued working-class Americans, but with dein-dustrialization and the introduction of crack cocaine, the problem became more pronounced (Sloane 2012, 95). By 1992, a variety of factors made the issue of liquor stores in South LA more inflammatory, the first of which was the rise in Black unemployment. As discussed in chapter 1, the recession disproportionately affected less educated Black men, which resulted in more visible instances of public drinking during this time period. In addition, ac-cording to a 1986 federal report by the National Institute on Alcohol Abuse and Alcoholism, alcohol abuse was the number one health problem in the Black community. While African Americans were less likely than Whites to drink alcohol, those who did were more likely to suffer alcohol-related prob-lems such as drunkenness and esophageal cancer, with low-income Black men at the highest risk.

Liquor stores were also concentrated in Latino communities in South LA, and heavy drinking may have been an even more pervasive problem among poor, male Mexican and Central American immigrants than among African Americans. Latinos were more likely to drink frequently and in larger quanti-ties than Whites or African Americans (Nielsen 2000). Among Latino men, Mexican Americans reported the most frequent and heavy drinking (at least once a week and consuming at least five drinks in one setting, at least once a year to weekly), and had the greatest prevalence of drunkenness and alcohol-related problems (Nielsen 2000, 301). In 1990, 10 times as many Latino juveniles as Black juveniles were arrested for alcohol-related offenses in LA County (Whitman 1993, 58).

An important factor with regards to alcohol abuse in South LA was the change in ethnicity of store owners. After the deregulation of liquor prices in 1978, Korean merchants started buying stores from Chinese, Japanese, Black, or other immigrant merchants.[17] This changeover followed a shift in ownership after the Watts Revolt in 1965, when merchants from different ethnic groups took over stores from predominantly Jewish merchants. There is little evidence that any particular group, such as Korean immigrants, aimed either to increase the number of liquor stores in South LA or to convert other markets into liquor stores: "There were fewer before this year's riots than during the Watts riots in 1965—but the fact that so many liquor stores were built in earlier generations remain" (*LAT* December 14, 1992). Neverthe-less, residents erroneously believed that Koreans were intentionally ruining the community with liquor. As one community leader stated: "One Korean merchant added to the despair of the inner city by flooding that community with a proliferation of liquor stores, adding to the growing chemical depen-dency problem already prevalent in South Central Los Angeles" (Hicks 1994, 81). As discussed in chapters 2–4, a racial and cultural chasm between the merchants and residents—along with local resentment over the immigrants' success—contributed to local perceptions of Koreans as the enemy and a symbol of oppression.

Beginning in the early 1980s, the South Central Organizing Committee mobilized thousands of homeowners, renters, and church members to protest problems associated with the overconcentration of liquor stores. Unlike the later established Community Coalition, the South Central Organizing Committee was not federally funded, and its achievements stopped short of appealing to City Hall. At the time, African Americans owned most of the liquor stores in South LA. In 1984, after trying unsuccessfully to have a number of problematic stores closed, the South Central Organizing Committee won the right to determine when and how alcohol was sold, and imposed conditions on lighting, security, and hours of operation (*LAT* November 23, 1992). A conditional-use permit was required both to open a new liquor store in South LA and to change an existing establishment's mode of operation. In 1987, the city made this interim ordinance permanent (Sonenshein 1996, 719).

Public pressure was then extended to crack down on alcoholism. In 1989, at a University of Southern California (USC) conference entitled "The Crack Crisis in the African American Community," a new group of community activists formed the Community Coalition for Substance Abuse Prevention and Treatment (Community Coalition). Founded by Karen Bass (and a group of community activists), who was a clinical instructor at USC, the Community Coalition led the effort to reduce the number of liquor stores in South LA. As a health professional, Bass had struggled to treat people whose lives had been torn apart by the crises of crack cocaine and alcohol, and she wanted to address the root causes of the crises (Abdullah and Freer 2010, 330). In 1990, with a five year, $1.5 million federal grant from the Center for Substance Abuse Prevention at the Department of Health and Human Services, the Community Coalition began devising programs to address drug and alcohol problems in South LA. The original mission of the Community Coalition was to "transform the hopelessness and despair that characterize parts of the South Los Angeles community into effective action and community building."[18]

Bass pointed to South LA's lack of control over the proliferation of liquor stores and questioned the public image of African Americans in need of moral reform:

> Over the past 12 to 15 years, African Americans have been portrayed as a community that's essentially in a morass—a community that can't get out from its own problems, that has weak family values, that needs to raise its moral standards, etc. . . . For the past several months, we have been attempting to address the problems related to the over-concentration of liquor stores within South LA...we understand that if we can reduce the number—it's not that people will stop drinking completely—you decrease the availability and it does improve the

health as well as the safety in that particular community . . . it's also the type
of alcohol that's sold. . . . If you go into West Los Angeles and ask for a "short
dog," a "Thunderbird," or "MD 20-20," you won't find those products. (Bass
1994, 69, 71).

Initially, the Community Coalition was composed of more than 250 groups,
agencies, churches, and individuals. Over time, it grew to include Latinos,
joined forces with a progressive Korean and Asian American community
organizations, and gained endorsements from Black politicians.

After the unrest, Community Coalition organizers were able to secure a
number of victories. They blocked, or at least inhibited, the rebuilding of
224 of the 728 liquor stores that were damaged or destroyed in the riots (K.
Park 2004). Activists claimed that the liquor store problem was not limited
to sheer number and overconcentration, but also to business practices: when,
to whom, and what kinds of alcohol were sold. Another concern was the
environment surrounding liquor stores and the safety of their customers.
Liquor stores were identified as a center of vice, public drunkenness, drug
dealing, rape, assault, and other criminal activities. The Community Coalition also achieved implementation of a "conditional-use variance" process
that required business owners to undergo a public hearing before reopening
their liquor store and forced them to limit store hours, hire uniformed security
guards, and provide parking lots for customers.

In one neighborhood, the Community Coalition found that 22 of the 64
burned-down stores had documented violations, many for selling liquor to
minors. In June 1992, when the Community Coalition began its petition
drive to "Rebuild South LA without Liquor Stores," it hoped to collect 1,000
signatures in two months. In merely five weeks, they had 25,700 names (*LAT*
July 27, 1992). According to a member of the Community Coalition: "It
was a blessing in disguise when so many liquor stores in South Los Angeles
burned down. Life is better without the drunkenness and crime that go with
alcohol sales and the city should forbid their rebuilding" (*LAT* July 27, 1992).
Activists also organized people to testify at public hearings, boycott certain
stores, set up candlelight vigils, and hold press conferences.[19] Moreover, the
Community Coalition pursued stricter controls on liquor stores by lobbying
both the city planning and zoning commissions (K. Park 1995/1996, 2004;
Sonenshein 1996). Key city bureaucrats and elected officials, in particular
Black politicians, threw their support behind the coalition, including City
Council members Rita Walters (9th District) and Mark Ridley-Thomas (8th
District), Assemblywoman Marguerite Archie-Hudson (48th District), and
State Senator Theresa Hughes.[20] Ridley-Thomas, who at the time represented
South LA, connected the presence of liquor stores to "[a]n institutionalized
form of oppression . . . the over-concentration of liquor outlets in my com-

munity drives down the quality of life" (*LAT* October 2, 1992). His analysis tied the abundance of liquor stores with broader, societal, anti-Black racism, arguing that they were a hindrance to upward mobility.

The Community Coalition's emphasis on social order, as seen in their condemnation of problematic liquor stores as a "public nuisance," built support among some conservatives as well, including members of the LAPD. All in all, the activists succeeded in blocking the rebuilding of many liquor stores, revoking liquor licenses, preventing the issuance of new liquor licenses, and getting the city to enact tough new regulations for proposed stores. These actions conflicted with Mayor Bradley's promise to merchants after the unrest that they would receive city support to rebuild as quickly as possible.[21] The City Council modified Mayor Bradley's emergency rebuilding ordinance by attaching a measure sponsored by Black council member Walters to exempt liquor stores and other "noxious" businesses from fast-track authority; public hearings would be required for these stores to be rebuilt. The city ended up compromising between these two opposing positions, setting up a plan-approval process that involved a protracted, case-by-case review of each request for rebuilding.

On the other side of the issue, the targeted liquor stores received support from the liquor industry, sympathetic politicians, and many Korean American community organizations. However, fewer than a dozen of the 175 Korean-owned liquor stores were able to reopen within two years of the unrest with the new restrictions in place (*LAT* July 21, 1994). While some merchants agreed that there were too many liquor stores in South LA, they felt it was unfair to revoke their right to engage in free enterprise without adequate compensation. Aside from the costs of relocating and retraining employees, the greatest expense came from the loss of liquor licenses, the value of which ranged from $10,000 to $100,000 or more. Finding support among some Republican politicians, a segment of the Korean American community mobilized to override the new City Council ordinance by appealing to the state legislature. However, due to strong opposition from Black elected officials, AB 1974, which would have overturned the city ordinance, was not passed.

## COUNTERMOBILIZATION:
## CALIFORNIA STATE ASSEMBLY BILL (AB) 1974

Many Korean Americans vigorously protested the Community Coalition's anti-liquor store campaign, condemning it as a cynical attempt to uplift Black residents by scapegoating Korean merchants. When city officials did not respond after the unrest, Korean merchants protested outside City Hall for days, demanding a meeting with the mayor. They beat on drums to attract attention, braving occasional objects thrown from inside the building. On July 1, 1992, they threatened to engage in civil disobedience, and on the next day, Mayor Bradley and Councilman Nate Holden agreed to meet with them (*KTLA* July 6, 1992).

Ryan Song, attorney and executive director of the Korean American Grocers' Association (KAGRO), Jerry Yu, executive director of the Korean American Coalition (KAC), and other Korean American community leaders spoke in defense of liquor store owners. At a public hearing on December 21, 1994, Song argued that there was no clear evidence that the stores encouraged crime: "Business owners have an absolute right to their livelihood, and small shop-owners can't afford to sell just food—they need the profit from alcohol. Besides, the protests smack of anti-Korean racism." These leaders also emphasized that Korean immigrant store owners were law-abiding citizens who had been victimized twice—once in the unrest and again in these policy changes. Similarly, Tong Soo Chung, an attorney and founding president of the Korean American Coalition (*LAT* May 24, 1992), stated:

> If you want to get rid of those businesses, do it legally. Buy them out! Pay them to leave. These people invested money to buy their businesses...But these special ordinances—singling out liquor stores and swap meets and requiring a public hearing in order to allow these businesses to reopen—the Korean Americans feel they are being victimized again.

According to Sonenshein, when Assembly Bill 40-X was killed, it was "a major turning point for the Korean American merchants" (1996, 726). Archie-Hudson's Assembly Bill 40-X would have invalidated licenses for liquor stores destroyed in the unrest if an excessive number of crimes occurred in their surrounding neighborhoods, or if they were located within 500 feet of another liquor store (*KTLA* July 6, 1992). When the City Council passed the emergency ordinance that required public hearings before rebuilding liquor stores, the store owners filed a lawsuit against the city, with the Community Coalition entering as an interested party in superior court in May 1993 (Sonenshein 1996, 727). The merchants' suit charged that the state had ultimate authority over liquor stores and that the city had overstepped its legal powers by requiring the planning commission hearings after the unrest. However, on June 1993, Judge O'Brien of the LA Superior Court ruled that the city could regulate land use even though it could not control licenses to sell liquor (*Sentinel* June 24–30, 1994).

Unsurprisingly, Korean Americans received support from Republicans as victims of an organized Black political coalition. Assemblyman Paul Horcher (R-60) introduced California State Assembly Bill 1974 in April 1993 to prevent the City of Los Angeles from imposing restrictions on the rebuilding and reopening of small businesses destroyed by the riots. The City Council required those businesses that had been burned down by the riots to meet up to 16 new conditions before reopening.[22] AB 1974 would have allowed small businesses to reopen without the two most restrictive conditions: mandated security guards and reduction of operating hours. The Korean American Coalition spearheaded a committee comprised of over 35 community organizations and individuals to support AB 1974. The committee conducted mass letter-writing and telephone-banking campaigns, coordinated media coverage, and organized lobbying delegations. The collective effort produced over 23,000 letters and hundreds of phone calls, and it proved to be effective (*KoreAm Journal* October 1994). However, after a hard-won victory in the State Assembly, the measure failed to pass the Senate due to strong opposition from LA's Black elected officials.

In his interview with *KoreAm* journal (November 1994), Jerry Yu described his involvement:

> AB 1974 is a perfect example of the kind of problems our community is facing because it is a political issue...We had pretty unanimous and solid backing from all the Korean American organizations. We even put some money together. We lobbied Sacramento. We lobbied City Hall. First of all, [the bill] wouldn't have even come up if we were empowered. The City Council would respect our community, and they would not have that kind of policy [that provoked legislation such as AB 1974]. But at this point [the city] did, and there is nothing we can do about it.

Yu's description of the countermobilization echoed the sentiments of the Korean American community: it diagnosed the anti-liquor store campaign as anti-Korean racism and a violation of Korean immigrant merchants' civil and property rights, similar to what they had suffered during the unrest.

> In terms of the merchants seeking approval to reopen liquor stores, the approval process often seemed arbitrary. In a public hearing, Mrs. Lee, the owner of Western Market and introduced in the previous chapter, received approval to resume her business despite some 20 residents' testimonies against her and some 500 residents' petitions for the city to reject her liquor license. Mrs. Lee's gas station and mini-market had been severely damaged in the unrest, with damages amounting to $220,000. She had also paid $80,000 to dispose of a gasoline storage tank in order to convert the station into a market. For Mrs. Lee, rebuilding her liquor store was a matter of life and death: "Since I lost my husband by armed robbery, I have run the business with my daughter's help. If I were not approved to sell liquor, I would end up with a huge debt. If the City Planning Committee disapproved, I wouldn't mind doing a hunger strike"

(*KTLA* June 26, 1993). Even the Korean immigrant merchants who attempted to rebuild by opening another type of business encountered problems. Once they had secured a loan from a bank or the Small Business Administration (SBA) for one kind of business, they were often unable to change it to a different activity and keep the loan. In other words, Mrs. Lee encountered more than one type of logistical problem in attempting to convert her liquor business into something else. Finally, business owners had already invested anywhere from $10,000 to $100,000 or more in a liquor license, which would be a huge loss to incur.[23]

## THE COMMUNITY COALITION'S RESPONSE TO AB 1974

The Community Coalition reacted angrily to AB 1974, stating: "Assembly-man Paul Horcher from Diamond Bar tried to pass legislation that would take away the City's power to regulate how stores were rebuilt." They pointed out that the corporate sector and the Republican Right were behind Korean liquor store owners:

Rumor has it Southland Corp (a.k.a. 7-11) and Arco Corp (AM/PM Mini-Mart) are really behind this legislation, and in classic racist fashion have put Korean grocers in front of the camera talking about the need to help the victims. The appearance is once again the "minorities" fighting each other when the truth is—the folks with the real money to help Horcher retire his campaign debts aren't African American, Latino, or Asian.

In a press release distributed at the public hearing of the City Planning Commission on October 15, 1992, the Community Coalition charged:

[S]ome business owners are utilizing the fast-track rebuilding process to expand and alter properties in ways that are detrimental to the community. A storeowner will propose the addition of a laundromat to a store. The Community Coalition is concerned that the loitering and public drinking common near South LA liquor stores will be increased and the laundry will essentially serve as a lounge or bar...The focus of the Community Coalition's Campaign to Rebuild South LA without Liquor Stores is directed at stores with histories of public *nuisance* [emphasis added] complaints from residents. Many stores were magnets for crime, loitering and violence. One of the stores requesting permission to reestablish alcohol sales is an example of this—a long-standing community nuisance. The Community surveyed residents who reported observing teenagers purchasing alcohol, people loitering and drug transactions inside and outside of the store. A number of residents reported that the quality of life has improved since the store was destroyed. One senior citizen reported that he no longer begins each morning cleaning up alcohol containers from his front yard, and he is no longer afraid to walk down the street now that the drinkers are gone.

Ironically, in the case mentioned by Community Coalition, the store owner who won approval for rebuilding was a Black woman. Other liquor store owners had no choice but to compromise and undergo several years of time-consuming hearings. For example, on April 23, 2002, at his fourth public hearing, Korean store owner of the now defunct B&O Liquor, who had been attempting to reopen his store since 1997, barely avoided a mandated closure of his business despite much opposition from the Community Coalition. He had run the business since 1986, demonstrated his harmonious relationship with the attending residents, had few documented problems surrounding the store, and pledged to hire a security guard. He also promised to only sell beer in six-packs and to stop selling single cans. The store owner expected his income to be halved by this restriction (*KTLA* May 24, 2002).

Middle-class homeowners and anti-liquor activists joined the Community Coalition in blocking the rebuilding of many liquor stores. The Community Coalition literature reported that on March 23, 1993, the City Council voted unanimously to overturn a Planning Commission decision that had approved the rebuilding of the historically dangerous Buckingham Liquor Store, which had a long history of "nuisance activity—narcotic arrests, burglaries, loitering, assaults, robberies and prostitution" (*LAT* November 23, 1992). Wearing green ribbons representing demands for a safe environment, over 150 residents and supporters greeted this victory with loud applause that filled City Hall. Supporters from the LA County Alcohol Policy Coalition, the West Valley Homeowners Association, the San Fernando Valley Alcohol Policy Coalition, and many others joined South LA residents in celebrating.

The Community Coalition made some efforts to ease racial tensions, since most of their targets were Korean-run liquor stores. The Coalition was cautious to avoid being accused of anti-Korean racism.

> Merchants are understandably upset when they discover that they are underinsured or uninsured, that they can't get emergency relief and that they face community opposition. They should not be driven into poverty, but neither should residents have to suffer from the return of problem stores.

In addition, the Community Coalition succeeded in recruiting some Latino and Korean American staff, as well as Latino members, in order to broaden their constituency and deflect charges of Black prejudice against Koreans.

All in all, the Community Coalition was quite successful in preventing liquor stores from being rebuilt. They borrowed strategies from the middle-class homeowners' and environmental movements, as well as some techniques from the Civil Rights Movement, while leaning heavily on political support from Black politicians. Unlike other Black community leaders and Black nationalists, the organization's leadership emphasized moral, environmental, and social impacts rather than racial ones.[24] For instance, Dale Goldsmith, the legal representative of the Community Coalition—who usually represented developers against challenges by slow-growth groups in the affluent West LA—used the California Environmental Quality Act of 1970 as an argument against rebuilding liquor stores (Sonenshein 1996, 729). Through tactical, race-neutral arguments, the Coalition prevented the rebuilding of over 150 liquor stores after the unrest. In addition, its members closed six motels, liquor stores, and recycling centers known for drug- and alcohol-related crimes, and supported the development of 44 non-alcohol related businesses that replaced liquor stores destroyed in 1992.[25]

The Community Coalition has actively opposed the proliferation of liquor stores in South LA for more than 20 years. In 2008, it helped persuade the LA City Council to approve the Nuisance Abatement Ordinance, allowing the city and residents more of a say in regards to the proximity of businesses, such as liquor stores and motels to parks and schools.[26] In 2009, the Coalition's campaign against the Korean-owned Century Liquor store at 39th Street and Western Ave—part of its 18-month Neighborhood Transformation Project, an effort to reduce crime and violence in an area known as King Estates—drew about 100 protesters, who called on Mayor Antonio Villaraigosa to revoke the store's permit to sell alcohol. In addition, teenage Coalition participants led a successful fight to reduce tobacco and alcohol advertising near South LA schools and replace offensive billboards with 120 billboards of their own anti-tobacco designs.

The Community Coalition's rationale for its movement has always focused on the harmful effects of alcohol. For instance, one of its pamphlets states that heavy drinking contributes to violent crimes like homicides, assaults, and rapes. The Coalition claims that it is single-handedly responsible for decreasing crime in the area of liquor stores by 16 percent.[27] However, it is aware that in the future it needs to prioritize building and organizing the community, as well as going beyond the current campaign against liquor stores to tackle larger problems, such as poverty, unemployment, and foreclosures.[28] As of early 2018, the Community Coalition is still on the frontline of grassroots organizing and has extended its focus to equity in the distribution of school-bond funding and reform within the foster care system. It is also planning a campaign to attract business to South LA, while organizing for welfare recipients and youth.

## FINDING COMMON GROUND

Established in 1976, the Asian Pacific Planning Council (APPCON) is a federation of committees and task forces whose purpose is to initiate action on major policy and planning issues that affect the APIA community. After the 1992 unrest, APPCON initiated a Liquor Store Task Force, chaired by Judy Nishimoto-Aguilera of the Little Tokyo Service Center Housing Program. The Task Force included representatives from the Korean Youth and Community Center, Koreatown Immigrant Workers Alliance, Chinatown Service Center, East West Community Partnership, and the Asian Pacific American Legal Center. Together with Asian Pacific Americans for a New L.A. (APANLA), the APPCON Liquor Store Task Force developed a position paper to identify common ground among Korean/Asian American, African American, and Latino communities based on principles of justice and fairness (K. Park 1995/1996, 2004; Sonenshein 1996).[29] The Task Force received the support of the Community Coalition, as well as a multiethnic list of other organizations.

The APPCON Task Force focused on developing a program to facilitate the conversion of liquor stores to other businesses.[30] On May 28, 1993, the City Council approved funding of $260,000 for the Liquor Store Business Conversion Program from money provided through the Community Development Department. In addition, the Council removed a crucial barrier to conversion by waiving the sewer hookup fee for new laundromats. Without that waiver, the conversion would have been far too costly—as much as $2,200 per machine (*LAT* June 3, 1993). The Liquor Store Business Conversion Program, administered by the Korean Youth and Community Center (KYCC), was open to enrollment by any liquor store owner in overconcentrated areas, with priority given to those whose stores were destroyed during the unrest.[31] The program combined individualized assistance to merchants with business training and community relations classes to help them research alternatives, select new businesses, and start up their new business. At the conclusion of the program, graduates were eligible for start-up grants and low-cost financing. Eric Nakano, a project manager of the Little Tokyo Service Center Community Development Corporation, chaired the APPCON Task Force and assessed the program's function, stating: "this program does not solve all the sources of conflict between communities nor does it wash away the continuing divisions over the liquor store issue. But it is an important step" (*LAT* June 3, 1993).

As a result of APPCON's success, the Alliance for Neighborhood Economic Development (ANED) launched the Liquor Store Business Conversion Program in July 1993, administered by KYCC and overseen by a multiethnic advisory committee.[32] As of June 1994, over 150 clients, mostly Korean American or Latino, were being served by ANED staff. About 25 percent of the total clients were owners of convenience and liquor stores seeking to convert or who had already converted to non-alcohol related businesses.

Among the program's successes were the opening of a self-service laundry, a mini-mall with five new businesses, and a garment shop. By the end of its first year of operation, the program's free technical assistance contributed to the opening of at least 18 new or expanded businesses. However, most of the merchants still needed loans between $50,000 and $300,000, and conventional lending institutions such as banks were often unwilling to provide capital (*LAT* May 8, 1994).

The alliance of KYCC with the Community Coalition to convert liquor stores engendered controversy within the rest of the Korean American community, which was divided over the project. Bong Hwan Kim, KYCC's executive director received criticism from other Korean American community leaders and resigned from his position in 1998, in part because of these ideological differences. While many Koreans saw him as a traitor who surrendered to Black political pressure at the expense of his community, Kim saw his action as a realistic compromise, which he hoped would provide an opportunity for Koreans to diversify their businesses. He stressed the importance of the coalition-building process with other minority groups, especially given the lack of Korean American political representation.

While progressive 1.5-generation community organizations such as KYCC and KIWA (Koreatown Immigrant Workers Alliance) applauded the conversion effort, many others, including conservative counterparts such as KAC and KAGRO, were quite critical. Korean American journalist Connie Kang of the *Los Angeles Times* (April 29, 1996) opined that the conversion project had not lived up to its billing as a "model" for the nation, as it had been described at the 1993 news conference announcing the project. She cited the figure that, as of 1996, only three Korean-owned liquor stores had converted to other businesses. Patrice Wong, general manager of the ANED, and Bong Hwan Kim himself also expressed concern about the practical limitations of this ambitious program:

> Impacted merchants who seek to convert their businesses are in need of three key elements: 1) access to capital, 2) viable business alternatives and 3) streamlined and expedited city permitting systems…The largest portion of the available money ($200 million) was set aside to create a Bridge Loan program for business[es] awaiting federal SBA loan assistance…only $8.8 million of the original $200 million was disbursed…The capital investment to convert a liquor store into a laundromat, for example, may be prohibitively high for most (roughly $750,000), with projected cash flows and profitability under comparable liquor store levels for several years. Conversion to less capital-intensive businesses, such as fast-food franchises or quick-print facilities, may not be viable because the forecasted returns are far below the earnings of liquor stores. In short, there are few realistic business alternatives that can replace the source

of livelihood for these merchants...Downzoning of commercial properties throughout impacted areas further complicates the rebuilding process. (*KoreAm* December 18, 1993)

As demonstrated by this history, the initiative and work of anti-liquor store campaigns stemmed from community efforts and cross-racial coalitions, and not from the city or state. Unlike the reaction to the 1965 Watts Revolt, intervention by the public sector was minimal and far from adequate.

## CONCLUSION

The anti-liquor campaign, which began as a consumer movement,[33] eventually expanded to include health, anti-racist, and environmental issues. The campaign had many of the attributes of the so-called "new social movements," and thus, indicates the continued importance of class analysis in the study of modern forms of power. As LaClau and Mouffe pointed out, "the struggle of the working class may take many different forms according to the conditions of the labor process and the discourses through which it constructs its interests and organizes its objectives at a given moment" (1992, 108). In other words, liquor stores connoted domination and the status quo in South LA. The Community Coalition, led by Black and Latino community leaders, symbolized an important struggle of anti-domination and resistance. Although this campaign was not considered a "worker's struggle," it did involve property owners and the urban poor.[34]

In addition, contrary to NSM theorists' predictions, this campaign was not merely oriented towards racial identity or inter-ethnic conflict. Although the Community Coalition challenged the owners of liquor stores, it also maintained that California state entities were directly culpable and therefore targets of their campaign. Thus, it illustrated how "new movements carry on the project of older movements in a vital aspect: they open up the political sphere, they articulate popular demands and they politicize issues previously confined to the private realm" (Weir 1993, 88). The Community Coalition not only carried out a consumer boycott, but it also succeeded in politicizing a racial minority movement.

More specifically, the Community Coalition challenged stereotypes about minorities and inner-city residents, contesting the view that people in South LA did not care about their environment and tolerated oppressive conditions, such as the overconcentration of liquor stores. Through participation in the Community Coalition, inner-city minorities and immigrants were able to spur change in the local liquor industry, especially with regards to the merchant middlemen. Targeting the third tier seemed to cause reverberations up the tiers. Accordingly, the Community Coalition constructed new political subjectivities. Secondly, this movement became part of broader coalitional politics going beyond ethnic separatism in LA, and led to the embrace of multiethnic organizing as a means to greater political empowerment. The Community Coalition was primarily a Black, female, grassroots movement that later expanded to include Latinos and even progressive Korean/Asian American community leaders and activists. In this way, it attempted to avoid charges of "anti-Korean" racism.

Third, the Community Coalition contested the dysfunctional, laissez-faire capitalism represented by liquor stores—capitalist endeavors that did not take into account the long-term impact of their business practices on the local community—and by the merchants who engaged in these practices. Refuting a media-driven, monolithic understanding of particular immigrant communities, young, progressive Korean American community leaders used moral reasoning as well as progressive political ideology to navigate a different course of economic empowerment for the Korean American community.[35] This new course of business practice forced many Korean small business owners to take into account long-term effects on their customers and to balance these practices using a sort of *moral compass* to determine if their businesses were healthy, ethical, and profitable.

This is the story of how inner-city residents mobilized to challenge and transform the liquor industry. The transformation wasn't initiated by multiethnic coalition, but it became one—one in which ethnic communities were not always monolithic in their actions, evidenced by the fact that members of the Korean community were on both sides of the liquor store debate. In the end, the ethnicity of South LA liquor store owners did become diversified, from predominantly Korean owners in the 1980s and 1990s to Armenian, South Asian, and Latino owners in the twenty-first century. Before the unrest, 45 percent of the liquor stores in South LA were operated by Koreans, according to a *Los Angeles Times* analysis of owners' names; as of 2012, only about one-third are Korean (*LAT* April 27, 2012). However, as *Los Angeles Times* columnist Sandy Banks writes, "The proliferation of liquor stores—not the ethnicity of owners—is what draws the community down."

There are nearly 70,000 more people today in South LA than there were 20 years ago, census figures show. The Community Coalition (2012) succeeded in closing all 24 liquor stores that it had identified as nuisances prior to the unrest and fought the reopening of some 200 liquor stores destroyed by the unrest; liquor license records show 174 fewer liquor stores. Notwithstanding the fact that there was a reduction in liquor stores in South LA, as David Sloane (2012) pointed out, the community's efforts to identify these businesses as sources of blight and disorder dovetail with the highly controversial, "broken windows theory" of policing and community health by James Q. Wilson.[36] This notion holds that maintaining and monitoring urban environments to prevent small crimes such as vandalism and public drinking helps to create an atmosphere of order and lawfulness, thereby preventing more serious crimes from happening. This notion is controversial, because this discourse dovetails with law and order rhetoric used by police, who are usually at odds with these communities. Community Coalition efforts did contribute to the perpetuation of ethnic tension, not to mention the economic disenfranchisement and social marginalization of Korean immigrant liquor store owners during the post-unrest period. Moreover, South LA still suffers from a disproportionate number of liquor stores as compared to LA County as a whole (Sloane 2012, 98).

Notwithstanding the drawbacks of this movement, it attempted to reestablish the social relationships of a community through a focus on the liquor store issue. Thus, I argue that the Community Coalition's effects went beyond preventing merchants from rebuilding liquor stores: it was a broader attempt to change capitalist relationships in Black and Latino communities. The Community Coalition challenged the capitalist idea that free enterprise is always a panacea.

This chapter and previous ones have explored Black-Korean tensions and, to a lesser extent, Korean-Latino relations. The next chapter will examine the perspective of Latinos on the ways their relations with Koreans have evolved, and compare them with Black-Korean tensions.

## NOTES

1. Chapter 7 was originally published as "Challenging the Liquor Industry in Los Angeles," *International Journal of Sociology and Public Policy* 24 (7/8) (2004): 103–36.

2. However, some scholars dispute such characterizations, questioning the notion that these are "new" social movements. See Weir (1993) for further discussion.

3. Until the early 1970s, the social-psychological tradition of the Chicago School was dominant, along with mass society theories (e.g., Kornhauser and Arendt) and Smelser's structural functionalist model of collective behavior (Cohen 1985, 671).

4. Resource mobilization theorists rejected the emphasis on feelings and grievances, the use of psychologizing categories, and the breakdown characteristic of the collective behavior approach. Instead, these theorists stressed "objective" variables such as organization, interests, resources, opportunities, and strategies to account for large-scale mobilization (Cohen 1985, 674).

5. 187 damaged liquor stores represented an estimated $42 million loss (*KTLA* May 11, 1992).

6. If one adopts the conservative figure of 300 Korean-owned grocery and liquor stores, these businesses would represent 44 percent of all grocery and liquor outlets in South LA.

7. In some states, government-run stores are the only places that can legally sell a bottle of scotch or gin.

8. As *Time* (November 8, 1999) reported, in 1999, a bill was submitted to Congress to let states sue in federal court for violations of bans on interstate shipments of alcohol. The Liquor Wholesalers and Distributors Association, concerned about Internet liquor sales to minors, gave $144,000 to Democratic Party committees and $209,000 to the Republican Party. Although the stated concern related to underage drinking, it was really about how e-commerce erodes the liquor manufacturers' business. Winemakers in California and elsewhere who hoped to sell wine over the Internet and allow tourists to ship wine home gave $1,339,000 to Democratic Party committees and $1,623,000 to the GOP. Both the House and the Senate passed the provision backed by wholesalers in 1999.

9. The ABC was rooted in the anti-salon movement of the late 1800s that was led by Carrie Nation, who later triumphed with the passage of nationwide Prohibition in 1920 (*LAT* December 27, 1996).

10. It had not been funded well before.

11. The Minor Decoy Program allows local law enforcement agencies such as the Department of ABC to use persons under 20 years of age as decoys to purchase alcoholic beverages from licensed premises in order to attack the problems associated with the unlawful purchase and consumption of alcoholic beverages by young people. http://www.abc.ca.gov/programs/minor_decoy.html. Accessed: January 27, 2018.

12. Half were "type 20" licenses for off-sale beer and wine only, and the other half were "type 21" licenses for off-sale beer, wine, and distilled spirits. The former type was held by most grocery stores, while only liquor stores held the full license.

13. New York State limits wine and liquor sales to liquor stores.

14. Grocery/Liquor Store (off-premise) Sale Hours are: Monday to Saturday: Beer: 24 hours; Wine & Liquor: 8:00 am to 12:00 am; Sunday: Beer: 24 hours; Wine & Liquor: 12:00 pm to 9:00 pm. "New York Liquor Laws," State Liquor Laws. http://www.stateliquorlaws.com/state/NY. Accessed: January 27, 2018.

15. The processing fee Korean merchants charge for cashing checks for customers is one of the many points of conflict.

16. A few merchants, including Koreans, were charged with illegally receiving food stamps for non-food items.

17. The data on number of stores changing hands is not available.

18. "Community Coalition," Community Coalition for Substance Abuse Prevention and Treatment. http://cocosouthla.org/. Accessed: January 27, 2018.

19. The zoning commission had the power to prevent the sale of liquor on the grounds that the store represented a public nuisance. The procedure required the imposition of conditions and a six-month evaluation period before the zoning commission could act, subject to override by the city council.

20. Ridley-Thomas and Walters joined forces to exempt liquor stores from fast-track authority in the rebuilding process, leading to a case-by-case consideration for

each reopening. Later on, they also defeated proposed state legislation (AB 1974) that would have stopped the city from imposing conditions on the rebuilding of businesses destroyed in the unrest. Nate Holden (10th District), who also represented part of Koreatown, took a more neutral position on the issue.

21. Mayor Bradley's South Central Community/Merchant Liquor Task Force's final report stated that the issue could not be resolved without outside money to buy out the store owners (Sonenshein 1996, 729).

22. New conditions included the hiring of security guards, restrictions on graffiti, as well as limits on the sale of cups and individual bottles.

23. The official fee for transference of a liquor license is anywhere between $5,000 to $10,000; however, they have been informally transferred at much higher prices. In contrast, in New York City, a liquor license is not transferable.

24. If liquor stores were shown to present an environmental hazard to public safety, then the rebuilding of liquor stores would require "negative declarations" or a more bulky, time-consuming Environmental Impact Act Report (Sonenshein 1996, 730).

25. "About CCSAT" Community Coalition for Substance Abuse Prevention and Treatment). http://www.cocosouthla.org/about/ourmission. Accessed: October 29, 2010.

26. Michael Brown, "After 20 years, the Community Coalition reflects on its efforts in South LA." http://www.ourweekly.com/los-angeles/after-20-years-community-coalition-reflects-its-efforts-south-la. Accessed: October 24, 2012.

27. "About CCSAT," Community Coalition for Substance Abuse Prevention and Treatment. http://www.cocosouthla.org/about/ourmission. Accessed: October 29, 2010.

28. According to the 2010 US Census, census tracts in South LA suffered from an official unemployment rate of almost 40 percent, and nearly 30 percent of residents lived below the federal poverty line.

29. APPCON was renamed A3PCON (Asian Pacific Policy and Planning Council) in 1996. APANLA (Asian Pacific Americans for a New LA) is now defunct.

30. The concept of conversion gained momentum when it became obvious that there were insufficient funds in public coffers or in the private sector to compensate liquor store owners for abandoning their businesses (Sonenshein 1996, 732).

31. KYCC was founded in 1975 and incorporated as a nonprofit agency in 1982. It aims to develop positive identity and leadership among youth, enhanced intergenerational relationships among Korean Americans, community socioeconomic empowerment, and constructive interethnic community relations (KYCC Fact Sheet 1994).

32. The advisory committee members represented a diverse section of community-based organizations, private sector companies, and elected officials, including Chinatown Service Center, Little Tokyo Service Center, Korean Immigrant Workers Advocates, Community Coalition for Substance Abuse Prevention and Treatment, Founders Bank, Bank of America, Community Development Bank, Dunbar Economic Development Corporation, and Councilman Mike Hernandez's office (*The Alliance for Neighborhood Economic Development Year End Report* 1994).

33. Labor group boycotts (23 percent) and boycotts sponsored by organizations representing racial minorities (21 percent) were the most common consumer boycotts in the 1970s (Friedman 1991, 152). It is important to note that, instead of price-oriented issues, quality-of-life considerations and "bioconsumer" issues (e.g., health or environmental issues) were a focus for boycotts in the 1990s (Friedman 1991, 166–67).

34. It should be noted that some residents of the neighborhood were happy to have the liquor stores rebuilt. However, most members of the community felt that the Community Coalition was speaking for them.

35. Korean Americans were not on the front lines of this fight.

36. James Q. Wilson, and George L Kelling, 1982, "Broken Windows: The police and neighborhood safety," The Atlantic. https://www.theatlantic.com/magazine/archive/1982/03/broken-windows/304465/. Accessed: January 27, 2018.

*Part IV*

# CONCLUSION

## Chapter Eight

# An Analysis of Latino-Korean Relations in the Workplace

## Latino Perspectives in the Aftermath of the 1992 Los Angeles Civil Unrest

A bad thing about them is that they are suspicious, they follow you around, and it is not a pleasant encounter. For instance, one time my aunt's blouse was ripped off because a merchant thought she was hiding something inside her clothes, tried to grab it, and ripped off her blouse. . . . However, one good thing we notice about the Koreans is that they learn Spanish and go out of their way to speak to you in Spanish—this makes us feel good, because it makes us more intimate with them and shows that they value us as their customers. (Emely and Bessy 1997)

Throughout this book, I have argued that race, citizenship, class, and culture—axes of inequality in a multitiered "racial cartography"—affected how LA residents thought about and interacted with each other before and after the 1992 unrest.[1] In this chapter, I focus on how structural inequality impacted relations between Koreans and Latinos. As I elaborate in the next chapter, race, class, citizenship, and culture are interwoven in hierarchical power relations among groups and evidenced in the processes of social inequality and conflict, including the LA unrest.

Since I conceptualize Black- and Latino-Korean tensions as racialized, classed, and cultural conflicts, it is critical to compare Latino-Korean relations with Black-Korean ones. How did Latino immigrants interact with Korean immigrants, in what ways did this differ from the latter group's relations with African Americans, and why? In short, Latinos were able to develop a better relationship with Korean immigrants and did not turn to the politics of protest, which African Americans employed. My analysis of the evolving relationship of Latinos with Korean immigrants is limited to the period after the unrest, as it was this event that brought my attention to this relationship. It is important to keep in mind that Latino-Korean relations have never been characterized by the same scope of conflict as that associated with Black-Korean tensions either before or after the unrest.

Mainstream representations of the 1992 Los Angeles unrest had little to say about Mexicans or Central Americans, the primary Latino ethnic groups who lived in South LA. Instead, the media honed in on Black-Korean tensions and the burning of Korean-owned businesses by African American rioters. As Jinah Kim points out, an overemphasis on the oppression of Black people ignored other systemic problems that led to the unrest and made Blackness both the focus of and the solution to the conflict (2008, 44). Although largely portrayed in the national media as a Black uprising, the unrest involved many Latinos, either as participants or as victims. First, Latinos were the initial victims of the crowd violence (see chapter 9). Out of 5,633 arrests, "51 percent of those arrested were Latino; 30 percent of those who died were Latino" (Pastor 1993, 1). Second, more than 12 percent of the damaged businesses were Latino-owned (Tierney 1994, 153). A third of the Latinos arrested were turned over to the Immigration and Naturalization Services (INS) and processed for deportation (Pastor 1993, 12). In the predominantly Central American Pico Union area, outsider-owned stores, particularly those owned by Korean Americans, were looted and destroyed by Latino residents (Navarro 1993, 79).

Latinos were a near majority in the neighborhoods most affected by the unrest: South LA, Koreatown, and Pico Union. Economic factors played an important role in the pattern of violence and property damage: in the areas where damage occurred, poverty and unemployment were twice as high as the rest of LA, while per capita income and home ownership were half the rate of the city overall (Pastor 1993). According to economist Manuel Pastor, these figures were related to the rapid growth of the Latino underclass. In LA, the number of Latino families falling below the poverty line was three times higher than that of non-Latino families. In 1989, the per capita income for Latinos in LA was $7,111, less than half the city's average; for Latinos living in South LA, the figure was much lower: $4,461 (Pastor 1993, 6).

Most studies on Latino-Korean relations at the time of the unrest are written from the Korean immigrant merchants' point of view, and for some time, discussion on Latino-Korean relations was limited to identifying cultural similarities between the two groups. However, the discussion has been considerably strengthened by recent scholarly interest in post-unrest multiracial coalition building (K. Park 1995; Yoon 1997; D. Kim 1999; Chang and Diaz-Veizades 1999; K. Park 2004; Min 2007; Chung 2007; N. Kim 2008). Cultural similarities alone cannot explain the social relations between Latinos and Koreans, just as Black-Korean tensions were not only rooted in cultural differences, but also in their divergent sociopolitical experiences in the US.

As discussed in chapters 2–5, Black-Korean tensions are interpenetrated by the four social categories of race, class, citizenship, and culture or four degrees of exclusion and divergence (see figure 8.1).

At the same time, as explained in chapters 4 and 5, class played an equally critical role in Korean-Black encounters between middle-class immigrant merchants and the inner-city poor. In addition, these inner-city African Americans contested the full membership—namely, citizenship—of recently immigrated Koreans within the US nation-state. They appeared to reap rewards too soon, without sufficient suffering or struggle. Finally, culture, in the form of business practices, seemed to contribute to the politicization of the tension (see chapter 3). Thus, the conflicts often appeared to be a matter of unbridgeable cultural difference. In short, complex urban problems were reduced to conflicts of culture, read reductively through race.

With regard to Latinos and Koreans, I argue that the different position of the two groups in relation to US racial hegemony, capitalism, and national identity created sociopolitical barriers and obstructed what could have been a productive social relationship, much like the case of Black-Korean relations. What emerged in interviewees' narratives was the recognition of the pivotal role of class, culture, and citizenship, rather than race and citizenship, in the development of Latino-Korean relations. Latino-Korean relations also

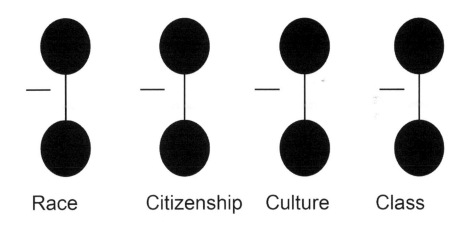

Race　　　Citizenship　Culture　　Class

Four Degree of Separation:

Ethnic Tension

Figure 8.1.　Korean-Black Relations

reflected aspects of patron-client relationships, as found in Latin America, indicating a dependent, symbiotic, and exploitative dynamic.

In keeping with the broader theme of the book, I examine how Latinos interacted with Koreans, how they interpreted such encounters, and, more importantly, what the implications of these interpretations are for understanding race/ethnicity, citizenship, class, and culture. Taking as a premise that the unrest, an extreme case of ethnic conflict, was a major turning point in race relations in LA, I first identify Latino-Korean relations as labor relations. Second, I examine the connection between the unrest and labor relations. Third, I discuss the importance of this link for interethnic relations, particularly as relates to post-unrest Latino-Korean labor organizing.

My earlier work (1995b) and chapter 6 provided a reference point for Latino-Korean encounters from the perspective of Korean immigrant merchants in South LA. However, this chapter focuses on Latino perspectives, which are analyzed in relation to historical and structural concepts such as racial ideology, the racialization process, class location, immigration, and citizenship, as well as notions of interracial social relationships. Special attention is given to public spaces where Latinos interacted with Korean immigrants, including store counters, neighborhoods, schools, workplaces, churches, and parks. Complementary interview narratives were obtained through grassroots community organizations. This study was not designed to reflect the most updated research on interethnic relations, but rather interviewees' experience of and response to the 1992 unrest.[2] Despite these limitations, this chapter provides an important glimpse into the phenomenon of Latinos working for Korean immigrant employers in the aftermath of the unrest. I am interested in explaining changing dynamics and relationships as well as individual opinions or attitudes. To date, no previous studies have explored how Latino clients, employees, schoolmates, or neighbors of Korean immigrant merchants experienced the unrest.

## "HIDDEN CONFLICT" BETWEEN LATINOS AND KOREANS

Since the 1970s, Korean merchants have employed Latino workers in LA as an alternative to co-ethnic labor, which is less available and more expensive.[3] This shift to employing outside one's own ethnic group has also been observed among other immigrant groups with high rates of self-employment (D. Kim 1999, 586). However, in 2007, Korean immigrants still had a greater dependence on Latino workers (38 percent) than either Chinese or Indian immigrant merchants (15 percent) (Min 2007, 399). As reported in previous chapters, before the 1992 unrest, Korean businesses in South LA also depended on Latino employees more than on Black employees (K. Park 1995b, 62).

Building on Lucie Cheng and Yen Le Espiritu's "immigrant hypothesis" (1989, 531), Chang and Diaz-Veizades (1999) writes that there was little ethnic conflict between Latinos and Korean immigrants, and that Latino informants admired Korean immigrants' work ethic and saw the employment opportunities they provided as beneficial for their neighborhoods (102). However, the authors were unable to explain why, despite these positive relations, Latinos also participated in looting Korean stores (Saito 2001, 79).

I should note that there may be no one causal relationship between Latinos looting Korean stores and Latino views on Koreans. First, post-unrest studies on Latino-Korean relations do not explain how Latino views of Koreans influenced their decision to loot. Second, despite having positive opinions, Latinos could have still participated in the looting of Korean stores for the purposes of self-interest. Third, it is possible that few Latinos interviewed in previous studies participated in looting Korean stores. After all, despite the low percentage of African Americans who expressed support for Black boycotts of Korean stores, Black-Korean tensions still developed. Thus, I examine both positive and negative Latino perspectives on Koreans, acknowledging that the relationship between the two could have been simultaneously respectful and contentious.

Pyong Gap Min (2007) attributes the positive relationship between Latinos and Koreans to a number of factors, including cultural similarities; mutual benefits derived from the employer-employee relationship; Korean American community organizations' establishment of cultural, social, and organizational linkages; and the provision of services to Latino immigrant workers and Latino children. He reported strong personal ties between Korean merchants and Latino employees, discussing various ways in which the former informally helped the latter, sometimes even sponsoring their applications for green cards (Min 2007, 402–4).

Notwithstanding these relatively good relations—and in part due to campaigns like the "Hotel Workers Justice Campaign," "Restaurant Workers Justice Campaign," and "Supermarket Workers Justice Campaign" by the Koreatown Immigrant Workers Alliance (KIWA)—an increasing number of Latino employees complained to government agencies about unfair/unlawful treatment and filed lawsuits against Korean employers. KIWA supported Latinos in these campaigns. Korean business owners typically depend on co-ethnic workers for managerial, supervisory, professional, or sales positions; they used Latino workers for more labor-intensive, low-wage jobs such as dishwashing, cooking, ironing, garment manufacturing, stocking retail items, cleaning, painting, moving, and construction work. However, Latinos were increasingly given managerial positions starting in the late 1990s. If cultural similarities is one of the reasons Koreans tended to hire Latinos, then why was there an ethno-racial division of labor and hierarchy in these workplaces, and why did that relationship gradually shift?

Larry Bobo et al. (1994) reported a "hidden conflict" between Latinos and Koreans, speculating that such tensions probably accounted for the level of violence directed at Korean merchants and businesses during the 1992 unrest. According to their focus group study, Latinos harbored the same grievances against Korean merchants and business owners that African Americans did. They also reported problems in employer-employee interactions, in coworker relations, and in neighborhood settings with Koreans (Bobo et al. 1994). Thus, cultural similarity—if it actually existed—may not have been sufficient to nurture a relationship between Latinos and Koreans. The argument regarding cultural similarity posed by Min needs to be understood as a politics of similarity, rather than a true indicator of similarity. Korean employers, rather than Latino workers, likely utilized a discourse of cultural similarity in order to gloss over economic inequalities between the two groups.

I believe it is more productive to examine the structural relationship between Latinos and Koreans, which is interdependent and symbiotic. One aspect of this relationship involves the patron-client dynamic between Korean employers and Latino employees, which might represent neo-feudal relations in which "patrons" gain the support of "clients" through the mutual exchange of benefits and obligations. The two groups work symbiotically, since the patron needs the client as much as the client needs the patron. In other words, Latino workers prove themselves indispensable to Korean employers due to their long tenure and reliable work performance. In return, Korean employers provide advice, gifts, and loans, while socializing and guaranteeing employment. That said, it is important to highlight Howard Stein's critique (1984) that the patron-client relationship is "dysfunctional in the long run" (30). According to Stein, no matter what the intent of those participating is, the mutuality of the patron-client relationship disguises a hierarchy of superior/inferior. As a result, civil unrest could become a way for the less powerful clients to address inequality.

Despite different racial and immigration histories, the Latin American patron-client relationship has been reproduced in some segments of the Mexican American community, according to some researchers. Octavio Ignacio Romano (1960), for instance, reported that White business owners functioned largely in the role of patron in rural Mexican American communities in South Texas during the 1950s, much in the same manner as occurred in Latin America between elites and peasants. More recently, Rachel Adler (2002) examines how traditional patterns initially found in Yucatan and throughout Mesoamerica have been adapted to fit transnational circumstances as migrants participate in patron-client relationships to achieve their goals in Dallas. Latino workers appear to use forms of patron-client relationships as a strategy for negotiating terms of employment.

As Roger Waldinger and Michael Lichter have noted (2003), employers in LA, including Korean immigrant employers, prefer to hire newly arrived immigrants because of their "personal qualifications—friendliness, enthusiasm, smiling, and subservience" (220). Unlike American-born White and Black workers, who are more likely to be aware of their labor rights, Mexican workers approach their Korean employers as clients. This type of relationship means that Korean employers, patrons in this case, perform favors by granting gifts, credit, loans, and providing assistance with immigration registration, income tax, social security applications, green cards, housing loans, and recommendations. However, Korean employers might not know they're expected to grant favors rather than just paying the workers for their work, or they might mistake Latino employees' friendliness for affection. When the patron-client relationship is not productive for Latino workers, they may choose to participate in the looting Korean stores, as they may anticipate less reprisal from their Korean employers who are not a part of the White-dominated establishment.

## THE POLITICS OF CULTURAL DIFFERENCE

My discussion on cultural similarity and difference is limited to the topic of economic and labor relations. These views represent a limited sample taken from recent immigrants to South LA from Mexico, El Salvador, Guatemala, and Honduras. Needless to say, in LA, where Latinos represent nearly half of the city's population, there are many ethnic and class differences: Latinos include immigrant and US-born Mexicans who can be either working or middle class, and Central Americans of Pico Union and South LA. My Latino interviewees were majority working-class immigrants, but some were US citizens.

Similarities between Latinos and the Korean immigrants include the experience of struggling to learn and become fluent in English. This not only limits immigrants' ability to communicate, but it also impedes their participation in the political process and integration into mainstream society. Equally important, both groups suffer from anti-immigrant sentiment and employment discrimination (Chang and Diaz-Veizades 1999, 104). Korean and Central American immigrants were also both subject to US imperialism, particularly military intervention, before immigration.[4] Furthermore, Latino perceptions of Koreans as hardworking resonate with how Americans view Mexicans or how Salvadorans view themselves. Ruth Gomberg-Muñoz (2010), for instance, suggests that American stereotypes of Mexicans emphasize "religiosity, family orientation, and work ethic" (301). Similarly, according to Beth Baker-Cristales (2004), "Salvadorans portray themselves as industrious workers, people who will do what it takes to earn a living, joking that they are the Japanese of Central America. Their nickname is 'guanaco,' meaning laborious, strong, [with the] stamina to toil like beasts of burden" (127).

Notwithstanding certain similarities, there are significant differences between Latinos and Koreans. Historically, individuals of Mexican origin were categorized officially as White (following the Mexican-American War), although they were certainly not treated as White; Asian immigrants and their children have historically been othered as non-White. Also unlike Koreans, Mexicans have a history of territorial annexation, since large swaths of the southwestern US were originally part of Mexico.

The data presented below is drawn from 18 interviews with Latino immigrants who were customers at Korean-owned stores. In addition to in-depth interviews conducted from 1995–1997 and archival analysis (*La Opinión*, 1990–2001), I participated in many social events such as dinners, picnics, weddings, and graduation ceremonies. Interviews were carried out in Spanish or English.[5]

In terms of the ways Latinos conceived of similarities between themselves and Koreans, they mentioned the following traits: Koreans were immigrants, hardworking, disciplined, family-oriented,[6] religious and mystical,[7] ate spicy food, and were partygoers. Table 8.1 presents a composite summary of Latino interviewees' opinions of the differences between themselves and Koreans.

The differences represented in Table 8.1 reflect stereotypes about Koreans and Asian Americans more generally. Some aspects simply reflect the larger society's dominant view of Koreans, while others are based on uniquely Latino observations. It should be noted that structural inequality often places Latinos in a lower socioeconomic status when compared to Asians (O'Brien 2008, 49), and they continue to enter the country largely as temporary labor-

Table 8.1.    Latino Discourse on Differences between Koreans and Themselves

| Koreans | Latinos |
|---|---|
| Strong belief in the American Dream | Weaker belief in the American Dream |
| Know and take advantage of the system | Ambivalent toward the system |
| Highly motivated | Conformist |
| Emphasize education and business | Emphasize employment and work |
| Business owners or middle class | Working poor or middle class |
| Greedy | Not greedy |

*Source:* Kyeyoung Park

ers ineligible for citizenship (Moran 1997, 1320). These differences might influence the fact that, although both Koreans and Latinos aspire to the "American Dream," Latinos believe that Koreans have a firmer and almost more naïve belief in it than they do. Regarding education and employment, Latinos feel that, while Koreans can afford to make education a priority, they cannot.[8] This sentiment does not mean that Latinos place little value on education, however.

Like Black interviewees, Latino interviewees pointed out cohesiveness and cultural retention among Korean immigrants. The concept of culture is broad and often misunderstood. However, my discussion is limited to the particular way Latino interviewees related to cultural traits as markers of difference; in other words, they recognized culture in terms of what worked or functioned. This discourse on cultural difference also needs to be understood as a politics of difference rather than a direct indicator of difference.

Interviewees Rafael, Emely, and Bessy, who are social workers at the Central American Resource Center (CARECEN), identified both similarities and differences between Latinos and Koreans.[9] Regarding similarities, Bessy said, "We are both hardworking, we are both immigrants. Moreover, we came here for the same purpose—to improve ourselves. We also face the same discrimination because of language barriers and because we are both ethnic minorities." Emely stated, "We have the same point of reference while Blacks do not. Another similarity is that we are both family-oriented." Regarding differences, Rafael stated, "Koreans stress education. We Latinos just stress working hard. After high school, many Korean parents stress their children to continue with the education." Rafael also discussed differences in communication style:

> Koreans learn and try to speak Spanish; they try to penetrate us and we do not know . . . they learn to speak our language and they own the businesses in our community, and we do not have much control or advantage towards Koreans. On the other hand, Latinos are more open and try to interact more with others but Koreans are not.[10]

Miguel, a 28-year-old who works at the nonprofit immigrant support organization *El Rescate*, had a similar take on Korean immigrants and their culture[11]:

> They look too tough, face too tough, serious. I do not see them happy, not at all. In addition, they just want to be with their own—no Latinos, no Blacks.
> (How do you characterize yourself?)
> Open-minded and disposed to learn other cultures.
> (How are they similar or different from you and your culture?)

No similarity. Latinos, we are too crazy, easygoing. We love dancing, sing-
ing, and partying too much. However, Koreans are too serious.

Paula, a 25-year-old second-generation Mexican American woman who
works as a sales assistant, put it bluntly:

There are no similarities between Koreans and Latinos. Koreans are greedy for
money. They are not conformist like we are, which is good. Most of the owners
of stores are Koreans, who are very rude and they have a funny body odor. They
are not trustworthy. I had a cousin that worked for a Korean, and he had a very
bad experience with them. They did not treat him right.

Although Latinos claim traits that can also be ascribed to Koreans, such
as family rapport and cultural maintenance (Telles and Ortiz 2008, 185),[12] a
number of Latinos I spoke with attributed the success of Korean immigrants
in business to the mobilization of their culture and social relations. Some
interviewees, like Melvin, a 45-year-old Salvadoran pastor, were critical not
of Koreans, but of Latinos:

I do not know much about the Korean culture, but I think it is good. They maintain their language, customs, they help each other out. . . . The difference is that
Latinos are not like that. Latinos do not have that unity, and they do not help
each other. Koreans are always helping each other.

In this vein, according to Chang and Diaz-Veizades (1999), Central Americans believe that Asians are able to run more profitable businesses because
they buy collectively. This might correspond with the admiration some Latino respondents had for the "unity" they identified in the Korean community
(Chang and Diaz-Veizades 1999, 91).

Jaime, an unemployed Salvadoran who had worked for a Korean business,
said he never had a problem with his boss. He worked at a Korean restaurant
doing maintenance work and helped in the kitchen. He held positive views of
his former Korean employer and Korean culture, although he resented their
suspicion of Latinos as criminals:

Well, I never see them getting drunk on the streets or doing bad stuff. . . . Well,
there are some differences. When someone passes by, Koreans do not say "hi"
or anything. They don't really care. . . . They take care of their own business
and that's it. . . . To make matters worse, when a Latino is walking around near
their home, they don't like it because they are suspicious and think that we are
criminals.

All in all, respondents' discourse about cultural differences reflected just as
much on economics and class differences. As one respondent put it vividly,

"They became successful owing to their magical culture." Latino interviewees also invoked cultural difference rhetorically as a way to problematize the capitalist segmentation of labor and ethnic hierarchies in workplaces. Only when such cultural differences were combined with different historical experiences and exacerbated by conflicting class/race relations did relations become explicitly antagonistic.

## LATINO PERSPECTIVES ON KOREANS

The multivalent encounters between Latinos and Korean immigrants have produced a more complex dynamic than has been observed with Black-Korean relations. A few Latino respondents reported having excellent relationships with their Korean employers, fellow employees, and merchants. Victor, a 33-year-old Salvadoran mechanic, had worked in the same Korean-owned gas station and mechanic shop since coming to the US in 1982:

> I am well treated here. There are six workers, three Koreans and three Latinos. My immediate supervisor is Korean. I am on good relations with both Korean employer and employees. I am well-treated, and they are good friends. Eighty percent of my friends are Koreans, good relations with them.

When he was asked to comment on his interaction with Korean merchants, he stated, "For me all has been good. . . . Never had any problems with Korean merchants. I always go to places I know, the merchants are like friends, and I am treated very well, same all the time." Similarly, Alfredo, a 37-year-old Mexican male, was in charge of building maintenance, repair, and security for a Korean-owned building, and he felt well-respected by his employer:

> My Korean employer, Mr. Kang, treats me well. There are five workers: two Koreans, two Latinos, and one European. . . . One of my Korean friends is my former apartment manager/owner. Even several years have passed since I moved out, but he is still my friend. We have good friendship.

However, a good number of Latino interviewees complained about merchant-customer relations like my Black interviewees, although they often provided a more nuanced view of Korean merchants. Antonio, a 38-year-old Honduran who did glasswork, noted that Korean merchants were suspicious of inner-city customers, even though his own experience with Korean merchants was neutral:

> I think Korean merchants have a hard time, they don't trust people and they can't trust, too many theft in the store, too many thieves around . . . look, if you

got the money, there is no problem. My experience with them is neither bad nor good. The problem is money, not the merchants.

Julio, a 40-year-old *El Rescate* staff member, attributed the problem with Korean merchants to cultural misunderstandings, but he stressed that the problem is limited to only certain Korean-owned stores:

> Not bad. Overall, interaction with Korean merchants is fine. Occasionally, though, unpleasant things happen due to misunderstandings. Merchants can be perceived as not very friendly. Koreans have to understand us better, our culture, but we also have to understand better their Korean culture as well.

Despite negative experiences with Korean merchants, the various encounters that Latinos had in many different social settings substantially diversified their understanding of Korean immigrants. My interview with three CARECEN social workers, who all had Korean friends at their schools, reflected the ambivalent nature of Latino-Korean relationships. For one respondent Rafael, these relations were "*nada malo* [not bad] and *nada bueno* [not good]." As is demonstrated in the opening quote for this chapter, the two other CARECEN employees also felt there were good and bad aspects to the Korean merchants.

Some Latinos reported a less than satisfactory relationship with their Korean employers. Most low-wage workers do not receive health insurance, paid vacations, and/or sick leave, because there is no legislation requiring employers to provide such benefits (Koreatown Immigrant Workers Alliance 2007, 17). Aurora, a 48-year-old Mexican woman who worked for a Korean market, identified low wages and lack of benefits and vacation as a source of interracial tension. When she once missed a workday due to illness, she was told her wages would be deducted or her employment would be terminated. Due to fear of termination, many of these workers are unable to recover adequately when an illness occurs. Interestingly though, Aurora also criticized the Latino community, in particular Latino employers, for paying less and discriminating against fellow Latinos:

> I have not had any big problem with them [Korean business owners].
> They do not demand too much from you as long as you are responsible. They treat me pretty well. Just too much work never ends. . . . Work is good. The thing is that we do not get vacations, and even if we did, it would not be paid. We do not get any kind of benefits, including medical. Can I ask you a question? What is the current minimum wage?
> (I believe it is $5.25.[13])
> My boss only pays me $5 an hour. I have never missed work, even one day, for the past four years of working for him. . . . Last month I fell and could not

use my right leg. I missed work for a week, but I do not think my boss is going to pay me for the missed week. . . . I believe it [the Latino community] is very selfish and egotistic. . . . Latino business owners pay less and discriminate against their own people.

Juan, a Mexican pastor, shared this grievance. There were 15 congregants of his church whose employers were Koreans. He noted that it took time for Latino workers to feel comfortable with Korean employers:

Some are good, but others are bad. They do not get any benefits. The place of work is usually clean and well-ventilated. If you compare Korean bosses with Chinese bosses, Koreans are better. Chinese are harsher. . . . In the beginning, they yell a lot. I knew one Korean woman . . . would yell in front of all the customers. Now that my friend has been working there for a while, things are better. . . . Another thing about Koreans is that they do not like giving raise, almost never. Moreover, when the Latino workers quit their jobs because of the low wage, the Korean employers just go find another Latino worker who is willing to work for the same low wage.

As these anecdotes show, although Latinos interact with Korean immigrants in diverse settings, workplace disputes are often the primary source of tension. For example, Miguel affirmed the presence of class tension: "Yes, there are differences. Economic differences—Koreans are employers and we Latinos their employees. We are under them, and they are above us. This is not a racial tension; it is strictly a class tension." Similarly, the CARECEN social workers I interviewed raised various problems with Korean immigrants, liquor store controversies (see previous chapter), and labor issues:

On two issues or cases, we can say there is some tension. One is the presence of liquor stores in the community. There are too many liquor stores in the neighborhood, mostly owned by Asians or Koreans. Around liquor stores, we see drug problems and drunkenness. Liquor stores give the neighborhood a bad image, and something has to be done about this. . . . The other problem is employer-employee relations. There are problems with workers' treatment; there are complaints about low pay and lack of recognition for [Latinos'] hard work. This problem is especially severe in the garment industry. This is economic or class tension, which is not racial. For other things, there is no problem between Koreans and Latinos.

The results of KIWA's Worker Empowerment Clinic survey buttressed interviewees' sentiments: the most common issue among the 50 Korean and 77 Latino workers surveyed in 2005 was wage and hour disputes; of the 127 cases, 88 percent corresponded to work hour disputes.[14]

## THE UNREST AND LABOR RELATIONS

Latino interviewees elaborated on their personal experiences with the unrest, which had much to do with their employment at Korean establishments. Some lost jobs or were left homeless by arson, while others joined Korean employers in defending their stores; this latter action may have not been a deliberate choice and should not necessarily be interpreted as a measure of loyalty, as they were at the store when the looting began. Take, for instance, the case of Antonio, who did glasswork in building construction. For him, the aftermath was quite traumatic and stressful because he lost his job; at the time, he was working for a Korean business that was burned down. During the riots, he stayed inside the house and spent several weeks desperate for another job.

Some Latinos were openly sympathetic with Korean immigrants and critical of the way the media portrayed them. As one respondent explained, the media "portrayed Koreans as trigger happy, gun-toting, and violent, but in reality, all they were doing was defending their property. I would have done the same thing if I were in their shoes." The image of Korean store owners protecting their property with guns in the face of the LAPD's complete abdication of responsibility was a powerful image for various Latino interviewees. Julio shared his changed perception of Korean immigrants after the unrest:

> We did not think or know that Koreans were so united. Koreans really defended their businesses well during the crisis. . . . . I thought Koreans just came here to live and better themselves, and are rather passive people. Their sense of unity and toughness during the crisis changed my perceptions of Koreans.

Many Latino informants, similar to Hunt's study (1997), argued that the Latinos who looted took advantage of the situation, bringing shame to the larger Latino community and expressing their anger in inappropriate and destructive ways (75). However, some of my respondents were disturbed with the negative perceptions held by Koreans and other ethnicities of Latinos as looters. Demonstrating tension between Latino groups, Mexican interviewees tended to blame the events on Blacks and Salvadorans. In particular, Mexican male interviewees strongly disapproved of Latino looting and felt it was morally wrong. Jose, a 41-year-old originally from Guadalajara who was unemployed at the time of interview, described the situation as disheartening. He felt that the people participating in the looting had no excuse:

> There are other ways of protesting, and that is not one of them. . . . I lived it, and the only word I can use to describe it is panic. I felt awful for my race because of what I saw in person and what I saw on television.

Gloria Alvarez, managing editor of Eastern Group Publications, the largest chain of Hispanic-owned bilingual newspapers in the US,[15] gave a similar response (2012):

> I'm ashamed of my people for participating in such a horrible event. In the end, my Raza victimized our own people all for what? For Rodney King? We did not care about him or any African Americans before this, yet we participated in rioting and looting for selfish gain! Shame on those cops that beat King . . . shame on the system . . . shame on my Raza who participated! (Alvarez, 2012)

Finally, some interviewees, like Antonio, were glad to see Korean employers treat their Latino employees better in the aftermath:

> Before the riot, the communication was not good. Koreans do not believe you. They do not believe, for instance, I am capable of doing certain things. Koreans think Latinos do not have brains, that everybody is stupid. However, this is not true, there are many Latinos who are smart, who go to college, etc.—not all Latinos are stupid. After the riot, since Koreans do not want that [to] happen to them again, there seem[s] to be more effort, better effort to communicate with Latinos, a more willingness to listen, and less willingness to dismiss us or ignore us.

In sum, being employed at Korean business establishments affected the way Latino interviewees experienced the unrest, producing more sympathetic views of Korean immigrant merchants and an appreciation for the better treatment of Latino workers by Korean employers in the aftermath.

## LATINO-KOREAN LABOR
## COLLABORATIONS AFTER THE UNREST

According to Chang and Diaz-Veizades (1999), "coalition building has emerged as the most viable option for Los Angeles's rebuilding process" after the 1992 unrest (105). Implications of a link between the unrest and labor relations can be found in the post-1992 cross-racial class formations, especially in the area of immigrant and labor organizing (I return to this topic in the next chapter). For instance, in 1994, a coalition of Korean American organizations came to the aid of 575 hotel union workers—predominantly Latinos—who were in danger of losing their jobs if the Downtown Los Angeles Hilton changed management firms to Hanjin, a subsidiary of one of South Korea's biggest conglomerates and the parent company of Korean Air. KIWA was instrumental in enlisting the support of other Korean American organizations, leading demonstrations in front of the Korean Air terminal at

Los Angeles International Airport (*LAT* November 18, 1994) and the South Korean Consulate, and picketing at Hanjin's shipping business. In this case, KIWA succeeded in forging what Edward Park (2004) has called "labor organizing beyond race and nation" by enlisting politicians, mainstream and ethnic media, and community organizations, and forming transnational labor solidarity between Local 11 and Hanjin unions in South Korea. It is important to note, as Park does, that "this campaign brought Latinos and Korean Americans together in universal terms of job security and corporate responsibility" (2004, 146).

There have been ongoing formalized efforts by KIWA to address common labor issues through the organization's advocacy of Latino and Korean/ Asian hotel, garment, restaurant, and supermarket workers. KIWA's series of cross-racial coalition endeavors has continued to spark scholarly attention. As Angie Chung (2007) noted, KIWA has promoted "class solidarity across racial and ethnic boundaries as a matter of social justice" (235). For example, KIWA has formed coalitions with various local and national Latino organizations, such as the Coalition for Humane Immigrant Rights LA (CHIRLA), CARECEN, the Mexican American Legal Defense and Educational Fund (MALDEF), and international labor organizations like Enlace (Chung 2007). Latino organizations in Koreatown and the neighboring Pico Union area lacking specialized services often refer Latino workers to KIWA. Although KIWA's primary mission has not centered on improving race relations, its efforts have nevertheless done so in significant ways. As these coalitions suggest, racial equality may be hard to achieve without addressing the class component that shapes and perpetuates many racial antagonisms.

Cross-racial labor organizing has provided Latinos with a broader range of experiences with Koreans, through relationships with Korean labor and community organizers who are committed to fighting against Korean employers on behalf of Latino workers. Interviewees' responses indicate that they have come to realize that bosses are bosses, and that these relationships have less to do with being Korean than with structural positioning. Moreover, efforts like those of KIWA have shown Latinos that Koreans are not a monolithic group. As one interviewee put it, "I couldn't believe how dead serious KIWA staff were committed to the Latino worker cause until they were arrested for protesting in front of the Korean Air at Los Angeles International Airport." KIWA's labor advocacy attracted attention from the local Spanish-language newspaper *La Opinión*, which reported that KIWA helped eight Latino restaurant employees receive $380,000 in compensation for nonpaid work hours (February 16, 1999; March 21, 2001). In addition, the paper covered KIWA's efforts to help 200 Latino garment and domestic workers demand protection against exploitation at the office of Governor Gray Davis (*La Opinión* June

30, 2001), and to aid 40 Latino workers petitioning for union recognition by the Korean immigrant supermarket chain Assi (*La Opinión* November 16, 2001).

## LATINO-KOREAN RELATIONS

Based on the ethnographic data presented in this chapter, Latino-Korean relations in post-unrest LA might be described as being separated by two degrees of exclusion in terms of class and culture, and two degrees of inclusion (or convergence) in terms of race and citizenship (see figure 8.2 below). This four-factor model of degrees of exclusion and inclusion can be used to analyze minority-minority relations and how different racial groups are positioned in relation to the US racial state, capitalist system, and national identity. That is, these axes of inequality contribute to create sociopolitical

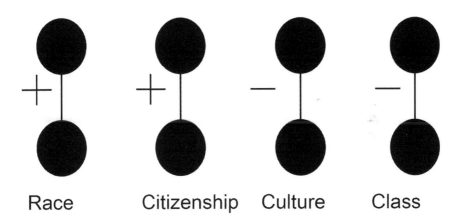

# Korean-Latino Relations

Race          Citizenship    Culture       Class

Two Degree of Separation and

Two Degree of Convergence:

Ethnic Distancing

Figure 8.2.    Korean-Latino Relations

distance, which affects interethnic dynamics. To some extent, there seems to be balance in Korean-Latino relations, but that balance may be transformed for better or for worse in the future. It is necessary to specify the different roles played by different factors in each relationship.

To assess the role of race in Latino-Korean relations, we should understand that both Latinos and Koreans are racialized in different ways from African Americans and from each other. Latinos come from pluralistic, multiethnic societies; however, "they were racialized in a particular way under the Spanish colonial context" (Almaguer 2012, 145). Latino interviewees did not generally turn to genetically based racial explanations of the relationship, but instead relied on ethnic/national differences in discussing Koreans. In contrast, Koreans come from a more or less racially homogeneous society marked by some form of ethnocentric bias. Moreover, some Korean immigrants assess other minority groups based on their perceived level of capitalism or development and how modernized their homelands are. In brief, Koreans often assume Latinos come from underdeveloped, poor countries.

As discussed in chapter 1, the racial status of the Mexican population in particular has been inconsistent, but at particular moments in US history they were classified as "White." From this, we may infer that Mexicans and other Latinos might rank the racial status of Korean/Asian immigrants lower than their own. For example, many Latinos use the term *chino* to refer to Asians, regardless of whether they are Japanese, Chinese, or Thai, and ethnic jokes abound (Navarro 1993, 80).[16] However, contradicting these stereotypes and assumptions about who ranks higher in the US racial hierarchy, one of the contemporary forms of racism in the US has been nativist racism. Although the term "illegal alien" does not signify a particular nationality, it is widely understood to refer to undocumented Latinos and relies on stereotypes about their criminality. Moreover, despite their racial diversity, Latinos are often assumed to have a particular physiognomy: olive/brown skin and dark, straight hair. The US government, mass media, police, and other major institutions refer to "Hispanics" or "Latinos" as distinct from both non-Hispanic Whites and African Americans, hinting at the racialization of Latin American immigrants and their children (Cobas, Duany, and Feagin 2009, 8), and ignoring the racial differences among Latinos. With regards to Latino-Korean relations in the workplace, these notions of race and stereotypes have not necessarily created distance between these two groups, although it is possible in the future that the differential racialization of Latinos and Koreans will create visible sociopolitical barriers between them.

The perceptions of Latinos as undocumented immigrants and cooperative workers add another dimension to the Latino-Korean relationship. Many Salvadoran immigrants and refugees hold temporary or undocumented status. Immigration status is significant with regards to the issue of unpaid wages, and the inability to communicate in English makes many workers susceptible to exploitative employment conditions. Like White employers, Korean employers identified undocumented workers as their favorite workers, because the economic, social, cultural and political vulnerabilities they face leave them no choice but to work hard, often without complaint. Interestingly, Nadia Kim's Korean American interviewees considered Latinos to be more visible than Korean and Asian Americans, in light of their greater population size and stronger political and cultural influence (N. Kim 2008, 163).[17] As mentioned earlier, Koreans (and all employers) exploited Latinos' undocumented status to pay them less. So this differential access to citizenship constitutes driving a wedge or straining the relationship. It may not have been something Latinos stated to their employers, but it clearly affected the relationship.

## POST-UNREST LATINO RACIAL FORMATION

Spanish-speaking Angelenos called the 1992 civil unrest *los quemazones*: the grand burning. Initially, the Latino community was relieved to see that East LA, the historic heart of Latino LA, remained relatively calm despite the region's economic difficulties, which were similar to those in South LA. East LA also had a history of relations with law enforcement officials because of numerous allegations of police brutality against Latinos. The early Latino reactions to the unrest turned out to be incorrect: "Despite the fact that thousands of Mexican immigrants participated, they blamed it on Salvadorans who are 'refugees' and not 'real immigrants' like Mexicans" (Davis 1993, 146). Latinos living in South LA, Pico Union, Koreatown, and other areas—many of whom were poor Salvadoran immigrants who engaged in extensive looting—both participated in and were deeply affected by the unrest. Undocumented immigrants accounted for more than 1,200 of the 15,000 people arrested (*LAT* May 11, 1992).[18]

The outburst of violence in areas with rapidly growing Latino populations caught community leaders and some elected officials by surprise. However, the Latino elected officials most likely realized that there was no common agenda between Eastside Latinos—who were predominantly Mexican in origin and less recently immigrated or born in the US—and their counterparts in South LA and Pico Union, who were more recent Central American immigrants. For one, like many other residents of this region, some working-class Latino citizens worried about increased competition in the labor market from recent immigrants who were willing to settle for lower wages.

Notwithstanding these differences, however, for the first time, immigrants from Central America were lumped together with Mexican Americans and Mexican immigrants, subject to pan-ethnic racialization from the top, courtesy of the media, politicians, and other state agents. To make matters worse, these new Latinos were viewed as a negative influence. In LA, a number of right-wing Republicans campaigning for office singled out Latino immigrants (Davis 1993, 145), exploiting the media's negative portrayal of them. They proposed to stop immigration to the US—in particular from Third World countries—while reiterating that nearly one-third of the first 6,000 suspects arrested were "illegal aliens" (*National Review* June 22, 1992, 46).

After the unrest, repairing the gaps between Mexican Americans and Central American immigrants and establishing an agenda for all Latinos in the LA area became a major focus for many elected officials and nascent community organizations. While Latinos did not appreciate the negative images of them as looters circulating in the media, they also pointed out positive outcomes, such as more emphasis on political organizing and efforts at forming a pan-Latino community. City Councilman Mike Hernandez, elected by the district that includes Pico Union, was the first Latino elected official to set up an assistance network; he also participated in the street cleanups and authored a proclamation in City Hall calling for an end to the INS raids (*LAT* December 11, 1993).

On May 4, 1992, LA County Supervisor Gloria Molina convened a group of about 25 Latino community leaders to form the Latino Unity Coalition. Similarly, Geraldine Zapata of Plaza Community Center, Professor Jorge Mancillas at the UCLA School of Medicine, and other Latinos organized a June 1992 conference to address social, economic, and political issues affecting Latinos and formed the Latino Unity Forum. While the Latino Unity Coalition and Latino Unity Forum did not last long, another effort emerged on September 14, 1992: the Latino Coalition for a New Los Angeles, numbering over 30 different organizations and representing a cross section of Latino political, social, and business leaders.[19]

The Central American community responded to the unrest with its own organizing efforts. El Rescate, originally established as a refugee center, organized a Pico Union Community Forum to solicit the neighborhood's views on the rebuilding process. Central American merchants joined a new association, the Unión de Comerciantes Latinos, to ensure that emergency and long-term relief efforts also met their needs. Before the unrest, these merchants' main concern had been to end the war in El Salvador and to stop illegal deportation. Central American communities also joined the larger Latino community in their efforts to be heard and participate in rebuilding efforts. In July 1992,

Latino office holders sent Mayor Tom Bradley a letter complaining that Latinos were being excluded from rebuilding efforts, while asserting that African American organizations had received disproportionate attention and post-riot aid due to their stronger ties to City Hall and the media's portrayal of the eruption as a Black vs. White or Black vs. Korean conflict. They also emphasized that the founding members and initial beneficiaries of corporate largesse via Rebuild LA (RLA) were Black organizations.[20] Many Latino-owned businesses, including taco carts, were affected along with Korean ones during the unrest. Overall, the denial rate for the federal grant and loan programs that was intended to serve victims of the unrest was 50 percent or higher. However, the rejection rate for Latino immigrants ranged between 75 and 90 percent, suggesting that a whole sector of the population was under-served by this relief effort (Pastor 1993, 28). Finally, Latino leaders called on business and industry leaders to create more job opportunities for Latinos (*LAT* July 22, 1992). Thus, for a brief period, the distinctions between Mexican vs. Central American, Mexican vs. Salvadoran, Salvadoran vs. Guatemalan, and Mexican vs. Oaxacan or Zapotec were set aside.

## CONCLUSION

As discussed in this chapter, Latino-Korean relations during and after the unrest were marked more by class, culture, and citizenship than race. The class dynamics between the Korean immigrant petite bourgeoisie small business owners and Latino workers were central to this relationship. Most complaints about Korean immigrants by Latino interviewees, at least the ones employed by Koreans, revolved around the issue of labor relations. Fortunately, there are more established channels (e.g., labor unions and community organizations such as KIWA) to address class-related problems, unlike the tensions between Korean merchants and African American customers. Tangentially, Korean remigrants from Latin America have also played a strategic role in Latino-Korean relations with their Spanish language and cultural competence, as well as their empathy towards Latino immigrants.[21] As Latinos came to experience Koreans not just as their employers, but also their advocates, they came to delink ethnic association from Korean employers.

Many Latinos were receptive toward other cultures, including Korean culture, and there appeared to be a genuine effort to avoid a racial argument and to adopt a cultural one instead. Perhaps this is because both groups come from less developed or newly developed countries, where reciprocity is more prevalent as a mode of interaction than in advanced capitalist societies such as the US.[22] Furthermore, some Korean immigrant employers developed a bond with their Latino employees, especially when the latter were longtime employees. In these multifaceted interactions, Korean and Latino immigrants not only shared cultural space by working together, but they also developed close relationships through socializing with and aiding one another. In this way, the concept of culture, which originally played a negative role in Latino-Korean relations, was transformed into a positive factor, although these cultural differences varied according to the ethnic and national origins of Latinos.[23]

As I posited above, I would argue that the relationship between Korean employers and Latino workers is reminiscent of the interdependent, symbiotic patron-client relations in Mexico and Latin America (Foster 1963; 1282–83).[24] While this type of relationship can be beneficial for both parties, it is important not to forget the inherent class and economic inequality entailed in patron-client relations. There is still a class hierarchy here, even though there are some positive feelings and collaborations. Overall, the Korean-Latino relations examined in this chapter are matters of "respectful caution." Many Latino interviewees encouraged Koreans to get to know and mingle with them. In general, there seemed to be less "othering" and "racializing" in Latino-Korean relations than in Black-Korean relations. Latino immigrants were able to develop a meaningful, courteous relationship with Korean immigrants via cross-racial labor and immigrant rights organizing.

To conclude, race, class, citizenship, and cultural differences disadvantage both Korean and Latino immigrants relative to the mainstream White population. Differences between the two groups as a result of their class status and culture often result in stereotypes propagated by each group about the other. It is these discourses that have played a central role in establishing differential categories of belonging, worthiness, and respectability. The next chapter will examine the overall impact of Latino immigration on post-unrest South LA. Over the past two decades, the most enduring change in South LA has been its transformation from a historically Black neighborhood to a predominantly Latino immigrant community. This transformation is referred to by some as the "Latin Americanization of South LA" (Sides 2012). By 2010, Latinos represented 66.3 percent of the population of South LA, and the "Black district" of South LA was only 31.8 percent Black. Therefore, the next chapter will examine the impact of this post-unrest Latin Americanization on race relations.

## NOTES

1. This chapter was originally published, in slightly different form, in *Amerasia Journal*, "Los Angeles Since 1992: Commemorating the 20th Anniversary of the Uprising," Issue 38, No. 1 (2012):143–169. Reprinted with permission.

2. By now, new residents are there that were not there during the unrest.

3. Dae Young Kim's study (1999) of Mexican and Ecuadorian employment in Korean-owned businesses in New York demonstrated that the initial shift toward hiring Mexicans and Latinos was an attempt to adapt to a diminishing supply of labor in the late 1980s.

4. It should be emphasized that US military interventions were quite different in nature: unlike in Korea, in Central America it involved funding and training, but not the official deployment of US troops. For example, $424 million in direct US military assistance from 1981 to 1984 led to a rapid escalation of the war in El Salvador and a major disruption of the economy and livelihood of many Salvadorans (Hamilton and Chinchilla 2001, 32).

5. As indicated in the introductory chapter, I used research assistants.

6. Koreans idealized a patrilineal and patrilateral kinship structure, while Mexicans upheld a bilateral kinship structure.

7. There are obvious religious differences, as most Latinos tend to be Catholic and most Koreans are Protestants. I have not heard about Latinos and Koreans forming a *compadre* (co-father or co-parent) relationship between the parents and godparents of a child when a child is baptized in Latino families, nor have I have heard of Koreans' ritual sponsorship of other Catholic sacraments (first communion, confirmation, and marriage) or a *quinceañera* celebration, for instance.

8. The preferred Korean path for social mobility is not via entrepreneurship, but education.

9. CARECEN was founded by a group of Salvadoran refugees whose mission was to secure legal status for the thousands of Central Americans fleeing civil war in the 1980s and 90s. As the largest Central American organization in the country, CARECEN has four major program areas: legal services, education, civic participation, and economic development. "CARECEN, The Central American Resource Center." http://www.carecen-la.org. Accessed: November 12, 2011.

10. It should be noted that this interviewee provided a contradictory argument: he felt Koreans tried to penetrate Latino culture but also that they didn't interact with other ethnic groups.

11. *El Rescate*, founded in 1981, was the first agency in the United States to respond with free legal and social services to the mass influx of refugees fleeing the war in El Salvador. "El Rescate," http://www.elrescate.org. Accessed: November 11, 2011.

12. Interviewees listed the following qualities: respect, family unity or closeness, family values, and to a lesser extent, culture or customs, language, religion, music, food, or fiestas. These traits are said to distinguish Mexican Americans from other races.

13. This was California's minimum wage in 1996. As of January 2018, it was $11.00.

14. Forty-five percent of workers were paid in cash, while cash and check, regular checks, and payroll checks corresponded to another 45 percent. Forty percent of workers were paid on an hourly basis, while another 55 percent were paid on a salary. Only 31 percent received itemized deduction slips from their employers. In addition,

62 percent of employers failed to keep time records, and 78 percent of workers had no benefits of any kind (Koreatown Immigrant Workers Alliance 2007, 5).

15. A Lincoln Heights-based chain of six bilingual newspapers, including the *Eastside Sun, Northeast Sun, Mexican American Sun, Bell Gardens Sun, Commerce Comet, Montebello Comet,* and *Vernon Sun.*

16. I was mistaken for a Filipina more than a couple of times by Latinos, perhaps because Filipinos are one of the largest Asian American groups in LA.

17. Nonetheless, I don't think anyone would argue Latinos' political influence is proportionate to their numbers.

18. On one occasion when 477 undocumented immigrants were picked up and handed over to the INS, 360 were from Mexico, 62 from El Salvador, 35 from Guatemala, 14 from Honduras, 2 from Jamaica, and the rest from other countries (*LAT* May 11, 1992).

19. A diverse group of organizations, including CARECEN, the Mexican American Political Association (MAPA), and La Unión de Comerciantes Latinos y Afiliados formed the Latino Coalition in the summer of 1992 (*LAT* May 29, 1993).

20. The Rebuilding LA program was top-down in its structure and program. Its ninety-four board members included a wide spectrum of business, government, civic, religious, and celebrity names, but it had no organic connection to the riot-torn neighborhoods (Dreier 2003, 40).

21. Mr. Kwang Choi, a case manager at KIWA since 1995, may be the best example. He is deeply grateful to the government of El Salvador for providing him with a full scholarship to attend university. His wife is also Salvadoran. He commands respect among Salvadoran workers. As for Koreans who lived in Latin America, see my other works (1999b).

22. Reciprocity is a principle often found in nonmarket economies; however, here it refers to a set of exchange relationships among individuals and groups.

23. Koreans tended to trust Mexicans more than Salvadorans, invoking Salvadoran criminality due to the notoriety of their gangs.

24. George Foster, in his seminal study of the Mexican peasant community of *Tzintzuntzan*, reported a patron-client relationship with an asymmetrical power differential, mobilized for the purposes of promoting villagers' security in a variety of life crises.

*Chapter Nine*

# The Racial Cartography
# of Post-Unrest LA

"Clearly the Black/White binary is central to racial and political thought and practice in the United States. . . . However, if we look at only this binary, we may misread the dynamics of white supremacy in different contexts" (Smith 2006, 71). The US is moving towards a society divided four-fold by color: Whites, African Americans, Latinos, and Asian Americans.[1] In order to address the increasing complexity of racial politics and racial identity today, we should recognize "antagonisms and alliances among racially defined minority groups" (Omi and Winant 1994, 154). An ethnographic examination of South LA communities between 1992 and 2002 demonstrated a complex negotiation of multipolar relationships, particularly between Koreans, Blacks, and Latinos. Given the data I collected, I want to view these relationships as an unfolding racial cartography, inflected on multiple axes by categories such as class, citizenship, and culture.

The 1992 unrest was widely characterized as a Black-Korean conflict, where African Americans demanded economic and social justice and protested punitive policing and the unfair distribution of development projects by damaging Korean-owned businesses and treating Koreans as a proxy for White power. However, the unrest and its aftermath were more complicated, involving not only Blacks, Koreans, and Whites,[2] but also Latinos, who accounted for over 50 percent of those arrested. Because they lived and worked in close proximity, Blacks, Koreans, and Latinos had to negotiate their own racial identities relative to each other. However, despite recognition of racial difference, overlaps and collaborations were present as well. While the 1992 unrest unearthed latent tensions between many Korean business owners and African Americans and Latinos, many Koreans have hired Blacks and Latinos as employees, leading to the development of certain alliances and affinities.

251

The LA unrest unveiled racial fault lines among oft-neglected racial/ethnic minorities—Koreans, Central Americans, and Mexicans—who were portrayed as both victims and victimizers. Before the unrest, antagonisms had risen to volatile levels, not only between Whites and Blacks over the issue of police brutality (as exemplified by the Rodney King beating), and between African Americans and Koreans (as displayed in the Du-Harlins case), but also between Latinos and African Americans over various issues, including the affirmative action program; reapportionment plans of the city, the county, and Board of Education; the hiring practices at institutions like Martin Luther King, Jr., Hospital; and competition for the position of Los Angeles police chief (Navarro 1993, 78).

As the American Anthropological Association's statement on race (1998, 3) concluded, contemporary inequalities between racial groups are not consequences of biological inheritance, but rather products of historical and contemporary social, economic, educational, and political circumstances. Economic position, political considerations, different positions within the US racial hierarchy, and legal status all shape how people understand others and themselves. Accordingly, this concluding chapter elucidates a regional racial cartography that focuses on social and political dynamics to answer the following question: how do people in South LA view others and themselves with regards to their racial status and rights/entitlements, racial distance (i.e., how close each racial/ethnic group feels to other groups), and racial tensions? I draw here on ethnographic data collected in the years following the unrest.

## REGIONAL RACIAL CARTOGRAPHY

In Los Angeles, racial distance is relative and relational, so the position of each locus can be mapped, as in figure 9.1. Like the national racial cartography (see figure 0.1), LA's racial cartography indicates lower positions for African Americans as compared with Koreans and Latinos (mostly Mexicans and Salvadorans).[3] Asian Americans hold the next highest position after Whites. During the last four decades, there has been increasing income inequality in LA despite economic growth in the 1970s and 1980s. As discussed in chapter 1, this economic inequality has been further translated into racial and ethnic inequality, along with the blight of inner-city poverty.

The Mexican-American War (1846–1848) ended with a peace treaty transferring New Mexico and California to the US and extending the Texas border southward; this resulted in the US incorporating nearly 80,000 Spanish speakers, mostly of mixed Spanish and Indian descent. Some Latinos invoke the fact that mestizos (people of mixed Spanish and Indian blood)

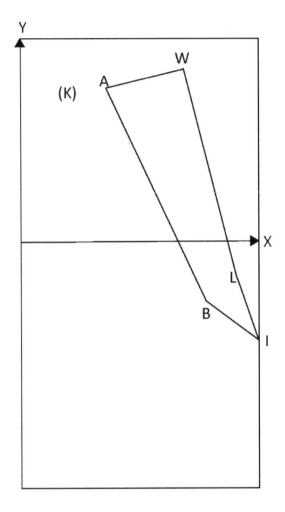

X: Centuries present within U.S. since 1776

Y: Household income above taxable minimum

    W: White

    A: Asian American (1840-50s)

    L: Latino

    B: Black

    I: American Indian (pre-1700s)

**Figure 9.1.   Racial Cartography in Los Angeles**

and Indians founded Los Angeles, along with a handful of descendants of Africans (Mason 2004). This origin story, advanced by leaders of the Chicano movement of the 1960s and 70s, highlights the presence of a multiracial group of settlers. It also presents a legal and primordial right to what they call "Aztlán," or the lands of Northern Mexico that were annexed by the US as a result of the Mexican-American War. As geographer Wendy Cheng (2013) writes, Latinos, and in particular Mexican Americans, are constructed as both more and less American than Asians are. Historically, Mexicans have been simultaneously erased from the southern California landscape (along with indigenous people) and fetishized via a Spanish colonial past. However, "in municipal politics, white elites were able to dictate the terms of belonging, often validating Spanish space as central to the identity of the area (though firmly relegated to the past), while continuing to treat Asian space as perpetually foreign" (Cheng, 2013, 132).

Sociologists Albert Bergesen and Max Herman (1998) hypothesized that there was a defensive, violent backlash by African Americans in South LA to the increasing in-migration by non-Black minorities during the unrest. They found that "controlling for economic conditions and racial/ethnic composition, there is a significant association between ethnic succession in neighborhoods (Latino and Asian in-migration and Black out-migration) and riot violence" (1998, 39).[4] Accordingly, while contesting the typical analyses of the unrest as merely a White-Black or Black-Korean conflict, my Latino interviewees said something similar to Gloria Alvarez's assertion (2012): "Latinos did not riot out of the verdict of Rodney King, rather their participation was based primarily as opportunistic and a bridge of cultural division between Hispanics and Blacks living in the area."

As discussed in previous chapters, some African Americans resent that Latinos have displaced them as workers in key sectors. In addition, not only are they losing political influence and control of major civil rights institutions to Latinos, but they now see themselves being displaced in the pecking order also by the Asian community, specifically Koreans. Thus, the unrest was seen by many African American interviewees as an act of resistance to the shifting racial cartography, whereas before the unrest, it was concerned with the indexing of racial status and entitlement in the field of racial positions. Notwithstanding these feelings of hostility among Black participants, some Latino interviewees felt that even though they now heavily populate the area that was once predominantly Black, interracial relations have improved over time.

Such resistance to the shifting racial cartography continued. By 1998, African Americans made up about 10 percent of the population in LA County, but held about a quarter of the jobs in city government and a third of those in county government. African Americans had held three seats on the fifteen-member City Council since the 1960s (*Newsweek* November 21, 1994, 57). Moreover, three of the region's representatives in Congress were Black. This may have been the high point of Black political power in LA. The newly arrived Latino immigrants complained about the lack of access to municipal jobs and leadership positions in local government, about staffing positions in the school system and the content of the curriculum, and about police brutality in Compton, where the chief and nearly all of the officers were Black (*Newsweek* November 21, 1994, 57).

The Black-White binary racial framework is unable to account for significant class-based realignments of the post-Civil Rights era, like the data portrayed in the Y dimension of the model, demonstrating what Susan Koshy has called "stratified minoritization" (2001, 155). In the post-Civil Rights era, Asian American-ness acquired a very different inflection. Hailed as the model minority, Asian American success had been attributed to Asians' unique cultural characteristics as well as "the increased economic strength of Asia [including South Korea] and the greater interconnectedness with and dependency of the U.S. on Asia" (Koshy 2001, 190). As Helen Jun (2011) argues, during the unrest, Black Orientalism or Black stereotypes about Asians interpreted "Asian labor, markets, and capital" both as evidence of the fulfillment of the American Dream and of the danger of the yellow peril (100).

## RACIAL DISTANCING

Social scientists have examined the shifting relationships between Whites, Blacks, Latinos, and Asian Americans in various ways, often with mixed results. I use the term racial distancing to refer to the closeness or social distance each racial/ethnic group feels with other groups. Larry Bobo and Vincent Hutchings (1996) found that both Blacks and Latinos feel more threatened by Asians than by each other, particularly in terms of economic power.[5] However, Blacks felt that Latinos were the group with whom they had the most conflict, listing street crime (especially gang violence), jobs, income, and access to higher education as sources of racial antagonism (Henry and Sears 2002). Researchers have also found that Latinos' feelings about African Americans are frequently characterized by competition for local resources such as jobs, housing, educational opportunities, and political representation (Johnson and Oliver 1989; McClain and Karnig 1990; Waldinger 1996). Several Latino respondents in this study sensed Blacks' feelings of hostility toward them, their sense of territoriality, and their view of Latinos as cultural outsiders and unwelcome interlopers in a competition for such limited resources. The animosity that both Korean and Latino respondents felt from the Black community contributed to their own hostility toward African Americans.

Other studies have shown that African Americans' views of Latinos are more favorable than those of Whites, and also more favorable of Latinos than Latinos' views of African Americans (Ribas 2016, 193). McClain et al. (2006) found not only that Latinos view Blacks less favorably than Blacks view Latinos, but also that they hold more negative views of Blacks than even Whites do. Similarly, Hernandez (2007) reported that Latinos preferred to maintain a social distance from African Americans and listed them as their least desirable marriage partners. Finally, Johnson, Farrell, and Guinn (1997) found that a large percentage of Latinos and a majority of Asian Americans viewed Black people as less intelligent and more welfare-dependent than their own groups.

There has been some critique of these studies as presenting analyses of immigrant incorporation processes in a simplistic good-versus-bad framework, particularly in terms of the quality of intergroup relations (Ribas 2016, 186). I agree with this assessment, which is why I attempted to understand the conditions that motivated the prod, rather than defining the relations between Korean immigrant merchants and their inner-city customers as either good or bad. Equally important is the fact that the above studies tend to ignore the overdetermining, if opaque, role of whiteness in the system of racialized stratification. For this reason, sociologist Vanesa Ribas (2016) frames intergroup relations among subordinated groups as "prismatic engagement," wherein emergent senses of group position are shaped through the "distorting optic of the prism" of white dominance (199). One example of the continuing dominance of Whiteness is the finding that Latinos feel greater discrimination from African Americans than from Whites (Ribas 2016, 196), and that some minorities feel closer to Whites than to other minorities: "the power wielded by whites over others in American society is in some sense legitimate: at worst an established fact one should accept with resignation, at best a prerogative to which one can aspire" (Ribas 2016, 185). Latinos likely understand that an approximation to Whiteness gives them greater social status and, internalizing anti-Black stereotypes, see Blackness as associated with oppression, discrimination, and marginality, and they wish to align themselves against these constructs.

Reframing the study of intergroup relations as prismatic engagement also recognizes that the social system into which a group enters is characterized by positions of unequal status. In other words, the process of belonging entails struggles over the positions that groups occupy within the American stratified system. Workplaces, the marketplace, and neighborhoods are key interactional arenas for the mutual construction of group identity through boundary processes, which are again informed by class, citizenship, history, and politics. This book sheds light on these dynamics, viewing the incorporation of both Korean and Latino immigrants as a process of adjustment by which groups both achieve and are assigned social positions in a stratified system of belonging.

As an alternative to more static cultural and biological theories of ethnic and racial difference, Barth's concept of "ethnic boundaries" has been frequently applied to study ethnic and racial inequality (Lamont and Molnar 2002, 174). The thrust of it is that racial minorities, as well as Whites, tend to draw symbolic boundaries, indicating how they understand and act on racial categories, to differentiate themselves from other groups, expressing varying views—from hostility to ambivalence to sympathy—as they are racialized by class and citizenship status. In my study, it is not just Blacks who are drawing symbolic boundaries against Korean and Latino immigrants. Korean immigrant merchants also draw symbolic boundaries against Black and Latino customers and residents, feeling "racially alienated" from them and from Whites (Bobo and Hutchings 1996). For Latino immigrants, despite their class proximity to African Americans, the imperatives of the American racial hierarchy means drawing strong symbolic boundaries between themselves and Blacks.

Racial minorities are placed in differential and unequal power relations to each other. African Americans and Latinos generally feel closer to Whites than to each other (Dyer et al. 1989, as cited in Barreto 2014, 207). Thus, Blacks felt the most affinity with American Indians (I), followed by Whites (W), then Latinos (L), and they had the least affinity with Asian Americans (A)—as you can see in my model. Black interviewees generally viewed Korean immigrants as more distant from them than Latinos. The reasons for this distance relate to racial, cultural, and class barriers, or what I call "four degrees of exclusion or segregation" in terms of race, class, culture, and citizenship (see previous chapter) that exist among Korean merchants and their Black customers (see chapters 2–5).

Black interviewees also believed that Korean immigrants were determined to rip them off, an accusation that echoes Black sentiment toward Arab American merchants in Detroit. Blacks devalued the Korean family enterprise "not as an economic accomplishment in the face of strong odds, but rather as an unearned opportunity at their expense" (Johnson, Farrell, and Guinn 1997, 1079). To make matters worse, "those poverty-stricken former peasants won't treat Blacks with respect, and some of the Korean immigrant merchants are *fake white*," one interviewee stated. For African Americans, Korean immigrant merchants appeared to be different culturally and physically, but they also reinforced stereotypes associated with nativist White sentiment. As indicated in this model of regional racial cartography, African Americans viewed

Korean Americans as more distant from them than Whites. I should point out the irony in this, given that African Americans were physically closer to Koreans in terms of living, working, and buying. Thus, they felt more distant from Koreans, even though they shared more daily encounters with them. Ussery, a Black business owner, noted how minority people rank each other:

> Whites rate all minorities below themselves, in all categories. But we should also ask the question, how do minorities look at themselves? Minorities rate Blacks and Hispanics about the same. Blacks rate themselves higher than Hispanics because they see Hispanics as immigrants who come in, grab the entry-level jobs, and work as cheap labor; an unfair misconception, no doubt. Asians rate themselves above Blacks and Hispanics, believing that they work harder, while Blacks are lazy and have no work ethic. Furthermore, Asians who come to America do not consider themselves a minority. And that's understandable because they come from a monocultural society, where there is no racial distinction. (1994, 93)

Ussery emphasized that ethnic stratification is more complicated than what can be read from socioeconomic indicators. He also reiterated the point that African Americans rate themselves higher than other minorities who are immigrants and read as non-Americans in terms of social status.[6]

Although non-Korean owned stores in South LA were affected by the unrest, Korean business owners were disproportionately targeted (R. Kim 2012, 17). They were targeted because Blacks felt exploited by them and because the stores were in their neighborhoods. A 37-year-old Chinese American grocery owner (1993) whose store was looted confirmed anti-Asian sentiments and distance from his Black customers, saying that "If he were a Korean, his store would be burnt." He continued,

> It is hard for immigrants, especially "Orientals," to do business because of culture and communication. New faces aren't treated well. We are lucky we have been here seven years, but if we were new store owner we get kicked out, especially Asians.
> Afro-Americans especially feel this way after the Soon Ja Du case. They feel that Orientals come here make money and not respect them. I hear this from the customers often.

## Latino-Black Racial Distancing

The phenomenon of ethnic succession in South LA has revealed underlying tensions particularly between Blacks and Latinos, as the former has long regarded the incursion of the latter as "threatening" (Morrison and Lowry 1994, 32). Indicating some evidence of this conflict, in 1994, Black voters backed

Proposition 187, which proposed instituting a screening system for citizenship as well as denied undocumented immigrants from using "non-emergency health care, public education," and other state services (Alvarez and Butterfield 2000). Some Black voters were also against the enforcement of equal opportunity laws for Latinos in LA (Barreto et al. 2014, 204). In 2001, African Americans uniformly voted against the Latino mayoral candidate in Los Angeles. However, with the election in 2005 of Antonio Villaraigosa, Black Angelenos joined his base of Latinos, labor unions, and liberal Whites, suggesting a return to coalitional politics in Los Angeles.

There are more recent statistics that evidence Black-Latino conflict in LA, such as the fact that although both groups make up the most frequent victims of hate crimes, the majority of Black victims were targeted by Latino suspects and vice versa (Los Angeles County Commission on Human Relations 2008, 10). A Latino man targeted African Americans in a spree of freeway shootings, and Florencia 13, a South LA Latino street gang, was charged with waging a murderous campaign—two hundred killings in three years—against rival African American gangs in their Florence-Firestone neighborhood, which is now 90 percent Latino (Quinones 2014). Finally, the Mexican mafia ordered attacks on Black inmates from inside prison. It is important to note that the more recent Black-Latino violence is related more to efforts by Latino gangs to control the drug market rather than to racial hatred of Blacks per se; in other words, economics are also in play (Quinones 2014).

Rebuilding efforts after the unrest brought Black-Latino conflicts to the fore. Of particular interest were the hostilities that erupted over the distribution of construction jobs and allocation of rebuilding resources. The situation was similar to that brought up by Mexican migrants in Chicago: "While plainly conscious of and commonly outspoken about the racialized discrimination and injustice that confront them, Mexican migrants in Chicago nonetheless have come to frequently articulate their perspectives in the hegemonic idiom of US racism against the African Americans who often appear to be their most palpable competitors for jobs and space" (de Genova 2005, 141). The tensions between African Americans and Latinos after the unrest were illustrated by the heated exchange between Danny Bakewell (see chapter 2), leader of the Brotherhood Crusade, and Xavier Hermosillo, leader of the group News for America. Bakewell demanded that job sites that had no Black workers be shut down, and he also marched with a group of Black contractors to a nearby site and attempted to stop demolition work. The incident resulted in Bakewell ordering a Latino worker off his bulldozer, allegedly in pidgin Spanish (*LAT* June 13, 1992).

Xavier Hermosillo responded heatedly by arguing that "[t]he Latino community will not tolerate, under any circumstances, the assault on the rights of

Latinos, Anglos, Asians or African Americans to work. Bakewell's actions smack of the same barbaric tactics employed by members of the Ku Klux Klan in removing Blacks from work sites" (*LAT* July 9, 1992). Hermosillo organized "sting teams" of undercover construction workers with video cameras that monitored work sites in order to record Bakewell's efforts to replace Latino workers with African Americans (Navarro 1993, 79). Unsurprisingly, although Bakewell and Hermosillo were controversial figures in the Black and Latino communities respectively, the mainstream media treated them as if they fully represented the opinions of each minority community.

Some community organizers acknowledged that Black-Brown conflict was a systematic problem caused by economic disinvestment by the public and private sectors in the inner cities, which contributed both to high unemployment rates of young African American males and the perception that Latinos were taking all the jobs (Villanueva 2017, 92). In addition, the LA Black Workers Center and Redeemer Community organized campaigns targeting the city government to enact a living wage policy and demanded environmental protections from fracking by private oil companies in the area, which would benefit both Black and Latino workers.

In a recently published book, Josh Kun and Laura Pulido (2014) urge us to move beyond the typical, teleological framing of "conflict" and "coalition": "Black LA and Brown LA coexist as much as they battle and see each other in the mirror as much as they refuse to look" (3). As they remind readers, in the late 1960s, both groups began seeing each other as potential partners and competitors, as was exemplified by the collaboration between the Black Panther Party and the Brown Berets. However, in the context of the post-Civil Rights Movement, Blacks and Latinos clashed over educational resources, political power, and access to employment. After the 1992 unrest, the relationship between the two groups, while initially fraught and discordant, has improved over time, as will be discussed below.

A good number of Black interviewees, like the following 64-year-old female arts coordinator for African American Community Organization (1996), blamed Latinos as well as Blacks for the unrest: "Latinos are just there. They did a lot of looting, but we got all credit for it. Like this kid I saw, he came out a store just holding up one shoe—what was he going to do with one shoe? But he had it." Similarly, a 32-year-old Black truck driver was asked in 1996 to comment on his perception of Koreans after the unrest. Instead, he mentioned Mexicans, unable to hide his dislike for *cholos*[7]:

> Koreans: Koreans are Korean, that's them. I have nothing against anyone; I'm not racist. No, that's not true. . . . I hate *cholos*, Mexican gangbangers with their hair greased back. I hate the way they talk, look, think, and everything about them. African Americans: No, they acted crazy and sick. There was no unity.

Whites: No, I have a love for Whites; two of my best friends are White. Latinos: Mexican Americans like these [nods and says hello to a woman and her son pushing a shopping cart and walking down the street], I have a love for these. But Mexican Americans with tattoos and all that stuff, I hate them.

In contrast to the relatively large racial distance between Blacks and Koreans and Blacks and Latinos, the greater closeness between Latino and Korean immigrants in the racial cartography model reflects a slightly more positive relationship, or what I call "two degrees of exclusion or segregation" in terms of class and culture and "two degrees of inclusion" in terms of race and citizenship (see previous chapter). Like Korean immigrants, Latinos have been subjected to less racism than African Americans. In addition, both groups often bring negative, biased perceptions of Black people from their home countries. Although large Black populations are found in certain areas of Latin America, like Cuba and Brazil, this is not the case for the major- ity of immigrants in South LA who are from Mexico and Central America. This partly explains the distance between the African American and Latino communities in the aftermath of the unrest. African Americans' grievances about immigrants from Mexico and Central America centered almost exclu- sively on economic issues, such as competition over community and school resources and jobs (Vargas 2006, 53). However, as Vargas (2006) points out, cheap immigrant labor is not generally the cause of Black unemployment, but rather another feature of exploitative capitalism that oppresses marginalized communities (2006, 52).

Returning to the ways racial distancing reflects patterns of residential seg- regation, Paul Ong et al. (2018, 6) note that as of 2016, segregation between Blacks and Whites in LA has decreased; however, it remains high. Latino residential segregation from Whites continues to also be relatively extreme, while Asians in LA are more moderately segregated from Whites.

## RACIAL CARTOGRAPHY OF
## TENSION AND UNREST IN SOUTH LA

As seen in figure 9.2, my South LA racial cartography indicates lower racial positions for Latinos than for African Americans and Koreans. Latinos are worse off than Blacks in South LA. Specifically, this concurs with what La- tinos said about their positions vis-à-vis African Americans. African Ameri- cans mistakenly believe they are worse off than Latinos.

Asian Americans are in a relatively high position, not including Whites, who are at the top of the hierarchy. Armando Navarro (1993) lamented the predicament of Latinos in South LA, which he felt were relegated to a quasi-

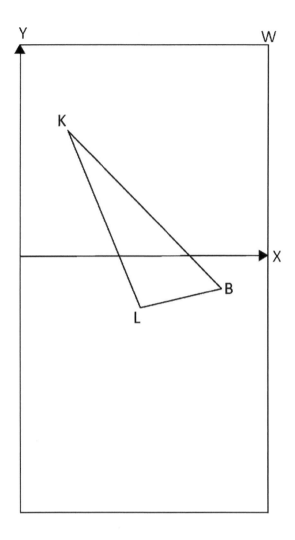

X: Centuries present within U.S. since 1776

Y: Household income above taxable minimum

    W: White

    A: Asian American (1840-50s)

    L: Latino

    B: Black

**Figure 9.2.**   **Racial Cartography in South LA.**

"South African syndrome" status, in that they constituted the majority of the population, yet they did not hold any economic or political power (81). As for interviewees' perceived economic position vis-à-vis Blacks, while Korean immigrant business owners clearly saw Black and Latino customers and residents as economically disadvantaged relative to themselves, Latinos perceived little or no difference between themselves and Blacks; in fact, they tended to perceive Blacks as slightly better off.

In their analyses of the causes of the unrest, both Black and Latino interviewees agreed on the importance of racism as a causal structure, alluding to police brutality and the racialized criminal justice system, as seen in the Rodney King verdict. Notwithstanding, the two groups disagreed on who were the victims of racism and who were the victimizers. Many Black interviewees spoke about the history of White racism and the central significance of Black-Korean tensions, particularly the controversial verdict in the Du-Harlins case, as one of the catalysts for the looting and aggression of the unrest. The majority of Black interviewees felt that while the Rodney King verdict was the most immediate cause for the unrest, the tensions had been latent for a long time. African Americans connected the Du verdict to that of Rodney King, feeling that neither she nor the White police officers were properly prosecuted, while Black men were facing high rates of incarceration. As discussed in chapter 2, Black interviewees felt that Judge Karlin's sentence sent the message that "Black life is worthless."

Individual experiences also varied, and each answer correlated with the greatest obstacle a given informant faced. A 27-year-old Black male program manager (1996) advocated for recycling Black dollars as a solution to inner-city problems, alluding to the popular Black capitalist ideology of self-help and a commitment to giving back:

> I call it the LA rebellion. Why? It was a result of racism and discrimination across the board, and unfortunately, Koreans were victims of victimization. We'll have to think about what caused the influx of Koreans. Whose place did they take? It was all about economics, discrimination, banks' redlining. . . . They learned that our dollars were just as green as everybody else's, so the dollars went out of the community. . . . Since they were here, we bought the goods. They don't share the same goals, familiarity, and commitments to the community.

Similar sentiments were presented by an African American man who participated in attacks upon Korean stores: "The riots were not riots at all, but a rebellion aimed at throwing off perceived economic and social oppression . . . we wanted to hurt [Koreans] physically, economically, raise their insurance rates—anything we could for payback" (*Christian Science Monitor* April 29,

2002). As discussed in chapters 1 and 2, this vision of civic and community-minded Black capitalism is an updated version of the Black nationalism advocated by the Garveyites of 1920s Los Angeles, who envisioned that Black-owned businesses would hire African Americans and provide useful services to Black consumers.

On the other hand, a 64-year-old Black female (1996) and art director for a community organization mentioned Latasha Harlins as the reason for the unrest (see chapter 2):

> It was because of Latasha Harlins, that Korean lady getting freed. Nobody outside of Los Angeles heard about that. It had nothing to do with (Rodney King); it was the straw that broke the camel's back. I mean she was walking out and the woman shot her in the back as she was leaving. I don't buy that shit. She couldn't handle it. It really makes me mad.

Talking about Latasha Harlins seemed to affect her deeply, and her voice tone changed. Despite her strong feelings concerning the Du-Harlins incident, she felt an affinity with Korean shopkeepers, telling one that she was glad they were rebuilding. For other African American interviewees, Latasha Harlins was not the only symbol of injustice that catalyzed the protest; neither was the Rodney King verdict. Some brought up the issue of institutional racism by the police and financial institutions or a long series of socioeconomic frustrations (e.g., poverty and despair) in the African American community as the underlying cause. An 18-year-old UCLA student (1993) believed that the cause was police brutality.

> People were fed up with the way the police treat minorities and fed up with the police getting away with bullshit. My uncle got killed by a cop in the street. There are so many unreported cases of police brutality. Prejudice. They think we're all in a gang, and they were tired of the police getting away with everything, especially when it's on videotape.

Many African Americans felt that outsiders—Latinos, Jews, and especially Koreans—controlled too much of the retail landscape in South LA. As a result, when these symbols of their own diminished control and limited retail options went up in smoke in the spring of 1992, some felt vindicated: "Maybe it had to burn . . . like how sometimes you have to burn a field. To make something new" (Simon 2011, 45). Finally, there were people like this 58-year-old Black liquor store owner (1993) who felt that multiple factors were responsible for the unrest, but he also felt that the issues were generational:

> I believe that the crisis happened because of a lot of hopelessness and drugs. Young people, it seems to me like they don't have anything to lose anymore.

No matter what race and ethnicity, young people today don't seem to care. The economy and jobs play a major role in this problem.

He also felt that class differences played a role: "When you are poor and you are locked in and you're seeing all these goodies around you and you want to get that quick, no patience. That's why you have a lot of drug problems." Unlike interviews with Korean merchants (see chapter 6), damage was not a common topic of discussion in the interviews with African Americans. Informants mentioned acquaintances that had lost jobs or businesses, but they had rebuilt and were moving on. All saw the Rodney King beating as an exaggerated example of routine police violence against Blacks in South LA, and they were outraged and saddened by this event. They often empathized with unrest participants, who presented themselves as "worthy protesters and freedom fighters" recognizing flaws in the system and the need for change (Murty et al. 1994). It prompted them to think of what it means to be Black in the US, to occupy the lowest stratum of the racial order (Hunt 1997, 78). Most concluded that "collective violence pays off" (Murty et al. 1994) and that there were positive results of the unrest.

After the unrest, my Black interviewees assessed their relationship with Koreans: "Efforts were made to build community relations [between Koreans and African Americans]." "They try to act nice, but you can tell it's fake. They come towards you and say 'hi' and 'have a nice day' too quickly."; "They [Koreans] became aware that they were in a community that they needed to try more."; "Brought them [African Americans] closer. Black on Black crime was cut down; it was a wake-up call." On the whole, for African Americans, the unrest was perceived as an necessary action to address injustice that did not do much harm or that led to positive changes in their community.

Unlike Black participants, Latino interviewees interpreted the unrest as an example of Black rage against Asians, Latinos, and Whites, even while identifying its causes in racism, capitalism, and the negative impact of economic restructuring. Looking at the riot victims at the corner of Florence and Normandie, George Sanchez (1997) suggested that the unrest was "an anti-immigrant spectacle from [the] very beginning" and an outpouring of resentment against increasing Latino and Asian immigrants in Black neighborhoods (1010). Sanchez noted that young Black Americans were heard saying that Latinos and Asians had invaded their territory, and that they would let Latinos off the hook but wanted to teach Koreans who ruled the neighborhood. Koreans "stood out as an easy target" because of a "Pacific Rim global economy," which was bringing change to LA as well as wealth for some new Asian immigrants (S. Lee 2015). At Florence and Normandie, while Black motorists appeared to pass without incident, others were attacked. Although the case of Reginald Denny, a White truck driver, was much publicized in the media, he was not the only person injured on that corner. One teenage girl exclaimed that a Japanese motorist, Takao Hirata, deserved to be injured as payback for the death of Latasha Harlins, calling him a "Korean motherfucker" (Alan-Williams 1994, 91, quoted in Watts 2010, 214).

Of a total 5,633 persons arrested during the unrest, Latinos constituted 50.6 percent whereas African Americans comprised only 36.2 percent of total arrests; however, 72 percent of those specific arrests were for curfew violations and property crimes (i.e., looting) (Pastor 1995, 239). Different motivations have been attributed to different participants, and there were distinct modes of participation, such as burning or looting, active or passive participation, and early or late participation. While some Black interviewees and commentators attributed the violence to Latino or Mexican participation, often invoking the large number of Latino participants, Mexican interviewees and commentators attributed it to Black or Salvadoran participation and carefully distinguished Latino participation from Black participation. David Hayes-Bautista et al. (1993) suggested a collective behavior approach in understanding Latino behavior: "Latino involvement is explained more by the fact of breakdown in municipal order than by anything else" (446). Thus, for many Latino interviewees, Latino participation in the unrest was not about anger, but more about opportunity. It was not until the third or fourth day, when the people could not get food or other things they needed due to the curfew, that Latinos became involved in the looting. Accordingly, economist Manuel Pastor (1995) claims that working-poor Latinos participated because of deep frustrations with the persistent economic inequality they saw in their neighborhoods, while the African American response was more closely tied to police-community relations. Some Latinos looted because the opportunity presented itself; some looted because they saw the chance to obtain an item they desired or needed. As mentioned in the previous chapter, Latinos generally were not protesting the Rodney King verdict, and many were opposed altogether to looting and arson, arguing that this response was not justified and would cause more problems in the long run and bring shame to the larger Latino community.[8]

For other Latino interviewees, the events represented participants' only "opportunity for oppressed people to be heard by the power structure" (Hunt 1997, 75, 76). They speculated that Latinos participated in the unrest with the same motivation as African Americans: protesting racist and classist treatment of Latinos and African Americans by the larger White society. One indicated, "Man [store owner] is rich, and we're poor." In many ways, Latinos were subjected to similar racial and economic conditions as Blacks, including unfair treatment by the LAPD and law enforcement. When a *Los Angeles Times* reporter approached one group of Latino workers who gathered every morning to look for work near the ruins of a construction supply store on Pico

Boulevard, some of the men responded with threats. One lobbed a small rock. One shouted, "Next time, bring us some food!" (April 21, 1997).

In short, the interpretation of the unrest as primarily a matter of Black-Korean tension, the Rodney King beating, or Black-Brown tension was not supported by interviewees. Instead, residents were likely to link the events to broader structural formations and a history of racial and economic marginalization rather than to the acquittal of the four White police officers.[9]

Although initially the motive of the rioters was attributed to racial tension, now race is considered to be one factor in a larger status quo conflict. If one looks at the situation and the parties more closely, however, this superficial appearance of White-Black and Korean-Black racial tension veils a class struggle, reminiscent of how Marx (1972/1954, 49) interpreted the events leading to the coup d'état of "Napoleon the Little" on December 2, 1851. The petite bourgeoisie did not feel sufficiently rewarded after the June Revolution of 1848, feeling that their material interests had been imperiled and that democratic guarantees had been undermined by the counterrevolution. Similarly, Korean immigrant merchants during the unrest were abandoned by state apparatuses, such as the police and government officials, and left to fend for themselves. The Revolutions of 1848 were led by an ad hoc coalition of reformers, the middle classes, and workers, which did not hold together for long. After the coup d'état, the peasants, whose interests were no longer aligned with those of the bourgeoisie, found their natural ally and leader in the urban proletariat, whose task was to overthrow the bourgeoisie order (Marx 1972/1954, 128). Likewise, Latino workers came to join the unrest as allies to African American residents.[10]

A massive and rapid residential demographic change occurred in the wake of the riots. Between 1970 and 1990, the South LA area had gone from being 80 percent Black and 9 percent Latino to 50.3 percent Black and 44 percent Latino (Grant et al. 1996). In the 2010 Census, the area of South Los Angeles had a population of about 768,456, with 64 percent of the residents Hispanic or Latino and 31.4 percent African American.[11] The majority of residents of South LA, like the rest of Angelenos, feel the city's economic situation has significantly worsened. South LA, whose residents had a per capita income of less than $14,000 per year, had the lowest income in the city. The per capita income of residents in affluent neighborhoods on the West side is 12 times higher than that of South LA residents (Los Angeles County Department of Public Health 2013). Male earnings have decreased dramatically in South LA since 1990 (Ong et al. 2018, 15). The community also has a higher concentration of low-wage jobs than the County as a whole (Ong et al. 2018, 9). In 2010, South LA had the highest rates of unemployment in the city at 13 percent (the city's average was 9.2 percent) and of people living below the

Federal Poverty Level (FPL) at 30 percent (as compared with the city average of 19 percent) (Los Angeles County Department of Public Health 2013). By 2016, the employment rate in South LA had improved, though it was still lower than the County and lower than 1960 levels (Ong et al. 2018, 14). The percentage of people over age 25 who did not graduate high school in South LA was over 50 percent, according to the 2010 US Census, while it was 26 percent for the city overall. Finally, on average, 30 percent of the population aged 25 and older in LA had a bachelor's degree, while the rate was 10 percent in South LA (Los Angeles County Department of Public Health 2013).

In general, after the unrest, about 100,000 jobs were lost and only 26,000 were generated through subsequent policies. Moreover, 60 percent of the new jobs went to non-Hispanic Whites, even though African Americans, Latinos, and Asians suffered 85 percent of the job loss (Spencer 2004, 98). De facto housing segregation remains intact, setting South LA apart from the rest of the city; in addition, homeownership of South LA residents remains low. Only 23 percent of the commercial buildings destroyed by the riots are back in business (Dreier 2003, 36); the majority of local stores were never rebuilt.[12] South LA after the unrest was characterized by even fewer supermarkets[13] and sit-down restaurants per capita than the rest of LA and suburban America, even though issues of retail justice and equity were one of the main topics of the 1992 unrest.

## FROM BIPOLAR TO MULTIPOLAR

By 2050, racial minorities may become a numeric majority in the US, and the Latino population is expected to increase to an estimated 128 million, or 29 percent of the country. The Black/White binary that defined race relations for centuries has evolved due to the influx of different minority groups and the ways they are racialized (Koshy 2008, 1548). I have argued that inequalities in power, privilege, and rights/entitlements should be a part of the discussion on racial difference. This study has examined how multiple racial/ethnic groups view one another and themselves in post-unrest Los Angeles. The post-unrest racial cartography of LA signals the future of race relations nationally: multipolar racial formation, race acting (e.g., acting White), and subaltern racism are all influenced by class inequality and immigrant/citizenship status.[14] The present race relations in the US are characterized by the complex interweaving of racial, class, and citizenship categories, making it hard to separate race from class as the predominant marker of differentiation.

First, immigrants from Asia and Latin America have been subject to differential racialization from Blacks and from each other, and from the state and civil society. In Omi and Winant's formulation, racial projects by the state form the basis for individual and collective identity formation, and at the same time become the site for political struggle between racially defined social movements and the racial state. Lack of protection of Korean immigrants' property and citizenship rights shifted the dynamics of racialization of Korean immigrants and their children. Koreans became a stand-in for all Asian Americans during the unrest—just as Mexicans or Salvadorans did for Latinos—and were subject to racialization. Although less visible than the case of Latino immigrants, Asian immigrants underwent a similar pan-ethnic racialization or racial interpellation, as seen in the formation of pan-ethnic Asian American community organizations.[15]

Mark Sawyer (2010) states, "Latinos are both potentially white and 'others'" (532). As discussed in the previous chapter, more than half of Latinos identified as White in the 2010 Census. For instance, in 2010, the ethnic Mexican population identified as 52.8 percent White and 39.5 percent SOR (Some Other Race), although Central Americans (largely Salvadorans and Guatemalans) were more likely to identify as SOR than as White (Pulido and Pastor 2013, 315). Latinos have not been always treated as White, but often as non-White racialized people with undesirable characteristics that make them "unassimilable" (Sawyer 2008, 43). Like Ong's (2003) poor Cambodian refugees, Latino immigrants in South LA were "Blackened" because their socioeconomic indicators were worse than those of African Americans, making them easier to exploit. Latinos are more likely to be poor than their Black neighbors who live in the same area, and Blacks have a much higher rate of high school graduation (Pastor 1993).

Second, it should be noted that White and Black roles do not only include people who identify racially as White and Black. In the post-Civil Rights era, different racial minorities are relegated to White/Black racial roles. Thus, Korean immigrants have been viewed as surrogate Whites without the White privilege (K. Park 1996). Similarly, some African Americans adopted a surrogate White role in responding with nativist sentiment to immigrant spatial and economic prominence[16]—in particular, the entrepreneurial presence of Korean business owners—and in supporting anti-immigrant policies such as California's Proposition 187 (which was later challenged and found unconstitutional by a federal court) and the federal Workfare bill. In Leimert Park, a traditionally Black neighborhood in South LA, a group called Choose Black America financially supported by the Federation for American Immigration Reform (a hate group with ties to white supremacist groups) led a march against illegal immigration in South LA.[17] However, it should be noted that African Americans have not been the principal sponsors of exclusionary immigration legislation or the primary promulgators of anti-immigrant movements (Ribas 2016, 193). It must be emphasized that racism espoused by Black people, while still racism, is not backed up by institutional power. Unfortunately, this "race acting" tends to produce charges of "subaltern racism" among racial minorities.[18] In sum, racial minorities are not immune to prejudice and bigotry. As activist and scholar Andrea Smith self-critically states, people of color are "victims of white supremacy, but complicit in it as well" (2006, 69).

Third, I have discussed post-unrest cross-racial class formation, in particular immigrant and labor organizing, as discussed in the previous chapter. Bobo et al.'s (2001) demographic findings call our attention to the semi-permanent formation of a multiracial working-class coalition. Employment trajectories demonstrate that Black, Asian, and Latino workers tend to be relegated to low-skill positions, while other ethnic groups such as Indians and Iranians acquire high-skill IT jobs (2001, 30–32). Also, except for Koreans, ethnic economies (such as food service and retail trade) are not linked to upward social mobility and do not offer protected economic niches. Immigrant and labor organizing often cuts across racial and ethnic boundaries, involving coalitions between Latinos and Korean/Asian Americans, as discussed in the previous chapter, and between Latinos and African Americans. A radicalized, largely immigrant population engaged in strikes, boycotts, and street theater. This multiracial movement emerged out of a series of concrete campaigns focusing on the struggles of the working poor, an expansive living-wage campaign, union drives among home care workers and janitors, and the fight for affordable public transportation, spearheaded by the Bus Riders Union.

Overall, in the mid-late 1990s, Los Angeles became the epicenter of labor organizing, particularly by Latino immigrant workers (Milkman as cited in Bonacich et al. 2010, 369). With the support of the public, media, public officials, clergy, and foundations, unions won better contracts for janitors, drywall workers, chambermaids, homecare and nursing home workers, municipal workers, social workers, librarians, and leisure industry employees, among others (Laslett 2012). The Justice for Janitors campaign organized a strike and a June 1990 demonstration in Central City, which drew an attack by police. However, the strike resulted in an unprecedented 25 percent increase in wages over a three-year period. In 1997, the revitalized union movement pushed the City Council to pass a living wage law (requiring firms with city contracts to pay decent wages and provide health benefits) over the opposition of Mayor Riordan and the Chamber of Commerce (Dreier 2003, 42). In 1999, more than 75,000 home health care aides won an organizing effort led by the Service Employees International Union (SEIU), which was the largest union victory in the country in more than 30 years (Dreier 2003, 42).

In 2002, the city's unions and anti-sweatshop activists (including clergy and college students) celebrated a victory when UNITE, the garment workers union, signed a contract with SweatX, a new local firm, to produce "sweat-free" clothing, backed by a foundation headed by the cofounder of Ben & Jerry. The United Food and Commercial Workers mounted a successful campaign among workers employed by Gigante, the Mexico-based chain of supermarkets (Dreier 2003, 42). Equally important, the Los Angeles Federation of Labor sought out strategies that would bring Black and Latino Angelenos together, while allying with African Americans and using their civil rights tradition of struggle for the cause of workers' rights (Bonacich et al. 2010, 369). South LA's Community Coalition, discussed in chapter 7, convinced the Los Angeles Unified School District to redirect funds to repair dilapidated school buildings in the city's poorest areas. The Bus Riders Union forced the Metropolitan Transit Authority to buy new buses and keep fares down. Action for Grassroots Empowerment and Neighborhood Development Alternatives (AGENDA) mobilized residents to challenge the city's federally funded job training program so that unskilled residents would be trained for work in industries with career leaders. In addition, Communities for a Better Environment defeated Sunlaw Energy Partners' plan to build a massive 550-megawatt power plant in South Gate, a predominantly Latino working-class city east of South LA (Dreier 2003, 42).

The Labor/Community Strategy Center, the Strategic Concepts in Organizing and Policy Education, and the Los Angeles Alliance for a New Economy have not only sought to foster class consciousness, but they have also prioritized the cultivation of interracial unity (Pastor 2014, 56).

For instance, the County Federation looked to groom African American leaders, raise the minimum wage, and reserve spots for African American workers in the sectors of building trades, janitorial services, and hotel employees. Special efforts were made to ensure that African Americans would not be left behind. The SEIU launched the Five Days for Freedom campaign to sign up thousands of licensed security guards—a sector that is 70 percent African American in the region—for union membership (Pastor 2014, 57). Similarly, UNITE-HERE! Local 11 used collective bargaining to ensure that African American workers were hired by the hotel industry. Labor unions wielded enormous political influence, culminating in the election of Latino Mayor Antonio Villaraigosa, who has deep roots in the progressive community and pushed "the entire center of political gravity of California to the left" (Laslett 2012, 313).

This cultivation of interracial unity is particularly important in South LA given its deep history of racial justice and civil rights struggles, particularly within the Black community. In light of the current demographic shift in South LA and rise in the Latino population, organizers such as Community Coalition felt that "they needed to embrace the changes but recognize the history of African American civil rights and social justice struggles" (Villanuerva 2017, 85). This cross-racial coalition focused on labor, class, and civil rights issues and cannot be explained solely by "racial formation"; rather, it must be analyzed as "racial and class formation."

## CONCLUSION

The media portrayal of Black-Korean tensions in South LA during and after the unrest—a battle between African Americans versus Koreans concentrated around the liquor stores of South LA—was overly simplistic. My research indicated that the "us versus them" mentality presented in the media was distorted. There are a number of factors that respondents spoke about that echo what the media was saying. The media's fixation on ethnic conflict seems to be related to "an attempt to portray all groups, and not just Whites, as having to overcome prejudice" and to shift the focus from racist structures to racist attitudes (Pastor 2014, 34). However, community members do not simply re-iterate what the media has fed them about their own community. Instead, they assess the situation based upon their own individual experiences. Thus, in theory, Korean merchants have the power to control their own destiny: if they are able to establish a better rapport with customers, relations may improve.

My research on African Americans' and Latinos' discussion of the unrest led me to conceive of a multitiered racial cartography, which exhibits stratified minoritization as the contestation of a hierarchy involving Whites, Asian Americans, African Americans, and Latinos in South LA. Since the 1980s, the conventional White/Black racial framework has expanded to include a four-tiered model where Latinos and Asian Americans occupy distinct racialized categories; because of their small numbers and high degree of marginalization, American Indians are often excluded in macro discussions of race in the US. Although multiculturalism is often the language used—it is presented as a positive alternative to white supremacy—it is still "governed by a normative logic that is racialized, classed, and gendered" (Jun 2011, 127). This four-tiered hierarchical racial classification system intersects with class structure, as different groups find themselves fighting for higher status. Although this new system—institutionalized via the census and other official policies— was introduced to avoid racial polarization, the groups involved are separated by presumed racial traits that serve as markers of privilege or subordination. There is still widespread racial segregation with respect to housing, and the four racial groups are ranked differently in the hierarchies of status and wealth.

In this hegemonic multitiered racial cartography, Whites are still at the top and African Americans are still at the bottom. Latinos seem to be as worse off as African Americans, at least in South LA, though. In between, two intermediate racial categories are positioned in a liminal state. As seen in this study, while Whites and African Americans are assumed to have full citizenship, Latinos' and Asians' political rights and legitimacy are often contested. Different races can occupy the role of Whites in particular situations, but they are still racialized by their bodies even if they have economic power!

This book has documented how interracial relationships and tensions between Blacks, Koreans, and Latinos involve an interplay of race, class, culture, and citizenship, specifically with regards to a particular conflict—the 1992 Los Angeles unrest. It explored how these relationships changed in the event's aftermath and charted a racial cartography to depict the relative position of Whites, African Americans, Latinos, and Koreans. The post-unrest racial cartography of LA is intended to reflect a multipolar racial formation, which is particularly impacted by the Latinization of South LA.[19] The future of race relations in the US will be characterized by the complex interweaving of racial, class, and citizenship categories, making it hard to separate race from class as the predominant marker of differentiation. Perhaps what is most important to note, however, is that despite reduced racial tension[20] and a modicum of economic growth, the structural conditions that led to the conflict have not changed substantially. The conditions in South LA are still dismal. Young, unarmed African Americans such as Ezell Ford in South LA are frequently killed by police. Therefore, another similar unrest could happen again.

## NOTES

1. I need to acknowledge indigenous people are still a part of this country even though their numbers might not be large.
2. I haven't focused on White people as a population group in this book, as the more relevant discussion relates to White-dominated institutions.
3. Regional racial cartography may be similar to a national racial cartography, but always diverges in specific ways.
4. Such defensive backlash was not exclusive to African Americans. Violence occurred against new Irish immigrants in the 1840s, against new arrivals from eastern and southern Europe at the turn of the century, against Black in-migrants from the South during the Great Migration, and more recently against the newest wave of immigrants, Latinos and Asians (Bergesen and Herman 1998).
5. Interestingly, Whites have been characterized as feeling they were engaged in the most conflict with African Americans rather than with Asians or Latinos (Henry and Sears 2002).
6. And yet, they rate Asians as higher in economic status.

7. *Cholo* is a Spanish term with various meanings. Its origin relates to a somewhat derogatory term for mixed-blood descendants in Latin America during the colonial era. In the United States, it most often refers to a Mexican-American youth who belongs to a street gang or dresses in the manner of the related subculture.

8. Darnell Hunt (1997) reported similar Latino perspectives on the unrest.

9. In response, during the June election of 1992, voters passed Charter Amendment F, which limited police chiefs to two five-year terms and set up a mechanism for more civilian review of officer misconduct.

10. I am speaking about racialized subjects—class is not the only factor here, as it was with Marx's example.

11. "South L.A.," Mapping L.A. website of the *Los Angeles Times*, http://maps.latimes.com/neighborhoods/region/south-la/. Accessed: January 29, 2018.

12. Patrick Range McDonald and Ted Soqui, "Then & Now: Images from the same spot as the L.A. riots, 20 years later," *LA Weekly*, http://www.laweekly.com/microsites/la-riots. Accessed: August 8, 2017.

13. There is now one less chain supermarket in the riot neighborhoods than in the 1992 (Dreier 2003, 41).

14. Work on Latinos and African Americans in LA say little about multipolar relations. For instance, a recently published anthology, *Black Los Angeles: American Dreams and Racial Realities* (2010), edited by Darnell Hunt and Ana-Christina Ramón, did not include a chapter on interracial relations. Scholarship about Latinos tends to include such discussion, as seen in Kun and Pulido (2014), but it is limited to the relationship between Latinos and African Americans.

15. The formation of a pan-ethnic Asian American identity emerged in the 1960s and 70s.

16. Of course, reinforcing nativist rhetoric does not necessarily mean Blacks can inhabit Whiteness, even temporarily. The burden of skin color is too great. It's different for Koreans who were economically privileged and thus held power over Blacks/Latinos.

17. "The compañeros have taken all the housing. If you don't speak Spanish they turn you down for jobs. Our children are jumped upon in the schools. They are trying to drive us out" (*LAT* August 17, 2013).

18. The word subaltern, as Gramsci calls it, refers to "the emergent class of the much greater mass of people ruled by coercive or sometimes mainly ideological domination from above" (Said 1988, vi).

19. The US racial hierarchy is becoming increasingly more fluid and gradational. Racial classification and the rules of racial recognition in the United States increasingly look like those of Latin American countries, which have long recognized racial mixture.

20. As of 2002, almost twice as many Angelenos believed the city has made progress toward improving race relations. Nearly three-quarters believed the city's racial and ethnic groups are getting along "very well" or "somewhat well"—compared with five years earlier, when only one-third rated race relations in Los Angeles as good (Dreier 2003, 45).

# References

Abelmann, Nancy. 1996. *Echoes of the Past, Epics of Dissent: A South Korean Social Movement*. Berkeley: University of California Press.

Abdullah, Melina and Regina Freer. 2010. "Bass to Bass: Relative Freedom and Womanist Leadership in Black Los Angeles." In *Black Los Angeles: American Dreams and Racial Realities*. Edited by Darnell Hunt and Ana-Christina Ramón, 323–342. New York and London: New York University Press.

Abelmann, Nancy and John Lie. 1995. *Blue Dreams: Korean Americans and the Los Angeles Riots*. Cambridge: Harvard University Press.

Adler, Rachel. 2002. "Patron-Client Ties, Ethnic Entrepreneurship and Transnational Migration: The Case of Yucatecans in Dallas, Texas." *Urban Anthropology and Studies of Cultural Systems and World Economic Development* 31: 129–161.

Alexander, Jeffrey and Steven Seidman, eds. 1990. *Culture and Society: Contemporary Debates*. Cambridge: Cambridge University Press.

Allen, Walter and Angie Chung. 2000. "'Your Blues Ain't like My Blues': Race, Ethnicity, and Social Inequality in America." *Contemporary Sociology* 29 (6): 796–805.

Almaguer, Tomas. 2012. "Race, Racialization, and Latino Populations in the United States." In *Racial Formation in the Twenty-First Century*. Edited by Daniel Ho-Sang, Oneka LaBennett, and Laura Pulido, 143–161. Berkeley: University of California Press.

Alonso, Alex. 2010. "Out of the Void: Street Gangs in Black Los Angeles." In *Black Los Angeles: American Dreams and Racial Realities*. Edited by Darnell Hunt and Ana-Christina Ramón, 140–167. New York and London: New York University Press.

Althusser, Louis. 1971. *Lenin and Philosophy, and Other Essays*. Translated by Ben Brewster. London: New Left Books.

Alvarez, R. Michael and Tara L. Butterfield. 2000. "The Resurgence of Nativism in California? The Case of Proposition 187 and Illegal Immigration." *Social Science Quarterly* 81 (1): 167–179.

American Anthropological Association. 1998. "AAA Statement on 'Race.'" *Anthropology Newsletter* 39 (9): 3–3.

APPCON/APANLA. 1992. *Statement of Position on Liquor Stores in South Central Los Angeles.* Los Angeles.

Ashman, Linda, Jaime de la Vega, Marc Dohan, Andy Fisher, Rosa Hippler, and Bill Romain. 1993. *Seeds of Change: Strategies for Food Security for the Inner City.* Los Angeles: UCLA Department of Urban Planning.

Atkinson, Will. 2009. "Rethinking the Work—Class Nexus: Theoretical Foundations for Recent Trends." *Sociology* 43 (5): 896–912.

Bailey, Benjamin. 1996. *Communication of Respect in Service Encounters Between Immigrant Korean Retailers and African-American Customers.* MA thesis, Department of Anthropology, University of California, Los Angeles.

Baker-Cristales, Beth. 2004. *Salvadoran Migration to Southern California: Redefining El Herman Lejano.* Gainesville: University Press of Florida.

Baldwin, James. 1969. "Negroes are Anti-Semitic Because They're Anti-White." In *Black Anti-Semitism and Jewish Racism*, 3–14. New York: Richard E. Baron.

Balibar, Etienne. 1991(1988). "Racism and Nationalism." In *Race, Nation, Class: Ambiguous Identities*, by Etienne Balibar and Immanuel Wallerstein, 37–68. London & New York: Verso.

Barker, Martin. 1981. *The New Racism.* London: Junction Books.

Barreto, Matt A., Ben F. Gonzalez, and Gabriel R. Sanchez. 2014. "Rainbow Coalition in the Golden State? Exposing Myths, Uncovering New Realities in Latino Attitudes toward Blacks." In *Black and Brown in Los Angeles: Beyond Conflict and Coalition.* Edited by Josh Kun and Laura Pulido, 203–232. Berkeley: University of California Press.

Barth, Fredrik. 1959. "Segmentary Opposition and the Theory of Games: A Study of Pathan Organization." *The Journal of the Royal Anthropological Institute of Great Britain and Ireland* 89 (1): 5–21.

———. 1969. *Ethnic Groups and Boundaries: The Social Organization of Cultural Difference.* Boston: Little, Brown.

Bass, Karen. 1994. "Alcohol's Relation to Urban Violence: When Free Enterprise Threatens Community Welfare." In *Black-Korean Encounter: Toward Understanding and Alliance.* Edited by Eui-Young Yu, 68–72. Los Angeles: Institute for Asian American and Pacific Asian Studies, California State University, Los Angeles.

Beauchamp, Dan. 1980. *Beyond Alcoholism: Alcohol and Public Health Policy.* Philadelphia: Temple University Press.

Bechhofer, Frank and Brian Elliott. 1985. "The Petit Bourgeoisie in Late Capitalism." *Annual Review of Sociology* 11: 181–207.

Bennett, Dionne. 2010. "Looking for the 'Hood and Finding Community: South Central, Race, and Media." In *Black Los Angeles: American Dreams and Racial Realities.* Edited by Darnell Hunt and Ana-Christina Ramón, 215–231. New York and London: New York University Press.

Bergesen, Albert and Max Herman. 1998. "Immigration, Race, and Riot: The 1992 Los Angeles Uprising." *American Sociological Review* 63 (1): 39–54.

Blalock, Hubert. 1967. *Toward a Theory of Minority-Group Relations*. New York: Wiley.

Blauner, Robert. 1989. *Black Lives, White Lives: Three Decades of Race Relations in America*. Berkeley, Los Angeles, and London: University of California Press.

Bluestone, Barry and Bennett Harrison. 1982. *The Deindustrialization of America: Plant Closings, Community Abandonment, and the Dismantling of Basic Industries*. New York: Basic Books.

Bobo, Lawrence, Camille Zubrinsky, James Johnson, and Melvin Oliver. 1994. "Public Opinion Before and After a Spring of Discontent." In *The Los Angeles Riots: Lessons for the Urban Future*. Edited by Mark Baldassare, 103–134. Boulder, CO: Westview Press.

Bobo, Lawrence and Vincent L. Hutchings. 1996. "Perceptions of Racial Group Competition: Extending Blumer's Theory of Group Position to a Multiracial Social Context." *American Sociological Review* 61 (6): 951–972.

Bobo, Lawrence, Melvin Oliver, and Michael P. Massagli. 2001. "Stereotypes and Urban Inequality." In *Urban Inequality: Evidence from Four Cities*. Edited by A. O'Connor, C. Tilly, and L. D. Bobo, 89–162. New York: Russell Sage Foundation.

Bonacich, Edna. 1972. "A Theory of Ethnic Antagonism: The Split Labor Market." *American Sociological Review* 37 (October): 547–59.

———. 1973. "A Theory of Middleman Minorities." *American Sociological Review* 38: 585–594.

———. 1980. "Class Approaches to Ethnicity and Race." *Insurgent Sociologist* X (2): 9–23.

———. 1987. "'Making It' in America: A Social Evaluation of the Ethics of Immigrant Entrepreneurship." *Sociological Perspectives* 30 (4): 446–466. https://doi.org/10.2307/1389213.

———. 1993. "The Other Side of Ethnic Entrepreneurship: A Dialogue with Waldinger, Aldrich, Ward and Associates." *The International Migration Review* 27 (3): 685–92.

Bonacich, Edna, Lola Smallwood-Cuevas, Lanita Morris, Steven Pitts, and Joshua Bloom. 2010. "A Common Project for a Just Society: Black Labor in Los Angeles." In *Black Los Angeles: American Dreams and Racial Realities*. Edited by Darnell Hunt and Ana-Christina Ramón, 360–381. New York and London: New York University Press.

Bottomore, Tom, ed. 1983. *A Dictionary of Marxist Thought*. Cambridge, MA: Harvard University Press.

Bourdieu, Pierre. 1977. *Outline of a Theory of Practice*. Cambridge: Cambridge University Press.

———. 1984. *Distinction: A Social Critique of the Judgment of Taste*. Translated by Richard Nice. Cambridge, MA: Harvard University Press.

———. 1990. *The Logic of Practice*. Stanford: Stanford University Press.

Brettell, Caroline, ed. 1993. "Introduction: Fieldwork, Text, and Audience." In *When They Read What We Write*. Edited by Caroline Brettell, 1–24. Westport, CT and London: Bergin & Garvey.

California Legislature, Assembly Special Committee. 1992. *To Rebuild Is Not Enough: Final Report and Recommendations of the Assembly Special Committee on the Los Angeles Crisis.*

Carbado, Devon W., Kimberlé Williams Crenshaw, Vickie M. Mays, and Barbara Tomlinson. 2013. "Intersectionality: Mapping the Movements of a Theory." *Du Bois Review: Social Science Research on Race* 10 (2): 303–312.

Chang, Edward. 1990. *New Urban Crisis: Korean-Black Conflicts in Los Angeles.* PhD Diss., Ethnic Studies, University of California at Berkeley.

———. 1993. "Jewish and Korean Merchants in African American Neighborhoods: A Comparative Perspective." *Amerasia Journal* 19 (2): 5–22.

Chang, Edward and Angela Oh. 1995. "Korean American Dilemma: Violence, Vengeance, Vision." In *Multicuralism from the Margins.* Edited by Dean A. Harris. Westport, CT: Bergin & Garvey.

Chang, Edward and Eui-Young Yu. 1994. "Chronology of Black-Korean Encounter." In *Black-Korean Encounter: Toward Understanding and Alliance.* Edited by Eui-Young Yu. Los Angeles: Institute for Asian American and Pacific Asian Studies, California State University at Los Angeles.

Chang, Edward and Jeannette Diaz-Veizades. 1999. *Ethnic Peace in the American City: Building Community in Los Angeles and Beyond.* New York and London: New York University Press.

Chang, Robert. 1994. "Toward an Asian American Legal Scholarship: Critical Race Theory, Post-Structuralism, and Narrative Space." *Asian Law Journal* 1 (1): 1241–1323.

Chapple, Reginald. 2010. "From Central Avenue to Leimert Park: The Shifting Center of Black Los Angeles." In *Black Los Angeles: American Dreams and Racial Realities.* Edited by Darnell Hunt and Ana-Christina Ramón, 60–80. New York and London: New York University Press.

Chavez, Leo. 1992. *Shadowed Lives: Undocumented Immigrants in American Society.* Fort Worth, Tex.: Harcourt Brace Jovanovich College Publishers.

Cheng, Lucie and Yen Lee Espiritu. 1989. "Korean Businesses in Black and Hispanic Neighborhood: A Study of Intergroup Relations." *Sociological Perspectives* 32: 521–534.

Cheng, Wendy. 2013. *The Changs Next Door to the Díazes: Remapping Race in Suburban California.* Minneapolis: University of Minnesota Press.

Cherkoss Donahoe, Myrna. 2005. "Indigenous Mexican Migrants in a Modern Metropolis: The Reconstruction of Zapotec Communities in Los Angeles." In *Latino Los Angeles: Transformations, Communities, and Activism.* Edited by Enrique C. Ochoa and Gilda L. Ochoa. Tucson: University of Arizona Press.

Cho, Sumi. 1993. "Korean Americans vs. African Americans: Conflict and Construction." In *Reading Rodney King /Reading Urban Uprising.* Edited by Robert Gooding-Williams, 196–214. New York and London: Routledge.

———. 2013. "Post-Intersectionality: The Curious Reception of Intersectionality in Legal Scholarship." *Du Bois Review: Social Science Research on Race* 10 (2): 385–404.

Chock, Phyllis. 1995. "Culturalism: Pluralism, Culture, and Race in the Harvard Encyclopedia of American Ethnic Groups." *Identities* 1 (14): 301–323.

Choi, Nora. 1992. "Between Black Rage and White Power." In *Inside the L.A. Riots: What really happened, and why it will happen again.* Edited by Don Hazen, 95–96. New York: The Institute for Alternative Journalism.

Choy, Christine, Elaine H. Kim, and Dai Sil Kim-Gibson. 1993. *Sa-I-Gu: From Korean Women's Perspectives.* A film, directed by Dai Sil Kim-Gibson; co-directed by Christine Choy. San Francisco: Center for Asian American Media.

Chung, Angie. 2007. *Legacies of Struggle: Conflict and Cooperation in Korean American Politics.* Stanford, CA: Stanford University Press.

City of Los Angeles. 1992. *Mayor Tom Bradley's South Central Community/Merchant Liquor Task Force.* Final Report.

Clarke, R. V. G. 1997. *Situational Crime Prevention: Successful Case Studies.* Albany, NY: Harrow and Heston.

Clifford, James and George E. Marcus. 1986. *Writing Culture: The Poetics and Politics of Ethnography.* A School of American Research Advanced Seminar. Berkeley: University of California Press.

Cobas, José, Jorge Duany, and Joe R. Feagin. 2009. *How the United States Racializes Latinos: White Hegemony and Its Consequences.* Boulder, CO: Paradigm.

Cohen, Jean. 1985. "Strategy or Identity: New Theoretical Paradigms and Contemporary Social Movements." *Social Research* 52 (4): 663–716.

Cohen, Jean, and Andrew Arato. 1997 (1992). *Civil Society and Political Theory.* Cambridge, MA, and London: The MIT Press.

Crenshaw, Kimberlé. 1989. "Demarginalizing the Intersection of Race and Sex: A Black Feminist Critique of Antidiscrimination Doctrine, Feminist Theory, and Antiracist Politics." *University of Chicago Legal Forum.*

———. 1991. "Mapping the Margins: Intersectionality, Identity Politics, and Violence against Women of Color." *Stanford Law Review* 43 (6): 1241–1299.

———. 2015. "Why Intersectionality Can't Wait." *Washington Post.* September 24.

Comaroff, John and Jean Comaroff. 1992. *Ethnography and the Historical Imagination.* Boulder, CO: Westview Press.

Coutin, Susan. 2007. *Nations of Emigrants: Shifting Boundaries of Citizenship in El Salvador and the United States.* Ithaca, NY: Cornell University Press.

Cumings, Bruce. 1981. *The Origins of the Korean War: Liberation and the Emergence of the Korean War.* Princeton, NJ: Princeton University Press.

Davis, Mike. 1990. *City of Quartz: Excavating the Future in Los Angeles.* Verso.

———. 1992. "In L.A., Burning All Illusions." *The Nation.* June 1: 743–746.

———. 1993. "Uprising and Repression in L.A." Interview by the Covert Action Information Bulletin. In *Reading Rodney King /Reading Urban Uprising.* Edited by Robert Gooding-Williams, 142–56. New York and London: Routledge.

De Certeau, Michel. 1984. *The Practice of Everyday Life.* Berkeley: University of California Press.

De Genova, Nicholas. 2005. *Working the Boundaries: Race, Space, and "Illegality" in Mexican Chicago.* Durham, NC: Duke University Press.

De Genova, Nicholas and Anna Y. Ramos-Zayas. 2003. *Latino Crossings: Mexicans, Puerto Ricans, and the Politics of Race and Citizenship.* New York: Routledge.

De Graaf, Lawrence and Quintard Taylor. 2001. "Introduction: African Americans in California History, California in African American History." In *Seeking El Dorado: African Americans in California.* Edited by Lawrence B. de Graaf, Kevin Mulroy, and Quintard Taylor, 3–69. Los Angeles: Autury Museum of Western Heritage.

Dikotter, Frank. 1990. *The Discourse of Race in Modern China.* Stanford, CA: Stanford University Press.

Douglas, Mary. *Constructive Drinking: Perspectives on Drink from Anthropology.* Cambridge: Cambridge University Press.

Dower, John W. 1986. *War without Mercy: Race & Power in the Pacific War.* New York: Pantheon Books.

Drake, St. Clair and Horace R. Cayton. 1993. *Black Metropolis: A Study of Negro Life in a Northern City.* Chicago: University of Chicago Press.

Dreier, Peter, John Mollenkopf and Todd Swanstrom. 2001. *Place Matters: Metropolitics for the Twenty-First Century.* Lawrence: University Press of Kansas.

Dreier, Peter. 2003. "America's Urban Crisis a Decade after the Los Angeles Riots." *National Civic Review* 92 (1): 35–55.

Edgell, Stephen. 1993. *Class.* London and New York: Routledge.

Espiritu, Yen. 1997. *Asian American Women and Men: Labor, Laws and Love.* Thousand Oaks, CA: Sage Publications.

Fanon, Franz. 1967. *Black Skin, White Masks.* New York: Grove Press.

Feagin, Joe and Hernán Vera. 1995. *White Racism: The Basics.* New York: Routledge.

Fogelson, Robert M. 1967. "White on Black: A Critique of the Mccone Commission Report on the Los Angeles Riots." *Political Science Quarterly* 82 (3): 337–367.

Foster, George. 1963. "The Dyadic Contract in Tzintzuntzan, II: Patron-Client Relationship." *American Anthropologist* 65 (6): 1280–1294.

Foster, SE. 2003. "Alcohol Consumption and Expenditures for Underage Drinking and Adult Excessive Drinking." *Jama-Journal of the American Medical Association* 289 (14): 1782–1782.

Foucault, Michel. 1977. *Discipline and Punishment: The Birth of the Prison.* New York: Vintage Books.

———. 1984. *The Foucault Reader.* Edited by Paul Rabinow. New York: Pantheon Books.

Fox, Richard, 1991. "Introduction: Working in the Present." In *Recapturing Anthropology: Working in the Present.* Edited by Richard Fox, 1–16. Santa Fe, NM: School of American Research Press.

Freer, Regina. 1994. "Black-Korean Conflict." In *The Los Angeles Riots: Lessons for the Urban Future.* Edited by Mark Baldassare, 175–204. Boulder, CO: Westview Press.

Friedman, Monroe. 1991. "Consumer Boycotts: A Conceptual Framework and Research Agenda." *Journal of Social Issues* 47 (1): 149–168.

Fuchs, Lawrence. 1990. "The Reactions of Black Americans to Immigration." In *Immigration Reconsidered: History, Sociology, and Politics*. Edited by Virginia Yans-McLaughlin, 293–314. New York: Oxford University Press.

Garcia, Arnoldo. 2000. "Race, Poverty, and Immigration." *Poverty & Race* November/December.

Garcia, David G and Tara J. Yosso. 2013. "Strictly in the Capacity of Servant: The Interconnection between Residential and School." *History of Education Quarterly* 53 (1): 64–89.

Gateward, Frances. 2003. "Breaking the Silences. An Interview with Dai Sil Kim-Gibson." *Quarterly Preview of Film and Video* 20 (2): 99–110.

George, Lynell. 1992. *No Crystal Stair: African-Americans in the City of Angels.* London and New York: Verso.

Glenn, Evelyn Nakano. 2002. *Unequal Freedom: How Race and Gender Shaped American Citizenship and Labor.* Cambridge, MA: Harvard University Press.

Goffman, Erving. 1956. *The Presentation of Self in Everyday Life.* Edinburgh: University of Edinburgh.

Gold, Steven. 2004. "Immigrant Entrepreneurs and Customers throughout the 20th Century." In *Not Just Black and White: Historical and Contemporary Perspectives on Immigration, Race and Ethnicity in the United States.* Edited by Nancy Foner and George M. Fredrickson, 315–340. New York: Russell Sage Foundation.

———. 2010. *The Store in the Hood: A Century of Ethnic Business and Conflict.* Lanham, MD: Roman and Littlefield.

Goldberg, David Theo, ed. 1990. *Anatomy of Racism.* Minneapolis: University of Minnesota Press.

———. 1993. *Racist Culture: Philosophy and the Politics of Meaning.* Oxford: Blackwell Publishers.

Gomberg-Muñoz, Ruth. 2010. "Willing to Work: Agency and Vulnerability in an Undocumented Immigrant Network." *American Anthropologist* 112 (2): 295–307.

Gonzalez, Cynthia. 2014. *Watts, Our Town: "Nothing about Us, without Us, Is for Us" An Auto-Ethnographic Account of Life in Watts, Los Angeles, California.* PhD diss., San Francisco: California Institute of Integral Studies.

Goodman, Alan H., Yolanda T. Moses, and Joseph L. Jones. 2012. *Race: Are We So Different?* Arlington, VA: American Anthropological Association.

Gotanda, Neil. 2000. "Multiculturalism and Racial Stratification." In *Asian American Studies: A Reader.* Edited by Jean Yu-wen Shen Wu and Min Song, 379–390. New Brunswick, NJ, and London: Rutgers University Press.

Gounis, Kostas. 1996. "Urban Marginality and Ethnographic Practice: on the Ethics of Fieldwork." *City & Society* 8: 108–118. doi:10.1525/ciso.1996.8.1.108.

Gramsci, Antonio. 1971. *Selections from the Prison Notebooks.* Translated by Q. Hoare and G. Smith. London: Lawrence and Wishart.

Grant, David M., Melvin L. Oliver, and Angela D. James. 1996. "African Americans: Social and Economic Bifurcation." In *Ethnic Los Angeles.* Edited by Roger Waldinger and Mehdi Bozorgmehr, 379–412. New York: Russell Sage Foundation.

Greenberg, James. 1995. "Capital, Ritual, and Boundaries of the Closed Corporate Community." In *Articulating Hidden Histories: Exploring the Influence of Eric*

*R. Wolf.* Jane Schneider and Rayna Rapp, eds., 67–81. Berkeley: University of California Press.

Gregory, Steven. 1992. "The Changing Significance of Race and Class in an African-American Community." *American Ethnologist* 19 (2): 255–274.

———. 1994. "Race, Rubbish, and Resistance: Empowering Difference in Community Politics." *Cultural Anthropology* 8 (1): 24–48.

———. 1998. *Black Corona: Race and the Politics of Place in an Urban Community.* Princeton, NJ: Princeton University Press.

Gusfield, Joseph. 1987. "Passage to Play: Rituals of Drinking time in American Society." In *Constructive Drinking: Perspectives on Drink from Anthropology.* Edited by Mary Douglas, 73–90. Cambridge: Cambridge University Press.

Gutmann, Mathew. 1996. *The Meanings of Macho: Being a Man in Mexico City.* Berkeley: University of California Press.

Habermas, Jürgen. 1989. *The Structural Transformation of the Public Sphere: An Inquiry into a Category of Bourgeois Society.* Translated by Thomas Burger with the assistance of Frederick Lawrence. Cambridge, MA: MIT Press.

Hall, Stuart. 1980. "Cultural Studies: Two Paradigms." *Media, Culture, and Society* 2: 57–72.

———. 1986. "Gramsci's Relevance for the Study of Race and Ethnicity." *Journal of Communication Inquiry* 10 (2): 5–27.

Hamilton, Nora and Norma Chinchilla. 2001. *Seeking Community in a Global City: Guatemalans and Salvadorans in Los Angeles.* Philadelphia: Temple University Press.

Han, Kyung-koo. 2007. "The Archaeology of the Ethnically Homogeneous Nation-State and Multiculturalism in Korea." *Korea Journal* 47 (4): 8–31.

Harris, Anne-Marie G., Geraldine R. Henderson, and Jerome D. Williams. 2005. "Courting Customers: Assessing Consumer Racial Profiling and Other Marketplace Discrimination." *Journal of Public Policy & Marketing* 24: 163–171.

Hartigan, Jr., John. 2010. *Race in the 21st Century: Ethnographic Approaches.* New York: Oxford University Press.

Hayes-Bautista, David. 1993. "Latinos and the 1992 Los Angeles Riots: A Behavioral Science Perspective." *Hispanic Journal of Behavioral Sciences* 15 (4): 427–448.

Henry, P. J. and David O. Sears. 2002. "The Symbolic Racism 2000 Scale." *Political Psychology* 23 (2): 253–283.

Hernandez, Tanya Kateri. 2007. "Latino Inter-Ethnic Employment Discrimination and the 'Diversity' Defense." *Harvard Civil Rights-Civil Liberties Law Review* 42 (2): 259–316.

Hicks, Joe. 1994. "Rebuilding in the Wake of Rebellion: The Need for Economic Conversion." In *Black-Korean Encounter: Toward Understanding and Alliance.* Edited by Eui-Young Yu, 79–82. Los Angeles: Institute for Asian American and Pacific Asian Studies, California State University, Los Angeles.

Hoffmann, Stanley. 1986. Review of *Distinction: A Social Critique of the Judgment of Taste,* by Pierre Bourdieu. *The New York Review of Books* 33: 45–49.

Horne, Gerald. 1997. *Fire this Time: The Watts Uprising and the 1960s.* New York: Da Capo Press.

————. 2001. "'Riot' and 'Revolt' in Los Angeles, 1965 and 1992." In *Seeking El Dorado: African Americans in California*. Edited by L. de Graaf, K. Mulroy, and Q. Taylor, 377–404. Los Angeles: Autury Museum of Western Heritage.

HoSang, Daniel, Oneka LaBennett, and Laura Pulido, eds. 2012. *Racial Formation in the Twenty-First Century*. Berkeley: University of California Press.

Hunt, Darnell. 1997. *Screening the Los Angeles "Riots": Race, Seeing, and Resistance*. Cambridge and New York: Cambridge University Press.

Hurt, Michael. 1999. "The Shape of Korean Ethnocentrism." Paper presented at the annual meeting of the Association for Asian American Studies. Philadelphia (April 1–3).

Hutchinson, Earl Ofari. 1991. "Fighting the Wrong Enemy: Blacks and Koreans." *The Nation*, December 4: 554–555.

Hymes, Dell. 1969. *Reinventing Anthropology*. New York: Vintage Books.

Ignatiev, Noel. 1995. *How the Irish Became White*. Cambridge, MA: Harvard University Press.

Jameson, Fredric. 1991. *Postmodernism or the Cultural Logic of Late Capitalism*. Durham, NC: Duke University Press.

Jenkins, R. 2001. "Ethnicity: Anthropological Aspects." In *International Encyclopedia of the Social & Behavioral Sciences*. Edited by Neil J. Smelser & Paul B. Baltes, 4824–4828. Amsterdam: Elsevier Science Ltd.

Jiménez, Tomás R. 2008. "Mexican Immigrant Replenishment and the Continuing Significance of Ethnicity and Race." *American Journal of Sociology* 113 (6): 1527–1567.

Jo, Moon H. 1992. "Korean Merchants in the Black Community: Prejudice among the Victims of Prejudice." *Ethnic and Racial Studies* 15 (3): 395–411.

Johnson, Jr., James H. and Melvin L. Oliver. 1989. "Interethnic Minority Conflict in Urban America: the Effects of Economic and Social Dislocations." *Urban Geography* 10 (5): 449–463.

Johnson, Jr., James H. and Curtis C. Roseman. 1990. "Increasing Black Outmigration from Los Angeles: The Role of Household Dynamics and Kinship Systems." *Annals of the Association of American Geographers* 80: 205–222.

Johnson, Jr., James H., C. K. Jones, W. C. Farrell, and Melvin Oliver. 1992. "The Los Angeles Crisis: A Retrospective View." *Economic Development Quarterly* 6 (4): 356–372.

Johnson, Jr., James H., Walter C. Farrell, Jr., and Chandra Guinn. 1997. "Immigration Reform and the Browning of America: Tensions, Conflicts, and Community Instability in Metropolitan Los Angeles." *International Migration Review* 31(4): 1055–1095.

Johnson, Kevin. 1997. "The New Nativism: Something Old, Something New, Something Borrowed, Something Blue." In *Immigrants Out!: The New Nativism and The Anti-Immigrant Impulse in the United States*. Edited by Juan F. Perea, 165–189. New York and London: New York University Press.

Joyce, Patrick. 2003. *No Fire Next Time: Black-Korean Conflicts and the Future of America's Cities*. Ithaca, NY: Cornell University Press.

Jun, Helen. 2011. *Race for Citizenship: Black Orientalism and Asian Uplift from Pre-Emancipation to Neoliberal America.* New York: New York University Press.

Jung, Moon-Kie. 2009. "The Racial Unconscious of Assimilation Theory." *Du Bois Review: Social Science Research on Race* 6: 375–395.

Kang, Miliann. 2010. *The Managed Hand: Race, Gender, and the Body in Beauty Service Work.* Berkeley and Los Angeles: University of California Press.

Karandinos, George, Laurie Kain Hart, Fernando Montero Castrillo, and Philippe Bourgois. 2014. "The Moral Economy of Violence in the US Inner City." *Current Anthropology* 55 (1): 1–18.

Kelly, Robin. 2012. "Separate and Unequal: a Conversation." In *Race: Are We So Different?* By Alan H. Goodman, Yolanda T. Moses, and Joseph L. Jones, 86–88. Arlington, VA: American Anthropological Association.

Kerner Commission. 1968. *Report of the National Advisory Commission on Civil Disorders.* Introduction by Tom Wicker. New York: Bantam Books.

Kim, Claire. 1999. "The Racial Triangulation of Asian Americans." *Politics and Society* 27 (1): 105–138.

———. 2000. *Bitter Fruit: The Politics of Black-Korean Conflict in New York City.* New Haven, CT: Yale University Press.

———. 2004. "Imagining Race and Nation in Multiculturalist America." *Ethnic and Racial Studies* 27 (6): 987–1005.

———. 2015. Dangerous Crossings: Race, Species, and Nature in a Multicultural Age. New York: Cambridge University Press.

Kim, Dae Young. 1999. "Beyond Co-Ethnic Solidarity: Mexican and Ecuadorian Employment in Korean-Owned Businesses in New York City." *Ethnic and Racial Studies* 22 (3): 581–605.

Kim, Elaine H. 1993. "Home Is Where the *Han* Is: A Korean American Perspective on the Los Angeles Upheavals." In *Reading Rodney King /Reading Urban Uprising.* Edited by Robert Gooding-Williams, 215–235. New York and London: Routledge.

Kim-Goh, Mikyong, Chong Suh, Dudley David Blake, and Bruce Hiley-Young. 1995. "Psychological Impact of the Los Angeles Riots on Korean American Victims: Implications for Treatment." *American Orthopsychiatric Association* 65(1): 138–146.

Kim, Jinah. 2008. "Immigrants, Racial Citizens, and the (Multi) Cultural Politics of Neoliberal Los Angeles." *Social Justice* 35 (2): 36–56.

Kim, Ju Yon. 2010. "The Difference a Smile Can Make: Interracial Conflict and Cross-Racial Performance in Kimchee and Chitlins." *Modern Drama* 53 (4): 533–556.

Kim, Nadia. 2008. *Imperial Citizens: Koreans and Race from Seoul to LA.* Stanford, CA: Stanford University Press.

Kim, Rose M. 2007. *Violence and Trauma as Constitutive Elements of Racial Identity Formation: The 1992 L.A Riots/Uprising/Saigu.* PhD diss., Department of Sociology, City University of New York.

———. 2012. "*Sa-I-Gu*, Twenty Years Later: I Still Love L.A." *Amerasia Journal* 38 (1): 63–82.

Kim, Sharon. 2010. *A Faith of our Own: Second-Generation Spirituality in Korean American Churches.* New Brunswick, NJ: Rutgers University Press.

Koreatown Immigrant Workers Alliance. 2007. KIWA Worker Empowerment Clinic, *Annual Report 2005.* Los Angeles: Koreatown Immigrant Workers Alliance.

Koshy, Susan. 2001. "Morphing Race into Ethnicity: Asian Americans and Critical Transformations of Whiteness." *Boundary* 2(28): 153–194.

———. 2008. "Why the Humanities Matter for Race Studies Today." *PMLA* 123 (5): 1542–1549.

Kurashige, Scott. 1996. *Locating Oppression and Resistance: Asian Americans and Racist Violence.* PhD diss., Department of History, UCLA.

———. 2008. *The Shifting Grounds of Race: Black and Japanese Americans in the Making of Multiethnic Los Angeles.* Princeton, NJ: Princeton University Press.

Kun, Josh and Laura Pulido, eds. 2014. *Black and Brown in Los Angeles: Beyond Conflict and Coalition.* Berkeley: University of California Press.

Kwon, Hyeyoung. 2015. "Intersectionality in Interaction: Immigrant Youth Doing American from an Outsider-Within Position." *Social Problems* 62 (4): 623–641.

Kwong, Peter. 1992. "The First Multicultural Riots." In *Inside the L.A. Riots: What really happened, and why it will happen again.* Edited by Don Hazen, 88–93. New York: The Institute for Alternative Journalism.

Labor/Community Strategy Center. 1993. *Reconstructing Los Angeles from the Bottom Up: A Long-Term Strategy for Workers, Low-Income People, and People of Color to Create an Alternative Vision of Urban Development.* Los Angeles: The Labor/Community Strategy Center.

LaFrance, Marianne and Clara Mayo. 1976. "Racial Differences in Gaze Behavior During Conversations: Two Systematic Observational Studies." *Journal of Personality and Social Psychology* 33 (5): 547–552.

Lamont, Michele and Virag Molnar. 2002. "The Study of Boundaries in the Social Sciences." *Annual Review of Sociology* 28: 167–195.

Laslett, John. 1996. "Historical Perspectives: Immigration and the Rise of a Distinctive Urban Region, 1900–1970." In *Ethnic Los Angeles.* Edited by Roger Waldinger and Mehdi Bozorgmehr. New York: Russell Sage Foundation.

Laslett, John H. M. 2012. *Sunshine Was Never Enough: Los Angeles Workers, 1880–2010.* Berkeley: University of California Press.

Latino Coalition. 1993. "Latinos and the Future of Los Angeles: A Guide to the Twenty- First Century." Los Angeles: The Latino Coalition for a New Los Angeles.

LaClau, Ernesto and Chantal Mouffe. 1992. "Beyond Emancipation." In *Emancipations, Modern and Post-Modern.* Edited by Jan Nederveen Pieterse. London and Newbury Park, CA: Sage.

LaVeist, Thomas A. and John M. Wallace. 2000. "Health Risk and Inequitable Distribution of Liquor Stores in African American Neighborhood." *Social Science & Medicine* 51: 613–617.

Leal, Jorge N. 2012. "Las plazas of South Los Angeles." In *Post-Ghetto: Reimagining South Los Angeles.* Edited by Josh Sides, 11–32. Berkeley: University of California Press.

Lee, Chang-rae. 1994. "My Low Korean Master." *Granta* 49: 122–132

Lee, Kapson. 1994. "Portrayal of Korean Americans in the Media." In *Community In Crisis: The Korean American Community After the Los Angeles Civil Unrest of April 1992.* Edited by George O. Totten III and H. Eric Schockman, 251–256. Los Angeles: Center for Multiethnic and Transnational Studies, University of Southern California.

Lee, Jennifer. 2000. "The Salience of Race in Everyday Life." *Work and Occupations* 27 (3): 353–376.

———. 2002. *Civility in the City: Blacks, Jews, and Koreans in Urban America.* Cambridge and London: Harvard University Press.

Lee, Jennifer and Frank Bean. 2004. "America's Changing Color Lines: Immigration, Race/Ethnicity, and Multiracial Identification." *Annual Review of Sociology* 30: 221–242.

Lee, Kun Jong. 2010. "Towards Interracial Understanding and Identification: Spike Lee's *Do the Right Thing* and Chang-rae Lee's *Native Speaker*." *Journal of American Studies* 44 (4): 741–757.

Lee, Kwang-rin (Yi Kwang-nin). 1978a. "Korea's Response to Social Darwinism (I)." *Korea Journal* 18 (4): 36–47.

———. 1978b. "Korea's Response to Social Darwinism (II)." *Korea Journal* 18 (5): 42–49.

Lee, K.W. 1999. "Legacy of Sa-ee-gur: Goodbye Hahn, Good Morning, Community Conscience." *Amerasia Journal* 25 (2): 43–45.

Lee, Shelley Sang-Hee. 2015. "Asian Americans and the 1992 Los Angeles Riots/Uprising." *Oxford Research Encyclopedia of American History.* http://oxfordre.com/americanhistory/view/10.1093/acrefore/9780199329175.001.0001/acrefore-9780199329175-e-15.

Lee, Taeku. 2000. "Racial Attitudes and the Color Line(s) at the Close of the Twentieth Century." In *The State of Asian Pacific Americans: Transforming Race Relations.* Edited by Paul Ong, 103–158. Los Angeles: LEAP/UCLA Asian Pacific American Public Policy Institute.

Leovy Jill. 2012. "Homicide, the New LAPD, and South Los Angeles." In *Post-Ghetto: Reimagining South Los Angeles.* Edited by Josh Sides, 191–208. Berkeley: University of California Press.

Lie, John. 2001. "Review of *Bitter Fruit: The Politics of Black-Korean Conflict in New York City,* by Claire Kim." *Journal of Asian Studies* 60 (4): 1126–1127.

Light, Ivan and Edna Bonacich. *Immigrant Entrepreneurs: Koreans in Los Angeles 1965–1982.* Berkeley and Los Angeles: University of California Press.

Lipsitz, George. 1998. *The Possessive Investment. In Whiteness: How White People Profit from Identity Politics.* Philadelphia: Temple University Press.

Lopez, David E., Eric Popkin, and Edward Telles. 1996. "Central Americans: At the Bottom, Struggling to Get Ahead." In *Ethnic Los Angeles.* Edited by Roger Waldinger and Mehdi Bozorgmehr, 279–304. New York: Russell Sage Foundation.

Los Angeles County Commission on Human Relations and Los Angeles City Human Relations Commission. 1985. *McCone Revisited: Focus on Solution to Continuing Problems in South Central Los Angeles.* Los Angeles, Independent Commission.

Los Angeles County Commission on Human Relations. 2008. *2007 Hate Crime Report*. http://humanrelations.co.la.ca.us/hatecrime/hatecrimereport.htm. Accessed March 20, 2009.

Los Angeles County Department of Public Health. 2013. Health Atlas for the City of Los Angeles. http://planning.lacity.org/cwd/framwk/healthwellness/text/healthatlas.pdf. Accessed March 24, 2015.

Lye, Colleen. 2008. "The Afro-Asian Analogy." *PMLA* 123(5):1732–1736.

Lynch, Kevin. 1960. *The Image of the City*. Cambridge, MA: MIT Press.

Maldonado, Marta Maria. 2009. "'It is Their Nature to Do Menial Labour': The Racialization of 'Latino/A Workers' by Agricultural Employers." *Ethnic and Racial Studies* 32 (6): 1017–1136.

Marable, Manning. 1995. *Beyond Black and White: Transforming African American Politics*. New York: Verso.

Marcus, George and Dick Cushman. 1982. "Ethnographies as Texts." *Annual Review of Anthropology* 11: 25–69.

Marcus, George and Michael M. Fischer. *Anthropology as Cultural Critique: An Experimental Moment in the Human Sciences.* Chicago: University of Chicago Press.

Marx, Karl. 1939. *The German Ideology*. Edited by R. Pascal. London: Lawrence and Wishart.

———. 1970. *Capital I*. London: Lawrence and Wishart.

———. 1972 (1954). *The Eighteenth Brumaire of Louis Napoleon*. 3rd. rev. Moscow: Progress Publishers.

Marx, Karl and Friedrich Engels. 1959. *Basic Writings on Politics and Philosophy*. Edited by Lewis S. Feuer. Garden City, NY: Doubleday.

Mason, William. 2004. *Los Angeles Under the Spanish Flag*. Burbank: Southern California Genealogical Society.

Massey, Douglas and Nancy Denton. 1993. *American Apartheid: Segregation and the Making of the Underclass*. Cambridge, MA: Harvard University Press.

McClain, Paula D. and Albert K. Karnig. 1990. "Black and Hispanic Socioeconomic and Political Competition." *American Political Science Review* 84 (2): 535–545.

McClain, Paula D., Niambi M. Carter, Victoria M. DeFrancesco Soto, Monique L. Lyle, Jeffrey D. Grynaviski, Shayla C. Nunnally, Thomas J. Scotto, J. Alan Kendrick, Gerald F. Lackey, and Kendra Davenport Cotton. 2006. "Racial Distancing in a Southern City: Latino Immigrants' Views of Black Americans." *The Journal of Politics* 68 (3): 571–584.

McCone Commission. 1966. *An Analysis of the McCone Commission Report*. Washington, DC.

McWilliams, Carey. 1973. *Southern California: An Island on the Land*. Santa Barbara, CA: Peregrine Smith.

Malpica, Daniel Melero. 2005. "Indigenous Mexican Migrants in A Modern Metropolis: The Reconstruction of Zapotec Communities in Los Angeles." In *Latino Los Angeles: Transformations, Communities, And Activism*. Edited by Enrique C. Ochoa and Gilda L. Ochoa, 111–136. Tucson: University of Arizona Press.

Merry, Sally. 2001. "Spatial Governmentality and the New Urban Social Order: Controlling Gender Violence through Law." *American Anthropologist* 103 (1): 16–29.

Meyerson, Harold. 1991. "Depression L.A.: City without a [Economic] Center." *LA Weekly* (December 19): 14–18.

Miles, Jack. 1992. "Blacks vs. Browns (African Americans and Latinos)." *The Atlantic* 270 (4): 41–60.

Min, Pyong Gap. 1996. *Caught in the Middle: Korean Communities in New York and Los Angeles.* Berkeley, Los Angeles, and London: University of California Press.

———. 2007. "Korean-Latino Relations in Los Angeles and New York." *Du Bois Review: Social Science Research on Race* 4: 395–411.

———. 2008. *Ethnic Solidarity for Economic Survival: Korean Greengrocers in New York City.* New York: Russell Sage Foundation.

Moran, Rachel. 1997. "What If Latinos Really Mattered in the Public Policy Debate?" *California Law Review* 85 (5): 1315–1345.

Morrison, Peter and Ira Lowry. 1994. "A Riot of Color: the Demographic Setting." In *The Los Angeles Riots: Lessons for the Urban Future.* Edited by Mark Baldassare, 19–46. Boulder, CO: Westview Press.

Morrison, Toni. 1994. "On the Backs of Blacks." In *Arguing Immigration: The Debate over the Changing Face of America.* Edited by Nicolaus Mills, 97–100. New York: Simon & Schuster.

Mosher, James F. and Joseph R. Mottl. 1981. "The Role of Nonalcohol Agencies in Federal Regulation of Drinking Behavior and Consequences." In *Alcohol and Public Policy: Beyond the Shadow of Prohibition.* Report of the Panel on Alternative Policies Affecting the Prevention of Alcohol Abuse and Alcoholism, National Research Council. Edited by I. Moore and D. Gerstein. Washington, DC: National Academy Press.

Mumford, Kevin. 2003. "Review of *Civility in the City: Blacks, Jews, and Koreans in Urban America*, by Jennifer Lee." *Urban Studies* 40 (13): 2802–2804.

Murguia, Edward. 1991. "On Latino/Hispanic Ethnic Identity." *Latino Studies Journal* 2 (3): 8–18.

Murty, K. S., L. B. Roebuck, and G. R. Armstrong. 1994. "The Black-Community Reactions to the 1992 Los-Angeles Riot." *Deviant Behavior* 15 (1): 85–104.

Nakano, Eric. 1993. "Building Common Ground—the Liquor Store Controversy." *Amerasia Journal* 19 (2): 167–170.

Navarro, Armando. 1993. "The South Central Los Angeles Eruption: A Latino Perspective." *Amerasia Journal* 19 (2): 69–86.

Nielsen, Amie. 2000. "Examining Drinking Patterns and Problems among Hispanic Groups: Results from a National Survey." *Journal of Studies on Alcohol* 61(2): 301–310.

Nopper, Tamara K. 2006. "The 1992 Los Angeles Riots and the Asian American Abandonment Narrative as Political Fiction." *CR: The New Centennial Review* 6 (2): 73–110.

O'Brien, Eileen, 2008. *The Racial Middle: Latinos and Asian Americans Living beyond the Racial Divide.* New York: New York University Press.

Okihiro, Gary. 1994. *Margins and Mainstreams: Asians in American History and Culture.* Seattle and London: University of Washington Press.

Oliver, Melvin, James Johnson, and Walter Farrell. 1993. "Anatomy of a Rebellion: A Political-Economic Analysis." In *Reading Rodney King/Reading Urban Uprising.* Edited by Robert Gooding-Williams, 117–141. New York and London: Routledge.

Oliver, Melvin and Thomas M. Shapiro. 1995. *Black Wealth/White Wealth: A New Perspective on Racial Inequality.* New York: Routledge.

Omatsu, Glenn. 1995. "Labor Organizing in Los Angeles: Confronting the Boundaries of Race and Ethnicity." In *Multiethnic Coalition Building in Los Angeles.* Edited by Eui-Young Yu and Edward Chang, 117–134. Claremont, CA: Regina Books for Institute for Asian American and Pacific Asian Studies, California State University, Los Angeles.

Omi, Michael and Howard Winant. 1993. "The Los Angeles 'Race Riot' and Contemporary U.S. Politics." In *Reading Rodney King/Reading Urban Uprising.* Edited by Robert Gooding-Williams, 97–116. New York and London: Routledge.

Omi, Michael and Howard Winant. 1994. *Racial Formation in the United States: From the 1960s to the 1990s.* 2nd edition. New York: Routledge.

Omi, Michael and Howard Winant. 2008. "Once More, with Feeling: Reflections on Racial Formation." *PMLA: Publications of the Modern Language Association of America* 123 (5): 1565–1572.

Omi, Michael and Howard Winant. 2011. "From Racial Formation in the United States." In *Race in an Era of Change: A Reader.* Edited by Heather Dalmage and Barbara Rothman, 3–17. New York and Oxford: Oxford University Press.

Ong, Aihwa. 1996. "Cultural Citizenship as Subject-Making: Immigrants Negotiate Racial and Cultural Boundaries in the United States." *Current Anthropology* 37(5): 737–762.

———. 2003. *Buddha is Hiding: Refugees, Citizenship, the New America.* Berkeley, Los Angeles and London: University of California Press.

Ong, Paul. 1990. *The Widening Divide: Income Inequality and Poverty in Los Angeles.* Los Angeles: The Research Group on the Los Angeles Economy, UCLA.

Ong, Paul, Kyeyoung Park, and Yasmin Tong. 1994. "The Korean-Black Conflict and the State." In *The New Asian Immigration in Los Angeles and Global Restructuring.* Edited by Paul Ong, Edna Bonacich, and Lucie Cheng, 264–294. Philadelphia: Temple University Press.

Ong, Paul, Andre Comandon, Alycia Cheng, and Silvia R. González. 2018. *South Los Angeles Since the Sixties.* Los Angeles: University of California Press.

Oquendo, Angel. 1995. "Re-Imagining the Latino/A Race." *Harvard BlackLetter Law Journal* 12: 93–129.

Ortner, Sherry. 1992. "Reading America: Preliminary Notes on Class and Culture." In *Recapturing Anthropology: Working in the Present.* Edited by Richard G. Fox, 163–190. Santa Fe, NM: School of American Research Press.

Palumbo-Liu, David. 1994. "Los Angeles, Asians, and Perverse Ventriloquisms: On the Functions of Asian America in the Recent American Imaginary." *Public Culture* 6: 365–381.

Park, Edward. 1998. "Competing Visions: Political Formation of Korean Americans In Los Angeles, 1992–1997." *Amerasia Journal* 24 (1): 41–58.

———. 2004. "Labor Organizing Beyond Race and Nation: The Los Angeles Hilton Case." *International Journal of Sociology and Social Research* 24 (7/8): 137–152.

Park, Edward and John S.W. Park. 2005. *Probationary Americans: Contemporary Immigration Policies and the Shaping of Asian American Communities*. New York: Routledge.

Park, Kyeyoung. 1994. "The Question of Culture in the Black-Korean American Conflict." In *Black-Korean Encounter: Toward Understanding and Alliance*. Edited by Eui-Young Yu, 40–48. Los Angeles: Institute for Asian American and Pacific Asian Studies, California State University, Los Angeles.

———. 1995. "The Re-Invention of Affirmative Action: Korean Immigrants' Changing Conceptions of African and Latin Americans." *Urban Anthropology* 24: 59–92.

———. 1995/96. "The Morality of a Commodity: A Case Study of "Rebuilding L.A. Without Liquor Stores." *Amerasia Journal* 21: 1–27.

———. 1996. "Use and Abuse of Race and Culture: Black-Korean Tension in America." *American Anthropologist* 98 (3): 492–499.

———. 1997. *The Korean American Dream: Immigrants and Small Business in New York City*. Ithaca, NY and London: Cornell University Press.

———. 1999a. "'I'm Floating in the Air': Creation of a Korean Transnational Space among Korean-Latino-American Re-Migrants." *Positions: East Asia Cultures Critique* 7 (3): 667–695.

———. 1999b. "'I Really Do Feel I'm 1.5!': The Construction of Self and Community by Young Korean Americans." *Amerasia Journal* 25 (1): 139–164.

———. 2004. "Challenging the Liquor Industry In Los Angeles." *International Journal of Sociology and Public Policy* 24 (7/8): 103–136.

———. 2010. "Sources and Resources of Korean Immigrant Entrepreneurship." *Critical Sociology* 36 (6): 891–896.

Parkin, Frank. 1979. *Marxism and Class Theory: A Bourgeois Critique.* New York: Columbia University Press.

Pastor, Manuel. 1993. *Latinos and the Los Angeles Uprising: The Economic Context*. Claremont, CA: Tomas Rivera Center.

———. 1995. "Economic Inequality, Latino Poverty, and the Civil Unrest in Los Angeles." *Economic Development Quarterly* 9 (3): 238–258.

———. 2014. "Keeping it Real: Demographics, Workforce, and Organizing for African Americans and Latinos in Los Angeles." In *Black and Brown in Los Angeles: Beyond Conflict and Coalition*. Edited by Josh Kun and Laura Pulido, 33–66. Berkeley: University of California Press.

Pattillo-McCoy, Mary. 1999. *Black Picket Fences: Privilege and Peril Among the Black Middle Class*. Chicago: University of Chicago Press.

Prashad, Vijay. 1998. "Anti-D'Souza: The Ends of Racism and the Asian American." *Amerasia Journal* 24 (1): 23–40.

———. 2001. *Everybody was Kung Fu Fighting: Afro-Asian Connections and the Myth of Cultural Purity*. Boston: Beacon Press.

Pulido, Laura and Manuel Pastor. 2013. "Where in the World Is Juan—and What Color Is He? The Geography of Latina/o Racial Identity in Southern California." *American Quarterly* 65 (2): 309–341.

Quinones, Sam. 2014. 'Race, Real Estate, and the Mexican Mafia: A Report from the Black and Latino Killing Fields." In *Black and Brown in Los Angeles: Beyond Conflict and Coalition.* Edited by Josh Kun and Laura Pulido, 261–300. Berkeley: University of California Press.

Ratcliff, Richard E., Melvin L. Oliver, and Thomas M. Shapiro, eds. 1995. *The Politics of Wealth and Inequality.* Greenwich, CT: JAI Press.

Rebuilding LA. 1997. *Rebuilding LA's Urban Communities: A Final Report from RLA.* Santa Monica, CA: Milken Institute.

Regalado, Jaime. 1995. "Creating Multicultural Harmony? A Critical Perspective on Coalition-building Efforts in Los Angeles." In *Multiethnic Coalition Building in Los Angeles.* Edited by Eui-Young Yu and Edward Chang, 35–54. Claremont, CA: Regina Books for Institute for Asian American and Pacific Asian Studies, California State University, Los Angeles.

Ribas, Vanesa. 2016. *On the Line: Slaughterhouse Lives and the Making of the New South.* Oakland: University of California Press.

Rieff, David. 1991. *Los Angeles: Capital of the Third World.* New York: Simon and Schuster.

Robinson, Paul. 2010. "Race, Space, and the Evolution of Black Los Angeles." In *Black Los Angeles: American Dreams and Racial Realities.* Edited by Darnell Hunt and Ana-Christina Ramón, 21–59. New York and London: New York University Press.

Rodriguez, Clara, Aida Castro, Oscar Garcia, and Analisa Torres. 1991. "Latino Racial Identity: In the Eye of the Beholder." *Latino Studies Journal* 2(3): 33–48

Rodriguez, Clara, 1992. "Race, Culture, and Latino 'Otherness' in the 1980 Census." *Social Science Quarterly* 73: 930–937.

Roediger, David. 1991. *The Wages of Whiteness: Race and the Making of the American Working Class.* London and New York: Verso.

Romano, Octavio Ignacio. 1960. "Donship in a Mexican-American Community in Texas." *American Anthropologist* 62(6): 966–976.

Rosaldo, Renato. 1988. "Ideology, Place, and People without Culture." *Cultural Anthropology* 3 (1): 77–87.

Roth, Wendy D. 2012. *Race Migrations: Latinos and the Cultural Transformation of Race.* Stanford, CA: Stanford University Press.

Roth, Wendy D. and Nadia Kim. 2013. "Relocating Prejudice: A Transnational Approach to Understanding Immigrants' Racial Attitudes." *International Migration Review* 47 (2): 330–373.

Ryoo, Hye-Kyung. 2005. "Achieving Friendly Interactions: A Study of Service Encounters between Korean Shopkeepers and African-American Customers." *Discourse & Society* 16 (1): 79–105.

Said, Edward. 1988. "Foreword." In *Selected Subaltern Studies.* Edited by Ranajit Guha and Gayatri Chakravorty Spivak, v–xii. New York and Oxford: Oxford University Press.

Saito, Leland. 2001. Review of *Ethnic Peace in the American City: Building Community in Los Angeles and Beyond*, by Edward Chang and Jeannette Diaz-Veizades. *Journal of Asian American Studies* 4 (1): 77–80.

Salas, Miguel Tinker. 1991. "El Immigrante Latino: Latin American Immigration and Pan-Ethnicity." *Latino Studies Journal* 2(3): 58–71.

Sanchez, George. 1997. "Face the Nation: Race, Immigration, and the Rise of Nativism in Late Twentieth Century America." *International Migration Review* 31(4): 1009–1030.

Sanjek, Roger. 1994. "The Enduring Inequalities of Race." In *Race*. Edited by S. Gregory and R. Sanjek, 1–17. New Brunswick, NJ: Rutgers University Press.

———. 1996. "Race." In *Encyclopedia of Social and Cultural Anthropology*. Edited by Alan Barnard and Jonathan Spencer, 462–465. London: Routledge.

———. 1998. *The Future of Us All: Race and Neighborhood Politics in New York City*. Ithaca, NY and London: Cornell University Press.

Sawyer, Mark. 2010. "Racial Politics in Multiethnic America: Black and Latina/o Identities and Coalitions." In *The Afro-Latin@ Reader: History and Culture in the United States*. Edited by Miriam Jiménez Román and Juan Flores, 527–539. Durham, NC: Duke University Press.

Saxton, Alexander. 1990. *The Rise and Fall of the White Republic: Class Politics and Mass Culture in Nineteenth-Century America*. London and New York: Verso.

Schreer, George E., Saundra Smith, and Kirsten Thomas. 2009. "Shopping While Black: Examining Racial Discrimination in a Retail Setting." *Journal of Applied Social Psychology* 39 (6): 1432–1444.

Scott, Allen J. and Edward W. Soja, eds. 1996. *The City: Los Angeles and Urban Theory at the End of the Twentieth Century*. Berkeley: University of California Press.

Scott, David. 1989. "Locating the Anthropological Subject: Postcolonial Anthropologists in Other Places." *Inscriptions* 5: 75–85.

Scott, James. 1976. *The Moral Economy of The Peasant: Rebellion and Subsistence in Southeast Asia*. New Haven, CT: Yale University Press.

———. 1985. *Weapons of the Weak: Everyday Forms of Peasant Resistance*. New Haven, CT: Yale University Press.

———. 1990. *Domination and the Arts of Resistance: Hidden Transcripts*. New Haven, CT: Yale University Press.

Sears, David. 1973. *The Politics of Violence: The New Urban Blacks and the Watts Riot*. Boston: Houghton Mifflin.

Sexton, Jared. 2010. "Proprieties of Coalition: Blacks, Asians, and the Politics of Policing." *Critical Sociology* 36 (1): 87–108.

Shin, Gi-Wook. 2006. *Ethnic Nationalism in Korea: Genealogy, Politics, and Legacy*. Stanford, CA: Stanford University Press.

Sides, Josh. 2003. *L.A. City Limits: African American Los Angeles from the Great Depression to the Present*. Berkeley: University of California Press.

Simon, Bryant. 2011. "'Down Brother': Earvin 'Magic' Johnson and the Quest for Retail Justice in Los Angeles." *Boom: A Journal of California* 1(2): 43–58. doi: 10.1525/boom.2011.1.2.43.

Sivanandan, Ambalavaner. 1973. "Race, Class and Power: An Outline for Study." *Race* 14 (4): 383–91.

Sloane, David C. 2012. "Alcohol Nuisances and Food Deserts: Combating Social Hazards in South Los Angeles Environment." In *Post-Ghetto: Reimagining South*

*Los Angeles*. Edited by Josh Sides, 93–108. Berkeley: University of California Press.

Smith, Andrea L. 2006. "Heteropatriarchy and the Three Pillars of White Supremacy: Rethinking Women of Color Organizing." In *The Color of Violence: The INCITE! Anthology*. Edited by Andrea Lee Smith, Beth E. Richie, Julia Sudbury, and Janelle White, 68–73. Cambridge, MA: South End Press.

Smith, Anna Devere. 2000 (1999). *Twilight Los Angeles*. PBS Home Video.

Soja, Edward. 1989. *Postmodern Geographies*. New York: Verso.

Soja, Edward, Rebecca Morales, and Goetz Wolff. 1983. "Urban Restructuring: An Analysis of Social and Spatial Change in Los Angeles." *Economic Geography* 58: 221–235.

Sonenshein, Raphael. 1993. *Politics in Black and White: Race and Power in Los Angeles*. Princeton, NJ: Princeton University Press.

———. 1996. "The Battle over Liquor Stores in South Central Los Angeles: The Management of an Interminority Conflict." *Urban Affairs* 31 (6): 710–737.

Sonu, Debbie. 2012. "Illusions of Compliance: Performing the Public and Hidden Transcripts of Social Justice Education in Neoliberal Times." *Curriculum Inquiry* 42 (2): 240–259.

Sowell, Thomas. 2004. *Affirmative Action around The World: An Empirical Study*. New Haven, CT: Yale University Press.

Spencer, James H. 2004. "Los Angeles since 1992: How Did the Economic Base of Riot-Torn Neighborhoods Fare after the Unrest?" *Race, Gender & Class* 11 (1): 94–115.

Stein, Howard. 1984. "A Note on Patron-Client Theory." *Ethos* 12(1): 30–36.

Steinberg, Stephen. 1989/81. *The Ethnic Myth: Race, Ethnicity, and Class in America*. Boston: Beacon Press.

Stevenson, Brenda. 2013. *The Contested Murder of Latasha Harlins: Justice, Gender, and the Origins of the LA Riots*. Oxford: Oxford University Press.

Stewart, Ella. 1989. "Ethnic Cultural Diversity: An Interpretive Study of Cultural Differences and Communication Styles between Korean Merchants/Employees and Black Patrons in South Los Angeles." MA thesis, Department of Communication Studies, California State University, Los Angeles.

———. 1994 (1993). "Communication between African Americans and Korean Americans: Before and After the Los Angeles Riots." In *Los Angeles—Struggles toward Multiethnic Community*. Edited by Edward Chang and Russell Leong, 23–54.

Stolcke, Verena. 1995. "Talking Culture: New Boundaries, New Rhetorics of Exclusion in Europe." *Current Anthropology* 36 (1): 1–24

Sturrock, John. 1979. *Structuralism and Since: From Lévi Strauss to Derrida*. Edited, by John Sturrock. Oxford and New York: Oxford University Press.

Szwed, John. 1975. "Race and the Embodiment of Culture." *Ethnicity* 2: 19–33.

Taguieff, Pierre-Andre. 1987. *Le force du prejuge: Essai sur le racisms et ses doubles*. Paris: Éditions La Découverte.

Telles, Edward and Vilma Ortiz. 2008. *Generations of Exclusion: Mexican Americans, Assimilation, and Race*. New York: Russell Sage Foundation.

Tilly, Charles. 1998. *Durable Inequality*. Berkeley: University of California Press.

Thompson, Anderson. 1993. "The Los Angeles Rebellion: Seizing the Historical Moment." In *Why L.A. Happened: Implications of the 92' Los Angeles Rebellion.* Edited by Haki R. Madhubuti, 49–60. Chicago: Third World Press.

Thompson, E. P. 1971. "The Moral Economy of the English Crowd in the Eighteenth Century." *Past and Present* 50: 76–136.

———. 1991. *Customs in Common*. New York: New Press.

Thornton, Michael C. and Robert J. Taylor. 1988. "Intergroup Attitudes: Black American Perceptions of Asian Americans." *Ethnic and Racial Studies* 11 (4): 474–488.

———. 2011. "Meaningful Dialogue? The Los Angeles Sentinel's Depiction of Black and Asian American Relations, 1993–2000." *Journal of Black Studies* 42 (8): 1275–1298.

Tierney, Kathleen. 1994. "Property Damage and Violence: A Collective Behavior Analysis." In *The Los Angeles Riots: Lessons for the Urban Future*. Edited by Mark Baldassare, 149–174. Boulder, CO: Westview Press.

Tong, Yasmin. 1992. "In the Middle: Mediating Black-Korean Conflict in South Central Los Angeles." MA thesis, Urban Planning, University of California, Los Angeles.

Turner, Bryan S. 1988. *Status*. Minneapolis: University of Minnesota Press.

Ussery, Terdema. 1994. "Small Business Ownership in South Central Los Angeles: Who Really Profits?" In *Black-Korean Encounter: Toward Understanding and Alliance*. Edited by Eui-Young Yu, 90–94. Los Angeles: Institute for Asian American and Pacific Asian Studies, California State University, Los Angeles.

Vargas, João. 2006. *Catching Hell in the City of Angels: Life and Meanings of Blackness in South Central Los Angeles*. Minneapolis: University of Minnesota Press.

Verkuyten, Maykel. 1997. "Cultural Discourses in the Netherlands: Talking about Ethnic Minorities in the Inner-City." *Identities* 4 (1): 99–132, 1997.

Villanueva, George. 2017. "Embodying Democratic Spaces: Community Organizer Alternative Narratives that Challenge the Mainstream Negative Stigma of South Los Angeles." In *Anthropology of Los Angeles: Place and Agency in an Urban Setting*. Edited by Jenny Banh and Melissa King, 73–98. Lanham, MD: Lexington Books.

Waldinger, Roger. 1996. *Still the Promised City?: African-Americans and New Immigrants in Postindustrial New York*. Cambridge, MA: Harvard University Press.

Waldinger, Roger and Michael Lichter. 2003. *How the Other Half Works: Immigration and the Social Organization of Labor*. Berkeley: University of California Press.

Watts, Paul R. 2010. "Mapping Narratives: The 1992 Los Angeles Riots as a Case Study for Narrative-Based Geovisualization." *Journal of Cultural Geography* 27 (2): 203–227.

Weber, Max. 1961 (1946). *From Max Weber: Essays in Sociology*. London: Routledge.

Webster, William H. 1992. *The City in Crisis: A Report by the Special Advisor to the Board of Police Commissioners on the Civil Disorder in Los Angeles*. Los Angeles: Special Advisor Study, Inc.

Wei, William. 1993. *The Asian American Movement*. Philadelphia: Temple University Press.

Weir, Lorna. 1993. "Limitations of New Social Movement Analysis." *Studies in Political Economy* 40 (Spring): 73–102.

Weitzer, Ronald. 1997. "Racial Prejudice among Korean Merchants in African American Community." *Sociological Quarterly* 38(4): 587–606.

Whitman, David and David Bowermaster. 1993. "A Potent Brew: Booze and Crime." *U.S. News & World Report*, May 31: 57–59.

Wicker, Tom. 1992. "The Persistence of Inequality." Review of *Two Nations: Black and White, Separate, Hostile, and Unequal*, by Andrew Hacker. *New York Times*, March 8.

Williams, Brackette. 1989. "A Class Act: Anthropology and the Race to Nation Across Ethnic Terrain." *Annual Review of Anthropology* 18: 401–444.

———. 1991. *Stains on My Name, War in My Veins: The Politics of Cultural Struggle in Guyana*. Durham, NC and London: Duke University Press.

———. 1993. "The Impact of the Precepts of Nationalism on the Concept of Culture, Making Grasshoppers of Naked Apes." *Cultural Critique* 24: 143–191.

———. 1994. "You Shall Reap What they Have Sown: The Producer/Work Ethic and the Moral Order of Subordinate Racisms in Interethnic Competition." Paper presented at the American Ethnological Society Meeting, Santa Monica, CA, April 14–17.

Williams, Raymond. 1974. *The Long Revolution*. London: Penguin.

———. 1976. *Keywords: A Vocabulary of Culture And Society*. London: Fontana.

Williams, Richard. 1988. "'Ethnicity' and 'Race' in Small Business." In *Racism, Sexism, and the World-System*. Edited by J. Smith, J. Collins, T. Hopkins, and A. Muhammad, 153–68. New York: Greenwood Press.

Wilson, William Julius. 1979. *The Declining Significance of Race?: A Dialogue among Black and White Social Scientists*. Edited by Joseph R. Washington. Philadelphia: University of Pennsylvania

———. 1987. *The Truly Disadvantaged: The Inner City, the Underclass, and Public Policy*. Chicago and London: The University of Chicago Press.

———. ed. 1989. *The Ghetto Underclass: Social Science Perspectives*. Newbury Park, CA: Sage Publications.

Winant, Howard. 1994. *Racial Conditions: Politics, Theory, Comparisons*. Minneapolis: University of Minnesota Press.

———. 1999. "The President's Initiative: Race-Conscious Judo Meets the Still Funky Reality." *Souls: A Critical Journal of Black Politics, Culture, and Society* 1 (3): 68–72.

———. 2001. *The World is a Ghetto: Race and Democracy since World War II*. New York: Basic Books.

Wolf, Eric. 1956. "Aspects of Group Relations in a Complex Society: Mexico." *American Anthropologist* 58 (6): 1065–1078.

———. 1982. *Europe and the People without History*. Berkeley: University of California Press.

———. 1990. "Distinguished Lecture: Facing Power–Old Insights, New Questions" *American Anthropologist* 92 (3): 586–596.

———. 1994. "Perilous Ideas: Race, Culture, People." *Current Anthropology* 35 (1): 1–12.

———. 1999. *Envisioning Power: Ideologies of Dominance and Crisis*. Los Angeles: University of California Press.

Wolff, Goetz. 1992. "The Making of a Third World City?: Latino Labor and the Restructuring of the Los Angeles Economy." Report prepared for the Latino American Studies Association.

Wong, Elizabeth. 1994. *Kimchee and Chitlins* (Play).

Wright, Erik Olin. 1985. *Classes*. London: Verso.

———. 2000. "Metatheoretical Foundations of Charles Tilly's 'Durable Inequality.'" *Comparative Studies in Society and History* 42 (2): 458–474.

X, Malcolm and Alex Haley. 1989/1964. *The Autobiography of Malcolm X*. New York: Ballantine Books.

Yi, Jeongduk. 1993. "Social Order and Contest in Meanings and Power: Black Boycotts against Korean Shopkeepers in Poor New York City Neighborhoods." PhD Diss., Department of Anthropology, City University of New York.

Yoon, In Jin. 1997. *On My Own: Korean Businesses and Race Relations in America*. Chicago and London: University of Chicago Press.

Zilberg, Elan. 2002. "Troubled Corner: The Ruined and Rebuilt Environment of a Central American Barrio in Post-Rodney-King-Riot Los Angeles." *City & Society* 14 (2): 185–210.

# Index

AB 1974. *See* California State Assembly Bill 1974

ABC. *See* California Department of Alcohol Beverage Control

Abelmann, Nancy, 7, 86n2, 201

ABIC Liquor Store, 186

abuse, alcohol, 203, 206–10

Ace liquor store, 73

Action for Grassroots Empowerment and Neighborhood Development Alternatives (AGENDA), 271

Adler, Rachel, 232–33

AFDC. *See* Aid to Families with Dependent Children

African American Community Based Organization, 260

African Americans: alcohol and, 207; as ambivalent other, 106–9; anti-Korean prejudice among, 81–83; BKA, 67, 70–71, 79–80; with Black-Jewish relations, 57n3; Black rage and, 23, 265; businesses owned by, 134–35, *187*; citizenship and, 15–16; customers, female, 94–95; customers, male, 92–94, 97; demographics, 34, 36–37; economic inequality and, 36; employees, 94, 102, 113n7; ethno-racial identities and, 44–48; as friendly "other," 99–102; in gangs, 41; hair salons and, 21–22, 23; homicides and, 36; income of, 14, 43, 121; intercessory ethnography and response from, 23–24; Korean Americans with prejudice against, 80–81; Latinos and relations with, 259–61; looting and, 178, 182–83; with political economic transformation, 38–39, 41; politics and, 33, 254–55; populations, 40; property damage by, 3; with race relations, 4; racial distancing with Latinos and, 258–61; as racial label, 15; racial triangulation and, 11; with rights of prior occupancy, 15; security guards, 94; slavery and, 14; White aggression and, 33. *See also* Black-Asian American relations; Black boycotts, of Korean stores; Black-Korean relations

AGENDA. *See* Action for Grassroots Empowerment and Neighborhood Development Alternatives

"agenda switching," 120

Aid to Families with Dependent Children (AFDC), 40, 143, 153

alcohol, 214; ABC, 204, 221n9, 221n11; abuse, 203, 206–10; African Americans and, 207; beer run,

# About the Author

**Kyeyoung Park** is associate professor of anthropology and Asian American studies at the University of California, Los Angeles. Her book, *The Korean American Dream: Immigrants and Small Business in New York City* (1997), by Cornell University Press, is the winner of the 1998 Outstanding Book Award from the Association for Asian American Studies.

Made in the USA
Middletown, DE
13 March 2023

26687564R00183